PERFECT
I'm Not

PERFECT
I'm Not

BOOMER
on Beer,
Brawls,
Backaches,
and Baseball

David Wells

WITH CHRIS KRESKI

Wm

WILLIAM MORROW
An Imprint of HarperCollins*Publishers*

PERFECT I'M NOT. Copyright © 2003 by BBL Enterprises, Inc.
All rights reserved. Printed in the United States of America.
No part of this book may be used or reproduced in any manner
whatsoever without written permission except in the case of
brief quotations embodied in critical articles and reviews.
For information address HarperCollins Publishers Inc.,
10 East 53rd Street, New York, NY 10022.

HarperCollins books may be purchased for educational,
business, or sales promotional use. For information please write:
Special Markets Department, HarperCollins Publishers Inc.,
10 East 53rd Street, New York, NY 10022.

FIRST EDITION

Designed by Adrian Leichter

Printed on acid-free paper

Library of Congress Cataloging-in-Publication Data
Wells, David, 1963–
Perfect I'm not: Boomer on beer, brawls, backaches,
and baseball/by David Wells with Chris Kreski.—1st ed.
p. cm.
ISBN 0-06-050824-8
1. Wells, David, 1963– 2. Baseball players—United States—Biography.
I. Kreski, Chris, 1962– II. Title.
GV865W434 A3 2003
796.357'092—dc21
[B]
2002035757

03 04 05 06 07 ❖/RRD 10 9 8 7 6 5 4 3

For Brandon and Lars
and, of course, Nina
—D.W.

For Amelia, Noah, Sammy, Tommy,
Tony, Tyler, Michael, Steven, and a pair of
players to be named later . . . an entire
lineup of rebels, troublemakers,
and attitude problems
—C.K.

Never quit
until every
base is uphill.
—BABE RUTH

CONTENTS

PERFECT
I'm Not

(Courtesy of Broadway Video Enterprises)

My Life as a Woman

Hello, ladies.
Your husbands are looking
very sexy tonight. I think
I'm gonna have sex
with them all!

—*Skank #1*

DECEMBER 1, 2001: NEW YORK CITY

Saturday night, 7:15 P.M. My frosted pink lipstick is layered on thick. My bleached blonde hair is moussed high and sprayed hard, like something you'd see wandering through a New Jersey shopping mall. Tight, black, patent leather pumps are squeezing my feet. Tight, black, queen-size panty hose are squeezing my groin. The cocktail dress I'm wearing feels at least two inches too short. My ass is freezing, but my big, fake boobs are smoking hot.

Thirty-eight Cs, these silicone girls are round, firm, full, and so incredibly perky they actually seem to defy gravity. They're better than perfect. They're fascinating, and strangely magnetic as well. All night long, I'll be happily copping feels of my own fake cleavage.

Right now though, I stand before a full-length mirror, sucking in my gut to get a long, first look at the full bosomy bloom of my own femininity. It's overwhelming. Quickly, and without any doubt whatsoever, I come to the realization that I may actually be the single ugliest woman ever to walk the face of this planet. Without the goatee I might rate a 2. With it, I'm a negative 6. At exactly this moment, someone shouts at me from across the room.

"Dude! You are one homely skank!"

I turn fast, and there's David Cone, red-faced, and laughing so hard the veins in his little pencil neck look like they're about to explode. He's doubled over. He's wheezing. He's even uglier than I am. Decked out in a black spandex miniskirt, polyester leopard-print halter top, and a bimbo-do that's even bigger, fluffier, and sluttier than mine, Coney's a mess. The dude looks like last call at Houlihan's. He makes dirt look pretty. Next to David Cone, I'm Pam Anderson. Side by side in the mirror now, we'll spend the better part of a half hour arguing over which of us is *really* more gruesome. Finally, rehoisting our bra straps, and readjusting our wigs, we call it a draw and go hunting for Derek Jeter.

Quickly, before you get the wrong idea, let me take a minute to explain that cross-dressing has never been high on my "things-to-do" list. Tonight's drag is a one-off; a command performance set into motion on the spur of the moment by *Saturday Night Live* producer Lorne Michaels. With Derek Jeter hosting this week's show, the *SNL* writers have concocted a sketch involving five Yankee wives and a sleazy pair of groupies who chase after their husbands. As the scene is cast, Jeter will be playing Alfonso Soriano's sweet, loving wife, "Candy." Guess who's playing "Skank #1" and "Skank #2"?

Less than three hours ago Coney and I were across the river in Jersey, happily serving as "honored guests" at a dignified, perfect-game-themed, autograph-signing appearance. Now we've both got purple mascara caked onto our lashes, and hairdos the size of sport-utility vehicles. How'd this happen? Simple. I opened my big mouth. Shocker there, huh? Let me backtrack.

I've been a rabid *SNL* fan ever since I was twelve years old, falling off the couch as John Belushi samurai-sliced his way through both the neighborhood deli and Buck Henry's forehead. With that in mind, it should come as no surprise that all through my first go-round with the Yankees, I was constantly weaseling myself invitations to *Saturday Night Live* tapings and also to the show's legendary after-parties. Loud and large and crammed with funny, talented writers, performers, and musicians, these things kick off right after *SNL* rolls its credits. They *end* right around the time the sun starts rising over the East River. They're great fun. I love being there, and through years of blatant party-crashing, I've slowly but surely developed a pretty solid "odd couple" friendship with Lorne Michaels, as well as the show's producers and some of the cast.

November 10, 2001. I'm in New York City making a personal appearance at a Manhattan Hooters franchise (tough work, but *somebody's* gotta do it), signing balls and posters and T-shirts, with the proceeds all going toward 9/11 relief. And since I'm in town on a Saturday, I *have* to call *SNL* producer Marci Klein, asking that she hook me up with tickets for tonight's show. As we chat, Marci runs through her usual song and dance about how funny tonight's host is gonna be, but then, from out of nowhere, she surprises me by asking for Derek Jeter's home phone number. I make the obvious joke about how she can't *possibly* be *that* hard up, but Marci keeps digging. She tells me *SNL* wants Derek to host their next live episode, which is scheduled to air the night of December 1. With one more bad, hook-up joke at Marci's expense, I pass along Derek's digits and make plans to be in the studio for "DJ's" debut.

Three weeks pass. Now it's December 1, and Coney and I are signing away in New Jersey, scrawling our names onto balls, baseball cards, T-shirts, and posters, one after another after another. That's when the cell phone rings. It's Marci, and *this* time she's all business, telling me there's been a great, last-minute sketch written for tonight's show, and it *really* needs me. She then reads me the whole "Yankee Wives" script over the phone while simultaneously giving me the full, hard-sell, used-car-dealer spin about how funny it'd be to close out the scene with me playing a sleazy ballpark groupie. Laughing into the phone, Marci presses me to commit, on the spot.

"Hell no!" I tell her, emphasis on the *hell*. It's not the drag that scares me, it's going *live* on national television with such short notice. I can't memorize a script. I can't read cue cards and act at the same time. I'll suck. I'm a baseball player, not an actor. You don't call Will Ferrell on a Saturday afternoon and ask him to pitch eight innings against the Red Sox that night. Tampa Bay *maybe,* but beyond that, it'd just be nuts!

"C'mon, David," she continues, "think of it as a challenge. Think of it as a big-game situation where you've gotta come through in the clutch." She's not giving up, charging at me now with a pocketful of transparent old sports clichés.

"Nice try, Marci, But I ain't biting. Sorry."

Next to me, Coney's been laughing all through this conversation, and in the end, he's *really* disappointed that I bagged. Coney swears that putting me in drag on national television will kill. For hours, I have to listen to the guy ranting about what a wimp I am, and about how hilariously bad I'd look in a dress. He's relentless, and so is Marci Klein, who calls me every forty-five minutes or so, retwisting my arm with each and every ring. I turn her down repeatedly, becoming a little less polite with each rejection.

By late afternoon, tired, hungry, our hands cramped into claws from writing our own names two thousand times over, Coney and I pile into a Town Car and head back into the city. Sitting together in the backseat, we're approaching the George Washington Bridge as my cell rings for what seems like the 187th time. Coney laughs, saying, "Not again!" I just grumble. Now it's annoying. Now it's too much.

Now it's Lorne Michaels. "David, it's Lor-r-r-r-rne," he says. "We need you to do this skit and that's all there is to it. You ARE appearing in this thing, so get your ass in here and get ready for dress rehearsal. I don't want to hear any more about it." I don't even get to protest. Lorne immediately hands the phone off to his assistant, and while I'm still just going "hominah-hominah-hominah" like Ralph Kramden, she chimes in with "Dude, you've *gotta* do this." From his side of the car, Coney gives me a thumbs-up and urges me on.

I sigh, trying hard to think of *some* tactful way to turn down Lorne's demand, when a great idea hits me from out of nowhere, and an abrupt left turn gets made. "Okay," I bark into my cell, "I'll do the sketch, but only if you write Coney into this thing too. That way at least I get to be 'the pretty one.'"

"Great," she says. "Lemme just get an approval on that and I'll call you right back." I hang up, look across the car, and notice Coney's gone white.

"Scumbag!" he yells, using his favorite nickname for me. "There's no way in hell I'm doing this."

"Bullshit, Scumbag!" I tend to use that same nickname back at him. "If I've gotta look like a slut on national TV, so do you."

We've barely made it to the West Side Highway when the phone rings again, this time with Lorne's official green light. Coney and I are now locked in as

"Skank #1" and "Skank #2." I give Coney the good news. He punches me in the shoulder and calls me a whole lot of terrible names I can't print.

Together, we hit the NBC Studios at Rockefeller Center. We hit Wardrobe. We hit Makeup, and by 7:45 P.M., Coney and I are in full skank regalia, bursting through the door of Derek Jeter's dressing room. "Hello, Shortstop," I shout. "Wanna visit third base with me?"

"Oh my God!" Derek moans 150 times in a row. "You guys are fugly with a capital *F*!" He should talk. I know Jeter's supposed to be "the cute Yankee," but honest to God, sitting there in his little sleeveless denim ensemble, the dude looks like the love child of J.Lo and a Sasquatch. The insults fly in every direction now, and the three of us are still joyfully ragging on one another when a stage manager shows up to drag our asses off to dress rehearsal. Heading through the hallways toward the stage, cast and crew all get into the act, each lobbing their own personal "ugly" jokes as the skank parade passes. Tracy Morgan tells me I look like I fell out of the ugly tree and hit every branch on the way down.

Onstage now, we get set into position. Coney and I stand off to the side as fear sets in and we wait for our cue. While we're there, I find myself repeating my one line over and over inside my own head. *"Hello-o-o-o, ladies. Your husbands are looking very sexy tonight. I think I'm gonna have sex with them all! Hello-o-o-o, ladies. Your husbands are looking very sexy tonight. I think I'm gonna have sex with them all!"*

I hear from the stage *"Hi, it's so nice to meet you,"* and that line snaps me out of my own head just in time to catch Derek's entrance. It floors me. I realize "Hi, it's so nice to meet you" isn't exactly a "joke," but I crumple anyway. Something about the combination of seeing Derek in drag, the soft "female" voice he's using onstage, and the feminine gestures he's trying to get across just shakes me to my bones. I laugh my ass off. Coney shushes me.

It gets worse when Derek, as "Candy Soriano," relates how "she" met her new husband, Alfonso. *"It's the cutest story, you guys! I was at Señor Frog's in Jamaica, and Alfonso was judging a bikini contest that I was in. And I went up to him and I was like 'You are the most beautiful man I've ever seen.' And he was like 'You're just saying that because I play for the Yankees.' And I was like 'You're right, I am!' And we fell in love."*

I laugh as "Candy" talks about Tino Martinez and how she's *"Studied THAT bulge."* I laugh as Chuck Knoblauch's wife is told that she doesn't have to worry about her husband's fidelity, because *"NOBODY wants to sleep with Chuck*

Knoblauch." Later, when "Candy Soriano" describes Derek Jeter's physical appearance by saying *"He looks like The Rock had sex with a Muppet,"* I'm gone. Tears are falling. As the audience howls, our dress rehearsal finishes like this:

Patrice Williams: Uh-oh, Clarice, you're not gonna like this, but those girls are back again.
Clarice Knoblauch: Which ones? The ones who flash their boobs on the JumboTron?
Patrice Williams: Mmm-hmm. They're coming this way.
Clarice Knoblauch: If those two skanks try to talk to my Chuck, I will take a bat to their teeth, I swear to God!

Silence. Then more silence; then still more.

Feverish whispering floats in now from offstage. At which point a stage manager runs up and gives me a push. "Go, go. GO!" she tells me. I was so busy laughing I completely forgot my own cue.

Into the scene I stumble, hands yet again at my own boobs. The crowd roars as they recognize me, which is good, because after all that laughing, I've momentarily forgotten my one line. It finally hits me. *"Hello-o-o, ladies. Your husbands are looking very sexy tonight. I think I'm gonna have sex with them all!"*

"You shut up!" say the wives.

Now here comes Coney, waving a pair of Jockey shorts over his head while trying pathetically to look hot. *"Aren't you Alfonso Soriano's wife?"* he/she asks Derek/Candy.

"I certainly am!" he/she replies.

"Well, tell him that he left his tightie-whities under my Tercel last night!"

And with that, a fistfight breaks out between the Yankee wives and us skanks. The audience roars, and there, under the lights, and in the middle of this phony brawl, Coney and Derek and I are literally giggling, swept away by the fun, and the humor and joy and the absolute silliness of it all. Four hours later, as the show is broadcast live across the country, the three of us duke it out again, this time in front of an even louder, rowdier live audience, and this time around, tens of millions of home viewers laugh along with them. Again, Derek kills. Again, the jokes all work. Again, I laugh too hard, lose focus, and miss my cue. This time, however, the stage managers are ready, and they give me a shove before my gaffe is even noticeable on-air. By midbrawl, I'm riding a huge adrenaline high, feeling absolutely great.

After-party with Dan Aykroyd and Lorne Michaels

Post *SNL,* Coney and I hit the show's after-party with Derek, then splinter off to hit a nightspot or two on our own. We laugh, we talk, we catch up with old friends at a few of our old favorite New York City "libraries and museums," and everywhere we go people tell us how funny our little cross-dressed cameo was. I can tell they're being honest, because almost everyone I talk to seems on the verge of laughing out loud as soon as they see me. Finally, just before 3 A.M., Coney cracks. He takes me to a mirror and shows me that I've forgotten to take off my *SNL* eye makeup. All night long I've been wandering through Manhattan with a big, bald head and skanky lavender eyelids. Coney's been loving every minute of it. Now I understand the cat-and-canary smiles I've been getting all night long. Quickly I decide to leave the Maybelline in place, milking my weird, purple makeover for a lot of late-night laughs.

Still later, when even the after-hours libraries and museums have closed for the night, I'm once again safely within the confines of my hotel room. I stand at the sink brushing my teeth, staring into my reflection with a glazed-over, semiconscious expression, when from out of nowhere I'm smacked in the head with an unexpected little wake-up call. It hits me hard. Tonight, I realize, for the first time in a LONG time, I'm free. Five full months after surgeons sliced open my spine, scraped around between a pair of vertebrae, and yanked a piece of broken bone out from under a nerve, there's been absolutely NO pain. I can walk, and move, and twist, and show up on TV in a dress, all without even *thinking* about my back. Tonight, the long-awaited confirmation finally sinks in; I'm gonna be okay. It's official. I take a long, deep, thoroughly satisfying breath, and feel the weight of the world rising from my shoulders.

Tonight, *hundreds* of hours of physical therapy, exercise, diet, jogging, stretching, and denial have all combined to buy me a few hours of freedom, a few hours of fun, a few hours of peace. Tonight, for the first time in a long time, I'm no longer a patient, I'm just Boomer. I can move. I can laugh. I can goof on Coney at will. Tonight, I feel like running downstairs, bolting outside in my boxers, and turning cartwheels down Broadway.

It's a very good sign.

TWO

Jabbed in the Back

David Wells is not
currently part of the Yankees'
plans for 2002.

—Yankees' general manager
Brian Cashman

JULY 1, 2001: COMISKEY PARK

Any time you're facedown, ass up in the trainer's room, the first thing you notice is the combination of smells. They're always the same. Betadyne, isopropyl, urinal cakes, atomic balm, hand sanitizer, guy stink. All these things are steeped indelibly into the walls of every trainer's room, in every ballpark in every major-league city. There are no exceptions. Trust me, *I* know. I spend a *lot* of time on these tables lately, and I notice this stuff. Mostly, I do it to take my mind off the six-inch needle being jammed up into my spine.

Cortisone and I go way back, and lemme tell you that beautiful little adrenal steroid hormone is a lifesaver. It eases pain. It keeps you off the disabled list. It may even let you toss a complete game shutout on a day where you wake up thinking that just putting on your shirt is gonna crack you in two. For an aging, perpetually husky pitcher like me, it's a godsend. It's baseball crack. In the mid 1990s, in Detroit, and Cincinnati and Baltimore, it helped me fight off occasional stiffness to become a successful major-league starter. With the Yankees in '98, it helped me pitch a perfect game. In Toronto, in 2000, it helped me win twenty games at the age of thirty-seven. Today, with the White Sox, it allows me to get out of bed in the morning . . . sometimes.

Without cortisone, I'd have long ago become a bent-over retiree, scouring Tampa Bay in search of early-bird dinner specials. With that in mind, I will never, *ever* fault a guy for helping his game, or extending his career, with the use of whatever drugs will get him over the hump. That said, I must add that drug use is an everyday fact of life in almost all major-league locker rooms, with most users falling into one of two categories.

First, "greenies" have been around for eons in the world of baseball, and while they're still just as illegal as they were when Jim Bouton first wrote about them in *Ball Four*, they're still every bit as prevalent. Cheap, and easy to find,* these little buggers will open your eyes, and sharpen your focus, and get your blood moving on demand, over and over again, right through a full 162-game season. Day game after a night game? A four-game series in the 102-degree heat of Arlington Stadium? A four-hour postgame flight followed by three hours of sleep and a one o'clock start? A *really* wild party at the hotel bar last night? Not a problem. A couple of greenies will get you sharp, and *keep* you sharp, right through nine innings of play.** Honestly, though I can't personally stomach anything more stimulating than a six-pack of Diet Coke, as a pitcher, I won't *ever* object to a sleepy-eyed middle infielder beaning up to help me win.

---

*A lot of guys will buy themselves a season-long stockpile at one time. We're talking about hundreds and hundreds and hundreds of pills. With that in mind, it really ain't hard to get connected. Stand in the middle of your clubhouse and walk ten feet in any direction. Chances are you'll find what you need.
**Over-the-counter eye-openers can include the gobbling of caffeine pills (sometimes by the fistful), Red Bull, and Ripped Fuel.

That may not be the politically correct spin on the practice, but I really couldn't care less. The only time I'll object is when it becomes obvious that a perpetually amped player has begun relying on alcohol or pot to mellow himself after a game. That's Elvis territory.

Less widespread, but much more dangerous, are the painkillers. Percocet, Vicodin, codeine, Darvocet—they're all interchangeable, equally addictive, and almost entirely unavoidable. If you're a pitcher, sooner or later, your shoulder *is* going to explode. If you're an outfielder, it'll be your knee, or your ankle. If you're a catcher, large parts of your body will probably fall off before you retire. But whatever your position, and whatever your injury, you're gonna need *something* to get you through the pain. That's how the painkillers take hold.

Nobody goes onto the DL without kicking and screaming. Nobody ever *chooses* season-ending surgery. And if you're lucky enough to be caught up in *any* kind of pennant race, there's no way in hell you'll *ever* pull yourself out of the lineup. With those things in mind, all over baseball, year in and year out, you'll find a whole lot of guys trying their best to play through a whole lot of pain. Pills keep them going. Pills keep them involved. But without being rested, these guys never *heal*. The pain obviously gets worse, and the cycle now repeats. Two Percocet become three. A twice-a-day dosage gets doubled, and pretty soon the habit's unbreakable. Trust me on this one, I've taken those drugs. I've *felt* them taking hold, and while I've always been able to step away, those bastards can eat you alive. It's amazing what guys will go through to keep playing baseball—an addiction far more powerful than anything I've just mentioned.

Throughout the years, the positive effects of my cortisone shots have become progressively shorter-lived. In 1995, for example, if my back were to tighten up in June, I knew I could get myself a shot, jump off the table doing somersaults, and forget all about pain until maybe Labor Day. By 1998, the cortisone-induced relief period was less than half that long. In 2001, in Toronto, after a blistering first half, where I went 15 and 2, the slide continued. Stiffness came on just after the All-Star Game, and as always, I'd fight through the pain as best I could, until finally, after a lousy start or two, I'd cave and go looking for my shot. As usual, the injections themselves worked wonders, but the window of their effectiveness was now dropping off fast. Let's put it this way: I pitched seven complete games for Toronto in 2000, each of them coming within twenty-four hours of being shot up. I also stood on the mound that summer during non-medicated, second-half starts where I got pounded for six runs in four innings, and seven over two. Sensing a pattern? I know I was, and maybe GM Gord Ash did too. By season's end, he had no qualms about shipping me (and my 20-8 record) off to Chicago.

Going into the 2001 season with a new team, I wanted desperately to keep myself functioning at a competitive level. With that in mind, I battled through my entire spring training with the White Sox while seeing a Tucson chiropractor three times a day. I'd wake up stiff, get dressed, and immediately drive to his office. Then I'd drive back over to the ballpark for my morning workout, then back to the chiropractor, then off to play golf, then back to the chiropractor. That was my day. I probably put two thousand miles on my rental car during those few short weeks, but it was absolutely worth it. The treatment kept me flexible, and as April approached, I started believing I might actually skate through yet another season without any real downtime. I was wrong.

By early summer, my relationship with the doctor giving me my cortisone fix was fast becoming a lot like that of Elvis and Dr. Nick. I'd gotten six shots in three months, and I needed more. I was in bad shape. Getting up in the morning, I'd literally have to crawl out of my bed. I couldn't stand. I couldn't even sit in a chair. Often, I looked more like a crab than a human, moving sideways around my hotel room on hands and knees. My body simply wouldn't straighten out. I'd be tilted. I'd be bent. I'd have to walk around hunched over like Quasimodo for an hour just to get loose enough to stand.

Out on the road there were days I wouldn't even get out of bed, it hurt so bad. With a dull ache in my spine, I'd just lay there in bed watching lousy movies on Spectravision hour after hour, hoping my next cortisone shot would finally get me back up to speed. Talk about torture. One day I actually watched *Deuce Bigalow, Male Gigolo* twice.

Throughout that 2001 season, while the injections worked pretty well *some* of the time, even the immediate effect of the cortisone hit had become a lot less miraculous. No longer did I jump off the trainer's table doing jumping jacks, just maybe sitting up, and walking and surviving six or seven innings with tolerable pain.

Clearly, if you put two and two together, you can't help but realize that after all those years of throwing 120 pitches every fifth night, and all those years of masking a degenerative back condition beneath a comforting blanket of cortisone, I'd finally reached a point of no return.

On June 28, 2001, after a couple of truly half-assed, truly painful starts against St. Louis and Baltimore, I was jonesing once more to be shot up. Three days later, I was back in my usual facedown/ass-up position with that goddamn spike sliding between my L4 and L5 vertebrae. I felt the stick, felt the burn of the fluid being forced between the bones, and then, right at that moment where I'd usually feel relief beginning to slide effortlessly down my back, I felt nothing. My shot was a dud. Ten minutes later I rolled off that table feeling like my best friend had rejected me.

The following day, going to the mound against the Minnesota Twins, I lasted all of two innings before my back seized up tight, locking in place and leaving me wide-eyed with pain. Unable to straighten up, unable to catch my breath, I ultimately tiptoed off the field, with a lightning bolt ripping through me. It was over. My body no longer would respond to cortisone, and something inside me was *really* messed up. Now it was scary. Now I was screwed. Five days later, I officially hit the disabled list.

I *hate* the DL simply because I LOVE pitching. I WANT the ball. Take those things away from me and I get royally pissed. I have pitched with raging hangovers. I have pitched with an explosive case of stomach flu. I have pitched a half season nursing a broken pinky. Let me say it again. Every fifth day, come hell or high water, I WANT the ball. It's that simple. You try and stop me, I kick your ass. With all that in mind, you *know* I went onto that gimp list roaring.

I looked for loopholes: newer, better, stronger drugs, mechanics adjustments, hydrotherapy, acupuncture, ANYTHING that might help me stay on the mound was fair game. Finally though, as the horizontal Spectravision days became more and more frequent, I had no choice. Unless the White Sox desperately needed a stiff body to weigh down the tarp during rain delays, there was *nothing* I could do anymore to help this team. I started rehab exercises the following morning, hoping for the best. That's not what I got.

I spent two full weeks stretching gently, getting massages, seeing chiropractors, soaking, sweating, and seething. Nothing helped. Nothing worked. Nothing eased the pain, not even a little bit.

On July 18, I went to see the White Sox team doctor, James Boscardin, who asked me to perform impossible stunts for him like walk, bend at the hips, and sit in a straight-backed chair. Watching me fail, with a sad, pitying demeanor, Boscardin quickly ordered a complete MRI series. When it was done, he showed me exactly how fucked up my back really was. I had a severely herniated disc between my L4 and L5 vertebrae. Worse, the disc was so swollen, it was now pressing constantly on a spinal nerve. While I had no idea what that actually meant, I knew it sounded *really* bad.

With charts, and pictures, and little plastic models, the good doctor patiently explained to this layman exactly what was at stake. My condition was grim: bad enough to keep me from walking someday if left untreated. That's all I needed to hear. My boys are eight and three, and on the very best days of my life, I serve as a sort of human trampoline for them. Even the *possibility* of losing my ability to run and jump and grab-ass and fake pro-wrestle with those monsters was enough to spur me onto the operating table. As terrifying as back surgery can be, there was nothing to think about, no hesitation. Though doctors assured me that after the surgery, and some rehab, I *would* more than likely be able to resume pitching, baseball was now the *last* thing on my mind. For the sake of my kids, and my wife, and our future together, I wanted this sucker done, now. There would be no debate and no second thoughts. With my eager blessing, Doctor Boscardin leapt into action, filleting me less than twenty-four hours later. Thankfully, the procedure went beautifully . . . sorta.

As expected, the disc between my L4 and L5 vertebrae was herniated. That was no problem. The doctors just went in and cleaned that little bugger up in no time. The problem came in that they *also* found a little piece of chipped bone lodged under a nerve in my spinal column. To get *that* sucker out of there, the doctors had to pull the nerve away from my spine, then scrape around and yank the bone out. The procedure ended up being a bigger deal than expected, which I realized the second I woke up after surgery.

I was in serious, stabbing, codeine-gobbling agony. My back was on fire, and because the doctors had to poke around at that nerve in my back, I now also had a nasty, burning pain shooting down through my ass and into my right leg.

Making matters worse was the fact that for the first six weeks after the surgery, my rehab routine consisted of doing absolutely nothing, beyond a tiny bit of "therapeutic walking." Wanna go stir-crazy sometime? Try shoving a knitting needle into your spine, then sitting in your house for the next forty-two days, in Florida, when it's 178 degrees outside, drizzling, with 100 percent humidity. The doctors wanted me to rest. I wanted to climb the walls. There was no way out.

I roll slowly through the worst July of my life, propped sideways, like a tree stump, on my living room couch. I lay there, depressed, watching the days unfold outside my patio doors. Cartoon Network blares from my TV set constantly as I watch endless episodes of *Scooby-Doo* with my little boy Lars. He likes that stupid old show almost as much as I do. He lays on top of me as we watch. My mind wanders. I wonder why I'm still in pain. I wonder what Velma looks like naked. I wonder if I'll ever pitch again, and I wonder if retirement would really be such a bad thing.

DAVID WELLS

Staring at Scooby-Doo

Spend a month on any couch, squashed up next to a three-year-old boy who loves you to death, and I promise you'll never want to go away on a ten-game road trip again. Sure, I'd hate to end my career with a rotten season and an aching back, but here at home, I know that even if my pitching days are done, I'm gonna be fine. With Lars in my lap, and Nina down the hall, humming in her office, the idea of early retirement actually seems kind of nice. After two decades on the road, life as a full-time, stay-at-home husband and father sounds pretty cool. It might drive my *wife and kids* nuts, but I'd love it.

On the other side of the coin, the surgery's done, and barring absolute disaster I *should* come away from this whole ordeal feeling a *lot* better than I have over the past four or five *years*. With determination, and discipline, a little bit of luck, and a *whole lot* of rehab, I *can* make it back to the bigs, not just as a survivor, not just as a hanger-on, but with full-bore, big-dog dominance. With all that in mind, I decide to work hard, get healthy, and let the chips fall where they may. Big-league pitcher, or stay-at-home dad, I win big either way.

Finally, right around Labor Day, I get the doctors' official okay to begin physical therapy. On day one, I'm nervous as hell. I weigh a monstrous 280 pounds. I'm stiff as a board. I have *no* idea how much better I'm gonna get, but I'm nonetheless thrilled with the idea of finally moving again. Gently, slowly, and with a lot of groaning and discomfort on my part, I start stretching, twisting, and getting my muscles reacquainted with one another. Almost immediately, I can feel my back loosening. The progress is microscopic but it's more than enough to get me excited. From there, my trainer and I discuss how important it's gonna be for me to strengthen my leg muscles and my abs as a way of protecting my back. Squats and sit-ups are going to be a big part of my rehab. I've always hated them both, but as of right now, I don't even care—if they're gonna help me get healthy again, I'll learn to *love* 'em.

Next we talk about how beneficial it'd be for me to drop five, or ten, or a solid thirty pounds. Believe it or not, even THAT news makes me smile. I'm not sure I can survive eating nonsupersized amounts of low-fat, healthy food, but with so much at stake, I'm certainly willing to try.

As the weeks pass, I'm shocking friends, family, and especially myself by sticking to a strict, high-maintenance workout regimen. Every single morning I run through an ass-kicking cardio routine: treadmill, bike, whatever it takes to get my heart pounding. After that, I hit my back exercises. Sit-ups are followed by Superman stretches, and *those* are followed by a weird-looking maneuver where I lay on the floor with my feet up on a big inflatable ball, then try to lift my hips up toward the ceiling. It feels awful, and it looks like some sort of low-rent, badly choreographed stripper-move.

I do my squats with a frown, then graduate to some even *more* heinous *one-legged* squats, which burn like hell. I bench-press, I curl, I crunch. I do calf raises until my legs feel like they're gonna explode all over the carpeting. Suddenly, I'm "yang" to the old David Wells's "yin," and I have to admit, I'm a little freaked out by the change.

Even more unbelievable is the fact that I've completely reinvented my own eating habits. Gone are the hot dogs, and the beer, and the pizza and the cookies and the nachos and the buffalo wings and the vodka and the lasagna and . . . you get the picture. Cap'n Crunch and bacon have both been banished from my breakfast table. In their place I'll scarf down a half-dozen egg whites and a chicken breast, maybe with a banana chaser. Friends now openly wonder if aliens have abducted the real David Wells and left some sort of evil, physically fit android in his place

Lunch, which used to consist of whatever cheese-covered, deep-fried, or sauce-covered all-you-can-eat entrée I could get my hands on, now consists of broiled chicken or fish or steak with a salsa-covered baked potato and a salad. Dinner's some variation on those same basic ingredients, and fake-chocolate protein shakes carry me through those times whenever and wherever I might suddenly find myself fighting off the desire to eat an entire meatball pizza.

What the hell is happening to me?

From early September through mid-October, I make slow, steady progress. Though I still sometimes waddle around the house as if I'm impersonating the Tin Man from *The Wizard of Oz*, I'm down twelve pounds, and my body-fat levels are practically free-falling. I can bend again, maybe not with full flexibility, but enough to know I'm gaining ground. I feel better than I have at any time since the surgery, and that's genuinely exciting. I start thinking about baseball again, and by the time the Yankees and Diamondbacks have squared off for the World Series, I'm definitely feeling left out.

I yell at the screen. I cheer. I want that ball . . . bad. Having been to the postseason in 1989, '91, '92, '95, '96, '97 and '98, I've got the fever. Come October, I want to be on that pitcher's mound every single year. That's *my* yard. That's *my* home. This year's no different. When Derek Jeter wins Game 4 of the World Series with a tenth-inning moon shot, I jump up off the couch to whoop at him. Catching myself in midair, I come down smiling, realizing this simple leaping expression of joy would have been absolutely impossible for me at any point over the past four or five years. I catch a twinge of pain for my cheerleading, but it's nothing major. Clearly I'm on the right track, and I'm more determined than ever to get back to the game. Oddly, within just weeks, both World Series opponents will become major players in jump-starting that return.

November. The two weeks following the World Series each year are notoriously quiet as team owners, GMs, scouts, and front-office personnel disappear from their offices, only to reappear nearly naked on sandy beaches all over the world. Wrinkles steaming, paunches protruding, man-boobs soaking up major UV rays, tropical coconut drinks in hand, baseball's big shots take their yearly hiatus. By the Monday after Thanksgiving, however, business as usual returns at full force. The suits are back at the table, and the chips start falling my way, fast.

Play number one comes from the Chicago White Sox, as they officially decline my option year. It's not at all unexpected, and I can't honestly blame them. I'd have cost the Sox $9 million in 2002, and right now, in mid-November, on paper, David Wells is still just a broken-down, overweight, thirty-eight-year-old lefty with a VERY uncertain future. I'd have dropped me too.

As Turkey Day fades into turkey leftovers, baseball's general managers start working their local media with a time-honored, annual lie. Like clockwork, these guys hit their local papers and helmet-haired TV sports reporters with claims their team isn't looking for any quick trades or easy fixes. They'll then give a quick spin on how their team, as assembled right now, is just a key player or two away from being a solid playoff contender. "We're calmly and carefully considering our options for the upcoming season," they'll say with a straight face, "and we won't be making ANY changes until at least the winter meetings." Their pants are on fire.

Nothing could be further from the truth. Heading into baseball's annual winter meetings, front-office types like nothing better than getting an early edge on the competition. With that in mind, it should come as no surprise that even at thirty-eight years old, coming off a bad season and invasive back surgery, I was suddenly becoming damn popular. Gregg Clifton, my agent, began taking "friendly" calls from a solid half-dozen GMs, each of them inquiring as to how I was feeling. During the course of those conversations, they'd inevitably ask about what I might be looking for in terms of a new contract. Oddly, neither Gregg nor I had really figured that out. With a beautiful wife, and two great kids, and a paid-off house and enough money to live very comfortably for the rest of my life, I was in no hurry to accept a lowball offer from some team looking to grab a bargain-basement pitcher hell-bent on returning to baseball. In a strange twist, that lack of desperation actually raised my price.

Gregg Clifton is an incredibly professional human being. He's organized, calculating, meticulous, and thorough. He's the anti-me, and I'm thrilled he's on my team. Gregg's known me since the late Mesozoic era, and after some serious, soul-searching chats, he got down to business with a really good idea of what it was gonna take to get me back on the mound. YES I wanted that ball. YES I wanted to go out on my own terms. YES I wanted to erase last year's stats, but not at *any* cost. Faced with the options of diving headfirst back into baseball, or staying home with the luxury of being around my family 24/7, my desire to get back onto the mound was by no means unconditional. If the offers coming in weren't gonna be irresistible, well, I really did have better things to do.

First and foremost, Gregg knew that I didn't want to ride out my career with a team that flat-out sucked. Good-bye Expos, sorry Devil Rays, it just wouldn't be worth it. Playing for a contender, in situations where every game means something and there's a solid chance of getting into the postseason, makes *every* player better. It also makes the season a lot more fun. Again, if I'm gonna get back on the horse and be away from home and my kids and my wife for the better part of seven months, I've gotta enjoy the process. Otherwise the money's just not worth it.

And speaking of money, while I'm by no means expecting a huge guaranteed contract, I'm not gonna let myself go at clearance-sale prices either. With fifteen years' experience and a proven ability to win, I feel that a guaranteed base salary coupled with a bunch of reasonable incentive clauses seems like a fair deal for both sides. I'm protected in the event I come back and give a team my all only to break down again, and the team's protected by not having to guarantee me a typical starter's salary. In my head, the hypothetical numbers that get me to bite are two or three million guaranteed, with another three or four million dangled over me as attainable incentives.

If I can throw 100 innings, fine, throw me a bone. Throw me another at 150 and another at 200. Let me prove myself by winning ten games, but bump my salary once I've done it. Bump me again at fifteen and twenty. Work out similar incentives for strikeouts and starts, and we can do business in a way that's fair to both sides. At today's prices, when guys who couldn't normally carry my jock out to the mound make $10 million a year (you know who you are), I'm a no-lose situation. Even if I come up big and gobble down every bonus you could possibly owe me, I'll still gonna be a huge fucking bargain.

Finally, as an extra added incentive, I'd love to hook up with a team whose spring training facilities are right here in Florida. That immediately buys me another six weeks at home with my family, and as you've no doubt figured out by now, that's important to me.

With those basic guidelines in place, Gregg and I sat back and waited for the phone to ring, which it did, practically off the hook. Every call started the same way. "How's David feeling? How's the back? Is it true he's lost weight?" The chitchat was almost identical. From there, it was time to put up or shut up. Teams inquiring as to whether or not I might be open to a nonroster, nonguaranteed invitation to camp are shooed away quickly. Teams willing to take more of a chance on me are schmoozed up big-time and encouraged to keep the gates of communication open. Before long, the Philadelphia Phillies, Texas Rangers, Atlanta Braves, and Arizona Diamondbacks are fast becoming front-runners. Oddly, the Yankees haven't called at all, which disappoints me.

Since August, I've been dropping hints in the press about how much I'd like to be a Yankee one more time. In fact I've even gone on the record as saying that I might consider dropping my asking price to help get the "David Wells/ New York Yankees Reunion Tour" kick-started. Obviously, the fairy-tale ending I'm dreaming about finds me back in the Bronx, back in pinstripes, back on the mound, back in front of the world's greatest fans, back in the greatest ballpark on earth: Yankee Stadium. I know it sounds corny, but somehow, deep down inside, I still *feel* like a Yankee. Clearly, I carry a torch. Still, with George Steinbrenner and Yankees' GM Brian Cashman currently neck deep in trying to yank Jason Giambi away from the Oakland A's, I know I'm back-burnered at best. Cashman has even gone so far as to declare in the New York papers that "David Wells is not currently part of the Yankees' plans for 2002." Short of wrapping myself in a bow and showing up at Yankee Stadium bearing flowers and candy, there's not much more I can do. At the same time, there's another heavy hitter who seems bound and determined to get my attention.

"Jerry Colangelo wants to talk to you personally," Gregg says through a lousy cell phone connection. "You up for that?"

"Of course I am!" I shout back. "Set it up."

Ten minutes later my phone rings. I let it go 'til the third ring in an attempt to avoid looking too anxious, and then I pick up. It's Colangelo. He asks, "No bullshit, do you think you're gonna be able to pitch?" which makes me smile, because after all the rehab and strengthening and conditioning I've been doing, I can honestly answer him with an "absolutely." We talk about his team's World Series victory, and Jerry makes it clear that he's working hard to make sure there's gonna be a lot more to come. We talk about his awesome pitching staff, and I have to admit, it gets me psyched. Y'know, the idea of joining a rotation that includes big-time studs like Randy Johnson and Curt Schilling gets your eyes open fast, and playing in front of a team as good as the 2002 Diamondbacks makes 15 to 20 wins a genuine possibility. Jerry closes out the call the way he started, by making it clear he wants me in Arizona, and inviting me to come meet with him in person. I agree without hesitation.

Three days later the trip's cancelled. Arizona's first offer has come in below expectations. There are plenty of incentives included in the deal, but the guaranteed base is very small. It's not an insulting offer, it's really not even all that bad, but as Gregg and I discuss the situation, we both agree it's unacceptable. For that reason, traveling to Phoenix seems pointless at this time, and meeting with Colangelo would more than likely just feel embarrassing to us both. We decline the offer and officially nix the meeting, though we make it clear that if the Diamondbacks remain interested, Gregg will be happy to counter their proposal with one of his own. More and more, I find myself hoping the deal works out.

On December 9, less than a week after our first phone call, it's time for round two. The Diamondbacks have restructured and raised their original offer, and Jerry Colangelo's called me at home twice more, trying to make sure the *is* are dotted, the *ts* are crossed, and the contract language is falling into place without any last-minute monkey wrenches. As it now stands, the new deal, while not overwhelming by any stretch of the imagination, is solid. I've got a million-dollar guarantee waiting for me, with incentive clauses that, with a little luck, could ultimately quintuple that amount. No other team has put an offer that serious on the table, and to play with the defending World Champs, I'm more than willing to bend. Once again Colangelo invites me to Phoenix for a face-to-face. Once again I accept. That's when the phone rings.

"Hey, Boomer, it's George." As in Steinbrenner.

"Dude. How are you?" I answer. Wondering what the hell's up.

"I'm in Tampa," he says. "Whatt'ya say we catch up over lunch tomorrow?"

"Uh, sure," I say while my brain calculates this phone call from 156 different angles. Is George looking to make me an offer? Does he *really* just want to catch up? Has he heard about Colangelo and the Diamondbacks calling me? No, that's crazy, even George isn't *that* well connected. *Is* George that well connected? Where should we eat?

"How 'bout Pete & Shorty's?" I suggest. George agrees, and we've got a date.

Time now to explain a couple of things you need to know. First, George Steinbrenner and I really *are* friends. After a strange start in New York, and one face-to-face encounter where we came dangerously close to punching each other's teeth out, our relationship has somehow evolved beyond that of owner and pitcher, ex-employer and former employee. I genuinely like the guy, and with all that in mind, a friendly lunch might really be all George is looking for. Second, George has a house down here in Tampa (actually it's more like a shopping mall with a living room—the sucker's humongous), so the fact that he's suddenly in Florida means nothing. An hour later, my head hurts. I still can't figure his game plan.

The following morning, I'm up and at it even earlier than usual, still obsessing over this mysterious lunch. Too nervous to eat, I skip breakfast entirely. I run through my cardio session and my stretching routine on fumes, then hit my upper body workout even harder than usual. It's a bad idea. With no food in my stomach, my blood sugar plummets, and even as I'm wobbling through my final three sets of bench presses, I'm toast. I'm burnt. I'm spent. I'm also late for my lunch date.

Now starving to death, I bolt out of the house and break at least fourteen local speed laws careening across Clearwater toward Pete & Shorty's. By the time I get there, I'm light-headed, belly growling. George is already there, smiling at me from a corner table.

"Boomer!" I hear from across the room as the smells off the restaurant's burger grill leave me weak-kneed. "How the hell are you, buddy?"

"Boss!" I call back, practically diving to the table. "You ready to order?"

"What? Uh, well, no, maybe if . . ."

I call the waitress over. "Y'know what's fun? Let's split a plate of those little Shorty burgers." George indulges me. I ask for them rare, knowing that'll get them to the table faster than "well done" would have.

"You look great!" George tells me. "You're down like what, fifteen pounds?"

"Almost twenty," I tell him, launching into a description of my new diet and exercise habits. Meanwhile I'm practically drooling in anticipation of lunch and simultaneously trying to read between the lines of everything George says, hoping to gain some insight into his real motivations behind this meeting. I want him to make me an offer. I want him to at least express *some* interest in bringing me back to Yankee Stadium. He does neither of those things.

Instead, we talk about our families and about hockey. We talk about the New Jersey Devils and their unexpected losing streak. We talk about the New Jersey Nets and their unexpected winning streak. We talk about hunting, and football, and how Florida is too fucking hot for human habitation. At that point, the burgers arrive and I dive on them like a hyena leaping onto a dead water buffalo. George laughs, saying, "Some things never change."

Embarrassed, I prove George wrong by cutting myself off after just two Shorty burgers (my record is thirteen) and by ordering myself a grilled chicken breast with salad and green beans.

"Wow, I'm impressed," George says. "You *can* live on something beside red meat and beer." Laughing now, George leans in and demands, "Come on, David. No bullshit, no spin, tell me how you feel."

"George," I say, "I feel better right now than I did last year, better than the year before, better than I did in '97 and '98. With no bullshit, and no spin, I can honestly say I feel ten years younger . . . maybe more."

"Ahh, that's fantastic," George says. "I'm so happy for you."

And then we talk baseball . . . for all of two minutes. George asks what teams are showing interest in me, and I tell him that the Phillies have called, and Texas, and Atlanta, and when I tell him about having a meeting set up the following week in Phoenix with Jerry Colangelo, George's eyes light up.

"Oh, be careful there," he says before I cut him off.

"Y'know," I say, feeling a lump growing in my throat, "it would be great to come back to New York too." There, I'd said it. Like the first "I love you" a lovestruck teenager tosses at a new girlfriend. I'd just kind of wound up, closed my eyes, and hurled my feelings through the air, even though I knew it was a dangerous move. Silence follows. The lump in my throat sinks down into my stomach.

"Welllllllllllll," George says, killing time, "in a perfect world, that *would* be great, but uhhhh, y'know for that to happen, other moves would have to be made, and the roster would need to be rearranged a little bit, and . . ." Yadda yadda yadda. It's a classic blow-off speech, after which George changes the subject. Forty minutes later, I leave Pete & Shorty's feeling like I'm gonna be an Arizona Diamondback.

Mark Newman, the Yankees' senior vice president of baseball operations, calls Gregg Clifton the following morning, saying "George reports that David looks great. We should talk about having him come back to Yankee Stadium in pinstripes." I laugh out loud when Gregg relays the news, loving the Yankees' interest and shaking my head in disbelief that George Steinbrenner, billionaire owner of the New York Yankees, has taken it upon himself to endure lunch at a burger joint and check me out in person. *This* is an owner who gives a shit. *This* is why the Yankees are THE YANKEES. Granted, a hundred-million-dollar payroll can make a contender out of any team, but there's more going on here. For all his faults, you can't deny that George Steinbrenner, the man, not just "the wallet," is a tangible, positive factor in the Yankees domination of baseball. His fingerprints are all over that team.

And honestly, who could blame George for wanting to squeeze the produce before purchasing? It's good business. I mean, George COULD have shown up to lunch and found that David Wells was now a six-hundred-pound shirtless guy in bib overalls, gnawing on a pork chop bone like Haystacks Calhoun. He could have found me nursing a useless, postsurgery, stick-up-the-ass posture. You get yourself a free agent in that kind of condition and the back page of the *New York Post* is gonna get ugly. I'm just surprised George didn't toss a ten-dollar bill on the ground to see if I could bend over and pick it up.

At any rate, there I was. In the course of two days, I'd gone from the wallflower nobody wanted to dance with, to the object of two suitors' affections. The Diamondbacks had made their intentions clear with hard, impressive numbers. The Yankees were still basically at the flirting stage. At this point, the bird in the hand, though less showy than the two black-and-white pinstriped birds in the bush, was still looking mighty attractive.

On December 20, I flew to Phoenix and finally had my face-to-face with Jerry Colangelo. Warm and smart and funny—it's impossible not to like this guy. He practically floated on air as he talked about how proud he was of his 2001 champs. Recounting practically every pitch of the World Series for me in vivid, elaborate detail, Colangelo took on the tone and demeanor of a proud father showing his guest an endless series of kid photos. He raved about his pitching staff, and his manager, and his coaches, and his stadium, and his hometown, and his bat boys, and his local supermarket. He threw hard numbers on the table that would have locked me up tight while allowing me to close out my career with a proven, solid winner.

Our courtship continued throughout most of the evening, first at a Phoenix Suns game, then at Colangelo's favorite pizza joint, and by the time this long, strange first date was over I have to admit that, yes, Jerry and I *did* shake hands

At the Suns game with Jerry Colangelo (*AP Photo/Paul Connors*)

on a tentative deal. Nothing was set in stone, or committed to paper, or leaked to the media, but we *had* agreed, at least in principle, to the bare-bones construction of a 2002 contract. I was in. I was back in baseball. I was pumped. Of course, I'd still have to go through the motions of passing a physical, with the Diamondbacks' team physician, but with the holidays getting close, my back feeling fine, and the good doctor out of the office on a two-week holiday vacation, *that* formality certainly could wait. Jerry and I would simply hold off on announcing the deal until after the New Year. No biggie. What could possibly happen? This transaction's done. I'm going to Phoenix. I need some SPF 30, fast.

David Wells was now a Diamondback, and that felt pretty good. The dollars were still decent, if unspectacular, and the team's West Coast spring training *was* gonna take me away from home for an extra six weeks, and it's *totally* fucking hot in Phoenix, but no deal's perfect, and the Diamondbacks' benefits were undeniable. Schilling, Johnson, Batista, Wells . . . this team was gonna win some ball games. I flew home on December 22 with a smile, wishing I could have knocked off the team physical and formally sealed the deal today. *Ich bin ein Diamondback.*

Less than twenty-four hours later, George is at it again. "Hey, Boomer, Pete & Shorty's for lunch again tomorrow?" he shouts into my phone.

"Uhhhhhhhh," I said, before squirting out a half-assed "Sure."

"Great. See you there." Now I'm REALLY confused. What the hell is he doing? He *can't* know about the Arizona deal. *Nobody* does. Does he want to make me an official offer? Does he want to give me a Christmas fruitcake? I'm clueless.

A quick call to Gregg Clifton's office throws me some leads. "Relax, buddy," Greg counsels. "Colangelo apparently leaked news of the deal at a charity function last night. George *must* have heard about it by now, and, you know, he probably just wants to wish you good luck. I'd say just go. Eat, enjoy your lunch, and don't worry." Easier said than done. With "the Boss" on my brain I spend the following twenty-four hours shopping for stocking stuffers while trying hard not to think about this meeting. I fail, miserably.

Christmas Eve, 12:55 in the afternoon; I pull into Pete & Shorty's five minutes early. George is already there, sitting at that same corner table with his back to the wall in classic Bugsy Siegel style. In an absolutely surreal moment, as I walk across the floor to join Steinbrenner, Alvin and the Chipmunks are singing loudly over the restaurant's speaker system. The two of us shake, sitting down for a meeting that could be worth multiple millions of dollars, but all I can hear is that little shit Alvin singing, "I-I-I still want a huuuuuuula hooooooooop!" Even stranger, one full hour into this power lunch, George still hasn't brought up the subject of baseball.

We've talked Christmas, and family, and we've split a pile of Shorty burgers.* Still, there's no sports talk. I slide the conversation sideways to baseball contraction, hoping the natural segue will snap George into "Boss" mode. No dice. Instead, George wishes me luck in the upcoming season, and in finding a good playing situation. He's smiling, a lot.

Now I'm lost. I genuinely like George, and normally, I'd love to have lunch with him and just shoot the shit. Today though, I have to admit I'm confused. Why would George waste his Christmas Eve with me in a hamburger joint if he wasn't gonna play Santa? Time to call the jolly old elf's bluff.

"Well," I say, trying hard to keep my fake grin screwed on straight, "I should probably go. I've still got like nine hundred Power Rangers toys to put together before tomorrow."

"All right," George says. "Oh, and by the way, what's your exact situation with the Diamondbacks?" We both light up. Somewhere in the distance, a choir of angels launches into the "Hallelujah Chorus."

"Well," I tell George, "Colangelo and I shook on a deal."

"Right!" George dives in. "But did you sign anything?"

I've barely chirped out my no before George is at it again.

Practically giggling, he reaches into his jacket, pulls out a sheet of yellow, lined paper, and beams. "This is what I want to do," he says. "I want to bring you back to the Yankees. These are the numbers that seemed to make sense to me." With that he slides the paper through the remnants of a dozen Shorty burgers, across the table so I can see.

"Ahhhhh," I say, biting the insides of my cheeks to keep from laughing, "lemme take a look." Outside, I'm cool. Inside I'm exploding.

Right now I want to get up and dance on the table. I want champagne. I want to shout "Whoo-hooo!!!" like Homer Simpson. I want to launch fireworks. I want to kiss George Steinbrenner square on the face.

Even before I've looked at the page, I know I'm a Yankee again, and honest to God, my heart just leaps with joy. Colangelo's gonna strangle me, and my agent may shoot me, but I just plain don't care. I ring Gregg Clifton's cell phone immediately. When I catch him, he's mid-mall, out of breath, frantically sprint-

---

* Okay, so Shorty burgers aren't exactly health food—it *is* Christmas Eve for crying out loud.

D A V I D   W E L L S

ing through an eleventh-hour toy run. "Sit down," I tell him. "You're not gonna believe this."

Taking a seat halfway between a discount shoe store and a skinny, department store Santa, Gregg hears my news, fights off the urge to kill, then patiently walks me through a whole song and dance about both the judicial and moral boundaries of my handshake deal with Colangelo. I glaze over. The whole time Gregg's talking, he sounds exactly like Charlie Brown's mother to me. *Yo no hablo legalese.* Finally, I just ask the obvious question of the day. "Gregg, yes or no, is a handshake deal officially binding?" And now there's a long "Hmmm-mmm" on Gregg's end of the line. "Listen to me," he begins, carefully constructing his next sentence in his head "Ethically, I'd say yes, but legally . . . no." That's all I need to hear. Three years after getting shipped off to live with the Canadian neighbors, I'm going home to Yankee Stadium! Across the table, George looks ready to burst. He knows how badly I wanted this. He knows what my answer's gonna be even if I do have to maintain an outward sense of dignified professionalism.

My head's spinning, and looking at George's proposal does nothing to stop it. Though I'd have been more than willing to cut the Yankees a discount, George's numbers are actually a lot higher than Colangelo's. George has two years on the table, with a nice guaranteed salary and a lot of incentive clauses thrown into the deal. If I can be successful with the Yankees this year (and let's face it, pitching in front of that 2002 lineup *you* could have probably won twelve games), my salary will be roughly equal to what I made last year. I'm thrilled. My only demand is that the Boss throw an ironclad "no-trade" clause into the soup. You remember that old saying about "Fool me once . . ."

I'm in heaven. Not only does George's deal include a guaranteed offer for the 2003 season, but there's an option tacked on for 2004 as well. I look at that piece of yellow paper and know that after stops in Toronto, Detroit, Cincinnati, Baltimore, New York, Toronto, and Chicago, I'm finally done moving. I'm gonna go out as a Yankee. It's hard to look cool when there are tears welling in your eyes.

By the time George and I had said our good-byes and headed our separate ways amid yet another eighty-five-degree, muggy, Bay Area Christmas Eve, George knew he'd made this my best Christmas ever. I've never actually believed in that old myth about how it's better to give than to receive, but judging by George's face, it really did seem he was enjoying all this at LEAST as much as me. In the weeks to come, I'll find out that George *himself* did the cheerleading for my return to New York, while many of his "baseball people" were less enthusiastic. That piece of news fuels my workouts for months to come. Now it's personal. I owe George big-time, and I AM gonna make him look good.

So it came without ribbons. It came without tags. It came without packages, boxes, or bags, but it came. My own Christmas miracle came just the same. I'm not in the car thirty seconds before I call home to Nina, who lets out a scream that nearly blows out my eardrum. She cries loudly. She actually shouts the word "Hooray!" She knows what this means to me. Even better, she's absolutely *thrilled* with the fact the Yankees' spring training complex is literally twelve minutes from our front door, and she *loves* the idea that New York City is just a two-hour flight away. During the season, Nina and my three-year-old son/Tasmanian devil-boy, Lars, can be with me anytime they want. At the same time, even though my older guy, Brandon, lives just down the road with *his* mom, he's officially old enough to join me in New York City for home stand weekends and for two-week blowouts during his summer vacation. He'll also accompany me through a Yankees' road trip or two. *Everybody*, it seems, got something really great this year for the holidays. Suddenly, I'm George Bailey at the end of *It's a Wonderful Life*. Now all I have to do is pass my Yankees physical.

Two days after Christmas, I've not only *passed* that test, I *aced* the mother-effer. Running through my daily workout with Yankees brass watching intently, I ran, and biked, and lifted, and twisted, and stretched and spun like there was no tomorrow. No dope, I knew those guys would be on their cells back to George and Joe Torre within minutes after my performance, and I was hell-bent on squeezing no-less-than-glowing reports out of them all. There's no way I wanted to go into spring training as a question mark.

As February slowly approaches, I know there's one last obstacle I've got to flatten. I haven't actually pitched in seven months now. I've long-tossed a little bit, and I played softball at a charity event, but despite the fact I'm feeling great, I still haven't reared back and let it fly. This is nothing new for me, and quite frankly, I'm usually the last pitcher to show up for camp, and the first guy ready, but this year's obviously different. I *should* be fine. I *should* have *no* problem. I *should* be just as loose and fluid and rubber-armed as ever. But I won't know that for sure 'til I chuck. Will my mechanics be affected by the back surgery? Will I unconsciously try to protect my back by altering my delivery? How will I hold up after tossing a few dozen fastballs? I can't answer ANY of these questions for sure until I get out on a local field and throw live . . . which I finally do on January 31.

Taking things slowly, I head out with a friend, and over the course of maybe thirty minutes, we graduate from catch, to long-toss, to actual pitching. And while I limit myself to twenty-five throws at maybe 75 percent velocity, I'm ecstatic with the results. My windup and delivery and follow-through are all smooth and comfortable, with absolutely no pain at all. Lighter, stronger, and healthier than I've been in years, I feel like I could go nine innings right now. I can't wait to get to camp.

Driving home, I find myself grinning broadly. My fastball still pops. My curveball still snaps, dropping off the table pretty consistently. My location is solid, and I have no doubt that by the time spring training's in full swing I'll be comfortably back at 92 or 93 miles per hour. In short, the tools are back in the box, and barring disaster (he said, knocking on the table and throwing salt over his left shoulder while crossing his fingers and toes) it looks like my back's gonna be just fine too. The last, lingering question marks have officially been erased, replaced now by large, black, Sharpie-markered exclamation points. I'm ready. The old confidence level is rising. The killer instinct is growling. Sitting here after just one brief home-grown outing, I can't wait for opening day. To the opposing batters, now striking out in my head, I silently holler, Just bring it! 'Cuz I ain't *nearly* finished yet.

Sitting in my car, cruising, Metallica blasting, I take a moment to reflect on my outing, and also to think about exactly how lucky I've been. Not just this winter, not just over the course of a major-league career, but *always*. For almost four decades now, through the great times, and the god-awful, I've *always* felt charmed. Somehow, no matter how chaotic or crazy my life has gotten, I've always managed to survive, thrive, and bounce back even better than before. As spring training 2002 drew closer, and that same basic scenario seemed ready to unfold yet again, I thought it might finally be time to document how chaos, disorder, confusion, pandemonium, turmoil, discord, anarchy, and insanity have somehow, time and again, worked their unexplainable magic in making me the luckiest man on earth.

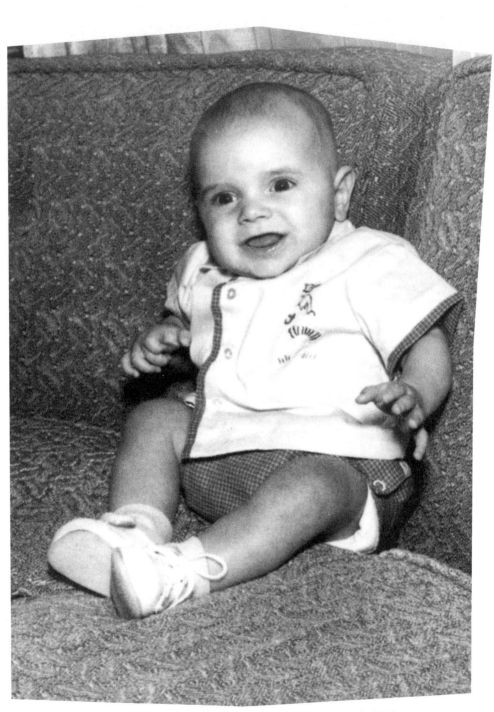

Me in 1963. Add a goatee and it looks just like me in 2003.

THREE

Growing Up with Hoggs

Listen, David, if you're
gonna drive my Harley, you've
got to wear a helmet . . .
at least until you're twelve.

—Crunch, Hells Angel pal

SPRING 1974: OCEAN BEACH, CALIFORNIA

The sun shines brightly . . . again. Seventy-eight degrees, under a cloudless, blue sky. Here in Ocean Beach, we've been blessed with another perfect, picture postcard of a day. This makes 46,447 in a row. Crossing the infield, toward my Little League pitcher's mound, I find myself wishing that just once a hurricane, or a tornado, or a tidal wave might rip through this town and heave a little variety into the local forecast. Sadly, that never happens.

Unfolding their lawn chairs, lined up on display along the visitors' side of the field, are the unfortunate results of human lives played out under such mind-numbingly ideal weather conditions. Power-tanned, soft-spoken, perpetually smiling moms and dads sit cross-legged in their razor-creased designer chinos. The moms all look like aging Barbies. The dads all look like game-show hosts. Down the foul line, as they play catch and stretch and warm up for today's game, their immaculate, soft, plastic children look like easy pickings.

With a sharp, high-schooler's fastball, an illegal curve, and a nasty habit of brushing back any hitter who tries crowding my plate, I'm the meanest son of a bitch in the league. I'm eleven years old. Tossing hard now as I finish warming up with my catcher, I watch those "Visitors" closely, slowly working up a nice, healthy hatred for today's unlucky opponents.

There's a nice little hop evolving on today's four-seamer when a faint rumbling floats in from right field. The noise grows louder, literally by the second. Across the field, the game-show hosts begin squinting, frowning off into the distance as they try to figure out what's coming. On the mound, I know the answer, and that top-secret intelligence allows an ear-to-ear smile to temporarily ruin my practiced, Bob Gibson scowl. They're coming again, right on schedule. Rolling in now, from the right-field side of the park, are ten fat Harley-Davidsons, every one of them lovingly customized to be as throaty and loud as mechanically possible. A group of heavy Electra Glides cruises in first, panheads roaring. Old 1957 XLs and Model Ks follow. A pair of *Easy Rider* choppers, wobbling badly at this low speed, thunders up in the rear.

Each Hogg is muscle-bound, black, and bearing its own personal super-size Hells Angel—Fat Ray, Snake, Crunch, Max, Fitzy, they're all stretched out down the line, large gap-toothed grins peeking out from behind their wild, fluffy beards. Distressed black leather is everywhere. Well-worn patches defiantly proclaim each man's Hells Angels status. Dark sunglasses make the group's combined first impression all the more ominous. The Barbie-moms squirm uncomfortably now as the bikers settle in to watch a little baseball. They squirm again when they see me leave the mound and greet the assembled gang members with enthusiastic high fives.

When you're eleven years old, and you're hanging with a squadron of guys who look as though they eat small children for breakfast, it's not hard to scare your sixth-grader opponents. It's even easier to frighten their naive, sheltered, boat-owning, sun-baked parents. In their eyes, I was immediately branded a delinquent by association, a rebel, an outsider, a bad influence. It was great! Even at eleven years old, those descriptions felt comfortable to me, even flattering. I was born to wear a black hat. The "hoodlum hurler" status also helped my pitching stats by supplying me a nice healthy dose of whiff-inducing intimidation. I owe these bikers big-time. They're my friends, my fans, my own heavily tattooed, rolling, roaring cheerleading squad.

At the front end of the lineup is Crazy Charlie. Tall and thin with long, wiry muscles, you can tell he's the boss just by looking at him. While the other guys laugh and goof around like extras off the set of any *Billy Jack* movie, Charlie carries himself with an air of authority and power and intelligence. Charlie's president of the local Hells Angels chapter, and he's also the strongest, most powerful, most positive male role model of my childhood. As always, my mom,

Me and Crunch

"Attitude Annie" Wells, sits behind Charlie on his Hogg, arms wrapped tightly around his waist. The pair will remain happily committed to each other for many years to come. I love them both like crazy. Fat Ray, Crunch, Snake, No-Neck, Skinny, Max; these guys came as part of the family package too, serving as a beer-bellied, hairy-faced battalion of large, noisy, make-believe uncles. Clearly, this ain't Ozzie and Harriet, but who the hell cares?

All of those guys really care about me, and they've been part of my life since I was five or six years old. I trust them. I *like* them. I confide in them, and never once do I feel shortchanged in the male-role-model department. What we lack in biological ties, the Angels and I make up for in genuine, shoulder-punching, guy-to-guy friendship. Often, as other kids are being picked up after school by Florence Henderson clones piloting station wagons, I'll be zipping through the school parking lot on the back of a Harley chopper, my hair blown straight back into a sort of unintentional Dracula-do. Later, in less public, less visibly illegal situations, the guys will sometimes let me take their Hoggs out for a solo spin.

Scared to death but riding a massive adrenaline rush, I roar over dunes, and parking lots, and godforsaken stretches of desert feeling like Evel Knievel. I spit like these guys whenever and wherever possible. I swear like them. I scratch and belch and fart like them, with hearty belly laughs following each of those well-performed bodily stunts. When friends ask where my "real" dad is, I tell them he's dead, consciously reasoning that if the guy wasn't smart enough, or cool enough, or man enough to stick with me and my mom, I was far better off hanging with my own personal band of bikers. That was especially true during Little League games.

Every baseball season, like clockwork, every one of those Hells Angels became my own personal bank. I'd start the yearly con right around the beginning of April, sweet-talking each one of the guys into supporting the success of my upcoming baseball season with generous fistfuls of cold, hard cash. The boys were always pushovers, and more often than not, I'd be bleeding a dozen leather-vested victims/benefactors at a time. The basic deal found each biker forking over five bucks every time I won a game, and another fifty cents for every strikeout.

At age eleven, I'd almost never lose, and over an average six-inning game, I'd strike out maybe eight batters. Do the math and you quickly realize I was pulling in roughly nine dollars a head. I was making a kid's fortune, joyfully fleecing twelve of the toughest bastards on earth for cash that would be immediately blown on such childhood staples as candy and fireworks and *Playboy*s. Nobody ever complained, and quite frankly, I think the guys all secretly enjoyed slipping me those few grimy bucks out of their perpetually dust-covered pockets. I'm sure they knew I needed it.

Tucked just south of San Diego and just north of the Mexican border, my hometown, Ocean Beach, California, was the exception to every single unwritten rule of Southern California beachfront living. There were no Beemers on my block, no lush, green, manicured landscapes, no luxury condominiums. In their place, we had dented junkers, a few sad-looking shrubs, and one rundown liquor store. Lined up around those landmarks, you'd have found endless, dead-straight rows of small, no-frills, single-family homes, mixed up with a few larger, stucco-spattered apartment complexes like the one I called home.

For nearly two decades, I lived just a block and a half from an absolutely gorgeous stretch of Pacific coastline, but somehow, despite all that "location, location, location," my neighborhood stubbornly avoided any and all attempts at urban renewal. Throughout my childhood, Ocean Beach remained steadfastly blue-collar, sometimes hanging on by a thread to its lower-middle-class status. Trendier, more fashionable, far more upscale communities boxed us in on all sides, but we never changed. Even as a kid I can remember feeling that an unwritten class distinction would always separate us Ocean Beachers from our more affluent neighbors. It was a fact of life. It was unavoidable, but being from the "wrong side of the tracks" actually strengthened our friendships, bonding us "OB Rats" with a very real "us against the world" sensibility.

Case in point: Ocean Beach was forever being overrun with bums, or as we called them, "trolls." I know it's politically incorrect to use those terms anymore, but I really don't care. They fit. All through the 1970s, they'd show up in waves, often shooed toward the shores of Ocean Beach by the police departments of neighboring towns. You'd hit the beach one morning, and from out of nowhere, there'd suddenly be dozens of these guys sleeping on the beach, under the piers, or up on the cliffs near the ocean. Sometimes you'd find them in the alley behind your house. They'd panhandle. They'd steal. You'd come home from school to find them hanging out in your backyard, or picking through your trash. It was ridiculous. The local lifeguards and police could sort of give these guys a hard time and tell them to "move along now," but that was the extent of their power. That wasn't the case with us kids. We could be as nasty as we wanted.

With that perpetual underachiever's chip on our shoulders, there was no way us kids of Ocean Beach were gonna suffer that sort of indignity quietly. Free from such obstacles as civil rights violations and compassion, my buddies and I would do our level best to make the lives of these obnoxious poor souls a living hell. We'd go from backyard to backyard, plucking lemons and limes and oranges and grapefruits off our neighbors' trees, then we'd head for the beach and launch a bombing mission. The trolls would piss and moan and yell at us as we splattered them with our overripe citrus bombs, but we never let up, and in the end they'd be bruised, and sticky, and running like hell down the beach. More often than not, they'd be back within hours. That's when things got even nastier.

Whenever the fruit-bombs failed, we'd simply upgrade our ammo to high-caliber mud clots and rocks. We were ruthless, and barbaric, and our aim was dead perfect (oddly enough, some of my earliest experimentation with breaking pitches came during these moments of human target practice). Banded together, our message was clear: "This is OUR territory! This is OUR town! YOU'RE not gonna make it worse." Sadly, there were plenty of locals up to that particular task.

Walking home from school one afternoon, three of us rounded a corner and stopped dead in our tracks. From inside a small house on one side of the street came the clear, infuriating sounds of a man just beating the shit out of a woman. "I don't need you!" he'd yell, and then you'd hear the smack, and then the scream. She'd beg the asshole to stop, but then he'd crack her another. Finally, I couldn't take any more, and I just shouted from the street, "Leave her alone, motherfucker!" Three seconds later, a gunshot rang out from inside the house, and it knocked the street sign behind us right off its pole. We scattered, literally running for our lives while a blinding rage burned through me. Given half a chance, I'd have liked nothing better than to kill that son of a bitch. Wouldn't have bothered me in the least. I'd have gone home whistling.

Next horror story, and this time the bad guy's me. Within just months of the bullet episode, me and a buddy (a guy so rotten he was even a bad influence on *me*) came across an abandoned car in a familiar empty lot. Our eyes widened. Our delinquent sides took over, and after busting out the headlights with rocks, and denting whatever quarter panels weren't already destroyed, we were both astounded to discover the junker still held about a quarter tank of gas. At that point, in a scene that would have looked right at home on any episode of MTV's *Jackass*, we idiots quickly decided to blow the mother up.

There was nobody around. There was no chance of anybody getting hurt (except for us), and with that in mind, we quickly lit up a rag, dumped it down into the tank, then ran like hell, hearts pounding, sprinting away from the blast like the hero in every Jerry Bruckheimer movie.

BOOOOOOOOOOOOOOOOOOOOOOOOOM! This thing went up bigger than either of us could possibly believe. We dove for cover. We watched open-mouthed as the sucker went blooey, and two seconds later, our shared, twisted mix of pride, accomplishment, and awe turned quickly to fear. This was too big for either of us. We were kids who might toilet paper your trees, or soap up your windows, but now we were in WAY over our heads. Scared to death, and shortcutting through backyards and woods, we hauled ass, putting a full ten blocks between us and the blast by the time the first sirens rang out. At that point, with my ears ringing and my lungs on fire, I promised God that I'd never misbehave again.

Still, though people as incorrigible as me and my friends made up a large percentage of the population, Ocean Beach really *was* a terrific place to grow up. With our close-packed homes and narrow, double-parked streets, *this* was a genuine community. Far removed from the sprawling isolation of upscale suburban living, here you almost HAD to know your neighbors. Walk to the corner grocery store and you'd bump into a half dozen acquaintances. Hit the beach on any day when the surf was raging and there'd be literally dozens of familiar-faced Boogie boarders all getting happily demolished by the same humongous curls. Nothing bonds strangers faster than shared, soggy, head-over-heels wipe-outs. In Ocean Beach, friendships were easily formed and easily maintained, especially among us kids. One big reason for that was the fact that none of us was ever home.

In 1974, kids lived on an entirely different planet Earth. We had no Internet, no PlayStation, no cable television, and absolutely no inclination to sit around the house all day like the current crop of twenty-first-century veal children. At the same time, our mothers thought nothing of getting us dressed in the morning, shoving some Cheerios down our gullets, then tossing us out the back door until lunch. One bologna and cheese sandwich later, we'd be tossed out again until dinner. The world wasn't nearly as scary a place in those days, and we kids took full advantage of our freedom. We were never bored. Toys don't come much better than the Pacific Ocean, and the beach was a huge draw for us all, with swimming, surfing, and girl watching all high priorities. Often, we'd trudge out onto the local jetties, sometimes to do a little fishing, sometimes to just throw rocks, sometimes to make out with whatever beach girl we could talk into such fantastic bad behavior.

The beach gave us all a fantastic neighborhood playground, but it was really just second best, its allure ranking just below that of our local Ocean Beach rec center. Every single day after school we'd descend like rats. On an average weekday afternoon, a mob of forty or fifty kids would be bouncing off the walls, doing arts and crafts, or playing basketball, or football, or soccer, or whatever other sport might allow us to run around like maniacs for a couple of happy hours. With volunteer coaches and referees, and nice equipment, and solid, well-maintained fields and courts to play on, nobody cared if we got loud. Nobody cared if we swore, or chewed gum, or went shirtless, or farted in public, or ranked on one another in the obnoxiously hilarious way only young smart-assed boys can get away with. Nobody nagged us about doing our homework or taking a bath. This was *Lord of the Flies*. This was heaven. This was tween nirvana.

From right after school until late afternoon, we ran blissfully amok at that place. Later, as our moms started calling us home for dinner, we'd scatter, scarf down whatever food they plopped in front of us, then run right back to the rec center until 8:30 or 9 P.M. With another two hours of sports-related screaming and running amok dangling over our heads, little nuisances like homework, grooming, basic hygiene, and chores all quickly got relegated to the "last-five-minutes-before-bed" portion of the day. I can't tell you how many crappy book reports I cranked out at midnight after playing six hours of H-O-R-S-E.

Weekends would find us playing organized games against other local rec center teams. Point Loma, Cabrillo, La Jolla, Sunset View: every one of those towns made Ocean Beach look like the armpit of San Diego County, but on the playing field, *we* had the edge. Football, basketball, soccer, baseball: the games varied with the seasons, but it didn't much matter. Ocean Beach Rec just rolled over everybody. Our opponents may have lived in big stucco-and-tile homes while we all slept in little wooden shit-boxes, but we took great pride and solace in doling out nasty, playing field ass-whuppings. We needed those victories a lot more than the other kids. Finally, when the last whistle of the night had sounded, we'd all guzzle down Pepsis, belch our lungs out, then straggle off laughing toward home. That's where my life got *really* unusual.

Here's the deal. By the time she was thirty years old, my mom had given birth to five children by four different fathers, none of whom bothered to stick around long after the fact. By 1974, three of those kids had moved out, each of them trading in the chaos of my mom's free-spirited/aspirin-inducing/biker-babe lifestyle in favor of the relative structure and blissful boredom of lives spent at the homes of their own various grandparents. My sister Jeannie and I stayed with my mom, the three of us sharing a two-bedroom apartment. But that's not the whole story.

Living with us as roommates in that tiny, crowded, loud, and happy rental, was an ever-evolving assortment of my mom's closest friends. Most notably there was P.J., a lovely, smart, funny, all-around *wonderful* woman who dated Crunch for a while and ended up living with us for more than a decade. My mom's pal Ann squeezed into our flat as well, bringing with her the single sexiest teenage daughter/goddess on earth. The girl's name was Kim, and with a face and body that made my Cheryl Tiegs poster look homely, she was always just *way* too hot for my own raging pubescent comfort. Honestly, I worked that angle right through puberty, flirting, dropping hints, forever hoping that one day the girl would finally wake up, come to her senses, and tear the pants off my body. It never happened. Still, with blue balls, bunk beds, and a body or two on the couch, the six of us squeezed into that apartment just fine. And then Mrs. Evans moved in.

Mrs. Evans started out doing some light housekeeping for us, which believe me, we couldn't afford but needed badly. After a while though, when Mrs. Evans started showing up for work looking as though she'd just gone twelve rounds with Joe Frazier, my mom did some digging. Pulling Mrs. E. aside, my mom learned that she shared a small apartment with her daughter. The two apparently fought like cats and dogs, often getting physical. Old Attitude Annie wouldn't stand for that, and she leapt into action immediately. By day's end, Mrs. Evans had packed her stuff, said good-bye to her daughter, and moved in with us. I was now the sole male, living with five women in a tiny two-bedroom apartment. Crunch and Snake prayed for me often, and it really seemed to help . . . except maybe for that day I broke my sister's jaw.

She totally had it coming. One Sunday Jeannie and her boyfriend were planning on taking a ride up to my Grandma Victor's house. Grandma Victor was my mom's mom, and while the two of *them* didn't always get along so great, the old woman was just nuts about us grandchildren. Typical grandma stuff—hugs and kisses and face pinching and overfeeding, the whole nine yards. Naturally, I LOVED going there, and when I found out at breakfast that Jeannie was heading that way, I whined, and moaned, and annoyed the poor girl until she finally cracked and promised to take me with her. With that, I gobbled down the last of my Fruity Pebbles and ran off to the beach.

There I spent the morning riding waves, and in an unusual twist, getting royally sunburned. By the time I got home, sand covered and shirtless, I was a bright red lobster with legs. It hurt like hell, but I just didn't care. I was too excited about seeing my grandma. I ran into the house with a huge smile cracking my own crispy, dehydrated lips. Jeannie stopped me at the stairs.

"You're not going," she told me.

"I am SO going!"

"Nope, sorry. Me and Jay decided we're gonna go out after we get done at Grandma's, and that leaves you shit outta luck."

So now I start yelling about how she'd promised to take me, and about how this was totally unfair. And when she STILL didn't budge I remember just yelling at her, "You're such a *bitch*!"

"Oh really?" she replied with a shove.

"Yeah, really!" I shouted, with a hard shove back. My sister fell down. I turned around and walked away. End of story, right? Wrong.

As I was walking away, this nightmare of an older sister sneaked up behind me, then took her long fingernails and scraped them as hard as she could right down the blistered red skin of my back. Man, you wanna talk about screaming bloody murder. I let out a yell that must have rattled windows in Nevada.

Without thinking, I turned around fast, wound up, and punched her as hard as I could right in the face. I broke her jaw. Meanwhile the big sister's boyfriend is standing right there watching, but the chicken-shit little creep never did a thing to help her. He was older than me, and bigger, but he knew if he messed with me I'd go get a bat and beat the shit out of him too. I was a feisty little bugger and I really had snapped.

Now my sister staggers up and goes running off to tell on me. Two minutes later she's crying like a banshee. She'd told my mom exactly what happened, and my mom's response was "Good, you deserved it."

God, I loved that woman.

With Mrs. Evans's arrival, we were crammed tighter than ever, but at the same time, my mom's life suddenly got easier. Mrs. E. worked wonders in keeping our house from degenerating into one giant pile of dirty laundry, dinner dishes, and dust, and at the same time, her presence finally allowed my mom to get the hell away from all of us every once in a while. More often than not, she'd take off roaring up the Pacific Coast Highway on Hells Angels trips with Charlie, disappearing for a weekend or a week at a time. Whenever she'd be gone, Mrs. E. filled in, watching me and my sister with an eagle eye.

I know what you're thinking, and while I have to admit the information squeezed into the last few paragraphs *does* sound like the bare-bones outline for some weepy network Movie of the Week, you're gonna have to trust me on this one: we were genuinely happy. Granted, my mom was a rolling, roaring, middle-finger-flipping biker babe, with her own loose, scattered, entirely *different* rules of parenting, but we *always* knew she loved us. Granted, we were piss poor, but we never, *ever* felt deprived. We always had a roof over our head and food and clothes and one another. Finally, while our little apartment may have been packed sardine style, it was always a joyful place, full of people who genuinely loved being with one another, even when things got a little wild.

For years, our apartment building stood unnoticed at 5109 Point Loma Boulevard, but over several years, thanks to my mom and Crazy Charlie and the boys, it slowly earned a well-deserved reputation as a slightly infamous Ocean Beach "party" address. Almost every Friday afternoon, Crazy Charlie, Fat Ray, Crunch, and the rest of my Hells Angels buds would come over to our place, and with the help of my mom, they'd launch a kick-ass marathon bash that rolled all weekend long, never quite ending until late Sunday night. There'd be Rolling Stones blaring on a close-n-play hi-fi. There'd be guys sleeping all night in outdoor chaise lounges. It was wild. It was free. It was just plain great.

The apartment complex we lived in had a little courtyard in the middle, and before long it seemed like *everybody* in the building (even the super and the landlord) started joining in the festivities too. Nobody called the cops. Nobody complained. Everybody was friendly. Everybody was sleeping together. Everybody was toking off the same joint. It was the mid-1970s, and this weekly event had been going on for years. I can remember them all the way back to the time I was six. Large and loud and full of smoke, it seemed like the whole world wanted to party in the cement courtyard of my apartment building.

On the opposite side of the coin, I should explain that my mom loved to party almost as much as she despised working. With that in mind, our perpetual poverty should come as no surprise. Charlie helped out as often as he could, but when money got especially tight, my mom would break down and catch some work at the liquor store across the street. She never went full-time, and never kept a set schedule, but for years, she worked there on and off, in little bursts of ambition, whenever we really needed the dough, or whenever one of us kids wanted something badly enough to get her feeling guilty. I remember one time my mom literally spent her last fifty bucks to buy me a Boogie board. I wanted one *so* bad that she finally just gave me the fifty and went into debt. The following morning she was back across the street, stocking cases of Bud into a walk-in cooler.

Mostly though, I grew up on welfare. The truck would roll in once a month, and we'd get the box that says CHEESE on it, or CORNED BEEF HASH (which was actually pretty damn good). We also got food stamps, which I *really* hated, because my mom would always make ME go to the store and buy groceries with them. *That* was embarrassing. Y'know, inevitably I'd get the wagon half-filled, and then I'd have to hide because there'd suddenly be people I knew in the aisles. I'd have to fill up the wagon bit by bit, and then wait until the coast was clear to run up to the register and pay with the goddamn food stamps. Sometimes it'd take me three hours just to get out of there, simply because I had to wait for everybody I knew to clear out. I hated being in that situation, but there was no way in hell I'd have let my mom do it either. She deserved better.

My mom still ranks as the smartest woman I've ever met—sharp, and funny, with a sense of humor that could double you over at a moment's notice. She was also loyal, outspoken, honest, and fiercely, joyfully, pridefully independent. She was *unique*, but never once did I wish she were a more traditional mom. I knew every minute, without any shadow of a doubt, that this woman loved me like crazy. And Jesus, she made it clear around our neighborhood that if *anybody* fucked with us kids, she'd flat-out knock 'em out. My mom would literally just come out of the house and smack people in the face. Didn't matter how big the guy was, or how little, if they messed with her kids, she'd get knee deep in their ass.

Talk shit to my mom and BAM! You'd take one. In a store, on the street, or at a party, if anybody ever got out of line, she wouldn't think twice about turning around, hauling off, and knocking them out. She wouldn't take the time to ask questions or discuss the situation, she'd just bust 'em. Looking on, I'd be standing there with my mouth open going, "Shit, Mom! Nice left!" With a watchdog like "Attitude Annie," *nobody* bothered us kids, ever. They were all too scared.

Anytime I had a squabble with my mom growing up, she'd be perfectly happy to deck me too. I'd take a pop and I'd be like "Damn, Mom, that hurt!" And then I'd poke at her—hit her back with a little love tap just to press her buttons until she'd attack. She had nails, man, long fingernails, and we'd get in wrestling matches all the time, messing around. I'd walk by her, feeling feisty, and push her or something, and she'd push me back, and I'd fall down, laughing. Then she'd gimme a slap and I'd slap her back and it was on—we'd be on the floor wrestling. She'd dig her nails into me. I'd yank her by the hair, but she was impervious. The woman was superhuman. I was *always* the one giving up. She'd laugh at me. She was just too tough for me—I was over-matched. We did that 'til I was like twenty-three or twenty-four years old, and that woman kicked my ass every single time. We'd both be laughing through the whole thing.

Crazy Charlie was a great guy too. He didn't wanna play dad, but I really knew he liked me—not in that condescending grown-up-kid way, but as a person. You always got the idea he really enjoyed hanging with you. Though Crazy Charlie never actually moved in with my mom and us (he wasn't THAT crazy), we spent huge amounts of time together.

Attitude Annie and Crazy Charlie

Charlie had a house of his own out in Cleremont, California, and it was an amazing place for a kid to hang out. In a back room, this guy had tanks full of rattlesnakes, scorpions, and tarantulas. He even had trained piranhas. I swear to God. Charlie could stick his hand right in the piranha tank, leave it there, swish it around, and those ugly little fish wouldn't bother him at all. If anybody else even went near those psycho little fuckers, they'd go nuts and try to get you right through the glass. Throw *anything* edible into their tank and they'd go crazy. A dead mouse wouldn't last thirty seconds in that water. It would be like a blender on "frappe" in there. My mom and my sister always hated those tanks. I loved 'em, even if I never *did* figure out how he trained those insane little monsters.

Even better than the animal carnage was the fact that Charlie was fascinated with Chevy Novas. He rebuilt them and customized those suckers constantly, and anytime you'd go to his place, he'd have at *least* one or two half-finished muscle cars to play with. Charlie tricked those mothers out like nobody's business. He'd put huge, 454 engines inside, and the end result was always a sort of hot-looking, supercharged muscle car on steroids. They don't come any cooler than that.

Another great thing about Charlie was the fact that he was every bit as protective toward us kids as my mom was. Oddly enough, it was Charlie's protective streak that finally broke the ice between my Hells Angels rooting section and the mortified local parents at my Little League games. I was pitching one afternoon, and in an effort to impress a girl that I liked named Kathy Newcombe, I invited her to my game. Kathy was friendly with my sister, and while I was pitching, the two of them ended up sitting together in the home-field bleachers. My mom and the Hells Angels hadn't shown up yet.

On the mound I was doing just fine, but I was distracted throughout the early innings, and then just pissed. Over in the bleachers, I could see two guys harassing my sister and Kathy, just really giving them shit, scaring the girls, being obnoxious. I could see some of the parents looking uncomfortable with the situation, but of course none of the game-show hosts actually *did* anything. They were afraid. And to be fair, I don't know that I blame them. These guys really were just assholes, dirty, stoned, loud derelicts, who were somehow getting their kicks by being thoroughly obnoxious to a couple of teenage girls. Solid six-footers, they were more than a little bit menacing. I was now pissed off to the point of walking two batters, but that's when the rumble rolled in. You could see this one coming a mile away.

My mom and the Hells Angels pulled up near the concession area, garnering their usual assortment of grimaces and eyeball rolling from the peanut gallery. At the same time, the two jackasses were down behind the bleachers now, behaving more rudely than ever—being loud and screaming insults at the players and a lot of sexually suggestive comments at the girls. I shot a look toward Charlie and was relieved to find him already scoping the situation hard, his eyes narrowed to slits, his jaw tightly clenched.

Two seconds later, Charlie and Max took a little stroll down toward the assholes. There, with pretend smiles glued onto their faces, they calmly and coolly grabbed these two dudes around their shoulders and with some friendly, not so gentle persuasion they ushered the jerks away from the girls and down behind the backstop. From the mound, I was ready to bust a gut. Charlie and Max were magnificent. They never raised their voices, never raised a hand in violence, they just swooped into an ugly situation and fixed it. Charlie simply explained to the morons that their behavior had been inappropriate, and that if they actually valued things like their spleens and the ability to chew solid food, they really should consider leaving the game immediately. From the mound, I think I also caught the words *coyote, shovel,* and *desert* in there too, but I can't be sure. All I know is that the end result found both degenerates white-faced and weeping as they sprinted away from Max and Charlie, away from the girls, down the right-field line, and out of sight. From the looks on their faces, I was convinced those guys might run all the way to China. That's when the miracle occurred.

Charlie and Max emerged from behind the backstop looking more than a little bit embarrassed by their little confrontation. They knew full well the other parents didn't approve of them, and to their credit, they always went out of their way to behave impeccably at my games. I'm sure they thought chasing off the locals, no matter how obnoxious, would just make them seem all the more villainous to the assembled parents. But that's not what happened. Instead, as Max and Charlie sheepishly walked back to their bikes, the entire bleacher section broke out in a spontaneous standing ovation. With one simple, two-minute burst of high-profile good behavior, my biker rooting section was reclassified from "Threats" to "Heroes." Max and Charlie were floored by the response, and they ended up taking little bows for the crowd. Suddenly, the whole "us versus them" vibe was gone from my arsenal. My guys went from "barely tolerated" to "beloved" in two minutes flat. I may have been the only person disappointed by that turn of events.

I honestly *loved* that undeserved edge the Hells Angels gave me. I loved their bad-boy mystique, and little by little, their biker lifestyle began influencing my own emerging sense of "cool." Slowly but surely my Partridge Family records got tossed out in favor of KISS and Zeppelin and Steppenwolf. My hair got longer. My clothes got blacker. Worst of all, in one gloriously antisocial plunge, I became a rabid fan of the New York Yankees.

In Southern California, you could run over your own grandmother with a forklift and the liberal majority would ultimately decide you were merely a little misguided. Rooting for the Yankees, however, immediately classified you as an evil, twisted, no-good son of a bitch. It probably still does. Babe Ruth became my first real hero. He could pitch, he could hit, he could eat seventeen hot dogs and launch a ball five hundred feet. He ate too much. He smoked too much. He drank too much. He rented his hookers by the dozen. What's not to love?

The Babe thumbed his nose at convention, and rules, and the conservative wisdom of his day. He rose up from the lowest possible upbringing to become the single greatest force the game has ever known, and he did it all without ever

kissing an ass, or politely tolerating those who'd attempt to tame him. Though the obvious psychological and aspirational connections soared *way* over my head at the time, they couldn't *possibly* be more obvious. The legendary Sultan of Swat embodied *everything* I wanted in life. He was a champion, a sympathetic character, and a "best-case-scenario" me. Every single year I'd find *some* way to turn an English, or history, or social studies paper into a thinly veiled, obsessive tribute to the Babe. He was always good for an B+ or better.

David Wells: the prettiest pitcher in the Sav-All Drugs 1974 rotation

As time passed and George Steinbrenner, Thurman Munson, Billy Martin, Reggie Jackson, and their seemingly endless ability to fight, cheat, talk trash, and ride roughshod over the rest of major-league baseball made the Yankees more hateable than ever, my attraction grew even larger. I was insatiable now. I studied box scores. I erected a small shrine of posters and pennants and glossy photos clipped from old issues of *Sports Illustrated* that I stole from the local library. I watched eight-millimeter movies of classic Yankees moments. I *lived* for those Saturdays when the Bombers' game would be broadcast as NBC's Saturday Game of the Week. Honestly, I know this sounds made up, and clichéd, but while most guys my age were busy staring one-handed at their Farrah Fawcett posters, *I* used to fantasize about someday playing for the New York Yankees, and about pitching in Yankee Stadium.

As America's Bicentennial celebration gave way to the disco revolution, my Yankee wish was fast evolving from fantasy into a distant but remotely possible goal. I was still skinny compared to my friends, but I was growing fast; and my fastball, as clocked by a junior high school girlfriend, was now approaching eighty miles per hour. Slowly, as Little League victories gave way to Pony League dominance, it began dawning on me: I might actually have "the stuff." Far from making me cocky, that knowledge just made me all the more determined to make it to the top. Come hell or high water, I was gonna *force* my dream to come true. I would *not* be denied.

Jason Scheff, a close childhood friend who'd grow up to one day become the lead singer for the band Chicago, remembers seeing that change firsthand:

> When I first met David, we were both sixth graders, and while he was a great athlete, he was short. He had long, long, LONG straight hair, and he was really slender. Honestly, the first time I saw him, I thought Dave was a girl. Worse than that, I remember I thought he was pretty. I saw him as a sort of attractive tomboy-type. It was ultimately kinda equal parts funny and disturbing.
>
> A few years later, though, I was playing Pony League ball, and Dave was just mauling my team, but I somehow managed to weasel myself a walk off him. And when I got to first base, my coach said to me, "Okay, Jason, let's make sure you take a nice, solid lead there." And so I did, and David never looked back at me, but *something* must have registered, because he took his windup, put a move on me, threw a bullet to the first baseman, and picked me off by four feet. I was humiliated. I never stood a chance. But the important thing here is that as I was leaving the field, there Dave was on the mound with that real killer instinct, eye-of-the-tiger kind of look on his face. Right there I knew he was playing at some level the rest of us would just never reach. Right there I could see tangible evidence of what separates the really great players from the rest of us mortals.

By my junior year of high school, a lot of major-league baseball scouts had started coming to my games. The only problem was they weren't actually coming to see *me*. The Point Loma Pointers were a perennial powerhouse of local high-school baseball, fielding multiple championship teams, multiple major leaguers, even going so far as to send one 1947 graduate on to a long and illustrious career with the New York Yankees. The kid's name was Don Larsen, and as you probably know, he's the man who pitched the Bombers' first ever perfect game, right smack in the middle of the '56 World Series. With all that in mind, scouts tended to monitor the team rather closely each year, hoping to find another diamond in the rough.

This year's diamond was a kid named Chris Correia. A big senior, Chris was a solid power hitter—fast, smart, and a really gifted defensive shortstop. A couple of other guys on that team drew scout interest too, but Chris was clearly "the man." Funny thing though, while Chris got busy waffling through a rather disappointing senior season, I actually had an unexpectedly terrific surge as a junior, going so far as to share the league's Player of the Year award with some senior first baseman from another high school. Completely by accident, I'd managed to get myself noticed by a handful of very important people.

The hype on me must have spread fast, because the following spring, it seemed like every team in baseball started sending scouts to my games. They weren't disappointed. We Pointers just rolled over the competition that year with a team that was flat-out awesome. And while my own stats were very good, there was a *solid* handful of guys on that team who could have absolutely gone on to play major-league ball.

Our catcher, Jimmy Pringle, was just awesome that year. So was our left-fielder, David Camara. Tommy Kamphonik, our Sherman tank of a first base-

On the mound for Point Loma High

man, had big-league stuff too, but he's probably best remembered for making our entire team quit baseball. I had thrown one perfect game early in that 1982 season, and in my next start, I had another one going into our final inning. I got the first batter to pop up to Tommy, and here he comes running the ball back to me shouting "Yeah!!!! All right, Dave! Two more outs and you've got another perfect game!!!" Every head on the field, and the bench, and the bleachers, and the grass, all just whipped toward Tommy now. I swear to God you could hear the necks going "whoosh." Everybody just shot daggers into the kid with horrified gasps.

Y'know, rule number one in baseball is that you never, EVER mention that a guy's throwing a perfect game or a no-hitter until it's over. If you mention it during the game, it's a major jinx, the ultimate whammy. The pitcher on the mound *will* give up a hit to the next batter, and it *WILL* be your fault—guaranteed. So now our coach is just throwing his hat down into the dirt, and he says, "Kamphonik, if this guy gets a hit, you're off the team!" Two pitches later the batter connects for a single. Worse yet, the ball just kind of skitters out into right field, just beyond the reach of my ex-pal Tommy. That was it. After the game, our coach threw Kamphonik off the team. He was *that* pissed.

Finally it got to the point where the rest of us literally had to go into his office and say, "Coach, if Kamphonik's off the team, the rest of us quit too." The skip caved pretty quick after that, and honestly, just between you and me, Tommy's gaffe never bothered me at all, not in the least. Tommy and I remain good friends even today, and I keep his blunder tucked away in some fold of my brain, mostly because it's still great ammunition for torturing the poor guy. As of right now, he's been officially tortured in print as well.

In that great old movie *The Pride of the Yankees,* Lou Gehrig's wife is forever clipping newspaper headlines about her man, and anytime the movie needs to flash forward, they just cut to a headlines montage, and blast us into another chapter. We should probably steal that idea right here, because quite frankly, my high school baseball team was so good, we were boring. We just went out and won, over and over again, without ever really having to work up much of a sweat. Honestly, the springtime of my senior year in high school is probably best represented with a fast montage of swirling headlines like: POINTERS POUND INDIANS 14–2, WELLS HURLS 10TH VICTORY IN SHUTOUT, POINTERS GO TWELVE AND 0, WELLS RACKS UP 14 DETENTIONS IN CAFETERIA FIRECRACKER FRACAS, WELLS SLAPPED DOWN IN BOTCHED BRA-REMOVAL EFFORT, WELLS DRINKS BEER WITH BUDDIES IN SUPERMARKET PARKING LOT—THIS KID'S A NATURAL!

All right, with those dull and/or embarrassing moments now irretrievably behind us, we're gonna fall into place somewhere around the beginning of May 1982. I'm on top of the world these days. Graduation's just around the corner, and I'm pleased with the knowledge that I'm passing EVERY-THING, even geometry. In even bigger news, I've also moved out of my mom's place, having stumbled into a fantastic condo share with a thirty-five-year-old local lawyer named Bill Reedhead. I'd known the guy forever, simply because he was always coaching or refereeing events at the rec center. When he found out I was rapidly becoming desperate to escape the dreaded Apartment of Multiple Females, he took pity on me and offered up a spare bedroom at his place—cheap! I moved in immediately.

By my standards, the place is amazing. There's shag carpet *everywhere*. In the living room, there's a color TV set the size of a Clydesdale, and best of all, the bathroom is completely free of stockings, bras, barrettes, Scrunchies, brushes, combs, hair spray cans, eyebrow tweezers, makeup, hair mousse, eyelash curlers, and tampon boxes. Heaven! Best of all, between work, workouts, and time spent dining and dancing with his hot little girlfriend, Barbara, Bill is hardly ever home. Seventy-five percent of the time, I'm the only guy in the place. After eighteen years in the sardine can, I've actually got room to spare in my own swingin' bachelor pad. I've got no *girls*, but it's a start anyway.

As May slides closer to June, I've also become convinced that I'm going to be the first player chosen in major-league baseball's yearly amateur draft. I've had a fantastic season, playing on a powerhouse of a team, and there have been scouts watching me now for two full seasons. Compiling all those factors, I'm just young enough, and naive enough, and ignorant enough, and cocky enough to decide I'm a lock to go round one, pick one. I'm gonna be a bonus baby of six-figure proportions. If all goes well, I should be a major leaguer in two years time.

Truth be told, I didn't go round one, pick one. I didn't go pick two either, or pick three, or four, or nine, or twenty-seven. Instead, I ultimately got drafted by the Toronto Blue Jays as the second pick of the second round. Al La Macchia, the Blue Jays' superscout, had flown in to watch me pitch on several occasions, and apparently he and every other scout who'd come to watch me play felt that round two, pick two, was right where I fell into the pecking order of this year's crop of rookies-to-be. Needless to say, after being untouchable on the field this season, I was more than a little bit pissed. My ego wasn't used to such reality checks.

Not having an agent and not really understanding what those guys did either, I asked my nifty new lawyer-roommate to handle my business dealings with the Blue Jays. It was simple enough. They'd offered me a $50,000 bonus to sign with their organization, and they made it clear that the figure was entirely nonnegotiable. They told me they knew I'd been offered full college scholarships, and they also told me they knew there was no way in hell a guy like me would want to spend the next four years vegetating at any Institution of Higher Learning. They were right. I was cooked. I had absolutely *no* bargaining power.

On the other hand, $50,000 was a TON of money, especially for a guy who'd never previously had two nickels to rub together, and I *did* want to play baseball more than anything else on the planet. With that in mind, less than ten minutes after the Blue Jays had delivered their offer, I dove on that sucker. I forgot all about the multiple six-figure bonus I'd been dreaming about, and ultimately I just said, "Fuck it." I signed with the Blue Jays.

A full decade later, I'd STILL be kicking myself for that decision.

Beers and Peers

AWOOOOOOOYIYIYIYIYIYIYIYIYI!
YEEEEEEAUGH!!!

—*My second roommate*

June: "Pomp and Circumstance" and mortarboards and gowns give way to raging high school graduation parties, then raging cheap-beer hangovers, then frantic clothes packing as I prepare to hook up with my brand spankin' new teammates somewhere up near the North Pole. Like all new Toronto draftees, I've been assigned to play my rookie ball with the Pioneer League's Medicine Hat Blue Jays, but less than twenty-four hours before traveling to join that team, I still haven't got the foggiest idea of where the town of Medicine Hat might actually be located. I know it's supposedly in western Canada, and I know Canada sits on top of the U.S.A., but that's as close as I get. Worse, as a recent high school graduate, I'm *completely* incapable of even finding Medicine Hat on a map. All I know is that it's far away, and WAY north. My knee-jerk reaction is to assume I'll be playing ball amid Eskimos and igloos, in a town where the locals probably chew on blubber and drink fresh-squeezed penguin juice for breakfast. I fully expect that polar bears will occasionally wander through left field. Thankfully, I'll soon be proven wrong . . . mostly.

At eighteen, I've never been outside of Southern California in my life. I've never been on a plane. Three-quarters of all the pants I own are shorts. My shirts fall into two basic categories: black concert Ts and Hawaiian prints. I own more flip-flops than shoes. It's hard to leave my Boogie board behind. Nothing gets folded or sorted or stacked as I pack, it all just goes headfirst into the same beat-up duffel bag. Black Sabbath and Ted Nugent eight-tracks get tossed inside, along with sweat socks, jock straps, a toothbrush, sneakers, and my one decent pair of lace-up shoes. Everything I own fits easily into that one bag, and there's even room for a bag lunch up top. I tie the duffel closed with a deep breath and a huge, anxious smile. The whole packing process takes me less than twenty minutes.

At the airport, I get a hug from my mom that nearly pops the eyeballs out of my head. I get slaps on the back from my bikers, some of whom actually look choked up to see me go. Even Jeannie, who's long ago healed from my face-crunching jaw jab, seems genuinely saddened that I'm going away. They're all rooting for me, dying to see me succeed, largely because they know as well as I do that if I blow this, I don't have a thing in the world to fall back on. They know as well as I do, this is my one real shot at moving above and beyond the confines of Ocean Beach.

I board the shuttle to L.A. like John Glenn boarding the *Friendship 7*. I strap in, undressing the stewardesses with my eyes as they halfheartedly mime their way through preflight crash-landing protocols. I get a shot of adrenaline as we lift off over San Diego, and by the time we land in L.A., I'm feeling like a seasoned traveler. Within minutes, I'm lost at LAX, ultimately stumbling onto my connecting flight with less than five minutes to spare.

Once aboard, I kick off my shoes, twist my right sock so that its hole in the toe isn't so visible, and relax all the way to . . . Montana. Short of Canada, I'll be joining my new teammates in Billings, right smack in the middle of a six-game road trip. And while tonight's matchup pits "us" against "our" arch rival—the Billings Mustangs—in the days to come we'll be taking on the Butte Copper Kings, a team captained by a moose-size, home-run-hitting stud named Cecil Fielder, and then the dreaded Idaho Falls A's.

Hooking up with the team, I learn right away that Idaho Falls is far and away the team to beat this year in the Pioneer division. They've got the league's best pitchers, the league's best hitters, and they're only glaring weakness comes in the form of a very tall, very skinny, slap-hitting third baseman. Ham-handed in the field and anemic at the plate, this kid looks exactly like Alfalfa from *The Little Rascals*. He has little power, no speed, and rumors are already circulating that this scrawny rookie's career is hanging by a thread. Staring down at this poor sap from the pitcher's mound, his uniform flapping loosely in the breeze, I remember thinking, Jesus Christ, this guy could Hula-Hoop inside a Cheerio. The toothpick's name was Jose Canseco,* and before this game was over, I'd beat him for four dribbled groundouts and a nice, fat K.

One year later, with both of us clawing our way up the minor-league food chain, Canseco and I would cross paths again, but *this* time around, I wasn't laughing. Instead, halfway through the first inning, with Canseco stepping into the batter's box for his first at bat, my eyes went wide, my jaw dropped to the rubber, and I was stunned to find that "the Idaho skinny guy" had somehow grown up to become a freaking Macy's balloon. Brand-new biceps ripped out from under his uniform sleeves. Thick slabs of beef padded his formerly bony frame. A pair of tree trunks now connected his hips to his ankles. Seven innings and two 450-foot moon shots later, I *still* had no idea what to make of this new improved mutant. Was this kind of super-size growth spurt even possible? What the hell was this monster eating?

Twenty years later, I've got a pretty good idea, mostly because a *lot* of mighty-morphing power hitters are now following in Canseco's pioneering, anabolically suspicious, triple-E-size footsteps. And that brings up the obvious hot-topic question of the day.

---

* Canseco would go on to become the only member of that Idaho Falls team to make it to the show. His greatest accomplishments would include hitting 462 career home runs, becoming the 1988 AL MVP, and, of course, dating Madonna.

Q: *Do major-league baseball players take steroids?*
A: *Hell yeah!*

Want proof? Sit down in front of your television set some Saturday afternoon and watch *any* rebroadcast of *any* "classic" baseball game. In two seconds flat, you'll find yourself wondering why the old-school players all look so tiny. The '78 Yankees look like a high school team when compared to today's players. The '86 Mets, for all their cocky, swaggering, hard-drinking machismo, look like pencil-necked pushovers. Even my '92 Blue Jays look like ninety-eight-pound weaklings. It's a genuine shocker. Those jocks of the 1970s, 1980s, and early 1990s actually have human proportions, average physiques, and believe it or not, every single player has a neck.

Okay, now flick your remote and look at whatever baseball game is playing on ESPN right now. At any given stadium you'll find that a lot of today's superstars are basically shaped like barrels with heads. Thick through the middle with big asses and pecs. Today's *shortstops* are bigger than Reggie Jackson, while today's outfielders often look like they ought to be pulling beer wagons for Budweiser. Should you believe these players when they tell you their brand-new bulk up is due to a well-focused, year-round training schedule? Should you believe the lifelong Mendoza-liner who attributes his forty-home-run season to good nutrition and God? If you do, please send me your address and phone number, because I've got some swampland outside of Tampa that you might want to think about purchasing.

Here's how it works. Imagine you're an average twenty-six-year-old second baseman with a good glove and a decent, if unspectacular, lifetime batting average. You make a lot of money, but you can't help but notice that the home run boys are now filling their eight-car garages with Brinks' trucks. You get jealous. You make a decision. You find yourself an honest, discreet drug trafficker (often a gym buddy or teammate), and you make your first buy. You run home, you shove a 22-gauge hypodermic needle deep into your ass, and bingo, your cherry's busted, and you've got yourself a nice, juicy, 400-milligram anabolic rush. Make a *habit* of those shots, and within months you're gonna need a bigger jersey. Puffy, round shoulders sprout fast, and they're followed by bazooka arms, chunky-chested man boobs, and thunder thighs that'd shame Tina Turner. At the same time, thanks to a case of raging, anabolically induced acne, you'll also grow a pizza face, a pizza back, and a pizza ass. Your jawline will get bigger. So will your forehead, your nose, your chin, and your knuckles.* Your balls, on the other hand, will disappear—which is actually no big deal, in the sense that after the steroids, they probably won't work all that well anyway.

Congratulations, now you're a freak, but with any luck at all, you're *also* an everyday player and a long-ball threat, and maybe an All-Star, or an MVP, or a Triple Crown winner.** Bigger dollars get thrown your way. Glory and fan adulation get heaped upon your batting helmet. Commercial deals may fall into place, and with all that smoke being blown in your direction, it's easy to overlook the butt-ugly, long-term effects of this stuff. Muscle tears? Joint failure? Liver damage? Death? Screw all that, your slugging percentage is up 25 points!

It's this simple. *Every* baseball player wants an advantage. *Every* baseball player wants a competitive edge, *every* player worries that someday soon a bigger, stronger, more talented teammate will sweep into the clubhouse and take their job away. With all that in mind, a syringe full of 'roids can make it a *whole* lot easier for a major leaguer to feel confident about his game. They're easy to score. They're easy to use. They really do work, and with fans falling in love with the new millennium's heavy-hitting, home-run-humping ball games, nobody in authority seems the least bit inclined to slow the phenomenon. As of right now, I'd estimate that somewhere between 10 and 25 percent of all major leaguers are juiced. But that number's rising fast, and down in the minors, where virtually *every* flat-broke, baloney-sandwich-eating AA prospect is chasing after the same elusive multimillion-dollar payday, the use of anabolic homer-helpers is flat-out booming. At just about twelve bucks per shot, those steroid vials must be seen as a *really* solid investment.

It's been said that with the aid of a good steroid program, mediocre ballplayers can finally get themselves hot, while good players may become superstars, and superstars might even become superhuman. Feel free to read between the lines on that last one. Those are the facts. That's the reality, and that's why the steroid business will absolutely continue to thrive. Watch a few spring training games next March, and I'll guarantee you that yet another wave of players will hit the fields of Florida carrying somewhere between fifteen and thirty pounds of newly minted mystery muscle. You've seen them. You know who they are. To

---

* Look at any photo of admitted steroid user Ken Caminiti from 1996 through 1998. He looks like the bastard sprawn of Janet Reno and Lurch, from *The Addams Family*.
** Or a Cy Young candidate. Pitchers are now using steroids almost as much as position players—look closely at the stat sheets, and you'll find a ton of older guys who are now throwing a lot faster than ever before.

a man, they'll attribute their brand-new inches to exercise, clean living, and proper nutrition. Who knows? Maybe some of them are actually telling the truth. Maybe some of them have found a way to defy every known law of biology and physiology in plumping up their torsos to previously impossible proportions. Maybe you should just accept their stories and marvel at what a wintertime full of squat thrusts can do for a guy.

Or maybe you're a lot smarter than I was back in 1982.

ANYWAY, BACK TO MEDICINE HAT. OVER THE NEXT FOUR DAYS, WE Medicine Hatters ultimately take two out of three games from those high-powered Idahoans, and as we make the thirteen-hour bus trip back "home," I'm feeling pretty good about this team.

Offensively, we Blue Jays are led by the bats of Chris Johnston, who leads the Pioneer League in RBIs, and by a good-looking klutz named Pat Borders. Pat's a tough guy, but with *manos de piedra* he's forever booting routine grounders to third into the visitors' dugout. When he's moved to first base, he makes Stevie Wonder look like Steve Garvey. In the outfield, where he's moved to minimize his potential for error, he loses balls in the sun, even during night games. Pat could hit like an absolute son of a bitch, but we just couldn't seem to find him a position. Years later, in an evolution that surprised us all, Pat would slowly emerge as one of the very best catchers in the major leagues, ultimately becoming Toronto's MVP in the 1992 World Series.

Meanwhile, our Medicine Hat pitching staff lines up like this. A guy named Keith Gilliam is clearly our ace. He throws nearly 90 miles per hour, and he'll lead the league in wins at season's end. Behind Gilliam, there's a solid righty named Daniel Gordon, and behind *him*, there's a slim, quiet, college graduate with glasses, who looks more like an accountant than a ballplayer. He *seems* like a nice guy, but we're oil and water, ammonia and chlorine, fat guys and thongs. At first glance, I assume he's stuck up. At first glance, he assumes I'm a devil worshiper. His name is Jimmy Key.

In Medicine Hat, I'm the fourth starter in a four-man rotation, and it quickly becomes apparent that I barely deserve even THAT standing. By the time I'm a week into my Rookie League career, I've had two lousy outings, and nearly all the overconfidence that came with me from San Diego to the Great White North is shot. For the first time in my life, I'm not dominant on the mound. I'm not intimidating. I'm not even good. I'm throwing smoke like I always do, but here in Billings and Idaho Falls that's not enough. Guys are raking my ass. Out on the mound, while still attempting to look tough, I'm thinking, God DAMN, man, this ain't high school! These motherfuckers are good! Only after I'd gotten thoroughly and repeatedly shelled did the obvious finally hit me: *nearly everybody* in this league was at *least* as good as me. Every single one of us used to be the dominant stud on our high school teams. I'd gone from "exceptional" to "barely average" overnight.

I came to Medicine Hat expecting business as usual. With a fifty-fifty mix of cockiness and ignorance, I'd just assumed I'd be as successful as ever, and with any luck at all, I'd be up in the bigs in a year. Obviously, that wasn't the case. Two losses and a couple of 400-foot dingers had opened my eyes pretty quick. This wasn't going to be easy. If I was going to make it at this level, I was going to have to pitch smarter. Getting by with a scowl and some decent velocity was a thing of the past. I needed to *work* at this—I needed to focus. Having my Hells Angels lined up down the sideline probably wouldn't have hurt either. I find myself wishing those guys might suddenly feel like a 2,200-mile road trip.

Calling home, I'd lie about my pitching stats while crossing my fingers in the hope that things would get better. I just couldn't bring myself to tell the truth and disappoint the people down in San Diego. I couldn't let them worry about me.

Back in Medicine Hat, my inconsistency on the mound was matched only by the inconsistency of my roommate situation. At six foot two, 185 pounds, with a hard, wiry frame and long, wild hair that just sort of exploded off my head in all directions Einstein-style, I really did look like a serial killer. At the same time, I wasn't nearly as well mannered, civilized, groomed, hygienic, and gentlemanly as I am today. Iron Maiden and Ozzy Osbourne used to blare from my boom box at all hours. I'd been known to occasionally enjoy a beer or twelve. I was also loud, pissed off, nocturnal, and all those things ultimately combined to make me . . . well, perhaps a tad difficult as a roomie.

During that first road trip with the team, I shared a room with a guy named Tim Kuziumko, a big corn-fed Canadian boy, affectionately nicknamed the Cooze, for reasons we don't need to explore. He was our third baseman and a solid guy, and I liked him a lot. Somehow though, after less than a week on the road together, he quickly came to the conclusion that he wanted out. By the time we got "home" to Medicine Hat, I'd been assigned a new roommate, whose name I won't print in this book, simply so I can legally tell you that I'd been paired off with a bona fide psycho-fucker. This guy made *me* look like Mr. Rogers.

Minor-league mayhem: I don't remember where this was taken . . . you can guess why

Imagine sharing a room with a guy who stands at the bathroom sink washing his hair with green Palmolive dishwashing liquid. Imagine when he's finished, he brushes his teeth with that stuff too. Imagine this same guy, in the middle of the night, just rolling around in his bed screaming, then grinding his teeth so loud you'd swear they were breaking out of his head. Imagine him howling in his sleep, with a sort of coyote/salsa singer feel, kinda like "AWOOOOOOOYIYIYIYIYIYIYIYIYI!" Imagine this goes on all night long. Suddenly, I'm "the reasonable roomie." I've gone from Oscar to Felix overnight.

In 1982 there were thirty ballplayers signed to the Medicine Hat Blue Jays, and *all* of us bunked, two to a room, in that town's Silver Buckle Hotel. Located just across the street from a hustling, bustling, diesel-scented, eardrum-rattling freight train hub, that place made Motel 6 seem like the Four Seasons. Just four stories tall, the Silver Buckle scattered us Blue Jays throughout the second floor. One story down was the hotel lobby, the front desk, and a big, kick-ass hotel bar, which featured live music most every night. Guess whose room sat directly over the bandstand. Have you ever tried sleeping while twelve feet below your head a shitty Canadian lounge band is plowing through a clumsy, twenty-two-minute cover of "Bette Davis Eyes"? It ain't easy. The situation would have been *really* annoying if I'd ever actually gone to bed.

Here's an experiment. Take thirty young males, most of whom have never lived away from home, and drag them all across an entire continent, to a land where the beer contains 5 percent alcohol and beer *drinking* is practically a national sport. Complete those scientific steps in order, and chaos is guaranteed to ensue. Up in Medicine Hat, we Blue Jays proved that hypothesis every single night. The ritual ran like clockwork. Just after our game, we'd hook up in the hotel lobby, pool our money, then head out to the nearest liquor store, where we'd buy ten, or twelve, or fifteen cases of bottled beer. Next, we'd lug 'em all up to the top floor of the hotel. Then we'd climb out a window and drag our foamy party supplies onto the roof. Out there, amid the Silver Buckle's air-conditioning condensers and fry-cooker vents, we'd relax, bond, and get royally ripped.

Maybe 75 by 150 feet, that barren little rectangle of roof quickly became sacred ground. Redecorating began almost immediately. We'd steal tables and chairs from the hotel bar, then drag 'em all up to the roof. We brought candles and coolers and boom boxes out there too. In time, hundreds of our empty beer bottles, lovingly arranged atop the four-foot cement wall that surrounded the roof, would add a nice, homey finishing touch. Some guys loved it so much out there on the roof, they'd actually drag their mattresses up the elevator, down the halls, and out the window so they could bed down under the stars. In the middle of the chaos, I'm happy as a clam. As aggravating as my short, rookie-league career has been on the mound, I quickly realize that when it comes to baseball nightlife, I'm an everyday player, maybe even an All-Star.

I love the guys, I love the laughter, I love the camaraderie, but far and away, the single most mind-blowing aspect of life as a brand-new professional base-baller is the fact that women are suddenly everywhere. Y'know, by Medicine Hat standards, we Blue Jays are pretty big celebrities. We're also young, red-blooded, athletic, reasonably attractive, and almost *completely* lacking in impulse control. Put guys like us around a flock of open, willing, sexually aggressive Canuck groupies, and all hell's gonna break loose. We were nuts, and like kids in a candy store, we ran completely amok.

Girls would find us at the ballpark, or in local bars, and when an entire baseball team lives in one hotel, it's pretty easy to track us down. We Hatters weren't exactly hiding from the ladies' advances either. We'd eagerly invite girls up to the roof with us. We'd hide 'em in our rooms. Sometimes we'd head off to their homes, where we'd be sure to eat everything in their refrigerators before diving upon their Yukon femininity. There wasn't a guy on the team older than twenty-three, and the vast majority of us were still teenagers. I mean really, less than a year ago, most of us were still trying and failing to find girls who'd let us touch their bras, and now, here in Medicine Hat, we're suddenly irresistible sex machines. You KNOW we worked that angle as hard as we could. It was beautiful.

Every single one of us (except maybe old green dishwashing-liquid head) knew that with a bit of effort, we could almost certainly hook up with *somebody* before the night was over, and with early 1980s morality mixing nicely with late-teens hormonal urges, we really didn't care who. One particularly popular flower of the north was a chain-chewing tobacco-dipper. I swear. A cute little redhead with a killer body, this girl could hit a spittoon from thirty feet, and guys were forever bumming Skoal and Copenhagen from her stash. Another girl had a whole stuffed moose standing in her living room, and I'm told that during more intimate moments, Mr. Moose always seemed to be staring, giving guys the evil eye for their sinful behavior.

Still, the most legendary of the local groupies was Medicine Hat Maggie (not her real name). This woman had become something of a Pioneer League legend, extending her own particular brand of highly gymnastic hometown hospitality to visiting teams anytime they'd stop in to visit her fair city. Though Maggie'd been a human Welcome Wagon for years, that all changed when she literally spilled her Molson on one of my horniest, loneliest, homeliest teammates. Sparks flew, steam rose, and the brand-new lovebirds ended up dating through most of that long, hot summer of '82.

Back on the field, after my initial disappointments, I managed a couple of decent no-decision outings, then went on the road and stepped things up with a complete game shutout against the Calgary Expos. Finally, I'd broken through. Finally, I could take a bit of a deep breath and convince myself that maybe I wasn't going to be a total washout. Getting onto the team bus after the game, our manager, Duane Larson, went out of his way to give me a very public pep talk, even going so far as to lead the team in a loud, heartfelt round of hip hip hoorays. At the back of the bus I was beaming, and another reality check was rapidly setting in. I *did* belong here, and with some work, and some smart pitching, I *might* even be able to thrive. I could feel my batteries recharging all through our relatively short, 300-kilometer drive back to Medicine Hat.

One *major* fact of minor-league life is the long, *long*, LONG hours you're inevitably going to spend rolling along highways in your team bus. On getaway days, we'd finish a home game at 10, or 10:30 P.M., then shower, shave, and ship out of Medicine Hat by eleven at the latest. Even with that speedy turnaround, we Jays would inevitably haul ass out of the locker room to find Dixie, our team bus driver, already steaming behind the wheel, swearing that we were *way* behind schedule. With that, we practically dove inside her bus.

Pulling out of the parking lot at the town's Athletic Park, we Medicine Hatters would roll across the tundra all through the night—seven hours to Helena, eight hours to Billings, eleven hours to Idaho Falls. It was an awful way to travel, but as weird as this sounds, it was fun too. With nothing else to do, guys would pass the time on those bus rides telling stories and jokes, slagging on one another, playing cards, listening to music, enjoying one another's company, and as the hours wore on, jockeying for sleep space.

Prime bedtime real estate was up in the luggage racks over the seats. Stretched out on the metal, overhead racks where commuters would normally stow their coats and briefcases, you could actually get a fairly decent night's sleep. With that in mind, those spots went fast. At the same time, guys would also be crawling over one another in hunting down a halfway sanitary stretch of unoccupied floor space. Stretched out down the center aisle of the bus, you'd ultimately find as many as six of us Blue Jays, all snoring loudly, looking not unlike a long, unconscious totem pole. Miss out on those prime spots and you'd be stuck curling up across a couple of hard, lumpy bus seats, or sleeping sitting up. Those guys would inevitably get off the bus hunched over, as if they were about to apply for a job as Dr. Frankenstein's assistant.

By midseason, despite a lingering homesickness, things were definitely looking up. The team was playing .600 ball, and my own stuff was coming along nicely too. From an 0–2 start I'd battled my way back to 2–2, with less reliance on my fastball and more work on the inside part of the plate. I'm still light-years away from my old overpowering status, but I'm holding my own and feeling pretty good about my progress. However, my revolving roommate situation shows no signs of stopping.

I put up with psycho boy until I literally thought I might have to murder the pine-scented mutant in his grinding/snoring/screaming sleep. He'd taken to unconsciously shouting something along the lines of "myuh-HOOOOO-awawawawa!" now, and it was all I could do not to smother the freak with my own pillow. I shipped out the following day, got myself paired off with a very nice guy by the name of Kash Beauchamp, and things quickly returned to normal—*he* couldn't stand living with *me*. We lasted almost two weeks, but while Kash and I would often go out drinking together, he never quite had my stamina after hours, and he just couldn't stand it when I'd come wobbling in at 5 A.M., wide awake with yet another raging case of the munchies.

I had a bad postdrunk, homecoming habit of pouring myself an enormous bowl of Cocoa Puffs, and then sitting on my bed, crunching and slurping and gobbling like a starving madman. One morning, after just such an impromptu prebreakfast feast, Kash packed up his stuff and left me flat. Oddly, it seemed that nobody else on the team wanted to live with me either, which was pretty insulting, considering that even my ex-psycho-fucker ultimately found himself a new roomie.

Normally, being obnoxious enough to scare off all potential roommates would just seem like a smart way of weaseling yourself a single room. Not here. In Medicine Hat, we Blue Jays paid $300 a month for our swanky, shared, sticky-floored accommodations. To live solo in the same room would cost a guy $600, which would have been just fine, except for the fact that my entire month's pay as a rookie-league ballplayer was exactly $600. With a private room, after paying the rent, I'd be left with exactly $0 each month for such staples as food, beer, clothing, beer, athletic supplies, beer, heavy metal eight-tracks, beer, girlie mags, toiletries, chewing tobacco, and of course, beer. I was screwed.

Obvious question: where was your 50k signing bonus? The answer: your guess is as good as mine. Floating rather aimlessly between the Blue Jays legal and human resources departments, my signing bonus had bounced back and forth between snail-assed accountants and Blue Jays bean counters for months. Nearly penniless now, and just a tiny bit desperate, I put on a clean shirt, screwed on a big, fake, cheese-eating grin, and hit up the hotel manager for whatever discount she could offer. Gazing with sympathy into the wide, wet eyes of the upstanding young man I was pretending to be, this chain-smoking, middle-aged angel of mercy took pity on my ass and told me I could keep my room, solo, at $300 a month for the rest of the season. I thanked her a hundred times over while silently kicking myself for not working this whole scam a lot earlier. Three days later, my bonus check finally showed up in Ocean Beach. My ex-roommate/lawyer immediately wired me a nice whopping chunk o' cash, and at that point, it was time to party.

For months I'd been stretching every last dime in order to make ends meet. However, as any guy who's ever worked on the Alaska pipeline can tell you, life in the far reaches of the Great White North is ridiculously expensive. Let's put it this way: even in 1982, a pack of hot dogs would run you six bucks at the grocery store. A jar of peanut butter would be even steeper. Hell, my Cocoa Puffs ran me almost five bucks a box. With all that in mind, it should come as no surprise that once my pockets got stuffed with cash, I went temporarily, gloriously, gluttonously insane. I'd be scarfing down ham and a half dozen eggs for breakfast, with fat steaks and baked potatoes and pitchers of beer for dinner. The day my bonus money arrived in Medicine Hat, I weighed a solid 185 pounds. By season's end, I'd go home at 210.

Still, despite the new love handles, or who knows, maybe even because of them, my pitching got better. Over the next eight weeks, with the team playing really well behind me, I managed to finish out the season at a decent, if not mind-boggling, 5–4, with a 5.71 earned run average. At the same time, our final *team* record was an awesome 44–26. We played .629 ball, finishing first in our division and edging out the mighty Great Falls Giants by one full game. One full week and two hellacious, eleven-hour bus rides later, we'd wiped out the Idaho Falls A's three games to one in the Pioneer League's Championship Series. Have you ever heard twenty-five drunken human beings sing "We Are the Champions" for eleven hours straight? Trust me, it makes you want to leap out the bus window into oncoming traffic.

Back in Medicine Hat, the team had rented a banquet hall for our victory celebration, and the combination of championship victory, adrenaline, and a real "last day at camp" atmosphere combined to make it one HELL of a party. NONE of us would be returning to Medicine Hat next season, and after seventy-four games as teammates, dozens of hours crammed into the same crummy bus, and endless nights spent together on the tar-papered roof of a crappy hotel, it really *was* hard to say good-bye. Gallons of free booze just made it harder.

The following morning, fighting off a hangover that felt like seven or eight weasels kickboxing in my head, I flew home to L.A. feeling like I'd accomplished something great. Granted, I hadn't exactly set the league on fire, but I'd held my own. I belonged, and that in and of itself felt pretty good. Already I found myself looking forward to next season. Already I could feel myself getting excited about improving upon this year's stats. Already I was dreaming of life as a full-bore, big-league Toronto Blue Jay (who might one day get traded to the New York Yankees). Touching down in San Diego, I hit the tarmac running, sucking in a huge, warm, cleansing breath of Southern California air—equal parts orange blossom and carbon monoxide. Some things never changed. I was home.

With plenty of bonus money left in the bank, I paid off some debt for my mom and then proceeded to spend my entire off-season doing absolutely nothing. My best friend, Chris Wheatley and I surfed every day and partied like rock stars. I hung, I chilled, I shot hoops, and as always, I tried really hard to find myself a girl or two. Oddly, the line "Hi, I'm a minor-league baseball player" doesn't work nearly as well in Southern California as it did up in Medicine Hat. It was a *long* winter; one in which I ultimately adopted a basic lifestyle pattern of *Surf-Eat-Party-Sleep-Repeat* for the better part of five months.

In mid-December I get my 1983 team assignment from the Toronto front office. And while I'm hoping that a Christmas miracle will leapfrog me up to AA

Chillin' in the stands back home at the Murph

ball in Knoxville, I get a lump of coal instead. First paragraph, second sentence, the letter tells me I'm headed for the Blue Jays' Class A baseball affiliate in Kinston, North Carolina. Disappointed, but not totally bummed, I did a little research and found that Kinston is located in the eastern half of North Carolina, amid the enormous tobacco farms of rural Lenoir County.

With an atlas laid out on the table, I find that while Kinston may seem a bit off the beaten track, its really just "down the road a'piece" from such metropolitan hubs as Beulaville, Tick Bite, Wheat Swamp, and Bucklesberry. In a flash, I've now got that freaky banjo boy from *Deliverance* playing "Dueling Banjos" in my head. Still trying like hell to find SOME ray of light among the day's disappointments, I reason that at the very least, Kinston IS part of the United States, and for that reason it can't *possibly* be any weirder than Medicine Hat. Rarely have I been so magnificently wrong.

Arriving in the Kinston, I was smacked with even *more* culture shock than I'd found up in Canada. There's grits for breakfast, and biscuits and ham. Waitresses call you "Sugar" and "Hunnnn" with voices that practically drool molasses. Skynrd is God, and seven out of every ten cars that pass on the street seem to have "Freebird" blaring out their open windows. Rebel flags hang everywhere. I actually hear the word *vittles* being used in a sentence. And while the town seems to be inhabited with roughly a fifty-fifty white/black mix, there's virtually NO mingling between the races. Night after night, at our home games in Grainger Park, I go out on the field, look up into the stands, and find the crowd split, just about right down the middle. All the white people sit together down the right-field line, the blacks down the left. There was no overt tension about it, no overwhelming sense this was wrong. It was just "the way things are," at least here in Kinston.

The Kinston Blue Jays were truly a mom-and-pop organization, owned and operated by a retired airline pilot named Ray Kuhlman and his funny, bright, charming better half, Ruth. Together they put a team on the field that included such future major leaguers as Cecil Fielder, Fred McGriff, Nelson Larriano, Alex Enfante, and me. Together, with all those big guns populating the lineup day in and day out . . . we were *still* pretty bad. Up one level from the entry-level players stumbling through their first year in rookie ball, the competition here in the Carolina League was absolutely fierce. In Alexandria, Winston-Salem, Hagerstown, and Durham, we'd routinely come up against pitchers who seemed untouchable, batters who seemed entirely incapable of making an out. Worst of all were our trips into Lynchburg, Virginia, where the nucleus of the 1986 World Champion Mets was rolling over everything in its path.

I'd stand in the dugout watching Dwight Gooden throw a 101-mile-per-hour fastball with pinpoint accuracy, and feel like maybe slow-pitch, beer-league softball might be a better career choice for me. On defense, Lenny Dykstra would drive our hitters nuts, diving around the outfield, covered in dirt and scabs and tobacco juice while he happily turned their singles and doubles into spectacular fly-ball outs. A half-inning later, he'd be doubling off the left-field wall, stealing third, distracting our pitcher, and just wreaking absolute havoc on the base paths. Guys like Mark Carreon and Randy Milligan, who'll go on to have respectable, if not spectacular, major-league careers are nonetheless racking up phenom numbers down here in Lynchburg. The effect was sobering, to say the least.

Still, despite the fact that my team is struggling, my work on the mound is actually progressing pretty well. I'm still not smart enough, or seasoned enough, or experienced enough to really understand the finer points of pitching, but I've definitely moved beyond the "haul back and heave" game plan that got me to Medicine Hat. With coaches watching my mechanics, my fastball gains a little more pop and my curve is starting to fall off the table with a nasty, late dive. Pitching a ton of innings that season, over the course of twenty-five starts, repetition alone practically forces me to get better. Like a five-year-old practicing her piano scales, there's muscle memory at work here, with a subconscious focus evolving over time.

One aspect of my game that's not changed an iota since Medicine Hat is that my living arrangements are perpetually screwed up. Unlike the hotel-bound Medicine Hatters, we Class A Blue Jays are free to rent rooms in the homes of local Kinstonites. I find myself a nice room in a pretty, sort of Victorian-era house, owned by a lovely older woman who's cute as a button, quiet as a mouse, sweet as candy, and absolutely out of her mind. Morning, noon, night, this woman would stand at the kitchen counter, silently opening and ingesting can after can of cold supermarket vegetables. Never fresh, never frozen, she'd just stand at the stove, humming while sucking down store-brand corn, or carrots, or beets, or even lima beans, which in and of itself pretty much confirmed her insanity. I moved out shortly before my second month's rent came due.

From the nuthouse, I moved into what seemed like a fantastic situation orchestrated by my teammate/buddy/fellow pitcher Perry Mader. Perry and I played together in Medicine Hat, but we never really connected as friends until midseason. Only then did I realize that Perry was as big a night owl as I was, while also rating as a world-class elbow-bender and a closet head-banger to boot. Here amid the southern belles and slack-jawed yokels of Kinston, I practically jumped at the chance to cohabitate with the maniac.

Perry had been sharing a huge old house with a couple we'll call "Fred and Cathy" (not their real names). Both were young, fun to hang with, and seemingly well off. Their house was beautiful, enormous, and constantly booming with a muscle-bound, bass-heavy stereo, and a premium-loaded cable-TV hookup. Hell, the house was even within walking distance of the ballpark. I couldn't have asked for a more comfortable place to live. Making things even better was the fact that Perry Leychick, yet another teammate who I actually liked, had just moved into the home's fourth bedroom.

The house was loud, and chaotic, and fantastic. Friends of Fred would show up at all hours of the day and night, but it never bothered any of us. The Perrys and I were all night owls, and most of the visitors actually seemed pretty cool. We never paid them much attention anyway, preferring to spend our time staring at MTV, debating whether Martha Quinn was a hottie (my claim) or just a weird-looking elf-girl. The debate raged for the better part of the summer until it finally got replaced by the classic "Debbie Gibson or Tiffany" arguments. What can I tell you, we had a lot of free time on our hands.

And then it got weird. Walking home from the park one night, Perry Mader and I are about three blocks away from the house, when some guy comes running up in the dark saying, "Yo, Dave! Perry! Stop! Don't go home!" And as this guy gets closer, under a streetlight, I recognize him as Fred's lawyer. He then tells me, "You can't go back to the house. There's cops everywhere. Just get in my car and we'll go to my house and hang out." Turns out Fred was supplying marijuana to every pothead in Lenoir County. The cops had been watching him forever, and now they had him dead to rights. He was cooked, and there was no way in hell any aspiring major leaguer needed to get into the middle of all that. Perry and I went to the lawyer's place and rode out the storm there.

At midnight, Fred gets thrown in jail. The cops search our house from top to bottom, but they don't find a whole lot of dope. Why not? Apparently Fred had gotten a last-minute tip that a squad car full of Kinston's finest Barney Fifes was coming after him, and in a frantic, panicked rush, he'd hidden his stash all over the house. That's how greedy the guy was. Rather than flush the shit, he hid it, hoping the local cops would be incompetent enough to miss it. Guess what: they were. I found that out the following day, when Fred came home after posting bail, opened up my closet, and said, "Sorry, dude, I left something in here." At that, he pulled out a bunch of my shirts on hangers, reached into the pockets, and produced what must have been a solid quarter pound of pot.

Fred laughed, then saw the veins throbbing in my forehead and realized he was about to die. "You stupid motherfucker!" I shouted, wrapping one hand entirely around his neck. "Do you have ANY idea how much trouble you could have gotten me into?" His toes were up off the floor by the time he started apologizing. I moved out that afternoon.

It wasn't even August yet, and here I was, moving for the third time. Thankfully I got lucky this time, when yet another teammate in shining armor came through in the clutch. Scott Elam was his name, and while he was having a difficult time catching on with the Blue Jays, he'd hit the absolute jackpot playing renters' roulette. Scott was renting one bedroom in the big-ass home of a

Du Pont executive we only ever knew as "Sweet Lou." Rich and single, with a suave, elegant playboy kind of vibe to him, Lou was constantly throwing small, elegant cocktail parties, all of them teeming with attractive, middle-aged bachelorettes. I swear to God, living with this guy was like living on the set of *The Dean Martin Show.* Sweet Lou may still rank as the single coolest man I've ever met. He drank manhattans. His shoes gleamed. He wore cuff links. He used Vitalis. Next to Sweet Lou, Scott and I looked like Tom Sawyer and Huckleberry Finn.

Believe it or not, Lou was also a gourmet chef, and every single morning, before leaving for work, he'd get up early, cook huge, gorgeous meals, and then leave them on the kitchen counter for Scott and me to scarf down like animals. Pot roasts, whole baked chickens, beef stews, pasta: these things were meant to be our dinner, but more often than not, we'd just gobble 'em down for breakfast. They sure as hell beat my Cocoa Puffs. I was busting out of my uniform by season's end, and as thrilled as I was about getting back to Ocean Beach, I was devastated at saying good-bye to Lou.

By the end of my season with that limp, shabby Kinston club, I'd racked up a barely winning record at 6–5. And while that's nothing to write home about, I'd also gained a little bit of attention for tossing a lot of innings by minor-league standards and compiling a solid 3.73 earned run average. This year I went home to Ocean Beach without a Championship hangover but smiling nonetheless, basking in the feeling that I'd now officially graduated one more step up the food chain of major-league baseball. Three weeks later, I was right back at the bottom.

This year's assignment letter came earlier than last, and when I stumbled upon it sitting in the mailbox, I was sure it had to be good news. I was almost positive I'd be playing AA ball at Knoxville next year, but my letter's early arrival actually kick-started a few wild AAA dreams percolating in my head. Still standing on the sidewalk, I ripped at the envelope so eagerly that I literally tore that letter in half. With two hands holding the pieces together now, and a huge smile on my face, I read that I had been assigned back to Kinston for the '84 season. I shuffled the papers, thinking maybe I'd misaligned them, and the message they bore got mixed up. No dice. At that point I released a screamed, high-volume expletive that carried all the way north to Disneyland. I was royally pissed.

After a solid three weeks of depression, door slamming, wall punching, and beer drinking, I emerged from my self-pitying cocoon more determined than ever to kick serious baseball ass. I work out. I jog, I swim, I surf, all the while obsessing about getting my baseball career into high gear. By winter's end, I report back to Kinston in great shape, focused and serious, with a "take-no-prisoners" attitude. I throw harder than ever. I snap my curve with even more wrist action. With every pitch, I practically launch my body toward home plate, wringing every last bit of velocity and movement from my delivery. Whatever it takes, I swear to myself, this is definitely my year.

By mid-May, I'm 1–6 with an earned run average of 4.71.

Obviously (at least from today's perspective), I'm trying *way* too hard. By overthrowing and forcing my release, I'm breaking two of the most basic rules of pitching. Little Leaguers know better. Somehow I've allowed my own pent-up frustration, determination, and maybe even desperation to combine over the past eight weeks and totally fuck with my pitching mechanics. Finally, with coaches hammering me about my mistakes, I decompress, returning to form with one decent outing that results in a no decision. It's an encouraging sign, but clearly, before we've even reached the season's halfway point, I've dug myself a deep hole. AA ball has never seemed so far away.

And then I got lucky. One floor up the pecking order in Knoxville, the Smokies' starting pitchers were dropping like flies. A couple of guys had been called up to AAA, a couple of guys had gone down with arm problems, and with all that happening, it was time to raid the Class A stock. Amazingly, just coming out from under the worst stretch of pitching in my brief, lackluster career, I found myself promoted. Stranger still, even amid the more intense competition and more talented players at AA, I thrived. I don't know whether it was the excitement of the move, or the fact that I was finally moving on to bigger and better things, but *something* definitely clicked. I made eight starts in Knoxville, with three complete games, a shutout, and a wicked earned run average of 2.59. That's right about where the bottom dropped out.

On June 20, I got shelled for the first time in my AA career. Five days later, I hit the mound again, eager to wipe the bad taste of that one bad start right out of my mouth. I blew out my elbow instead.

Tossing a simple curve, down and away, toward home plate, I suddenly felt a sharp, burning pain, sort of like someone had run a lawn mower over my elbow, *then* scraped a fork around inside the open wound, *then* poured molten lead on top to seal it up. I saw stars. I tried to shake it off, but that just sent a wave of agony shooting up my arm. Tears welled in my eyes. A knot clamped tight in my stomach. I was fucked and I knew it. By the time the trainers got to me, I was already pretty sure my season was over. My career seemed to be on life support as well.

Two and a half seasons into what has so far been an entirely unremarkable minor-league career, I've lost an elbow and blown *any* chance of getting myself to the big show, or even AAA ball, anytime soon. Team doctors examine my arm and they quickly come away frowning, with two options for me. Telling me there's ligament damage and some muscle tears on either side of the elbow joint, they claim surgery is the most efficient way to go. I couldn't wait for option two.

In the experts' opinion, shutting the arm down, going home, and letting the muscles heal themselves *completely* over an extended winter break seems a plausible alternative to surgery. It keeps me from getting cut, and it will more than likely allow me to hit spring training 1985 back at full strength. I don't know what sort of miracle cure I was expecting, but *both* those scenarios hit me like a ton of bricks. Ultimately opting to avoid the knife if at all possible, I flew home to San Diego trying hard to remain optimistic, trying hard not to feel like my dream was now dying.

To my mom, and my friends, I do nothing but smile, pooh-poohing my injury as nothing to worry about. Privately, however, I can't help feeling like damaged goods. Endless appointments with sports medicine specialists, physical therapists, and trainers do nothing to squash that perspective. Only after I begin rehabbing the elbow at La Jolla's fantastic Scripps Institute do I see any tangible signs that I might actually beat this thing. With talented therapists guiding my recovery, I gain mobility in the elbow faster than expected. I progress to soft tossing shortly thereafter.

By late summer, the Padres have consented to let me use their facilities at Jack Murphy Stadium for daily workouts. By Christmastime, I've made enough progress to begin throwing for real, and I get a real boost when the Pods backup catcher (and future manager) Bruce Bochy agrees to catch me. This guy's made the show. This guy's just two months removed from playing in the Padres' first-ever World Series, and yet he's been kind enough to catch me as I rehab. Over the next two months, Bruce is endlessly optimistic, helpful, and a bit of a cheer-leader for me. Together, we're both astonished to find my stuff quickly returning to preinjury form. Pain free and excited, I can't wait to get back to camp.

As February approaches, I thank Bruce endlessly for his help, then pack my bags, run to the airport, and hit spring training feeling like Ebenezer Scrooge on Christmas morning. Savoring this second chance, with a huge genuine smile in place, I know I've now successfully dodged what *could* have been a career-ending bullet. Throwing heat through my first Florida workout, the Blue Jays' coaches seem genuinely impressed. "Great stuff today, kid!" they shout at me from the sidelines. "Way to throw!" I'm walking on air as I head for the showers, and later *drinking* on air as the team spends that evening practicing the fundamentals of running frozen margaritas through a hotel blender.

Three days pass. I've tossed well on the sidelines, done my running, teased my teammates, talked shop with Blue Jays' pitching coach Larry Hardy, girl-watched for hours, and finally it's my turn to crank it up again. Riding a wave of my own momentum, I hit the mound and launch eight strikes in a row, each one tracking at better than 95 miles per. Pitch nine is the exception. Pitch nine never makes it to home plate. Pitch nine turns my throwing arm into ground chuck. Pitch nine rips muscle from my bones, and tears ligaments on either side of my elbow. If last September's injury rated a 7 on a scale of 1 to 10, this one's maybe a 49. It's one of those moment's so bad it seems to play out in slow motion. I hit the grass. I scream. The arm flops, dead at my side. Trainers and coaches and teammates run in from every direction. They help me off the field, keeping the arm immobile as we head straight to the hospital. I want to cry. I want to kill. I want to wake up and realize this whole thing's a bad dream.

Preliminary MRIs lay the wound out in all its muscle-tearing, ligament-snapping glory. At the same time, a dozen bone chips make their world premiere appearance, scattered all over my elbow like sprinkles on an ice cream cone. I get plastic smiles from doctors and coaches alike. I get stories about how a Dr. James Andrews is doing remarkable things these days surgically repairing pitchers' arms. I get pats on the back and endless words of encouragement. Meanwhile, I'm fucked and I know it.

From the time I was ten years old, my *only* dream (except for the one about me and all three of Charlie's Angels in a Budweiser-filled hot tub), has been to make it as a major leaguer. I've been working toward it all my life, eating, breathing, and sleeping baseball 24/7/365. Could I *really* just let myself walk away? Could I *really* just give up? The answer was obvious.

"Yes." Right then and there, I decided to quit.

FIVE

Minor Indiscretions

Y'see, David. When you
work your hacksaw properly,
you can rip through the leg bone
with one clean slice.

—*My boss*

JULY 1985: KNOXVILLE, TENNESSEE

And then Larry Hardy smacked me out of it. A great, no-nonsense, straight-shooting pitching coach who spoke his mind almost as loudly and bluntly as I did, Larry found out I was quitting baseball and got in my face immediately.

"Come with me," he told me, pushing me toward a corner. "Now, look me in the face and tell me you're quitting."

"I'm quitting." I don't think he expected that.

"Tell me something," he said. "Once you're out of here, what do you think you're gonna do?"

"Well, I guess, maybe . . ."

"Lemme rephrase that. What the hell CAN you do?"

He'd stumped me.

"You gonna flip burgers? Christ, you'd eat more than you'd ever sell. You gonna bang nails up on a hundred-and-ten-degree roof in San Diego all day? You good with a mop? 'Cuz maybe, if you've got a connection somewhere, you might be able to score a bathroom-cleaner position."

I stood there, pissed off to no end by the things Larry was saying, not so much for their tone but for their dead-on, undeniable accuracy. Mercifully, Larry changed directions at that point.

"Look," he said. "I'm not gonna kid you. Your elbow's a fucking mess right now. It's gonna take surgery, and a boatload of physical therapy, and prayers, and luck, and maybe voodoo and a human sacrifice or two to get it back one hundred percent, but you owe yourself the shot. I won't bullshit you, David, and I wouldn't say this to ninety-nine percent of the guys who've pitched for me over the years, but I see real, solid, major-league potential in you. I know right now it seems hard to believe, but I really do think you can make it and be successful in the bigs. Quitting is obviously your call, but before you go, I wanted you to know exactly what you're walking away from. The obvious question here is 'How bad do you want it?' "

And I stood there. And I took one deep breath. And I asked Larry if he'd help me set up a surgical consultation with Dr. Andrews. He nodded with the barest perceptible hint of a grin. That's when he told me he'd already done it. Three days later, I'd already been on and off the table, wide awake through three hours of surgery that was deemed a complete success. Three *weeks* later, I was back back in Ocean Beach, nursing both a badly swollen elbow and a severely shrunken wallet.

Almost three years had passed now since I'd received that fifty-thousand-dollar signing bonus from the Blue Jays. Almost nothing was left. I'd paid off my mom's debts, bought a car, and used what was left to avoid having to get a job through the winters of 1982, 1983, and 1984. Heading now into an unemployed summer of 1985, I was running on fumes. In an effort to beat paying rent, I'd even moved in with my sister. Married, with two small kids of her own, she was currently living in a tiny, two-bedroom Ocean Beach house. With a husband channel-surfing on the couch, kids crawling *everywhere*, and toddler toys, bottles, and diapers all over the place, adding me into the chaos would have been cramped even under the best of circumstances. Making matters crazier was Jeannie's habit of saving *everything*. Newspapers, paperbacks, cardboard boxes, recycling cans; every square inch of that tiny house seemed waist deep in various piles of vaguely sorted stuff.

At the same time, the house was right behind a Jack in the Box fast-food joint, and I mean *right* behind. From my crash spot on the couch, I could literally hear that cheesy little "drive-thru clown" going off 'til two in the morning. At six, he'd start all over again for the breakfast rush. "Hello, may I take your order?"

"Yeah, I want you to die."

"Hello, may I take your order?"

"Yes, I order you to shut the fuck up!"

"Hello, may I take your order?"

"Kiss my ass, Clowny!"

Awakened by the evil clown yet again, I stumbled into the kitchen one morning, poured myself a glass of the kids' Juicy Juice, then walked out the front door to grab the morning paper. Eyes still half-closed, ratty T-shirt hanging over equally ratty boxers, I trudged through my sister's tiny front yard, grunting like a Neanderthal. Grabbing the paper, I turned, took one step back toward the house, then snapped back around. The driveway was empty, and even in my semiconscious state, I knew immediately that my car had been repossessed.

It was now officially time to get a job.

One quick peek at the local classifieds proved beyond a shadow of a doubt that Larry Hardy wasn't far off base when he acted as my own private guidance counselor. I was qualified for nothing, and after two weeks of failing in job interview after job interview, I ended up working as a busboy, making $2.35 an hour and swiping the uneaten dinner rolls from every basket in the place. I hated every minute of that job, and I quit as soon as something infinitely better came along.

Price Club needed a guy to walk around their gigantic parking lot, rounding up customers' empty shopping carts and rolling them back up to the front of the store. I *loved* that job! I'm not kidding. Every day I'd show up eager to start pushing my carts. It was a job that let me spend the day outside. It was a job where I didn't need to wear a shirt.

Best of all, "cart-pusher" was the one Price Club position where you didn't have to deal with customers. *That* was sweet. Headphones on, I could spend the whole day working up a sweat to "Panama" and "Hot for Teacher" while I air-guitared across the pavement, rocking and rolling thirty racked-up shopping carts back toward the store's front entrance. Bare-chested, beer-bellied, with wild hair billowing, I looked like a very happy escaped mental patient. Sadly though, despite all the perks and benefits of the job, my Price Club party ended too soon, when my mom had a heart attack.

Diabetic for years, "Attitude Annie" had finally fallen victim to the devastating effects of that disease. Thankfully, with fast, competent paramedics on the scene and coronary specialists who really seemed to care about the tough old broad in their care, my mom pulled through just fine, beginning a slow, steady recuperation at home. I stayed with her as often as I could, and when Price Club assistant manager types started giving me a hard time about days off, I just laughed at them and quit. I mean really, what kind of asshole sells out his sickly mom for $3.85 an hour?

In the weeks that followed, I divided my time between my mother's house and the big stretch of beach down her block. There, I'd swim for distance, gently coaxing the muscles in my left arm back into business. Later, as my strength began returning, I found that simply paddling a surfboard gave the arm an almost perfect workout. At the same time, pickup basketball games at the rec center kept my weight down and my stamina strong, and daily torture sessions with slave-driving flexibility trainers had me back near full mobility in just a few months. By late fall, with my mom feeling better and my own health worries fading, the future was once again looking bright—at least if you overlooked the fact that I was now dead broke and homeless.

Having finally bolted from my sister's House o' Toddlers, stanky diapers, and mechanical clowns, I spent the late summer and early fall bumming space on friends' couches, floors, and sometimes even their patio furniture. It was uncomfortable at best, but with a grand total of two responsibilities on this planet (my mom and my arm), my no-frills/no-rent mooch-packed lifestyle allowed me to take good care of both without ever having to deal with bills, landlords, or a nine-to-five job. The situation got even better the day I moved into a buddy's SUV.

Dennis Crowley was a navy chemist who spent his evenings volunteering at the rec center. I'd known him forever, and when he found out that I'd actually spent a night sleeping on an inflatable raft next to a buddy's aboveground pool, caught me mid-layup and, through his nephew Chris Georgio, offered me a rent-free, month-to-month lease in the back of his Chevy Suburban. Forty-five minutes later I moved in and immediately loved the place.*

With the middle seats folded down, the Suburban was nothing short of huge. Honestly, if this thing were listed as a studio apartment in Manhattan, it'd go for at least $1,400 a month. Every night, he'd have the truck parked in front of his tiny, one-bedroom apartment, waiting for me with the lift gate unlocked. Every night I'd stumble in sooner or later, crashing for a few hours 'til a quarter of nine, the time Dennis needed to throw me out of the vehicle and drive it to work. At that point, I'd head inside the guy's apartment, raid his refrigerator, and catch a few more Z's on his couch. Dennis kept me going at a time when I really needed the help, and to this day I feel indebted to the man.

During early November, with a roof over my head, not to mention a roof *rack*, and an arm that was undeniably on the mend, the David Wells story settles into a nice, quiet, predictable routine . . . for maybe three days. Sound asleep one night in the Suburban, I have an amazing, even life-changing dream. In it, I'm walking down a sidewalk along a wide, pretty residential street. Tree-lined and peppered on both sides with big homes and picket fences, my dream road looks an awful lot like Disneyland's Main Street U.S.A. or maybe something out of an old Norman Rockwell painting. I walk through my dream with a purpose, eyes darting along the street, from house to house. I'm searching for my dad's house.

Though I've never met the man in my life, for some reason, the dream version of me knows my dad lives in West Virginia and has his street address written on a slip of paper. As the dream rolls on, I find my dad's street, and I start running, counting down house numbers as I look for his place . . . which ultimately fails to exist. Every other house on the street is right where you'd expect it to be, but his is simply nonexistent. I could not, for the life of me, find my dad.

Standard stuff, right? Wrong! While I've since been told that any Psych 101 student could explain away my dream as "a classic example of the subconscious mind expressing feelings of parental abandonment," I can honestly tell *you* that's not the whole story. Waking up shaken, I made a beeline for my mom's place and surprised her by asking flat out, "Hey, Ma, does my dad live in West Virginia?" She looked like she'd just seen a ghost.

"Yeah," she said. "Your dad lives in West Virginia. How'd you know that?"

* So did my roommate, my buddy Robert Rubio.

"I had a dream."

My mom sat down. Taking one long breath, she then launched into the first "real" discussion we'd ever had about exactly where I'd come from. For my whole life, I'd simply assumed that my "dad" was the ex-husband who'd given my mom the last name Wells. I was wrong. *My* biological father, a man named David Pritt, came into the picture long after those two had divorced. Though they obviously had a child together, David Pritt and "Attitude Annie" never actually got along well enough to marry, and their relationship ultimately lasted less than two years. He left town just before my first birthday. They hadn't spoken since. My last name is Wells simply because my mom hung on to that surname throughout her adult life.

With my head spinning, I sat down next to my mom. That's when she handed me the phone number.

Out from the back corner of an old catch-all drawer, my mom handed me a crumpled, yellowed sheet of notepaper bearing the last known phone number she'd had for David Pritt. Less than an hour later, I called it and got hold of his sister (*my aunt?*), who told me Pritt had moved, at which point she passed along his new number. I thanked her and dialed immediately. It rang four times, which seemed like forty.

"Hello."

"Hi," I said. "Um, is this Dave Pritt?"

"Yessir. Who wants to know?"

"Well, this is your son . . . from California." And now there was a long pause.

"Hi, son."

And I lost it. It was just overwhelming to hear his voice, and to suddenly have him be real. I wasn't prepared for the emotion of the moment, and I fell apart fast. He followed suit, and together, with him drying his eyes and wiping his nose into Kleenex, and me doing the same exact thing into my sweatshirt sleeve, we made plans to meet. I wasn't looking for any kind of big relationship or anything, but I really *did* want to see him, and to meet him, and maybe even *know* him a little bit before he died. When he invited me to West Virginia for Thanksgiving with him and his wife, I accepted without any reservations at all. I was looking forward to the adventure.

Oddly, I had no real chip on my shoulder toward this guy, and with a little soul-searching, I came to realize that it probably had to do with the fact that even though *he* wasn't part of my life, I had always had a *lot* of father figures around. They may have been six foot four and covered in biker tatts, but they cared about

David Pritt and his lovely Priscilla

me, and hung with me, and always made me feel wanted. In short, I was never completely fatherless, and somehow that made meeting David Pritt more of a curiosity than a calling or an obsession, or a vendetta. I really had nothing to lose.

I flew into Cincinnati the day before Thanksgiving, and my "dad" met me at the airport. Together, with me silently marveling over the fact that we really *did* sort of resemble each other, we made the awkward, ninety-minute drive to his home, talking the whole way, learning about each other's lives, trying hard to keep things up and pleasant and light. Pulling into his driveway, I was quickly introduced to David's wife, Priscilla, a smart, good, funny lady, and I fell for her immediately. Jolly and beautiful, with huge eyes that twinkle all the time, she's impossible not to love. Over the course of the next four days, she bounced back and forth between us like a Super Ball, steeping us guys in turkey, pie, and mashed potatoes, while making us laugh and steadfastly refusing to let this first meeting be anything but 100 percent positive.

Priscilla succeeded, and despite an unavoidable "where the hell were you?" moment or two, Mr. David Pritt and I came away feeling pretty good about each other. Slowly but surely, over the years to follow, we'd ultimately build a really solid relationship. As of this writing, the man's a huge part of my life, and we're closer than ever.

Back in Ocean Beach, I slept in Dennis Crowley's big-ass Chevy right through the late fall and winter of 1985. Christmas Eve, nursing a minor eggnog headache, I listened to carols through the dashboard speaker while peeking through the sunroof for rum-induced reindeer. One week later, in the exact same spot, with a champagne buzz still glowing, I made myself the same New Year's resolution as the last year, vowing to myself that the upcoming season would find me healthy, effective, and taking yet another step toward a full-bore career in the bigs. Come hell or high water, the year 1986 was mine. I'd *make* good things happen. And that's exactly what I did . . . sorta. First, I was offered a dirt-cheap share in a dirt-covered apartment by my buddies Tony Laragonie and Albert Carreon. I was in heaven, sleeping on a real bed for the first time in months, and without a tire in my back. Then I stumbled into another great job . . . working with dead cows.

Out of the blue, my buddy Tom Rawls was kind enough to hook me up with some entry-level work at Ocean Beach's Sea and Shore Market. With pockets now completely lacking in date cash and beer money, I jumped at the job. Sick to death of my perpetual mooching, I was doubly intrigued by this particular offer of work, largely because I figured there'd probably be a lot of free, recently expired food in it for me as well.

From day one, I loved that job. A small corner store with the best meat department in town, the Sea and Shore took great pride in the cleanliness and quality of its produce. The floors shined. The deli counter gleamed. The eggplants were stacked into perfect purple pyramids.* The staff, except for me, was fresh faced, smiling, and impossibly well groomed, which may actually explain why the manager quickly decided to train me as the store butcher. Chops, ribs, filets, T-bones—give me a side of beef and a band saw, and I'd have you barbecue-ready in no time.

With my pitching fingers just inches away from steel blades, cleavers, and meat grinders through most of my workday, the Blue Jays would have freaked to see my hacking, chopping, flesh-ripping artistry, but I didn't care. The pride I took in my perfect little stew cubes, sausage links, and veal cutlets more than justified the risk of absentmindedly lopping off a pinky. Back behind the counter, I literally reconstructed the bones of the cows on my cutting board, rotating their joints in an effort to better understand my own healing process. I stayed at that job right up until I left for spring training 1986, where I quickly found myself right back at square one.

---

* It wasn't that clean but Tim Cabana and I did our best. Now, every time I see stacked fruit, my heart swells.

Dr. Andrews's official line on my elbow surgery described it as "repairing the ulnar collateral ligament" in my left arm. Loosely translated into layman's terms, that phrase means "turning a meat loaf back into an elbow." And while the Blue Jays' front office was optimistic regarding my recovery, they were by no means expecting a miracle. With that in mind, I'd been assigned to start the 1986 season with the team's "Low A" affiliate in Florence, South Carolina. One rung below Kinston on the Blue Jays' food chain, this was as low as a player could get and still call himself a professional. It was the kind of assignment where the catered dinner after a game often consisted of Campbell's tomato soup and one-slice bologna sandwiches. It was the kind of assignment where you bought your own soap for the shower. It was a league full of long shots, raw kids, last-chancers, and of course, guys trying to come back from career-threatening injuries.

The plan, as laid out by the Blue Jays' GM, Pat Gillick, and his assistant, Gord Ash, was to slowly ease me back into throwing shape amid the gentle, less competitive atmosphere of Low A Florence. Once I felt comfortable throwing all my old stuff, I'd graduate up to a High A affiliate, and we'd take it one step at a time from there. It seemed logical, and fair, and I have to admit I was secretly relieved that my rehab starts would fly in under the radar amid the largely ignored hinterlands of Florence. My "comeback" was by no means a sure thing, and if I was going to be rusty, if my velocity was going to be mush, if my control was going to be ferkakta, it was definitely better to work through those problems while hiding inside a league where game starts were sometimes delayed due to cows in the outfield.

As it turned out, I was up and out of Florence within three weeks. I did feel a *little* bit of tenderness in my elbow whenever I threw live, but that was to be expected. Scar tissue *needs* to get broken up, and it hurts. That's why God invented ice and Advil. Throwing from the mound, I adjusted my mechanics a little bit to favor the elbow, but my velocity was solid, the pop on my fastball was back with a vengeance, and my curve returned to form with a drop-off-the-table snap. After just three short relief appearances, and one comfortable, dominant start, I got two happy surprises. First, I was being sent up to a High A affiliate, and second, that affiliate wasn't Kinston. Instead, I was being shipped out to the California League, and the Ventura Gulls. For the first time in a long time, I'd be playing near home, once again tossing my innings beneath bright blue boring SoCal skies. I flew cross-country less than twenty-four hours later, but honestly, I probably could have just floated there. I was that happy.

Playing out of the California League, we Gulls made the standard, marathon bus trips, rolling to lush, manicured, well-loved ballparks from Reno, Nevada, to Rancho Cucamonga. Home stands, however, were an entirely different story. With no ballpark of its own, the Ventura franchise played all its home games on the baseball diamonds of Ventura Community College. Yankee Stadium, this wasn't. With fences short enough for even *me* to clock a homer or two, the park was oddly shaped, with a rocky, perpetually dusty infield, and an outfield that boasted a mountain in deep right. I'm not talking about a gradual incline, or a bump, I'm talking an actual hill, rising maybe three and a half feet above the ground level at first base. Anytime there'd be a fly ball hit deep to right, Rob Ducey, who played right field for us, would inevitably turn, run like hell, hit that hill, and wind up facedown in the grass. Seconds later, he'd be swearing up a storm while a benchful of us dugout degenerates would be laughing our asses off at his painful, but always entertaining, crash landings.

The VCCC ballpark had no lights whatsoever, and that meant we played every single one of our home games during the day. Like bankers or business-men, we Blue Jays would be home by 5 P.M. By now you've *gotta* know that's a recipe for trouble. Throwing gasoline onto that fire was the fact I ended up shar-ing a four-bedroom waterfront apartment with semi-wildman teammates Todd Stottlemyre, Jeff Musselman, and Todd Provence. With time on our hands every single night at home, we hit that town hard, cruising the Pacific Coast Highway both north and south on an endless quest to raise as much hell as humanly pos-sible. In an odd twist of fate, all four of us ended up finding real live girlfriends that summer. In an even odder twist, all four of them were named Karen. Odd-est twist of all, *my* Karen was hands down "the cute one." You might want to call the *Ripley's Believe It or Not!* people on that one.

I ultimately spent only about a month in Ventura, making a handful of starts and feeling absolutely great on the mound. With an earned run average of 1.89 under my belt, I got called up yet again. This time, getting shipped back across the country, to AA Knoxville. We hadn't even reached Memorial Day yet, and already I was making big progress. I was psyched about the promotion, though *way* disappointed to be leaving the insanity of Ventura behind.

I hit the locker room at Knoxville with a genuine sense of accomplishment. After coming desperately close to giving up on baseball entirely, I'd now spent a little more than a year "getting back on the horse." And while that process had entailed everything from endless therapy, to living in a car, to hacking the hooves off dead cattle, I'd survived. I wasn't back in the stadium two minutes before Larry Hardy found me, beaming with a smile that showed he was every bit as glad to see me as I was to be back. I practically bear-hugged the poor guy, knowing full well that I owed him my career. Seventeen years later, I still feel that way.

For almost two months I pitched well in Knoxville, winning consistently with no pain at all in my recycled elbow. I'd had a bit of soreness in my left *shoulder* from time to time, but it was nothing terrible, nothing to worry about. The situation was actually more annoying than painful, in that I'd made this quick, clean comeback from a nasty elbow injury, only to be saddled with a sporadically sore shoulder. Still, when that tenderness got more severe over my next couple of starts, Larry Hardy came to the rescue again. Watching my mechanics closely one afternoon, he noticed that I had shifted the angle of my delivery in the year since the elbow injury. In subconsciously protecting my elbow, I'd sacrificed my shoulder to an unnatural release point. The result was a pretty nasty case of tendinitis. Larry shut me down that afternoon, unwilling to let me do further damage to myself. And though I bitched and swore and moaned like a banshee, he ultimately put me on the disabled list from the Fourth of July weekend all the way through mid-August.

Traveling with the team, I slowly but surely began soft tossing, then throwing, then pitching from the mound as Coach Hardy watched my mechanics like a hawk, making sure I was free of bad habits and returning to my original form. When he was finally satisfied that I was once again ready to go, I rejoined the rotation and had two really strong outings before a surprise phone call pulled me north to Syracuse, New York, and the Jays' AAA affiliate. At that point, there was no way in hell I was gonna tell *anybody* how bad my shoulder still hurt.

I arrived in Syracuse on August 25, and over the course of the following week, I struggled through three increasingly weak, increasingly painful relief appearances before getting the shock of a lifetime. On August 31, 1986, I, David Wells, got *"the call."* I was gonna be a September 1 call-up with the Toronto Blue Jays. From out of the blue, a lifelong dream was suddenly being handed to me on a silver platter. My head spun, my heart raced, my hands perspired, but my brain finally took over and put a stop to all that. After battling so hard, for so long to get myself invited to the dance, I knew there was no way I could accept the Blue Jays' offer.

It practically killed me to say no, but with my shoulder feeling worse with each outing, and my performances on the mound going downhill fast, I knew my trip to the show would have been nothing short of disastrous. Major-league batters would have eaten my lunch, and after last year's elbow disaster, I'd lost all my illusions of immortality. I knew that another month of abuse would very probably turn my aching shoulder into an aching ball of mush. That's not exactly the major-league debut I'd been dreaming about. For all those reasons, I finally just choked out my refusal along with an honest confession of just how bad my shoulder was hurting.

Within twenty-four hours, Jeff Musselman got called up from Knoxville to take my place with the Jays. Meanwhile, I was headed straight back to the offices of my friend and career savior, Dr. James Andrews. With a barrage of X rays and MRIs, and a lot of chin scratching and fatherly "harumphing," Dr. Andrews informed me that in overcompensating for my elbow injury, I'd actually managed to tear my shoulder's cuff and labrum. It wasn't nearly as bad an injury as last year's disaster, but getting me back to 100 percent would once again require a bit of his inspired, nearly magical slicing and dicing. One deep sigh, seven curses, and two kicked chairs later, I was ready for yet another miracle.

Once again I entrusted my body and my career to Dr. Andrews, and once again he came through big-time. Honestly, within just a week or two of this surgery, I felt significantly better. By Halloween, I was back in Ocean Beach, paddling through another off-season of intensive splashing/tanning/shelf-stocking/cow-cutting/beer-drinking rehab.* By spring training, I felt like a million bucks. Really, even after completing the last two seasons by having various parts of my arm gutted and crocheted, I roared into camp in 1987 a new-improved monster.

For the first time in years, my fastball was clocked as high as 97 miles per hour. And with my delivery once again comfortable and pain free, the snap on my breaking pitches began sending batters back to the dugout just shaking their heads in frustration. An evil grin sat with me through every mound appearance these days. The old black hat was squarely back on my head.

From Florida, I eagerly packed my bags and flew due north, maybe not all the way to Toronto, but at least as far as Syracuse and AAA ball. With the arm feeling strong, and my confidence now once again bordering on cockiness, I couldn't wait to start chucking. Perennial teammates Rob Ducey and Todd Stottlemyre made the leap to AAA with me, and we quickly settled down together

* All I did was get drunk and play basketball with my pal Chris Wheatley. We ruled the courts all winter long.

as roommates in yet another makeshift bachelor pad/hovel. Together we all spent the next couple of months happily defiling that college town's friendliest coeds, while simultaneously lowering both their grades and their brain-cell counts. We also combined to rack up terrific AAA stats.

Ducey, protected now in the lineup by hard-ass hitters like Glenallen Hill and Lou Thornton, was thriving even in his earliest days at AAA. Todd Stottlemyre, having now grown out of his wild, fireballing ways, was much smarter on the mound, much more in control. As for me, while still more of a thrower than a pitcher, I'm nonetheless mowing down opposing batters with the sort of dominance I hadn't experienced since the last time I had Hells Angels cheering me on down the right-field line. I don't really understand why it's happening, but I sure as hell ain't complaining.

I'm pitching well in Syracuse, and my fast start catches the attention of Blue Jays' GM Pat Gillick, who somehow manages to *entirely* overlook the positive progress of my season in favor of deciding I'm fat. Effective immediately, as per Mr. Gillick's direct order, I now have to be weighed-in before every game and fined twenty dollars each time I top the 220 mark. My jaw drops. My ass clenches. This is the dumbest, most distracting bit of bullshit I've ever heard. Of course, at this point in my career I was still very young, and there *were* a lot more Toronto seasons in my future.

At Gillick's command, team trainers actually began lugging heavy medical scales on all our road trips for the sole purpose of having me step up and be measured like some prize heifer at a county fair. It was humiliating. It was demeaning. And obviously, it got to be a real pain in the ass. I'd go out there on the mound and try to concentrate on the game, but that petty, ignorant nonsense would be eating away at me. My numbers on the field were getting stronger all the time, but somehow, at least in the eyes of this one particular GM, that was all secondary to his own misguided crusade to tighten my belt.

Finally, I decided that if Pat Gillick really wanted me to weigh in every day at 220 or less, I should probably go out of my way to make sure I'd never let him down. I leaped into action immediately, hitting the weight room, where I looked long and hard at the treadmills and Stairmaster . . . then opened up the back of the team scale and jimmied it to read 8 pounds light. The following afternoon I hopped onto that sucker with a big smile on my face. "Way to go, Dave!" the trainers yelped. "You've lost six pounds!"

"Be sure Mr. Gillick hears about that," I told them. "It took a lot of hard work."

For a solid ten weeks, I felt unstoppable on that Syracuse mound, and with a May earned run average of 0.87, the gossip started flying. "David's going to the show." "Gillick's looking for arms." Every once in a while, amid the standard fart jokes and sex talk of the Syracuse locker room, those rumors sneaked in. I knew they were most likely false, but I couldn't help hoping to be proven wrong. I was so close now, I could smell it. I wanted that call more than anything. Three weeks later, it finally came.

We were in the middle of a ten-day road trip, staying in Tidewater, and if you can believe *this*, a bunch of us were out drinking that night. Stumbling through a very confusing revolving door, back into the hotel lobby, I found the team manager waiting for me. First response: "Oh shit!" Second response: "Why's he smiling at me?"

"David, congratulations. You're going to the big leagues!"

Right then and there, it took all the strength I could muster just to fight off my own, overwhelming urge to squeal and scream and jump up and down like every fat housewife who's ever won a new refrigerator on *The Price Is Right*. With a fist in the air and a "Yessssssssss!" that shot out of my chest like a cannonball, I ran to my room and practically dove at my phone. "Ma! Guess what! I'm going to the show!"

Two thousand miles away, my mom did the *Price Is Right* squealing for me. Then she laughed. Then she cried. Then she laughed some more, squealed, cried, laughed, squealed, and ultimately the whole pattern just repeated itself for the better part of an hour. From there, I stayed up all night long, calling friends, then relatives, then a ridiculously long line of acquaintances, waking them all, to share my major-league news. I finally hung up the phone, simply because I was now officially late for my plane. I've got to be on time, I thought. Got to make a good impression when I join my new team on the road. My heart racing, my hands shaking, I know for a fact that in the history of man on earth, NO human being has EVER been this excited about visiting Milwaukee.

SIX

El Torturo Grande

**Ha HAAA, mi
amigo. Pollos locos!
Pollos LOCOS!**
—*My Venezuelan
cabdriver*

JUNE 1987: EXHIBITION STADIUM, TORONTO

Like the concrete offspring of a male low-rent housing project, and a female medium-security prison, Exhibition Stadium rose gray and ugly from the Canadian landscape. It's huge, dark corridors looked like they were purchased wholesale from a slaughterhouse distributor. Its ridiculous, shocking green AstroTurf looked even more phony than the stuff you used to see in the backyard of the Brady Bunch. The whole place felt cold, even in summer.

Constructed eons ago, Exhibition Stadium was the official home field of the Canadian Football League's Toronto Argonauts. Baseball got "temporarily" shoehorned into the building when the Blue Jays expanded the American League in 1977. A decade later, with the space-age confines of the Skydome still more than two years away, the Blue Jays continued renting this big cement monster while dreaming of a brighter, more comfortable, less mildew-stained future.

Meanwhile, deep within the poured-slab bowels of the building, I was just thrilled to be "home." Joining the Jays in Milwaukee, for a set of three against the Brewers, I arrived equal parts eager, excited, nauseated, and nervous. Meeting manager Jimy Williams for the first time, I smiled through his obligatory "welcome aboard" speech, then gritted my teeth through a quick, strained meet-and-greet with "Chief of the Fat Police"/Toronto GM Pat Gillick. Finally, with the formalities and ass kissing aside, I got down to the business of meeting my new major-league teammates.

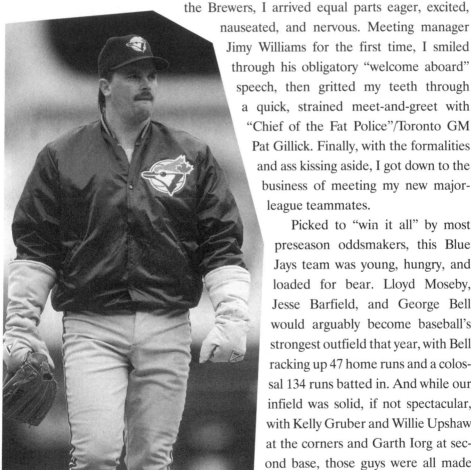

Greener than the AstroTurf
(© Mitchell Layton/Newsport)

Picked to "win it all" by most preseason oddsmakers, this Blue Jays team was young, hungry, and loaded for bear. Lloyd Moseby, Jesse Barfield, and George Bell would arguably become baseball's strongest outfield that year, with Bell racking up 47 home runs and a colossal 134 runs batted in. And while our infield was solid, if not spectacular, with Kelly Gruber and Willie Upshaw at the corners and Garth Iorg at second base, those guys were all made instantly and significantly better, just by playing on the same diamond as our absolutely fantastic shortstop, Tony Fernandez. At DH, rookie slugger Fred McGriff impressed from day one, while a monumentally underutilized Cecil Fielder got into about half of our games, spot starting at first base while also DHing, and making a mercifully aborted stab at becoming the world's biggest, most ham-handed third baseman.

Veteran backstop Ernie Whitt was doing the catching. And while years of abuse behind home plate had slowly turned the man's fingers into cocktail franks and his knees into creaking, cracking wrecks, the man's knowledge of baseball was mind-boggling. Coaches, managers, other pitchers, *nobody* I'd ever met seemed quite as brainy in the sweet science of striking motherfuckers out.

Skilled as he was, Whitt had his mitts full that year in guiding a pitching staff that might best be described as "almost very good." With a bullpen led by super-closer Tom Henke, and assisted by Mark Eichhorn and ex-roomie Jeff Mussel-man playing the roles of righty/lefty setup men, our relievers were hands down the best in baseball. Over the course of that 1987 season, the Blue Jays bullpen would throw 454 innings, with a jaw-dropping won-loss record of 38–17. Having those guys in our pen was like adding a pair of All-Star starters to the team . . . and that's exactly what we needed.

We were solid at the top of the rotation, with veteran righty Dave Stieb at the ace position, followed by ex–Medicine Hatter Jimmy Key. Jimmy made it to the show as a reliever in 1984, and ultimately threw well enough to join the Jay's rotation in '85. By the end of the 1987 season, Key will have a 2.76 earned run average in his pocket and nearly fifty career victories under his belt. All of that's encouraging for me (in a dark, twisted sort of way), because I know for a *fact* I was better than that guy back in Canada.

From there, the Toronto starters went downhill fast. Jim Clancy, a career Blue Jay with a sub-500 ten-year career, waffled through his regular starts, keeping the team close as often as he could. After him, a guy named Joe Johnson began the season as the Jays' fourth starter, but with injuries mounting, and a skyrocketing ERA, the dude was fading fast. By mid-June, with the start of baseball's serious trading season still at least a month away, the Jays were just desperate enough to hoist me up to the Great White North and hope for a miracle.

Within days, Jays' skipper Jimy Williams had penciled me in for my first start, Sunday, June 30, at home, against the New York Yankees. With some quick mental math, he then checked the schedule and told me I'd more than likely be pitching against "Louisiana Lightning" himself, Ron Guidry. I practically turned a backflip in his office.

Guidry had long been an idol. One of my favorite Bronx Bombers, Guidry was literally front and center in almost all my old Ocean Beach bedroom Yankee shrines. To be making my first major-league start against this man was an honor that knocked me for a loop, much like the Yankees would do four days later.

A crowd of just about 30,000 showed up at Exhibition Stadium that day, breaking my old "largest crowd" record by perhaps 25,000 people. Warming up, backup catcher Charlie Moore tells me my stuff looks pretty good then tries his level best to relax me. He fails, miserably. Waiting for the game to start, "Oh Canada" seems longer than "Stairway to Heaven," and team introductions last maybe six and a half weeks. Finally, with a cry of "play ball" and a long, loud stadium cheer, I sprint to the mound, immediately tipping the fact I'm nervous to leadoff hitter Rickey Henderson. Stepping into the batter's box, he's already got me beat.

When a player as smart as Rickey Henderson finds out he's leading off against a guy who's never thrown a major-league pitch, he might as well drag a lawn chair into the batter's box. He knows I'm nervous. He knows I'm pressing. He knows I'm gonna be trying too hard, aiming the ball and/or overthrowing every pitch. Even if it only takes me a minute or two to settle down, right now he knows I'm right where he wants me. He knows he's not swinging at *anything* until I prove I can throw a strike. If he gets lucky, I might even get behind in the count and toss him a nice fat grapefruit down the middle.

Sweating, I throw Rickey ball one, followed by ball two. He's smiling now, and even at that infantile stage of my career, it pisses me off.

Strike one follows, with a sweet, sweeping curve. A second curve, this one even better than the first, rings up strike two. Rickey's not smiling anymore. Even better, with the count even, I know he's probably sitting on another curve. Instead, I throw him a fastball, on the inside corner of the plate. It's pretty clearly a strike, but with a little Rickey Henderson body English and the fact that I'm a rookie both working against me, the umpire calls "ball three." I refuse to let myself throw Rickey the fastball he's waiting for, and I go back to the curve, which I overthrow badly. Rickey connects with a single that drops in front of George Bell in left. Willie Randolph comes to the plate.

Within seconds, Rickey's dancing off the bag, trying his level best to rattle my concentration. He succeeds, big-time. I know full well that Rickey's gonna try to take second from me. I also know he'll probably succeed. On top of all that, I've now got a great contact hitter at the plate, and if I'm not careful, in about two minutes, a steal and a single will combine to put me down 1–0 before I've even recorded my first major-league out. Worst of all, with his large lead off the first-base bag, I know it's almost a given that right now, Rickey's peeking down toward home, trying his level best to steal Charlie Moore's signs. With any success at all, Rickey will quickly begin using his eyeballs and/or fingertips to signal Randolph as to whether he's being set up inside or out. All of these things go into making that royal pain in my ass the single greatest leadoff man in the majors. My first pitch to Randolph misses the outside corner. Rickey stays put, though he surely realizes that second base would have been easy pickings.

And then I get lucky. With Rickey more confident than ever as he dances off the first-base bag, I stare into home plate, nod, then whip a throw over to Willie Upshaw at first. Somehow, I'm blessed with a minimiracle and we catch Rickey by a half-step. Rickey goes through the motions of arguing the call, but he's picked off, and he knows it. He walks back to the Yankees' bench shaking his head, with what appears to be the faintest glimmer of a "you got me" grin. One man down. Three pitches later, Willie Randolph walks. I still haven't gotten anybody out at the plate.

Don Mattingly steps into the batter's box now, and I'm face-to-face with another idol. For years, I've imagined what it might be like pitching to this man, dreaming of the day it might happen for real. That day is here, and I'm ready. I know what Mattingly likes. I know where his strengths are, and for the first time all day, I feel like I know exactly what to do. Slowly, carefully, I work the Yankees' biggest offensive threat up and down, inside and out, and six pitches later, I get him to nick a little dribbler between first and second. Willie Upshaw grabs it, and we get Randolph with a fielder's choice at second. Buoyed now, with two outs under my belt, and a moral victory against Mattingly, I take a deep breath and stare down Dave Winfield.

Another Yankee, another tough out. I haven't faced a pushover yet. Winfield stands tall in the box, watching and waiting for my first pitch. Charlie Moore calls for my change-up, knowing full well it'll be the last thing Winfield's expecting. I wind up. I toss. I throw a butterfly toward home plate that finds Winfield reaching, lunging, and losing his bat. It heads straight for me.

"LOOK O-O-O-O-O-O-O-U-T!!!" Winfield yells from home plate.

I leap over the whooshing, windmilling Louisville Slugger with just enough unintentional comedic talent to pull some big laughs and a mock ovation from the assembled crowd. Three pitches later, Winny beats me with a single into deep right as Don Mattingly chugs and wheezes all the way to third.

On the mound now, while I *could* be panicking, I manage to keep my head together, telling myself that one simple out lets me escape the inning unharmed. One pitch later, Yankees center fielder Gary Ward slaps a little deke single into right. Mattingly scores, and Winfield goes to second.

Shit! I'm pressing now, trying to keep this thing from getting ugly, fast. Charlie Moore takes a walk to the mound, just to check in and keep my brains from exploding out the top of my head. When he's satisfied I'm cool, he heads back to the plate with a thumbs-up. With DH Ron Kittle at the plate, we turn a first-pitch fastball into a neat little groundout to third. Down 1–0, I'd now survived a whole half-inning of major-league baseball relatively unscathed. Sadly, that would be the high point of my game.

Over the next three innings, the Yankees slapped me around pretty good, with eight more hits and four earned runs. Winfield, Rickey Henderson, Mattingly: they all got their revenge on me, and it wasn't long before Jimy Williams took a slow, stone-faced, pep-talk-free walk to the mound demanding the ball. I went to the showers, rationalizing all the way. It wasn't *too* bad for a first start. I *had* gotten four Yankee strikeouts, and my control *had* been pretty good, and I *did* manage to pick Rickey Henderson off at first base. Still, beneath all that spin, I knew I'd been hittable. All I could do was hope for a better outing next time around.

Five days later, spending Independence Day at the home of the league-leading Kansas City Royals, I got lit up like a bottle rocket. It was nasty; an ugly start where I just didn't feel like I had anything working. I don't even want to write about it. Let's just leave it at the numbers. I lasted only an inning and a third that day, giving up five runs on six hits. Jimy Williams looked even more unhappy making his walk *this* time around. Again I went to the showers looking for positives, and again I hoped for some better luck in my next start . . . which ultimately came almost two years later.

Two starts, two losses, and I was sent back down to Syracuse, and the slings and arrows, and bus trips, and poverty, and bad hotels, and cold bologna sandwiches of minor-league ball. Pissed and embarrassed that the Blue Jays gave up on me so fast, I was also pissed and embarrassed at my own shitty performance. When guys like Ernie Whitt and Cecil Fielder and Dave Stieb tried to console me in the locker room with words like "Don't worry, buddy, you'll be back here in no time," I found them hard to believe. When Jimmy Key shook my hand and wished me well, I'd never felt more jealous in my life. I knew it was wrong, and completely unfair, but I just couldn't help feeling like *I* should be enjoying the same successes *he* had. Without the blown elbow and the blown shoulder, maybe I could be the one having the incredible year. Maybe I could be the hot young phenom instead of the major-league washout. Twenty-four hours later, I settled back into Syracuse as a decidedly unhappy camper. Thankfully, one coach refused to let me sulk.

For fourteen seasons, Dave LaRoche pitched all over the major leagues, working out of the bullpen, as a closer, a setup man, a long reliever, even a spot starter. And while he never threw smoke, from 1970 right through 1983, he was often just about unhittable. By '87, he'd found a home working as our Syracuse pitching coach, and I would soon become the man's pet project.

Dave immediately demanded that I put my short, bad experience in Toronto behind me, refocusing instead on all the positives that got me called up in the first place. We worked on my mechanics a little bit, we sharpened the break on my curve, we talked about my competitive edge and the fact I threw hard and was never rattled too badly by high-pressure situations. Slowly but surely, the old reliever began trying to reinvent me as one of his own.

He talked up the fact that it took me no time at all to warm up before a game. He talked up the fact that I seemed to thrive whenever a game was on the line. And he talked up the possibility that it might be a lot easier for me to break back into the bigs as a reliever. That last one made me a convert. If working out of the bullpen would help this team, and get me back to the Blue Jays, it was all just fine with me. I started relieving that night, and all through July and August, the Dave LaRoche experiment seemed to pay off big-time.

My arm held up fine. My stuff stayed sharp with the extra work, and mentally, I found that I really liked the idea of riding in like the cavalry to shoot down an attack. My stats as a reliever were *much* better than any starting numbers I'd ever racked up, and on September 1, as major-league rosters expanded, Toronto took notice, bringing me back north to get busy in their pen. Unlike my last go-round, this time I made the most of my shot.

After getting burned twice during my last trip north, there was no way in hell Jimy Williams was gonna let me into anything close. His Jays had been running neck and neck with the Detroit Tigers, battling over first place in the AL East for several weeks now, and with September unrolling fast, there was no time to experiment. However, after scoring my first major-league victory in a surprise, come-from-behind victory against the Angels, and following that performance with a couple of strong appearances in glorified mop-up spots, I started getting some regular work . . . and thriving.

Working as a left-handed, long reliever, I began seeing action almost every other day, ultimately going 4–1 for the month of September with an ERA of just 1.50. I was contributing—making a difference and succeeding at the major-league level for a team that was still hanging tight through a late-season pennant race. As an extra perk, on September 18, my first major-league save came against the New York Yankees, *in* Yankee Stadium, with a performance so strong it *almost* made me forget how badly they'd kicked my ass back in June.

Oddly though, despite having a lot of late success out of the pen, my proudest moment of the '87 season actually came during a loss. Going into a VERY big series in Detroit, Jim Clancy had given up three runs in just two and a third innings, and he'd gotten into trouble again in the third. With men on first and second, and no outs, Jimy Williams came to the mound and called for me. With the game tied at 3–3, this was a big spot, in a big game, and I was proud to be asked to stop the bleeding.

Alan Trammell was at the plate as I came into the game, and I ultimately worked him well, but not well enough to stop him from blooping a single just over the outstretched glove of Garth Iorg. One run scored, and the Tigers went up 4–3. With men on first and third with no outs, I was still in big trouble, but somehow, something fierce kicked in and I was able to wriggle out of that rough patch with no further bleeding.

Coming back to the bench, with backslaps and congratulations all around, Jimy pulled me aside to tell me the game was now officially mine to win or lose. It was as proud a moment as I'd ever had in baseball. Working hard over the next six innings, I was able to shut the door on Detroit, scattering just a handful of hits. We ultimately lost that game 4–3, but even with the loss, I knew I'd really accomplished something. I'd gone out onto a major-league mound, against a first-place team, and flat-out kicked ass. The realization hit me like a ton of bricks, and somehow, it finally allowed me to take a deep breath and relax. Y'know, in my own head, I now officially had "the stuff." I *could* compete successfully at a major-league level. I now had genuine, tangible evidence.

In a perfect world, I'd now spend the better part of this paragraph talking about how we Blue Jays mounted a dramatic late-season winning streak, ultimately passing the Tigers on the last day of the season. Sorry, can't do that. The world being an imperfect place, I must report that none of those things actually happened. Instead, though we played solid ball the rest of the way, we Blue Jays got swept in a season-ending series against the Tigers, going from one game up, to two back in the process. The final lesson I learned that year was that while a tie may feel like kissing your sister, second place feels more like kissing your weird uncle Jimbo.

The Jays' season ended on a cold, nasty, drizzly Sunday afternoon, and as dusk rolled in, I was already daydreaming about getting back to the beach. For the first time in a long time, I could go home this winter as a returning success, a hero, free to do absolutely nothing. I could live off the little bit of cash I'd made up here in the bigs, while spending my days surfing, baking in the sun, and daydreaming about better things to come in 1988. And then I heard about "winter ball."

As the season was winding down, Pat Gillick and Gord Ash began gently "suggesting" that certain young players might want to take advantage of the "supplemental training opportunities" that could be found as part of a fun-filled off-season playing winter ball in Venezuela, for the Barquisimeto Division's Cardenales de Lara. To put it mildly, I was less than thrilled. However, once the idea of cold, hard cash, money-money entered the equation, I started thinking about how nice it might be to get out of Southern California and maybe see a little bit of South America.

Los Cardenales were offering six thousand bucks in exchange for my services throughout their short, six-week season. And while that dollar amount sounds tiny by today's standards, it was eyebrow-raising in 1987, especially when you take into consideration the fact that I'd now endured a solid five years of playing for minor-league money that maxed out at $18K. And yes, embarrassing as it sounds, I *did* like the idea that my participation might stroke the Jays front office a little bit. With all that in mind, I bounced home to Ocean Beach just long enough to kiss my mom, catch a handful of six-foot curls, and drag my friends through one marathon nonstop, screaming, totally obnoxious tour of all the city's can't-miss degenerate hangouts. With those absolute requirements out of the way, I was now free to ship out and play ball.

From the airport in San Diego, I hopped a plane to Houston. There, I got on a smaller plane to Caracas, where I boarded a little puddle jumper into Barquisimeto. Nearly nine hours after the journey began, I stepped out onto the melting tarmac and immediately began wondering if maybe I'd made a big mistake.

Looking like guerrilla fighters out of some old Chuck Norris movie, dirty, camouflage-clad soldiers were all over the airport. Every one of them carried a machine gun, and *none* of those guys looked the least bit capable of operating it safely. Sweating now, I grabbed up my bags and endured a ride to the ballpark that did *nothing* to calm my fears. For the better part of twenty miles, we hit potholes bigger than the car we were driving. We slowed down in a traffic jam caused by chickens in the street. "Ha HAAA, *mi amigo. Pollos locos! Pollos LOCOS!*" my driver shouted, laughing as he bumped a curb, lit a cigarillo, and kept on driving.

I've been warned never to drink the water. I've had 742 separate innoculations, but very quickly, I'm feeling decidedly unsafe down here near the equator. A quick stop at the team hotel does nothing to change my mind. We bounce into the parking lot with worn-out shocks meeting equally worn-out pavement. Grabbing my bags from the cab trunk, I pay a wildly inflated fare, then trudge through a broken glass door into a lobby that looks like the tragic aftermath of a medium-size earthquake, maybe a 6.5 on the Richter scale.

A stained, orange velour couch is surrounded on either side by large, bent, plastic plants. An old TV set stands in a corner, rabbit ears twisted into a configuration just perfect for receiving the old, dubbed episode of *The Beverly Hillbillies* currently offered by the local station. In a mild state of shock, I stare at the sitcom while a clerk in a sweat-stained, yellowed, formerly white T-shirt checks me in. Oddly, I notice that Jethro's voice sounds like it's been dubbed into Spanish by a husky, teenaged girl, and the phrase "CEE-ment pond" remains "CEE-ment pond" even after the translation. I get my key and head upstairs with my bag, daydreams immediately returning to the SoCal beaches I left behind.

I turn the key and enter my room, hoping for a miracle. No dice. Saggy, grimy twin beds lay on either side of a painted, green night table. A small, portable television set is already turned on, tuned in to the same *Beverly Hillbillies* episode I saw downstairs. At this point, the bathroom door swings open, and I get another shocking surprise. My roomie for the next six weeks is gonna be Cecil Fielder.

"Hey, Boomer,"* he says with his usual, gigantic grin. "I've got dibs on the bed near the window, 'cuz yours has a big, nasty stain on the comforter." At this point, disgust kicks in, on two completely unrelated levels. First, the idea of sleeping on somebody else's mystery stain makes my skin crawl (I mean, just imagine the possibilities). Second, I'm equally disgusted by the fact that even at my size, I *know* I can't argue with Cecil, because quite frankly, the man could

---

* I was loud, so people called me Boomer. Go figure.

kick my ass from here to Caracas without ever breaking a sweat. The stained bed is mine, whether I like it or not.

Taking a deep breath to relax myself, I instead notice the room's striking, vaguely familiar odor, which, after one more whiff, I recognize as an odd combination of mildew and maybe cheese. My first words follow. "Holy shit, Cecil," I say, "how the fuck are we supposed to live here?"

"I don't know, but trust me on this one, you're gonna want to wear your flip-flops in that bathtub. You hungry, man?"

Honestly, at that point I wasn't sure that I'd ever be hungry again. However, in a conscious effort to just plain get the hell out of the hotel, Cecil and I hit a local bar and grill, where we chowed down like animals on two supersize orders of plain, safe, well-done grilled chicken. We also gobbled up the attention we suddenly began receiving from the local señoritas.

Clearly American, clearly athletes here to play winter ball, even a couple of imperfect beauties like me and Cecil became suddenly irresistible to the vast majority of local girls competing for our hunky, he-manly companionship. We weren't stupid. We knew the girls' attraction was almost entirely rooted in the fact that if they played their cards right, we could conceivably offer them a much better life in the United States. We knew their friendly gestures and flirty, aggressive body language were most likely phony. However, with black hair flowing, olive skin glowing, and dark eyes sparkling at us in the light of our mosquito-repellant candles, we just didn't care. These girls made it crystal clear that Venezuela's most breathtaking natural resource was its bumper crop of stunningly gorgeous women. In an instant, the hotel horrors and the airport soldiers seemed like distant, trivial, deeply repressed memories.

Stumbling back down the street to our hotel when we were both sufficiently inebriated and sleepy enough to overlook our room's obvious faults, Cecil and I flopped onto our cheap, thin mattresses, pulled up our threadbare sheets, and drifted off into a peaceful sleep. Forty minutes later, I woke up screaming. Something was crawling into my nostril.

Jumping out of the bed with arms flailing, I hit the floor hard and immediately squished something crunchy with my foot. I clicked on the light and thought I was gonna die. HUNDREDS of big-assed, nasty brown cockroaches went skittering in every direction. I slapped Cecil awake while the little bastards were all still running for cover.

"Oh shit," he said. "We better leave a light on." At which point he rolled over and went back to sleep.

All night long, while Cecil snored, I laid there under my mystery stain, trying and failing to lull myself back into unconsciousness. Less than twenty-four hours after leaving my hometown, I was officially miserable. First thing in the morning, I bolted across the street, buying up every can of Raid in the local bodega. I then launched a full-tilt war on the invading *cucarachas*. Only when the air quality in the hotel room reached toxicity levels that left me dizzy, did I finally call a cease-fire and head off to the ballpark. Once there, I quickly realized that my new home field was every bit as wonderful as my hotel room had been.

The base paths were rocky. The outfield grass, where it existed at all, was brown and scraggly. The backstop was made of chicken wire strips, pieced together with the help of garbage bag ties. The locker room floors were wall-to-wall sticky. One day ago, I would have been shocked to find such conditions, but today I took it in stride. Honestly, at this point, nothing short of two burros salsa dancing on the pitcher's mound would have raised my eyebrows.

Settling into my warped, plywood locker, I compared hotel horror stories with Cardenales teammates like David Justice, Rob Ducey, Glenallen Hill, Luis Sojo, Luis Leal, and Alex Infante, taking comfort in the fact they all seemed to be enduring their own personal hordes of uninvited, six-legged demons. At the same time, being young and male and obsessed with sex, we shifted gears rapidly, forgetting all about our bug problems in favor of cheerleading about the fact that here in Venezuela, the local, superhuman gene pool seems entirely incapable of producing any female who's not drop-dead stunning. Rob Ducey is halfway through telling us about how he's already met the girl of his dreams,* when the Cardenales equipment manager starts tossing uniforms at us.

Sizing us up with a quick once-over, he outfitted the whole team in the span of ten minutes, which seemed impressive, until it became obvious that nobody's uniform actually fit. They were *all* too small, especially on guys like me and Cecil. By team picture time, we looked like a bunch of dads trick-or-treating in our kids' Pony League uniforms. We smiled for the camera, shouting *"Queso,"* rolling with the punches through one more misadventure in what was quickly becoming an endless comedy of errors.

Within days we began our first home stand, playing ball against local teams from Aragua to Zulia. And while a few of those franchises fielded a decent starting lineup, our Barquisimeto Bombers, as captained by our Torontonian band of

---

* Rob ended up marrying her.

D A V I D   W E L L S

ringers, just mopped up every bit of the competition. At the same time, free from the pressures of pitching in big-game situations, I was cleared to experiment. Tossing my curve from different angles simply to see the effect, toying with different speeds on my change-up; here in Venezuela, I didn't have to worry about making mistakes to a Mattingly, or a Kirk Gibson, or a George Brett. Here, amid the rocks and the weeds, the beautiful girls, and the friendly, rabid fans, I could just relax, have fun, and play ball. For three hours a day, I really enjoyed my experience in winter ball. It was the other twenty-one that nearly killed me.

First and foremost, the bug situation was making me certifiably nuts. The Raid offensive had failed miserably, and follow-up attacks with boric acid, boiling water, and the soles of my Nikes had proven even more pitiful. Finally, when I awoke one night to find a huge roach on one eyelid, I'd had enough. Packing my stuff as fast as I could (though I did take a moment to make sure my bag was bug free) I checked out of the team hotel and cabbed it across town to a nicer place. Now paying my own housing bills, I began seriously dipping into my winter ball money just to cover the rent. In short order, I was back to barely making ends meet. Still, if the brink of poverty was gonna keep bugs from eating my face while I slept, I was more than willing to go there.

Alone now in my brand-new room, I was vermin free but also bored to death. With no teammates in the building and no Spanish in my vocabulary, killing time became a daily chore. Honestly, once I'd finished brushing my teeth in the morning, my daily planner would be completely blank until game time. With no American television channels, no local theaters showing English-language movies, and the nearest beach more than a hundred miles away, I mostly just sat, like a lump, in my room. I'd play garbage can basketball, seeing how many paper wads I could sink in a hundred tries. I'd nap, like a three-year-old. I'd listen to my KISS tapes until even *I* got tired of them. It was pitiful. And then Luis Sojo saved my sanity.

Born and raised in Venezuela, Luis mentioned in passing one day that even though the boxes on the VHS tapes for rent in town were printed in Spanish, the movies inside were always in English. I could have kissed him. The following morning I spent way too much money on a decent VCR and started renting myself anywhere from five to seven movies a day. Within weeks, I'd become a Roger Ebert–size expert on cheesy, mid–1980s American cinema.

One after another they'd roll out in my room: *Rocky* I, II, III, and IV, *Rambo* I and II, *Police Academy*, *Porky's*. I didn't care if they were good, bad, or horrible; if a movie could kill two hours, it was definitely worth watching. By late afternoon, bleary eyed, and squinting into the afternoon sun, I'd walk to the ballpark while a little voice inside my head whispered, What the hell are you doing here? Each day that voice got a little louder.

On road trips, the whole Cardenales team would pile into a secondhand minibus, captained by a driver who had a large, plastic Jesus on the dashboard and crosses Krazy Glued over each rearview mirror. It didn't instill a whole lot of confidence in his driving. Later, as the man careened through the countryside, on mountain roads that seemed better suited to donkeys than bus traffic, I half expected plastic Jesus to jump down off the dashboard, force open the doors, and leap out into the relative safety of a sixty-mile-per-hour bailout.

What the hell are you doing here?

And then came the riot. Beginning a brand-new home stand, I was walking toward the ballpark, like I always did, but on this day I wandered into a full-blown riot. Local university students had apparently decided to air their grievances against the Venezuelan government by breaking store windows, turning over cars, and burning large piles of tires in the street. Thick clouds of black smoke billowed up, while a heavy police presence seemed to be growing larger and angrier by the minute.

What the hell are you doing here? The voice was back, this time louder than before.

Still blocks away from the park, I watched a police car get flipped, then did a quick about-face and jogged back to the relative safety of my hotel, where I spent the night watching *The Natural* three times in a row.

And then, I nearly got killed.

On the mound one night, pitching against Los Leones del Caracas, I've got a runner on first, with the league's best hitter, Andres Galarraga, at the plate. Bearing down, I decide to heave a 95-mile-per-hour fastball toward "the Big Cat." I wind up, I throw, and even before I'm done following through, Galarraga's connected with a line shot back up the middle that somehow miraculously ends up in my glove, which somehow, even more miraculously, was right in front of my face.

The impact of the ball sends the mitt crushing into my face, redesigning my nose while simultaneously unlocking floodgates of blood. I've never had a ball hit that hard at me before (or since). In shock, on the mound, I've inexplicably got the presence of mind to throw over to first and double up the runner, but I'm fast becoming a dazed, broken, bloody mess. I wobble to the bench and collapse in a heap.

What the hell are you doing here? It's practically shouting now.

And then I got dysentery.

It was my fault. For weeks I'd been really careful about drinking the local water, even going so far as to brush my teeth with bottled water. But one absent-minded slip at the locker room water fountain quickly introduced me to a raging case of the Barquisimeto Bowel Blaster. Though I'll spare you the explosive details, you can probably judge for yourself how bad I was feeling by remembering the worst stomach flu you've ever had, and quadrupling it. I was green, exploding from both ends every thirty minutes like some geyser at Yellowstone, and the team was set to start a new road trip the following morning.

Ten A.M. I'm now feeling even worse than I did last night. I'm sweating uncontrollably. I'm incapable of keeping any food or drink in my system. I smell worse than you can possibly imagine. I am by no means someone you'd want sitting next to you on a small, crowded, no-bathroom/non-air-conditioned bus for the next five hours. I call in to the clubhouse, saying that there's no way I can travel with the team this morning, explaining my illness with enough vivid detail to make grown men beg for mercy.

Amazingly, within minutes I've got team officials on the phone shouting at me in broken English that I *must* travel with the team. Again I lay out the horrifying realities of my intestinal distress, but this time, there's no sympathy on the other end. Instead, I'm advised to take Pepto-Bismol, to suck it up, to think about the team, and to be on the bus within a half hour. The call is so bizarre, I'm literally laughing between cramps.

In the end, I thank the executives for their concern but tell them I won't be able to honor their (insane) request. I hang up the phone, flopping back onto my bed, where if I'm lucky, I'll die soon.

Twenty minutes pass, and sadly, I'm still alive. Now the phone rings again, and this time it's Blue Jays' general manager Pat Gillick, who speaks to me like I'm a dog who's just shit the carpet. Apparently the Cardenales front office has called Pat at home to complain about my insubordination. After a brief hello, and some forced chitchat wherein the man pretended to care about how I was feeling, Gillick strongly suggested that it'd be in the best interests of both the Cardenales and me if I could find some way to haul my ass onto that bus. The message between the lines could not have been clearer. If I wanted to stay in the good graces of the Blue Jays' front office, I was gonna have to play ball, both literally and figuratively.

I got on the bus. I'm not proud of that fact, but as a young player still strug- gling to gain a foothold in major-league baseball, I weighed the consequences of standing up for myself against incurring the wrath of a major-league GM, and I caved. With a shower, some mouthwash, and a pair of mismatched sweats com- bining to make me at least marginally presentable, I stumbled down to the bus and took a seat, praying to plastic Jesus that I wouldn't actually explode in front of my teammates.

Cross-legged and pale, clutching a bucket at all times, I endured yet another bumping, weaving, pot-hole-packed voyage into the Venezuelan heartland. Nobody else sits within two rows of me, but with an absolutely classic example of mind over matter, I'm somehow able to control my bodily blowouts through- out the entire trip, throwing up only during regularly scheduled rest stops at gas stations, Porta Pottis, and the odd, occasional shrubbery along the way.

WHAT . . . THE HELL . . . ARE YOU DOING HERE?!!! This time the voice won me over. After the bugs, and the bad food, and the boredom, and the ill-fitting uniforms, and the smashed-in nose, and the riot, and the worst case of diarrhea in the history of man on earth, I'd finally had enough. I launched an escape plan almost immediately.

From the very beginning of winter ball, I'd made it clear that on one week- end, about halfway through the season, I was going to have to fly home to San Diego to serve as best man at the wedding of my good buddy and fellow Ocean Beach monster Chris Wheatly. I'd rejoin the team two days later. Both the Car- denales and Blue Jays had agreed to that request up front, but now, with the date drawing near and every single day seeming to unleash a bigger, badder hor- ror story, I realized I could use the trip as my bulletproof way out. I'd just stay in San Diego after the wedding ceremony, going AWOL from the Cardenales before this season in hell leaves me with permanent brain damage.

And then I waffled. Honest to God, even with all the nightmarish events of my sentence here in Venezuela, I really *did* enjoy playing ball for the Carde- nales, and I felt like an asshole for even *considering* running out on my team. Thoughts of the incredible local women and equally incredible local rum made it even harder to decide. Finally, even on the day of my trip home, I still hadn't made up my mind what to do.

Packing for the airport, I put everything I had with me (minus the VCR) into two huge duffel bags and called Cecil Fielder. In an odd coincidence, Cecil was going back home to Los Angeles for the weekend, with a family obligation of his own, and we'd made plans to head for the airport together. Less than halfway there, I told him about my possible escape plan, and he laughed.

"I had a feeling," he told me. "You've been quiet the past few days, so I knew *something* was up."

By the time we'd reached the airport, Cecil and I had spent the better part of an hour debating my choices. "Big Daddy" wasn't thrilled with the idea of my leaving the team in midseason, but he *was* open-minded. Better than anybody else on the Cardenales, he'd seen firsthand, bug-in-the-nose evidence of how miserable I'd been, and he knew that hanging around Venezuela for another month would probably just make things a lot worse.

At the same time, Cecil also calmed my fears about upsetting the Blue Jays' front office. Never a big fan of the suits and bean counters running that club, Cecil just kind of wrapped one giant hand around my shoulder and guaranteed me that even with Pat Gillick behind the big desk, there was no way in hell I'd be left off the '88 roster. I'd *earned* my spot by coming up to the bigs and kicking serious ass, in relief, all through the month of September. Sane people *never* argue with Cecil, so I just smiled, thanked the man, then hit the duty-free shop.

Loading up two shopping bags with fantastic Venezuelan rum, and grabbing up a few tacky souvenirs to pass out back home, I caught up with Cecil as he hurried toward our flight gate and the one empty wooden bench in the whole packed airport. He interrogated and jogged at the same time.

"So?" he asked

"So what?"

"What's the verdict?"

"I don't know," I told him. "I think I just have to do a lot of soul-searching this weekend and wait for a sign."

And at that point I dropped my duffels, hitched up my shorts, and sat down next to Cecil. The bench broke in half.

With a CRA-A-ACK! that rang out loudly in all directions, that bench snapped right down the middle and dumped both of our fat asses on the airport floor. My rum bottles rolled across the tile. My coconuts carved into monkeys fell out of their bag. Cecil lost a shoe. And now, from what seemed like all corners of the terminal, dozens of locals just ran up in stitches, pointing and whooping, and having a great time laughing at our shared, ridiculous misfortune.

Flat on my back, I had to smile. I'd asked for a sign, and ten seconds later it came through loud and clear. My decision was made. I went home to Ocean Beach and rode out the winter blendering my stockpiled rum into fantastic mai tais and piña coladas, while dodging angry, long-distance phone calls from both Venezuela and Toronto. I never went back.

Pitchers and catchers were due to report in less than a hundred days.

SEVEN

Big Leagues
and Bad Behavior

Mr. Wells, you have the
right to remain silent. Anything
you say can and will be used
against you in a court of law.

—Oompa Loompa–size
Chicago police officer

MARCH 1988: DUNEDIN, FLORIDA

It's not even April 1, but already Jimy Williams looks mid-August miserable. Granted, even on his best day, the man hangs a cranky, slightly constipated look on his face, but today's different. Today he's alternating between cursing loudly and muttering under his breath. Today he's messed with George Bell.

With 47 home runs and 134 RBIs, the Blue Jays All-Star left fielder was voted 1987's American League MVP. He was also just about terrible in the field. Bad arm, bad speed, bad skills, bad attitude, George was awesome at the dish, but he really did play half-assed, lazy defense in left. He drove Jimy Williams nuts, and with that in mind, our Blue Jays' skip came to spring training '88 with a plan to make George our everyday DH. Within days of arriving in Dunedin, Jimy'd unveiled his plan to the press but apparently not to George Bell . . . who quickly threw what might best be described as a balls-out, freaky-deaky, mid-locker-room hissy fit.

Shouting mostly in Spanish, with generous doses of the expletives I'd learned in Barquisimeto, Bell was furious, but to his credit, Jimy Williams stuck to his guns, going nose to nose with the big left fielder, telling George in no uncertain terms *exactly* why he was planning the switch. Chests puffed, jaws jacked, nostrils flared; though coaches intervened, neither one of these guys was about to back down. Williams had flat-out told the press that moving George to DH would make the Jays a much better defensive team. The truth hurt. Bell felt insulted, and before long there was an unwritten locker room jihad flowing back and forth between these guys.

George was a team leader in that dysfunctional Blue Jays locker room, especially among the Latin guys, and that fact caused a lot of managerial second-guessing to start bouncing off the walls. Williams had always distanced himself from his players, often disappearing into his office for some quiet time with a paperback novel, and now, with the grumbling growing, that lack of warmth was coming back to haunt him. Players began openly aligning themselves in George Bell's camp, griping about Jimy's DH plan, then slowly expanding their complaint department to include pitching changes (Jimy was a notorious Captain Hook in that regard), batting orders, team practices, and strategy. A line was fast being drawn in the sand between the captain of the S.S. *Blue Jay* and his mutiny-minded crew.

And then the front office got involved. Faced with bad press, nasty rumors, and a clubhouse where tension hung thick in the air, Gillick and Gord Ash ultimately decided to go with the money, nipping Williams's plan in the bud and rescuing George Bell from the shame and dishonor of designated hitting. MVPs were obviously a lot harder to replace than managers. With that in mind, George Bell quickly returned to left field, where he hit three humongous home runs on opening day, seeming to circle the bases more slowly with each mammoth blast, while clearly turning the screws to the now-castrated Jimy Williams.

George would hit 33 more homers that season, while also committing a whopping 15 errors in left. Tensions never entirely cooled between Williams and Bell, and throughout the rest of that season, those guys seemed to erupt at six-week intervals, reigniting their feud at the drop of a hat, or a routine fly ball to left. Each time the flare-up would quickly be swept under the rug, but with every outburst, Jimy Williams lost a little more control of his players. It was a stupid, ugly situation that destroyed team chemistry and really hurt us on the field throughout the first half of that long, strange season. By mid-July, the "power-house" Jays were 10 games under 500, and running 11½ games behind the front-running Red Sox.

For now though, even as the Dunedin humidity does its level best to turn me into soup, I'm just happy to be alive. For the first time in my life I find myself spring training with the big boys, Working out on the *good* field, with the *major-league* club, long after the minor-league reassignments start dropping into place. I'm pitching well. The arm feels great. Nobody's said a word to me about my Venezuelan great escape, and I'm quickly starting to harbor the feeling I've got this club made as a reliever. And though I do catch a few players giving me the old hairy eyeball, most of my teammates actually seem to like me. Dave Stieb and Mike Flanagan offer pitching advice. Ernie Whitt tells me my stuff looks better than ever. Best of all, I've now begun hanging with the big club guys through their daily excursions to the absolute finest in Central Floridian titty bars.

Forget all the media hype about guys "sweating themselves back into shape," or "getting mentally prepared for the upcoming season," because here's the God's honest truth: the first weeks of spring training are a fucking breeze, especially for pitchers. You get to the park by 7:30 or 8:00 A.M. You get some work in, you throw a little, *some* guys pretend to jog around the outfield for a little while, and that's that. You're done. By 11:30 or noon at the latest, most guys are at the golf course. Nine holes later, they may eat a little lunch, and that's followed by maybe some more golf, or a movie matinee, or some mall shopping, dinner, and then barring absolute disaster, it's major-league naked lady time.

From all parts of the hotel, guys start congregating in groups of four or five, piling into their rental cars for a quick trip to the finest local strip clubs. I'm thrilled when I'm finally invited along for a Blue Jays adventure at the Doll House, and my jaw drops to the floor as I enter.

Don't get me wrong. As a young, single, red-blooded, All-American horn-dog, I've been to plenty of strip clubs during my time in the minors. However, tucked into the backwoods of North Carolina, Alberta, Canada, and upstate New York, those were low-rent, hole-in-the-wall dives full of bald old men and bored strippers who looked as though they could probably make a better living hanging Sheetrock.

This place is different. *This* place is packed with literally dozens of the most beautiful women I've ever seen in my life, and, as an extra added bonus, every single one of them is butt-naked. This, I'm told, is an "upscale gentleman's club." And while I don't qualify as either "upscale" *or* a "gentleman," I'm quickly mesmerized. One drink in that place costs more than I used to earn in two hours as a shopping cart wrangler, but I quickly find that veteran players almost never let a rookie buy his own beer. On occasion, I'm told, those guys might even bring a smile to that young rookie's face by surprising him with the gift of a redheaded lap dance . . . or two, or eleven. This *definitely* ain't Medicine Hat.

And now the official disclaimer: despite all my starry-eyed, slack-jawed, nudie-bar cheerleading, I have to go on the record and say that by and large, the time most ballplayers spend in "gentlemen's establishments" is really not all that lecherous. YES, we're guys. YES, we like looking, but the vast majority of major-league veterans, especially the guys with wives and kids, and divisible assets, are NOT looking to touch. We're not that stupid.

We're just bored out of our skulls. Faced with the nightly challenge of filling the six or seven empty hours between dinner and sleep, a squadron of young, affluent athletes gets antsy, fast. Should we sit in the hotel and watch sitcoms? Excuse me while I hang myself. Movies? Books? Jigsaw puzzles? No, thank you. No, thank you. No, thank you!

However, a couple of other suggestions are virtually guaranteed to get you a positive response. A few beers with the guys? Sure! A few beers with the guys in the middle of a hundred pole-dancing beauty queens? Now we're talking! Beer + Boobs + Buddies = Blast! It's that simple, and trust me on this one, in *any* given major-league city, on *any* given night, *somewhere* within a ten-mile radius of the team hotel, you WILL find a gentlemen's club packed with ballplayers. And while nobody's looking to get laid (well, *almost* nobody), neither will any of us complain about the chance to hang, talk shop, catch *SportsCenter,* bend an elbow, and tease the hell out of each other, all while happily nestled amid a pack of gorgeous, thong-wearing hotties.*

---

* I should probably add that *another* reason ballplayers and strippers rarely hook up is the fact that the girls are just not interested. Trust me, nobody's losing a night's tips to chitchat with some lame, transparent horn-dog, even if he *is* a major leaguer.

We're guys. That's how we're wired. What can I tell you?

Meanwhile, back amid the more wholesome confines of Grant Field, Williams and Bell have now formally declared war, and a large chunk of the team has begun openly railing against the manager who kept us in the pennant race until the last day of last season. Still, despite the turmoil and distraction, we Blue Jays are once again shaping up as the team to beat in the AL East (at least on paper). Offensively, we're fielding an even better lineup than last year's team, with two noteworthy improvements. Fred McGriff moves to first base, and as a huge, pleasant surprise, when the largely unheralded Rance Mulliniks becomes our DH (instead of George Bell), he immediately begins a season-long tear, batting .317 for the year. On the bench Cecil Fielder sits, grumbles, and picks up a lot more splinters.

On the mound, Dave Stieb's back at the one spot, with thirty-six-year-old veteran Mike Flanagan in from Baltimore to back him up. Deeper down, Jim Clancy's back again, and after some time on the DL following elbow surgery, Jimmy Key returns better than ever. In Key's absence, my buddy Jeff Mussel-man makes the big leap from reliever to starter, and my ex-roomie Todd Stot-tlemyre finally busts into the bigs as our brand-new "fifth man." In the pen, Tom Henke's nastier than ever as our closer, with Duane Ward playing our righty setup man. On the left-hand side is a handsome, talented, charming young gentleman, who's had a fantastic spring, mowing down the competition while securing himself a one-way ticket to Toronto. His name is David Wells. He has no idea what he's in for.

Riding a huge wave of adrenaline into the season, I've never been happier. Running through the Grant Field complex, I find Dave LaRoche, and yet another coach/savior gets bear-hugged to rib-cracking lengths. His patient, creative coaching has turned me from an also-ran starter into a major-league reliever, and I'm not about to forget it. Though Dave plays it cool, he can't suppress one big-time smile as he gives me the standard "just doin' my job" routine. With a minor-league workout in progress, I manage just one more "thank you" before Dave shoos me away and turns his attentions toward yet another hopeful young pitcher. I head back to the big-league side of the complex, wondering how many more careers that man will rescue in seasons to come.

April 11. This year's home opener finds the Yankees in town, and yours truly winning his first game of the season, in relief, but it's a roller-coaster ride from there. I'll pitch ten more times in April, giving up 11 earned runs in 17 innings while an increasingly cantankerous Jimy Williams frowns, shakes his head, and begins scooping me out of games at the first sign of trouble. It's frustrating as hell, but I honestly can't say that I blame him. He knows as well as I do that at this point in my career, I'm just not smart enough to succeed on the mound with anything less than my best stuff.

I wasn't a pitcher. I was a thrower. I had no game plan. I had no strategy. I'd basically just haul back and heave and hope to get lucky. Behind in the count, or working with runners on base, I simply didn't have the experience or the street smarts to out-think the stick at the plate. As a result, I was predictable. I was ordinary. And from a managerial perspective, I was maddeningly inconsistent. With my A game cooking, I'd go out to the mound and kick ass. With anything less, I'd be lucky to survive an inning. For the better part of a month, I'd throw one good appearance, then a couple bad ones, then one good, then a couple bad. That was my rhythm. That's what put me in the doghouse.

With less than a month under my belt, I could already feel my stay in the bigs falling out from under my feet. Jimy Williams used me less and less now, and almost never in any sort of competitive situation. Down 12–1, I'd get the call and throw an inning. Up 6–5, my ass was nailed to the bullpen bench. Jimy took no chances. He showed no confidence in me, no faith. I was deep in the shithouse, and I knew it. That's when I finally went looking for help.

By 1988, Mike Flanagan had been winning major-league ball games for four-teen seasons. He'd seen it all, done it all, and when I approached him one after-noon, hoping to pick his brain for a few small crumbs of real world advice, I was thrilled to find him open, willing, even eager to help me. Within minutes, Dave Stieb had been sucked into the conversation as well, and suddenly I was Luke Skywalker, sponging up a vast stockpile of battlefield knowledge from this pair of rubbery-armed old Yodas. Our chats became frequent events.

We talked about pitch selection, and strategy, but more often than not, those guys gave me free psychology lessons. Three on a bench, we'd huddle up and perform hypothetical brain surgery on a Paul Molitor, or a Kirby Puckett or a Kent Hrbek. It was all about unscrewing the skull of the man at the plate and digging around inside to understand what he'd be thinking. With a combined 749 years in the bigs, Stieb and Flanagan knew from good *and bad* experience how most sluggers, and pull hitters, and contact guys, and free swingers ticked. As a result, these two didn't *need* their A game, overpowering stuff every time out to be successful. They had more tools than me, more smarts, more tricks, more insight. These guys could hack into a batter's head at any time, pull out that guy's probable plan of attack, and then make adjustments on the mound to ultimately confuse, frustrate, and kill that guy's threat.

A simple example: let's assume that the first time you face Wade Boggs, he yanks your best fastball and pulls it down the line for a base hit. Three innings later, he's back at the plate, assuming there's no way in hell he's getting another one. Instead, nine times out of ten, the guy's gonna look for a curveball, or something away. He's logically going to expect that you're gonna do whatever you can to keep him from getting around and pulling another line drive. He'll always have a mental image in his head of what he's expecting, and he may even crowd the plate in anticipation. With that knowledge working for you, a pitcher can readjust, surprise the hitter, and stay one step ahead.

Jam the guy inside. Work him up. Work him in. Work him fast. Best of all, you could even come right back at him with another well-placed "fuck-you" fastball. He won't expect that, and more often than not, he'll just stand there and eat it. You hear pitchers talk all the time about "keeping batters off balance," and while that seems like a simple concept, it's actually a unique undertaking for *every* batter, in *every* situation, in *every* game. In a sense, it's all about exploiting a hitter's anticipation. The human brain is forever attempting to organize chaos. The human baseball pitcher is forever screwing with that mental process.

As a final, added bonus, once a pitcher's proven himself a difficult read on the mound, a lot of batters come to the plate with a defensive "don't let him make me look like an idiot" mind-set. They may swing more freely, trying to slap at any toss that looks halfway decent, or they may tighten up, simply picking a spot, waiting, and hoping you'll hand deliver a nice, fat, hittable present. Either way, they're on the hook. You're in command, and your own "probability of success" rate just soars.

Stieb and Flanagan yanked me from "novice" to "beginner" in terms of my head game, and when he returned to the team after elbow surgery, Jimmy Key did some tutorial work on me too. He may not have been crazy about hanging around with any human being in a black Ted Nugent concert T-shirt, but he saw me struggling, and when I came to him looking to talk shop, he was more than willing to help me out. It was a little ego bruising to approach a peer (as opposed to a veteran) looking for advice, but Jimmy couldn't have been cooler about it.

A heavy-duty student of the game, Jimmy would watch me pitch and make mental notes, then afterward we could sort of dissect my performance, pitch by pitch, batter by batter. With Key looking a lot like a high school math teacher, and me looking a lot like a kid who was failing summer school algebra, we'd dig through my game and learn from my mistakes. Suddenly, my ex-teammate's quick road to success made a lot more sense, and for a while it started to seem like I'd soon be joining him in the fast lane.

With Stieb and Flanagan and Key working me over like some brainy, Indy 500 pit crew, I bolted through May like a raging, roaring mound monster. Jimy Williams even took notice, and I slowly began getting into as many as four games each week. Still, even with my game on fire and my confidence soaring, none of those veterans *ever* let me forget I was still a rookie, and still subject to all the pranks, abuse, harassment, and humiliation that every one of us first-year guys is honor bound to endure. As low men on the totem pole, we live by a time-honored set of sacred, inflexible, thoroughly insane, locker room commandments.

COMMANDMENT NUMBER ONE: "Sit down, shut up, and learn something." Nothing in the world drives a veteran player crazier than a rookie who struts around the locker room running his mouth. Like fraternity pledges, or military cadets, rookie ballplayers are to be seen and not heard. Smart, game-specific questions are generally tolerated, and with a little ego stroking even embraced by most big-league vets, but beyond that, smart rookies spend most of their time trying hard to blend in with the wallpaper. Legend has it that New York Mets rookie Timo Perez spent the first part of his 2001 season loudly chatting up older teammates while dancing through the Shea Stadium locker room in heavy gold chains, flip-flops, and underpants. Don't for one minute think that didn't have a lot to do with the fact he spent the second half back down in AAA.

COMMANDMENT NUMBER TWO: If a veteran tells you to do something, you do it, preferably with a smile. We rookies fetch coffee and/or donuts and/or sandwiches and/or sunflower seeds and/or Skoal and/or beer, whenever and wherever asked. Got any of the above items in your hand? Those are free for the taking too. What time is it when Cecil Fielder spots your hoagie? Time to get a new hoagie.

COMMANDMENT NUMBER THREE: Keep the beer cold and readily available. This one's important. After games and especially during getaway days, it's up to us rookies to play brewmeister. In the locker room, we organize and maintain (and guzzle down) team inventory. On the road, we rookies lug case after case (after case after case) of beer onto the team bus. At the airport, we then carefully transport that precious cargo onto the plane. Once aboard the airliner, the beer is iced, the veterans growl, and we quickly shift into "distributor" mode (see Commandment Number Two).

COMMANDMENT NUMBER FOUR: You are fair game. Take any large group of males, force them to spend way too much time together, and I flat-out guarantee that a boatload of funny, embarrassing, joyfully antisocial pranks are just around the corner. Baseball teams offer a textbook example of that theory, and at the bottom of the food chain, we rookies often became walking, talking, human punch lines.

I'd come back to my locker after the game on a getaway day and find that Ernie Whitt and Dave Stieb had taken my suit pants and cut them into shorts. So now, with the team rushing out to the airport, and the Blue Jays sticking tight to an asinine "suits and neckwear at all times" dress code, I'd literally have to fly across the country in a jacket and tie and these amputated shorts. Even worse, while those guys would always leave a hundred bucks in your pants pocket to cover the cost of a new pair, the Toronto management was so anal, you'd get fined $500 for being dressed in shorts on the team plane.

Other times, guys would sneak up to my locker and hammer little tap-dancing taps into my shoes; or they'd dig around in my bags and put hot balm in my underpants. Worst-case scenario, I'd end up running across some airport tarmac with my toes tapping and great balls of fire. Sometimes, they'd even steal the clothes out of rookies' lockers and replace them with outfits that were just plain ridiculous. Trust me, if you ever see a big guy running through your local airport in orange bell-bottoms and a purple tube top, he's more than likely a major-league rookie on his way to catch a plane.

On the flip side, once you've been pranked, the vets who've tortured you will almost always make it up to you. Stieb and Moseby, for example, took me out to dinner all through my rookie year and never let me pay for a thing. It was great of them, but no matter how nice your tormentors may be, once you become the butt of somebody else's joke, it's only natural to seek revenge. Which leads me to our fifth and final commandment.

COMMANDMENT NUMBER FIVE: Rookies never prank the vets. I never actually abided by this one. I mean really, when you've had your pants cut, your shoes tapped, and your testicles tortured, you'd have to be a total pussy not to get even. At the same time, still stumbling through life as rookie slime, I knew I had to be careful. Getting caught would have unlocked floodgates of abuse. I picked my spots wisely, carefully, and to this day, I've never been found out.

On road trips, as soon as we'd get into a new city, I'd always call down to the front desk and find out which rooms everybody was in. Then I'd keep watch, waiting until I was pretty sure everybody was in their rooms, sleeping. At that point, on a pretty regular basis, I'd take a stack of those little breakfast room-service cards that you hang on your door, and order up gigantic breakfasts for all those guys, each specifically requesting a 4:45 A.M. delivery. At the same time, I'd take little stacks of pennies and then use a butter knife to wedge them tight between the vets' room doors and the jambs. On a good night, I could booby-trap five or six rooms at a clip.

At a quarter to five, room-service waiters would inevitably come knocking, and my groggy teammates would come stumbling to the door, wondering what the hell was going on. The "room service"/"I didn't order any room service" argument would inevitably ensue, at which point the player would try to open his door, only to find it wouldn't budge. The jammed pennies actually make it impossible for the door's dead bolt to turn. Ten minutes later, long before the sun was even close to rising, hotel maintenance guys would have screwdrivers dug into the door frame, with pennies tinkling out onto the hallway carpeting. From inside each room, loud, muffled swearing would be rolling out into the hallway.

Just down the corridor, I'm laughing my ass off. Barfield, Moseby, Bell, Fernandez, Clancy, Gruber, and Stieb . . . it's official. Your mystery's finally been solved. With a smile on my face, and my nose happily thumbed in your collective direction, I now confess. And while I'm clearing the air, please be advised that if you happened to encounter any Vaseline-covered toilet seats, stink bombs, or large, unexplained hotel bar tabs during that 1988 season, they were more than likely my handiwork too. They say revenge is a dish best served cold, but I have to tell you, I hate leftovers. Secretly driving you guys nuts was the highlight of this rookie's season.

As Memorial Day rolled in, I was flying high, thrilled with my success, and also the fact that I now felt more in control, smarter, and more confident on the mound. It seemed as if I'd gone from the scrap heap to the *top* of the heap in less than one month. I know they say that a little knowledge goes a long way, but could it really be this easy?

No.

As good as I'd been in May, I was horrendous in June. All the mind games, all the strategy, all the lessons that had worked so well for me just weeks ago, seemed to backfire on me now with every single appearance. Somehow I'd lost my magic. I'd lost my edge. I'd lost my ability to retire even the suckiest of batters. I'd changed nothing. I felt fine. I just suddenly had a big black cloud over the pitcher's mound. While Stieb and Flanagan and Key were busy telling me to stick to my guns, remain confident, and work through this bullshit without getting down on myself, I lost two games, blew two leads, and watched my ERA balloon up to 6.00. The mysterious, mind-fucking gods of baseball had apparently conspired to teach me a lesson in humility, taking my newfound baseball smarts and turning them to shit right before my eyes. At the same time, Jimy Williams bailed on me.

A workhorse in May, I'd spent the latter half of June back on the dung pile, getting into maybe one game a week, almost always in blowout situations. By mid-July I had pitched in a grand total of two ball games that month, and had been shelled at Comiskey Park. Todd Stottlemyre surveyed my miserable demeanor and decided that a rip-roaring drunk might snap me back to form. I agreed wholeheartedly, and forty minutes after the game, we'd already made our way to a wildly popular local nightspot called P.S. Chicago.

On the books to earn a mind-boggling $82,000 dollars that season, I felt absolutely rich. I'd never seen that kind of money before, and as much as I liked *getting* those checks, I loved spending them even more. With Todd feeling rookie-rich as well, you can well understand how the idea of moderation never actually entered our minds that night.

With mousse in our hair, and thin neckties dangling, Todd and I head-bobbed into that club feeling like world-class 1980s big shots. We had cash in our pockets. We had fancy, imported beers in our hands. We had Wang Chung thumping through a muscle-bound sound system. Life was good, baby. Big-haired, glossy-lipped women were packed near the bar, and we were shamelessly trolling the waters. Pickup lines blazing (*"Y'know, if I could, I'd rearrange the alphabet so I could be next to U"*), we'd faux-casually mention our big-time baseball player status to any woman who didn't immediately kick us in the leg and run for the hills.

Three hours later, with both of us still single, Todd and I are both just drunk off our asses and ready to pack it in for the night. Todd heads for the door while I take one final, desperation lap of the bar, hoping for a last-second hookup. When it doesn't come, I take my walk of shame toward the exit, where I find Todd screaming at the biggest motherfucker I've ever seen. This guy's like six foot six and WAY ripped. My eyes go wide, and the words *Oh shit!* fly out of my mouth. Todd's seconds away from a biggie-size ass-whupping. He's nose-to-chest with the guy, expletives flying, as I come running to make the save.

"Come on, guys, why don't we just end this right now?" I say to them both. "My friend don't want no part of you. You're too damn big." I'm chuckling now at my own bad joke, but neither guy budges. "What'ya say guys? C'mon, we're not looking for trouble here, we're just leaving."

The big ape speaks. "Who the fuck are you?" he growls, big hairy knuckles dragging on the floor

"It doesn't matter who I am," I tell him, now trying to *hide* the fact we're ballplayers. "We don't want any trouble."

"I don't give a shit *what* you want, asshole." Then WHAM! I take a monkey fist to the chest, which sends me backward two steps, then down onto the floor. Now I'm steaming. I get up fast, and I pop the guy in the face. Smoked him. Dropped him. People around me went "Ohhhhh!!!!!" It was awesome. Honest to God, for one split second, I actually had my own, really cool, action-movie-hero moment. Y'know, I'd dropped the bad guy with one punch, and now I was gonna be free to stroll off into the sunset with somebody like Linda Hamilton or Sigourney Weaver, or . . . uh-oh.

I'm still fantasizing as the monster gets back up. He's towering over me three seconds later.

Oh shit! I think to myself. I'm gonna die!

But that never happened, because now, instead of killing me, the big, punched-out pussy goes and gets the cops. Meanwhile, I'm laughing, because this idiot hit me first. The cops will be fine.

He comes back now with a pair of cops, one of whom immediately asks, "What the hell do you think you're doing?" The sarge is all of five foot seven and maybe 160 pounds soaking wet. My eyebrows rise.

I explain the situation as calmly and clearly as I can, but right from the get-go, this cop's being a total asshole. "I know who you are," he tells me, "and I don't *care* if you play baseball, you're not gonna come into *this* bar, in *this* city, and cause trouble!"

"Wait . . . 'cause trouble'? I hardly—"

"Shut up! And get the fuck out of here now!" I take one final stab at setting the record straight, but he's not interested. "You heard me," he says, cutting me off. "Now, I want to see you two RUN back to your hotel!" He's smiling now, and it's all I can do not to punch him in his little yellow teeth.

"Fuck that!" I tell him. "I ain't running. We're leaving, but we didn't start the trouble here. There's no reason for us to run."

He stares. "I'm waiting. You gonna get the fuck outta here, or am I gonna arrest you and *make* you get the fuck outta here?"

I take a long, deep breath. "Fine," I say, knowing full well I'm not gonna win this one. "Just let me get my coat."

Now I go back inside, I get my jacket, and I carry it under my arm, outside the club. I catch up with Todd, and the two of us start walking. We get like twenty feet away, and I stop to put my coat on. The sleeve is inside out, so it's taking me a minute, and somehow this idiot cop sees me standing there, and comes to the insane conclusion that by stopping momentarily I'm being a smart-ass and showing him up. This jackass thinks I'm somehow making a statement, openly defying his authority. I'm still jiggling one arm through a sleeve as he grabs me from behind.

"Hey!" the little shit yells. "I told you to leave. You didn't go. Now you're in trouble." With one hand on my wrist, he's actually trying to throw me down onto the ground. I've got nine inches and nearly a hundred pounds on the guy, but he's going Randy "Macho Man" Savage on my ass.

"What the fuck are you doing?!" I shout at him, trying hard not to laugh. Two more cops join the cause by the time I finish the sentence. Three on one now, these guys get rough. They push me through a barricade, and they're all still trying to get me down on the ground. They fail. I'm still standing, still protesting as they push me across the street and shove me face first into the side of a paddy wagon. At that point, one of the cops takes my left arm and yanks it so far up behind my back that I swear I could see myself waving.

I was yelling now. "All right! All right!" Twenty feet behind me, Todd's pinned on the ground, apprehended.

"What the FUCK is the problem?!!!" I shout.

"I'll tell you what's the problem. You're a fucking smart-ass! When I tell you to go back to your hotel, you DO it. You don't stand still in the road and show me up!!!"

"Dude! Let my arm down! I wasn't being a smart-ass! I was putting on my coat!"

He's "go to hell-ing" me now. I'm "mother-fuckering" him. He grabs my wallet, takes out my driver's license, and says, "San Diego, huh? Are all the jocks in San Diego little pussies like you?"

I say, "What in the world is that supposed to mean? I'll tell you one thing, the cops in San Diego know how to handle things a lot better than *you* piece-of-shit cocksuckers."

In retrospect, that was probably a poor choice of words.

The cops physically pick me up off the ground now, and they throw me in the back of the paddy wagon. Todd (who'd been smart enough to keep his mouth shut) gets released and goes back to the hotel. There he wakes up our team play-ers' rep, Ernie Whitt, who calls the Blue Jays' team lawyers, who get out of their beds and work the phones all night, trying to get me released. By 6 A.M. I'm free. Having perpetrated nothing worse than standing in the street and putting on a jacket, I was never officially arrested. With no charges pressed, I go back to my hotel and catch a nap before heading off to the ballpark. I'm not inside the locker room five minutes when Jimy Williams hauls me into his office, looking

Pitcher. Blue Jay. Trusted political adviser.

more constipated and cranky than I'd ever seen him. He tells me I'm being sent back down to AAA as a disciplinary measure. Todd Stottlemyre, who started the whole bust-up, skates under the radar without so much as a reprimand. Lucky stiff.

Twenty-four hours later, I'm back in Syracuse, and my pitching arm, the one that got twirled up over my head by the cops, hurts like hell. I won't pitch at all for the next twenty-eight days. If ever there was an award handed out for most infuriating way to get yourself demoted to the minors, I'd have won it hands down. I was dejected, depressed, sulking through games as I obsessed about when and if I'd ever pitch in the bigs again. Thankfully, the tenderness in my arm turned out to be relatively minor—no tears, no sprains, no lasting damage—and by mid-August, I was back on the hill, dominating AAA batters as a big pissed-off fish in a very small pond.

When major-league rosters expanded at the end of August, I got called back to Toronto one more time. There, Jimy Williams was waiting for me with open . . . doghouse. Right from the beginning, it was clear the stench of my June had not yet cleared, and that Captain Hook would be taking no chances with me. After a long slow start, the Jays had gone on a second-half tear, and as I rejoined the asylum, they were fast reapproaching the .500 mark. With the AL East standings now clustered with Boston, Detroit, Milwaukee, the Yankees, and the Blue Jays all within five games of first place, Jimy wasn't letting my shaky, unreliable stuff anywhere near his mound. I got into a grand total of four of our last thirty-one games, at one point going nearly three weeks without an appearance. Without me, all the Jays did was go 23–7. After a difficult start, and one great month, my season was now dissolving away in a brilliant blaze of boredom.

At the same time, despite being smack in the middle of a pennant race, the Jays' surly locker room *still* found ways to be unhappy. Cliques of the Latin players were forever huddling to piss and moan and complain in Spanish about Jimy Williams. Lose a game, it was Jimy's fault. Win a game, "we saved his ass." Across the floor, other players complained that the infighting was distracting the team's focus from breaking to the front of the AL East traffic jam. Locked away in his office, Williams interacted as little as possible now with his attitudinally challenged team, and that fanned the flames of dissension even higher.

Meanwhile, the Jays just kept on winning, and in an absolutely bizarre season-ending twist, Dave Stieb goes out to the mound twice during our final week, pitching 8⅔ innings of no-hit ball . . . *both times*. Twice in five days, he loses a potential no-hitter at the last possible moment. We take both games, but it's heartbreaking to watch.

The '88 Jays finished the season at 87–75, two games back of the goddamn Red Sox. And though our third-place finish was considered an underachieving disappointment for the team picked to "win it all" back in April, our last-minute scorching streak undoubtedly saved Jimy Williams's job. Whether Jimy deserved *any* of the bullshit dumped upon him through that long, strange season is more than debatable. But the fact he kept his mutiny-minded malcontents playing near the top of the standings stands as solid proof of the man's managerial talent. He may not have *liked* us. He may not have been a people person. He may not have played well with others, but the man won ball games. That was his job, and *that* he did well . . . for three dozen more games.

EIGHT

The Big Hump

Shopping for future ex-wives.

*—Standard player slang
for groupie hunting*

APRIL 1989: EXHIBITION STADIUM

With the Toronto Skydome fast approaching its June 5 grand opening, and every single Canuck within a thousand miles seemingly desperate for a ticket, the Blue Jays front office is hell-bent on getting the '89 season off to a fast start. They've got a humongous new stadium to fill, and another disappointing season just won't cut it this year. Closing out the team's final days at Exhibition Stadium, the Jays pulled out all the stops in getting the Dome sold out for as long as humanly possible. TV ads blared. So did radio and print and gigantic billboard hard sells. Blue Jay fever spread across Canada like pinkeye through a kindergarten class. You simply couldn't escape all the hype. Barring absolute disaster, baseball fans all over the Great White North would soon be going oot and aboot to the Skydome, where every one of them could enjoy a grand old expensive time at the ballpark. There was just one problem. We sucked.

Despite coming back for the season with a lineup virtually identical to last September's world-beaters, the team stumbled badly through the first month of the season. Immediately, the Jays front office personnel began having nightmares about paying the rent on 49,000 empty, bright blue Skydome seats. Panic set in fast. Knees jerked, players moved, and even before the month was out, Toronto sent slumping slugger Jesse Barfield to the New York Yankees in exchange for top-notch pitching prospect Al Leiter, who promptly arrived in Toronto, made one start, destroyed his elbow, and sat out for the better part of the next *four years*.

Meanwhile, as we just kept losing, vultures began circling Jimy Williams's office daily. After the previous year's endlessly embarrassing clubhouse problems, he'd started the season on a short, tight leash. With his team's bad start now taking the piss out of the Blue Jays' pre-Skydome hype, Jimy's leash was fast becoming a noose. On May 15, when his team sinks to a lousy 12–24, Williams is released, replaced on an interim basis by team batting coach Cito Gaston. Almost immediately, far off in the dysfunctional corners of the Blue Jays' locker room, a fiesta kicks in, and the team celebrates our changing-of-the-skippers with a 17–10 run that brings us right back to respectability.

By the time we move into the Skydome's two-million-square-foot, bright-blue, plastic-covered, entirely charm-free confines, we Blue Jays are playing kick-ass ball. George Bell and Fred McGriff are *both* roaring toward monster years, and while our team pitching hasn't been *quite* as solid as last year, my own outings are *finally* consistent, well pitched, and successful. I've stepped up. My stuff's less streaky and erratic than it used to be. My focus feels better, and with continued tutorials from Stieb, Flanagan, and Key, I'd have to be an idiot *not* to make *some* progress. By season's end, I'll have appeared in 54 games, going 7–4, with a 2.40 earned run average.

Even better, I'm really starting to enjoy life in the bullpen. Far away from the intensity, stress, and authority figures of the dugout, we pen-dwellers are free to give each other hot foots, talk trash, fart loudly, nurse our hangovers, chat with friends, and troll for hot women in the stands. In the Skydome, on a surprisingly regular basis, we can even get them topless.

In an architectural hiccup, one whole section of seats at the Skydome hangs right over one edge of the Blue Jays' bullpen. Way down the line, and sort of tilted toward the outfield, they're horrible seats if you have any interest in watching the game. However, when friends are in town, they're the best seats in the house. Ass parked in those babies, your guest can sit almost right above you and chat all night long. Even better, from the dugout, no Blue Jays' official can see you ignoring the game to chat back. Even in the middle of a 50,000-seat stadium, it's a really secluded spot. That's exactly what made it so great for talking up groupies.

Every single night girls would migrate over toward that section, trying to get up close and personal with the pitchers below. They'd wave. We'd wave back. They'd yell "Give us a ball!" and we'd launch into a little pantomime that made it clear if they wanted a baseball, they'd have to lift up their top and give us a flash. At *least* twice a night, they'd happily agree, with the length and enthusiasm of the free show generally corresponding to exactly how many LaBatts they'd recently consumed.

It was a perfect scam until one evening, one particularly gifted young lady saw our little mime, laughed like a sailor, took off her top, yanked out a pair of absolutely enormous, superwobbly, uh . . . assets and just kind of flopped 'em over the side of the railing and left 'em dangling. We threw her a ball immediately. Now cheering and bouncing up and down with her ball for the better part of a minute, this girl's got no shame. Even worse, released from their cages, her boobs turn out to be just plain scary, dangling to her navel, with purple veins all over the place and nipples the size of DVDs. The crowd roars, with a large group chanting, "Put it back ON!! Put it back ON!!!"

At that point, instead of being shocked back into a more modest posture, this woman is loving every minute of the attention. Now the cops come running. They grab the girl, cover her up, take her ball, and arrest her for *very* indecent exposure. Needless to say, that put at least a temporary hold on our bullpen peeping. It did nothing, however, to keep our raging, roaring, horn-dog status in check.

Give any kid unlimited candy, and he'll eat himself sick. Dump too much goldfish food into a bowl, and your beloved little pet WILL just keep sucking it down till he explodes. When it comes to sex, young, single baseball players are no different. Just like in Medicine Hat, Toronto fans quickly discovered which restaurants, bars, and nightclubs attracted their local heroes on a regular basis. With that in mind, almost anywhere we'd go, fans, autograph hounds, and groupies would all be waiting for us. Gawking from a distance at first, the groupies always seemed to get braver as the night wore on and their blood-alcohol levels rose. Dressed to thrill, tipsy, beautiful, and by no means shy, these girls all came looking to make their own personal love connection.

On the road, it's every bit as crazy. First comes the eye contact, followed by flirting, and maybe a carefully placed hand on your knee. From there, in a time-honored, small-talk-skipping tradition, the friendly young lady will inevitably find some way to bring the topic of conversation around to your hotel. "Are you guys staying at the Marriott?" she might ask. And of course that's your cue to say, "Yes, in fact I was just heading back there now. Wanna join me for a drink?" (Which of course translates into: "Message received, now let's go hump.") Honest to God it's that simple, and when you're young and single and an athlete and a celebrity, that perpetually available smorgasbord is absolutely impossible to resist. For a while, it's goddamn fantastic.

I know that's not the politically correct take on the situation, but fuck it, I'm not gonna lie. You want sex with a redhead on a Tuesday night in Milwaukee? You've got it. You want a big-busted brunette in Boston? No problem. Want twin blondes in Anaheim? You might need to put some effort into the hunt, but you can probably swing that too. Honestly, there are a lot of situations where a well-known player can literally just point and wink and find himself nose to nose with a great-looking new "girlfriend." Out on the road, we late-1980s Jays live out whole scenarios that sound like letters to *Penthouse* forum. It's a wonderful perk of the trade.

Before I go any further, I should probably take a moment to explain that for most players (as implausible as this may sound to you guys reading this book), the "kid in the candy store" fascination with groupies wears off pretty quickly. Guys find girlfriends. Guys get married. Guys have kids, and all of those things quickly make the idea of just following your dick around like a compass seem pretty fucking lame. Sooner or later, most guys just get lucky and move on to something better. Once that happens, they lose interest in nameless, commitment-free sex—at least *most* of the time.

Other times, guys will stumble into a situation where they'll sleep with a sweet, genuinely nice person, whose feelings end up being shattered when they finally realize the player's not into their relationship for the long haul. Unless you're a total asshole (and some guys are), that's a surefire way to end up feeling like shit.

Finally, there's that small minority of guys who just won't leave the booty buffet until they're literally scared away. I know this is gonna sound like the stuff of urban legends, but there *are* groupies out there looking for a lot more than just a roll in the hay. Some are just nuts, rejected stalkers looking for a ballplayer not so much to rent, but to own. They'll call a guy's cell phone a hundred times a day. They'll phone team officials, pretending to be family, sending messages to "Call Home: URGENT!" followed by their own home number. They'll threaten and curse and cry and beg, and when all else fails, they often get really nasty. I know of one American League All-Star whose parents actually got a phone call saying he'd died in a car accident. They were obviously devastated, and it wasn't until hours later, when their son phoned home just to say hello, that they realized the call had been faked. A simple check of phone records revealed the obvious culprit.

Worse than that are the groupies who aren't looking for love or sex but big money. Married guys who slip up on the road have been known to find themselves presented with photographs or a videotape of their one-nighter, with a cash payment demanded in exchange for the evidence. Another scam finds a groupie slipping a powerful sedative into a player's drink, then stealing his wallet, spending his cash, and running up enormous charges on his credit cards during the ten or twelve hours he'll remain unconscious. That one happens far more often than you'd imagine, and on one occasion, I personally rescued a teammate who hung out a little too long at the bar and began passing out before his "date" could get him upstairs. Oddly, she disappeared from the scene at the first sign of trouble.

Worst of all, I will swear to you that at least two players I know have fallen victim to a particularly nasty variation on the basic blackmail photos theme. It starts with the same drugged drink, and the standard trip upstairs for sex. Once there, the girl inevitably heads into the bathroom to "slip into something more comfortable" while the player quickly drifts into unconsciousness. At that point, she uses a cell phone to call an accomplice who'll arrive five minutes later with a camera in tow. While she waits, the girl will help herself to whatever cash and plastic the player's got in his wallet. It's business as usual so far.

Now the partner arrives, hands the camera to the groupie, and undresses *himself. He'll* then slide into bed with the knocked-out player and spend some time posing for a set of staged, homosexually explicit photos. By the time the girl's finished shooting a roll or two, they've got more than enough ammunition to blackmail the player for serious cash. Knowing full well that pro jocks are a proud, ego-driven, often homophobic bunch, they know there's almost no chance their victim will report the crime to the police. And while I know this particular story bears more than a passing resemblance to that old urban legend about the businessman who wakes up missing a kidney, I know for a *fact* it happens. I *also* know that throughout my entire career, I've seen only one instance where a player was brave enough to seek help, with police quietly apprehending the perpetrators.

Back on the subject of baseball, I should tell you that as our long, cool Canadian summer wore on, the Jays' newly appointed Gaston regime flourished on the field. By the All-Star break, we Blue Jays had begun a slow but steady jog toward the top of the pack. Though still in fourth place, and just barely flirting with the .500 mark, there really *was* a sense that the winds had changed. Fred McGriff's bat caught fire, Dave Stieb (maybe the single most underrated pitcher in modern baseball history) was once again blowing away the opposition, and in time, this team actually began "finding ways to win."

I know that sounds like a hollow cliché, but I swear to you it's a genuine reality of the game. It's a combination of talent, motivation, and heart, really. Watch the Yankees or the Braves or the Diamondbacks sometime. Down 5–0 in the sixth, they'll NEVER go down without a fight. They scratch and claw and give the game their all, and when a team's got balls that big, all that effort often combines to make them really "lucky." In June, we Jays overcame a 10–0 deficit to beat the Red Sox 13–11 in 12 innings. In July, we exorcised the ghosts of last season by coming from behind to whomp the Detroit Tigers in a three-game sweep at Tiger Stadium. In August, Dave Stieb destroys the Yankees, but ultimately loses yet *another* no-hitter after 8⅔. At any rate, over the course of just three months, this team had gone from sleepy and mediocre to pumped, powerful, and full of piss and vinegar. Cito Gaston had obviously done something right.

Intense and vocal, with a real gung-ho, hands-on "Let's get out there and kick some ass!" spirit, Cito was the exact opposite of Jimy Williams. Well liked by most of the Blue Jays' everyday players, Cito's experience as the team's batting coach found him coming into the manager's job with a lot of close player relationships already in place. However, when it came to the pitching staff, Cito and his underlings were like oil and water.

Cito just didn't like his pitchers. I know that's a broad statement, but I can back it up. We rarely talked with the man, and we *never* talked shop.* Don't get me wrong, Cito's a good guy, but to me, he's just an average manager. Our awkward relationship (which was easily the *most* strained of Cito's manager/pitcher alliances) would come back to haunt us both *big-time* in seasons to come. For now, though, I was just thrilled that my stuff was working, and my team was winning . . . a lot.

Early August found us right back in the thick of the hunt for first place, and with that goal now squarely in sight, we Jays got even better. Mookie Wilson joined the team as an exile from a rapidly imploding Mets team, and his hits, stolen bases, outfield defense, and gigantic, ever-present, thoroughly infectious smile all seemed to help get us over the hump. I'd never met Mookie before the trade, but when he finally got to Toronto, it took me all of two minutes to figure out why the New York fans were so crazy about the guy. You just couldn't resist.

At month's end, righty reliever Jim Acker joined the team from Atlanta, and while his lifetime stats are just a little better than average, the guy's nothing short of awesome for us all month long. He pitches fourteen times in September, winning two games while stomping the opposition with an ERA of just 1.59. *Now* it feels like destiny. *Everybody* at *every* position seems to be playing at the top of their game. Across the continent, a stacked Oakland A's team is running away with the West, but with the way our team's cooking, I have to believe we'll just charge right through them in the ALCS.

Finally, on August 31, after going 20–7 for the month, we caught Baltimore and tied for first. Serious momentum followed. This really did feel like it was going to be "our year." All through September, the Orioles and Jays both jockeyed for first, with the season ultimately being decided by two head-to-head meetings during the season's final weekend . . . which we won, *easily*. The Blue Jays were now officially heading for postseason play, and so was I.

I learned three important lessons that weekend. One: clinching a division feels ten times better than *anything* else I've ever experienced in baseball. Two: a champagne bottle makes one hell of a squirt gun (I swear to God I nailed "Terminator" Henke smack in the head from a full twenty feet away). And Three: champagne in the eyes hurts like hell. One thing you *never* see on televised locker room celebrations are the three or four guys who'll inevitably take

---

* Cito and I were friends and still are, but he was tough on pitchers. He didn't hate us, he just didn't understand us, especially when it came down to our pitch selection. He couldn't understand it at all.

a bad squirt in the eyes, and end up crouching in the corner blinking and weeping through the better part of the party.

With confidence brimming, we Jays flew to Oakland, where the A's would serve as our hosts for Games 1 and 2 of the 1989 American League Championship Series. The press descended, the bunting was hung, the network television guys lined the Oakland Coliseum with like 742 extra cameramen. The stage was set for the Blue Jays' moment of triumph, which never came, thanks in large part to that fucking Rickey Henderson.

The '89 A's were an awesome team, stacked with humongous bats like Mark McGwire, Jose Canseco, Dave Henderson, and Carney Lansford, and pitchers as good as Dave Stewart, Mike Moore, and Bob Welch. However, over the course of that five-game series, Rickey racked up an on-base percentage of nearly .600! He stole eight bases (ultimately running catcher Ernie Whitt out of town—he'd be traded shortly after the season). He had a slugging percentage of 1.000 (that's *not* a typo). All told, Rickey scored 8 runs, and as the series MVP, the man just kneed us in the balls, day in and day out.

We lost both games at the Coliseum, with Dave Stieb picking up the loss in Game 1 against Dave Stewart, and Todd Stottlemyre struggling through a 6–3 Game 2 disaster that saw Rickey steal four bases. Out in the bullpen, where I'd been very comfortable all season long, I was climbing the walls. Here in the postseason, with my team struggling, and my own stuff stronger than ever, I experienced my first real bout of "gimmetheballitis." Buoyed by the big-game atmosphere, and the crowd, and the fact that everything we'd worked for all season long was now on the line, I was *dying* to get into the game.

For the first time all season I envied our starters and wished like hell I was one of 'em. Standing in the bullpen 300 feet removed from the action, I chewed my nails down to the nubs. I spit sunflower seeds like an Uzi. I bobbed up and down, blew bubbles, and hoped like hell I could get into the game. Finally, with the Jays already down 5–1 in the sixth inning of Game 2, Cito gives me the call. I practically fly to the mound.

Riding a tsunami of adrenaline, I hit that mound, reared back, and . . . walked two batters. It wasn't that I was nervous, it was more a problem of being overly excited. My heart racing, ambition, joy, and confidence soaring just for the fact I'm even playing in a game this big, it took me longer than usual to get a handle on my stuff. And while that's a dangerous thing when you're facing a team where Jose Canseco and Mark McGwire bat back to back, I ultimately managed to get through the inning without any real trouble. Jogging back into the dugout, I was feeling great, ready to go back out there and knock 'em down all over again in the seventh, eighth, and ninth, but I never got the chance. Going into the seventh, Cito replaced me on the mound with the Terminator, and as eager as I was to help my team, I wouldn't pitch again 'til spring training.

Coming back into the Skydome down two games to zip, the Jays try hard to remain positive, a process that gets a whole lot easier when Jimmy Key gifts us with a solid, easy 7–3 victory in Game 3. Now we're back in the hunt. Now the momentum is back on our side of the field.

Game 4. Jose Canseco shuts up 50,000 rip-roaring Canucks by clocking a home run so monstrous it may actually still be orbiting the planet. Not allowing *anyone* to muscle in on his series thunder, Rickey Henderson steps up and clobbers two! And while we Jays do manage to slowly chop the A's early lead from 6–2 to 6–5, a bullpen call to super-fireman Dennis Eckersley snuffs out our comeback in two minutes flat. Mike Flanagan, Duane Ward, John Cerutti, and Jim Acker all pitch in the game while I sit on my ass and eat another pound and a half of seeds. I'm less than thrilled.

Flattened now, manhandled, and beaten up by a team that's rapidly proving themselves a *lot* better than we are, the Jays locker room quickly begins resembling any scene from *Night of the Living Dead*. We still talk the talk, and a few guys shout the "It aint over yet!" rhetoric, but for all intents and purposes, we're zombies. While nobody will say it out loud, or in the press, most guys are focused now, not so much on winning the series, but on not being embarrassed. Still, despite the handwriting on the wall, this team's not going down without a fight. We proved that the following day.

Down 4–0 to Oakland ace Dave Stewart in the eighth inning, this team's still not packing it in. With home runs from George Bell and Lloyd Moseby, we get the crowd crazy while getting ourselves back as close as 4–3 . . . at which point Dennis Eckersley seemed to exert almost no effort in slamming the door shut on our season. A's win. Jays come up short. That said, we Jays take the long walk back to our locker room knowing we've got nothing to be ashamed of, but clearly, the best team really has won.*

Oddly, while the mood in our loser's locker room is somber, it's not depressed, or despondent, or ugly. Instead, having come back from a terrible start to make it this far, we really can find positives. For the first time *ever*, the obligatory season-ending cries of "Wait'll next year" don't just seem half-assed

* Those no-good A's would go on to sweep San Francisco in the '89 World Series.

and hollow. In a strange, backward way, closing out the '89 season is kind of exciting in that it seems entirely possible, maybe even *probable*, that we'll be at *least* this good again next year.

Swigging from the losers' beer cans, as opposed to the A's champagne bottles, I head out into another off-season feeling pretty good about my year. Coming into this sucker not even sure I'd make the team, I'd gone on to throw my best stuff ever. Even in the minors, my numbers weren't anywhere near as good as my 7–4, 2.40 stats of '88. In a very real sense, I proved myself this year, not just as a guy who might be able to pitch his way *into* the major leagues, but also as a guy who might just end up doing pretty well for himself.

As I exit the Skydome for the final time that year, the mental positives *almost* let me forget about how little faith Cito seemed to have in me during the playoffs. That nagging aggravation will linger all through a fantastic off-season, where I'll reap the benefits of my seemingly enormous $107,000 Blue Jays' salary by partying with friends, picking up bar tabs, and traveling to Hawaii with my boy David Allen on a long bleary-eyed quest to find Miss Hawaii. I also helped drag my mom out of debt once and for all—that easily qualifies as the highlight of my year.

Spring. The 1989 season rolls in with a whole lot of winter-fat, wheezing Blue Jays (me among them) returning to Dunedin after an absolutely asinine owners' lockout. With that in mind, we've now got a grand total of three weeks to get ready for baseball. Finally, I think to myself, a spring training schedule that makes sense. For once, I won't be wasting weeks halfheartedly pretending to touch my toes, and hiding from running drills. This year, without the luxury of wasteable time, we get down to business fast, and for once, even on day one, I not only have this team made, but I also know exactly where I'll fit in.

Nobody had better numbers out of the pen last year than me, but with my lack of playing time in last year's playoffs still poking at my ego, I was bound and determined to take my game up one more notch. This year, come hell or high water, I was gonna establish myself as a dominant force in the Jays' bullpen.

That idea survived only until May, at which point, things took an abrupt turn . . . for the better. At thirty-eight, Mike Flanagan started the season pitching .500 ball, but after just five starts, arm problems shut him down for the season. From there, with Al Leiter's arm still held together by Scotch tape and bobby pins, and the high minors lacking any obvious breakout starter, Cito was forced to juggle his rotation. Over the next few weeks, a couple of different relievers got a couple of spot starts, but when their outings ultimately failed to satisfy, Cito surprised me one afternoon by penciling *my* name onto his lineup card as a starter. It was that simple. No pomp, no circumstance, no news conference, the man just took a chance, handed me the ball, and hoped for the best. That's exactly what he got.

To say I was thrilled out of my fucking mind at the prospect of becoming a starter would be an understatement. Mind you, I really didn't *mind* being in the bullpen, but after spending 95 percent of my time out in a little Cyclone-fenced kennel, two steps removed from the action, being "the man" really seems like a lot more fun. It was easy to get lost out there in the bullpen, fading out during dull ball games, daydreaming, sleeping, often spending whole day games sitting on a bad hangover while praying to God I wouldn't be called into the action. The whole thing just felt like a part-time job. Starting was a whole different story.

Since I was making my first major-league start in Anaheim, just about an hour's drive from Ocean Beach, it was a piece of cake to have my mom front and center in the best seats in the house. I'd papered almost one whole section of the park with freebie seats for friends, relatives, even a couple of old girlfriends. Sadly though, a reunion of my old Hells Angels cheerleading section was gonna be impossible. Crazy Charlie didn't live long enough to see me pitch in the major leagues. Cancer took him about a year earlier, and Crunch, Snake, and the rest of the old Hells Angels turned out to be nearly impossible finds on such short notice. With that in mind, on the mound, right before the game started, I said a quick little prayer for all of them, thanking each guy individually for their help in getting me here.

I lost that game, but I actually threw pretty well, keeping us close throughout seven innings of work. With competent throwing, and a few scattered flashes of power, I came away feeling surprisingly good for a guy who'd just taken a loss. Five days later, closing out the road trip, I tossed the game of my career (up to that point), racking up a 2–1 revenge victory over Oakland, and allowing just two hits over six innings, with strikeouts against both McGwire *and* Canseco. The win couldn't possibly have been any sweeter, and when I managed to win three more starts over the next ten days, I was able to firmly establish myself as more than just a flash in the pan. Even Cito took notice. I was walking on air, smiling even wider than Mookie . . . except maybe on getaway days.

When you play ball in Toronto, there's no such thing as a short hop on travel days. First, no matter where we were headed, we always had to go through Canadian customs, and there was *always* a delay. We always expected it, and while it was never a surprise, that did nothing to lower the situation's "suck factor." Worst of all were the times we'd get into Toronto at two or three in the morning, coming off a road trip, then *still* have to spend another hour and a half having some guy in a tan, polyester customs uniform pick through our dirty socks and underwear. "Just another reminder" we used to shout to one another across the sleepy airport. "Yep, just another reminder" the reply would come back. Unknown to the customs agents and airline personnel around us, "Just another reminder" was actually team shorthand, an abbreviation for the full phrase "Just another reminder that it sucks to play baseball in Canada."

While travel was *always* a nightmare with the Blue Jays, at times it got absolutely insane. Case in point? On one occasion, with the team heading out on a ten-day West Coast trip, customs agents were shocked to find that one unnamed Blue Jay had actually chosen to pack a handgun with his pajamas. I know it sounds nuts that this idiot actually thought he could breeze through security with a snub-nosed .38, but what you've got to realize is that at the time, the dope and his handgun were *both* fully loaded.

Now he gets caught, and this unnamed teammate actually says to the airport security types, "What's the matter? They let me right through with my gun in Boston."

Word apparently travels fast among FAA employees. Two weeks later, flying into Boston's Logan Airport after a game, airport security treated our whole Blue Jays team to a baggage inspection so painstakingly meticulous and thorough that the process took the better part of three and a half hours. We didn't get to our hotel 'til ten after five in the morning.

Still, after all that pissing and moaning, I should take a moment to add that as painful as the *logistics* of team travel can be, a major leaguer's time spent in the *air* is actually pretty great. Jets are chartered by each team, and *all* of them are equipped with big, fat La-Z-Boy-style first-class seats throughout. It's nothing like flying commercial. The flight attendants are friendly and helpful, the food's fantastic, the movies are brand-new, and best of all, scattered around the back of the plane, there's generally a card table or two, packed solid with teammates engaged in yet another hotly contested, season-long poker marathon.

Y'know, when you're spending several hours in the air every few days for the better part of six months, guys have a lot of time to try and pick up that inside straight. With that in mind, a *lot* of these games become travel-day traditions, with the same guys sitting in the same chairs from liftoff to landing. In Toronto, Dave Stieb was always a player, and Pat Borders and Rob Ducey never failed to rank as the two luckiest human beings on earth. Neither one of them would *ever* fold, and just at the exact point you were damn sure you had them beat, they'd magically pick up the exact card they were waiting on, and take you to the cleaners. They regularly defied every known law of seven-card-stud probability.

The stakes: yes, there were times I won big, but there were a lot more games where I got my ass kicked, sometimes astronomically. More often though, over the course of a four-hour flight, you'd find yourself winning a few thousand or losing a few thousand. This wasn't Monte Carlo, but it wasn't penny-ante either.

Still, anytime we played air-poker, it was controlled, and careful, and laid-back. If anybody got possessive, or started losing and barking, we'd shut 'em down right away and say, "No more." We didn't want anybody getting into bad habits. There was no fighting, and nobody got addicted to the action. It was really just a way for guys who could afford to be in the game to sit back, relax, and have a good time.

We never let the young guys play, simply because they'd be making so much less money than the other guys at the table, it'd just have seemed nasty to take their cake. Nobody wanted to get into a situation where a teammate would end up borrowing to cover his losses. This game was *only* for fun, and with that in mind, I want to make sure and spill a disclaimer that our games never *ever* left the plane. We Blue Jays *never* played poker in our hotel, never in clubs, never at other players' homes. Gambling is an illegal activity, and none of us guys would ever condone breaking the sacred laws of the Royal Canadian Mounted Police. And that, my friends, is the God's honest truth—or I could be lying.

Running through that 1990 season, we Blue Jays fielded a team nearly identical to the '89 squad, with former Medicine Hatter Pat Borders taking over behind the plate for Ernie Whitt. However, where the previous year's team routinely ran up monster winning streaks, this time around, we never quite pulled our whole game together. It seemed like we'd hit for a while and lose games 9–7, or we'd waste a Dave Stieb gem by losing 1–0. We weren't bad at all, but for whatever reason, we just didn't feel like the "team of destiny" that year. And while we hung tight near the top of the AL East right up until late September, a last, disastrous road trip through Baltimore, New York, and Boston wiped us completely out of the hunt. We closed out the season at 86–76, two games back of the Red Sox.

Personally, the season was an unqualified success. I threw nearly 200 innings as both a starter and out of the pen, going 11–6 with an earned run average of 3.14. I'd come into the season hoping to improve my standing in the Jays' bullpen, and six months later, I'd surpassed that goal by leaps and bounds, not just holding my own as a makeshift starter, but also kicking some *serious* ass. I'd stepped up my game for the second year in a row, and that felt fantastic. Finally, if I'm gonna be totally honest here, I have to admit that on a crass, lowest-common-denominator level, I also loved the fact that this year's performance was just about guaranteed to get me one hell of a raise next year.

There are really just two more highlights of that 1990 season worth writing about here. One found Dave Stieb *finally* getting his no-hitter in an awesome effort against Cleveland. The other, *also* taking place in Cleveland, finds me and Pat Borders eating like pigs at his aunt's house. I'm not sure which of those highlights was actually more enjoyable.

Pat Borders has relatives all over Cleveland, and every single one of them always took insane, almost sadistic pleasure in feeding the two of us until we were both just one pierogi away from exploding. Every single day, every time we came into Cleveland, Pat's relatives would just kind of show up at our hotel, push us into their cars, and kidnap us. Heading off to their homes, as we sat like kids in the backseat, the two of us were in heaven, smiling in anticipation of the baked ziti, kielbasa, stuffed cabbage, turkey, ham, corn on the cob, mashed potatoes, stuffing, shrimp, apple pies, blueberry pies, cherry pies, and humongous chocolate cakes we knew they'd stockpiled for our visit. I was never so happy to be Pat Borders's friend.

Pulling into their driveway, Pat and I would bolt the car and practically sprint inside the house, where after getting hugged by 622 aunts and uncles and cousins and mimas, we'd spend the rest of our day acting as gluttonous food vacuums. The aunts and grandmas would inevitably have this enormous smorgasbord laid out for us, and we'd just graze there like starving hippos until it was time to hit the couch, watch crappy daytime TV, and fall asleep. Heaven. We'd ultimately waddle back toward the park somewhere in the late afternoon, praying to God that we wouldn't have to run at all during that night's game.

Honestly, when you're a guy who spends every day alone in a hotel room or bachelor apartment, those few hours spent in a well-loved, knickknack-filled living room, with good food, and laughter, and people who clearly love being around one another, are appreciated above and beyond belief. I mean really, here it is foureen years later, and I can *still* smell the manicotti.

Heading out into another worry-free, lazy-assed, debauchery-packed off-season, I can distinctly recall feeling like I'd finally "made it." I'd proven how good I could be as a starter. My job security was a lock, and after four years with the team, I was actually starting to "feel" like a Blue Jays' lifer. People recognized me on the streets of Toronto now. The team was strong, and with those things in mind, who cared if the stadium looked like a kitchen countertop on crack, and my manager still ducked any conversation with his pitchers beyond "Hey." Finally, with the Yankees having lost 95 games in 1990, and looking like shoo-ins to do it again in '91, even *that* dream seemed to be losing its lustre. Sure, I still fantasized about playing in pinstripes every once in a while, but all things considered, Toronto seemed like the kind of place where a guy could very happily play out his career.

Within a year's time, I'd be desperate to escape.

NINE

Canada: At War

Toward the end of his stay in Toronto,
Boomer was openly unhappy, constantly expressing
his anger and frustration about being yanked back and forth
from the starting rotation to the bullpen. But, y'know, David would
"express anger and frustration" if it was raining outside, or if
it was too hot, or if his jacket didn't fit right, and believe
me, with Boomer's body, it never did.

—*Rob Ducey*

WINTER 1990: SKYDOME

The 1990 Jays drew a mind-boggling 3,885,284 fans into Skydome, and at least according to the local press, our performance on the field had disappointed every last toque-wearing one of them. Columnists whined about the

(© Mitchell Layton/Newsport)

team's saggy finish. Beat writers painted the team as a perennial also-ran in the AL East. And GM Pat Gillick was unceremoniously nicknamed "Stand Pat," for his lack of bold moves in getting this "good" Jays team over the top. With negative press swirling, a gigantic ballpark to keep filled, and a province full of life-long hockey and curling hosers slowly being retrained to appreciate baseball, the Toronto front office immediately took steps to remedy the team's "close but no cigar" reputation.

In time-honored baseball tradition, the Jays front office was silent in the weeks immediately following the World Series. Then came the standard "calmly and carefully considering our options" routine, which was quickly proven a work of fiction, with a December 5 trade that sent the Jays' two best everyday players to San Diego, in exchange for *that* team's premier duo. Coming out of the 1990 season, Fred McGriff and shortstop Tony Fernandez were clearly the Jays' most valuable position guys. Across a continent, and on an entirely separate cultural planet, San Diego's MVPs were just as easy to spot.

Joe Carter was a humongous, homer-hitting outfielder with a beautiful swing, and Roberto Alomar was flat-out phenomenal at second base. Two for two, straight up, neither team could have been unhappy. And while now, thirteen years removed from the trade, you can make, and probably win, the argument that the Jays got the better of that deal, in 1990 terms, with Robby Alomar still just a thumb-sucking toddler of twenty-two, this one was too close to call. Stand Pat and the Toronto media got their shake-up, and in a swirl of positive press, Toronto fans actually spent a good portion of that hallowed, holy Maple Leafs' season talking baseball. Talk about a "miracle on ice." By early spring, with preseason ticket sales booming, the Jays' front-office types were beside themselves with glee.

With free agent George Bell exiting Toronto for the greener pastures of free agency and the Chicago White Sox (where George would soon alienate yet *another* manager, this time over the fact he *wasn't* being asked to DH), the Jays yanked another Southern Californian north of the border. Devon White, a speedy, underachieving outfielder from the Angels, joined the Jays in exchange for Junior Felix, our own *homegrown* underachieving outfielder. This time around, there was no argument. We robbed the pants off California.

Faster than a speeding bullet, "Devo" became a sponge in the Jays' outfield, soaking up fly balls for miles in any direction. And while his numbers grew slowly at the plate, his feet and his glove routinely turned singles and doubles and triples into outs. He turned pitchers' mistakes into long, fly-ball, over-the-head putouts. He turned rallies into runners left on base. He turned defeat into victory. He made us a much better team.

While I've always approached spring training with the same sort of queasy heebie-jeebies kids associate with "back-to-school" week, I have to admit that heading into the eighty-degree sunshine of Dunedin that year, I was every bit as caught up in Blue Jays mania as your average ice-fishing Canuck. I really felt like *this* team was significantly better than last year's model. Even on March 1, I had October squarely in my sights. This team really seemed capable of going all the way, and nothing on earth would have made me happier than a few big-game, October starts. The season hadn't even begun yet, and already I wanted the ball for Game 1 of the World Series.

I flew through spring training as the Jays' fourth starter, with stuff good enough to pass for a number two or three man on most major-league clubs. As always, Dave Stieb was back on the mound making the rest of us look bad in comparison, while Jimmy Key and Todd Stottlemyre locked up the two and three slots. I'm penciled in at the four, with shaky young prospect Denis Boucher hanging on at number five. At least until the new kid gets called up.

All through spring training, from the bottom of the starting staff food chain, and without a whole lot of attention at first, one rookie is fast becoming a camp phenomenon. Juan Guzman is his name, and he spends the better part of the next six weeks in Florida opening eyes and mouths all over camp. It's almost impossible to watch the kid pitch without having your jaw drop. He's awesome, throwing smoke with "drop off the table" movement. It's immediately clear he'll be joining the big club as soon as he gets a few starts under his belt at the AAA level. I can't help smiling. That old "team of destiny" tingle is already nibbling at the back of my brain. It falls off a bit when I start the '91 campaign sucking royal ass.

Four starts into the season, I'm 1–3 with a 5.16 ERA. Worse, I'm suddenly giving up big, nasty home runs at an alarming rate. Cito, like Jimy before him, begins yanking me at the first sign of trouble. It's a frustrating, confusing situation, in that I've never been prone to this kind of long-ball shellacking before. I don't think I'm pitching any differently than I had during my 1990 untouchable streak, and my stuff *feels* pretty good, but somehow, something's clearly out of whack. Am I tipping my pitches? Are my mechanics off? Am I getting too cute around the edges of the plate? I never get my answer because somehow, without ever actually figuring out what I'm doing *wrong*, or making any real adjustments to "fix" my stuff, the ever-mysterious gods of baseball smile down on me and slap me right back to the top of my game.

I wish I could explain how it happened, but the truth is, I've no idea. All I know is that after some of the worst starts of my career, I woke up on the morning of May 3, as a roaring, raging, born-again mound monster. In May, I win four starts in a row, before losing a 2–1 heartbreaker. Seven more Ws rack up in a row after that. Best of all, the gopher ball seems to have disappeared from my arsenal. From early May through late July, I'm 11–1 with an ERA hovering right around 2.00. I'm as close to perfect as I've ever been.

Meanwhile, though virtually every position player on the team seems stuck in a minor slump, we "new improved" Blue Jays are stomping through the American League like world-beaters. And when in late May Dave Stieb goes down for the year with back and arm problems, even this potentially devastating loss turns into a positive, as boy wonder Juan Guzman makes the show and spends the rest of the season just wiping out the competition. Shortly after that, in an effort to upgrade the number five spot on our pitching staff, Denis Boucher gets banished to Cleveland, along with Mark Whiten and Glenallen Hill, in exchange for veteran knuckler Tom Candiotti.* In two weeks time, our staff's lost its ace, and gotten significantly better in the process . . . at least until August, when the gods of baseball returned, smiting my ass in its hour of triumph.

My late-summer slide came on fast. I lost five in a row, with home runs once again flying out of the Skydome like regularly scheduled 747s. On the mound, though I was clearly struggling, and frustrated, and pissed, *this* time around, past experience assured me that I'd work through the doldrums sooner or later. Cito wasn't so sure, and shortly after one godawful game against the White Sox, where I'd given up four home runs, each one of them a tape measure shot, he made his feelings abundantly clear. That's when our perpetually awkward relationship finally got ugly. That's when things finally came to a head.

I'm on the mound in Toronto, pitching against the Boston Red Sox, but I don't have a whole lot working today. My curve is flat, and my other stuff just kind of feels "off." Mixing things up as best I can, I've avoided a total disaster, but by the top of the seventh inning, we're losing 4–0, with one man out, and runners on first and second. Mike Greenwell, a .300-hitting lefty, is at the plate. It's a tough spot. I look to Pat Borders for his sign, and he calls for a change-up, which is completely fucking insane. The change is a *terrible* pitch in that situation, because any halfway decent lefty is gonna get around on the ball, slap it into right field, and advance the runners. Honestly, if I were to walk down to

---

* He was the best jokester in all of baseball.

home plate right now and say, "Excuse me, Mr. Greenwell. What would you like my next pitch to be?" he'd answer, "The change, please." It's just that ridiculous.

Even stranger, having caught me as far back as 1982, Pat knows for a fact that I'd never in a million years throw a change-up in this situation. I shake off his sign, assuming that Pat must be crossed up in his signals.

I look in again now from the mound, and I see Pat carefully, and very deliberately, signal again for the change. "What the fuck?" I say out loud as I shake him off again. Now Pat calls time and he comes running out to the mound.

"Hey man, just throw this," he says.

"Fuck that, I don't throw left-handers change-ups. You know that."

"Dude, just throw it, all right? It's coming from Cito."

Unhappy with my less-than-stellar performance, Cito Gaston's now taken it upon himself to call pitches *for* me. I'm screwed. His "request" for the change-up is more like a demand. It's non-negotiable. I look toward our dugout, where I find Cito staring at me.

"The change, huh?" I say to Borders. "Maybe Cito ought to be charged with the two runs Greenwell's gonna drive in, instead of me."

"I hear ya," says Borders.

"All right," I tell him. "Get the fuck outta here. I've got a ball game to lose."

I look into the dugout now with a hard, nasty glare, making absolutely sure Cito knows how much I hate throwing this pitch. He watches me, burning, trying hard not to acknowledge my anger.

Now I throw the change-up. Greenwell connects for a triple. I cross the infield to back up third, and from there, even while the play at third is still unfolding, I'm staring at Cito. "You happy now?" I'm screaming at him in my head. I walk slowly back to the mound scowling at my beloved manager the whole time. Cito comes running out now, pissed.

"You looking at me?!" he shouts.

"You're goddamn right I'm looking at you, asshole!"

"You don't EVER show me up! That's totally unprofessional! Who the fuck do you think you are?!"

"Listen, motherfucker! I don't need nobody calling my pitches! You don't get the loss, I do!"

"What, are you padding your stats? Making sure you've got a good win-loss record?"

"Fuck that shit!"

"Gimme the ball. You're out of the game."

"What?!" Now I just snap. This guy's actually pulling me out of a game because of his own idiotic strategy mistake. "You want the ball?" I ask him. "You want this ball right here?"

"Gimme the ball," he answers. Cito's grabbing at the ball in my hand now, but I've got it squeezed tight, and I'm not letting go. He's furious. The crowd's loving it.

"You want this ball?" I shout at him. "Go get it, motherfucker!" And at that point I just kind of wound up and heaved a screamer into foul territory, down the right-field line. Thousands of fans laugh and cheer. Cito's eyes go wide.

Now I leave the mound. I storm through the dugout and right through the locker room, into Cito's office. I knew he'd be coming, and I wanted to make sure I'd be easy to find. I wanted his head on a stick. Two minutes later, I see him walk past, just outside the door, looking all over the locker room for me. "I'm in *here*, motherfucker!" I shout out the door.

Cito flies in now like an express train. He gets into my face immediately, and we both just go at it like pro wrestlers. It was really ugly. Coach Gene Tenace and Juan Guzman ultimately get between us, but Cito just keeps yelling at me as they pull him out of the room. "How fucking dare you show me up like that, you son of a . . ." It went on forever, and when Cito finally came up for air, he just kind of slammed his own office door on me. I ended up sitting alone on the man's desk.

But I wasn't done yet. I shout at the door, "Hey, you chickenshit mother-fucker! You running out on this argument?" Now the door flies open and it's time for round two. Cito dives through the air, ready to kill me. Juan Guzman grabbed him before he could get to me, and he and Tenace ultimately ended up sort of dragging the skip back up to the dugout. I was so pissed, I just showered, grabbed a bag full of beer, and left. The game wasn't even over yet, and I got fined like a motherfucker for leaving, but I think my getting out of the building may actually have been the only thing that kept me and Cito from killing each other that day.

By the time my losing streak seemed ready to right itself, the Jays were knee-deep in September, holding court at the top of the AL East with a bit of breathing room between us and the slumping Red Sox. At the same time, Cito Gaston had gone down with a badly herniated disk in his back, and coach Gene Tenace was running the show (well) in his absence. With the team firing on all cylinders, "Tenace the Menace" (as the papers called him) had a very pleasant month-long tenure at the helm, with only one real sore spot spoiling his ride.

Say hello to Mr. Sore Spot.

With the Jays' lead in the AL East widening past five games, and the clinching of the division fast approaching, Tenace, with the approval and assistance and prodding of Cito Gaston and the Jays' front office, began realigning us Jays for the ALCS. Part of that readjustment, coming just days before Cito's return to the bench, demoted me back to the bullpen. Sure, I'd been struggling, but with my stats at 14–10 with a 3.75 ERA, clearly there was more going on here. After the blowup with Cito, I was branded "difficult" and "unprofessional." My banishment to baseball Siberia immediately cleared the Jays' pitching mound of any and all potential for controversy. With me in the pen, there'd be one less struggling pitcher to baby-sit, and one less pain in Cito's aching lower back. Coolers were kicked. Beers were guzzled. Curses were shouted, but nothing changed. I was now officially, and irrevocably, the odd man out of the Jays' postseason rotation. Case "F"ing closed.

Spending the final two weeks of the season as a reliever, I had a tough time readjusting to the old daydreaming, girl-hunting, hangover-nursing ways of the pen. These days I wanted the ball, and the responsibility, and the W—and life in the bullpen felt a LOT like riding the bench. Oddly, though I was unhappy with the move, I did get into a lot of games over those final days of the '91 season, and with all that work, my game righted itself pretty damn fast. For a change, Cito actually seemed eager to get me the ball, and I almost never disappointed. Though I hated this particular fact of life, I knew that coming into the ALCS, I really could help my team win from the pen. Heading into the postseason, against the surprisingly strong Minnesota Twins, that was my job. Getting myself back into the rotation would have to wait until spring.

Traveling into the old Hubert H. Humphrey Metrodome, with momentum building and our confidence sky-high, we Jays take to the turf charging toward a no-holds-barred grab at well-deserved baseball supremacy. Three innings later, with Tom Candiotti on the hill, we're already losing 5–0. With the knuckler's knuckler mushy, Cito makes an early call to the pen, bringing in his designated "long" guy . . . aka me. Coming into the game in the third, I'm pumped and primed and high on adrenaline. Over the course of the next three innings, I've got the A game working while my teammates do everything they can to get us back in the game.

With Twins' ace Jack Morris getting tired on the mound, we Jays battle back to 5–4, but when Rick Aguilera clamps the lid tight, through the seventh, eighth, and ninth, we Jays head for the hotel down one game to zip.

In Game 2, Juan Guzman pitches an awesome six innings, and with Terminator and Duane Ward backing him up, Kelly Gruber tattooing *everything* tossed his way, and Devo scoring three runs, we head back to Toronto with a 5–2 victory, and the series tied at 1–1.

Feeling like the series momentum was definitely back on our side, we Jays showed up for Game 3 high-fiving, forearm smashing, ready, willing, and eager to tear the Skydome up. But, of course, that didn't happen. Instead, we lost Games 3, 4, and 5, getting royally pummelled in each.

Personally, I came out of the pen in four of the series' five games, giving up just two runs in 7⅔ innings. It's a hollow, completely insignificant positive, and packing up my locker, I remember I actually felt shitty even thinking about it. It felt like going to a funeral and *really* enjoying the lunch.

And there we were. Six months of solid play, commitment, undying dedication, and collective personal sacrifice had once again amounted to a great, big, steaming pile of "second best." At the same time, with my spot in the rotation now officially blown, I settled in to hibernate, depressed, wondering if at twenty-eight years old, my best days in baseball were already behind me. Thankfully, huge, unexpected doings up north quickly slapped me out of my winter doldrums.

In 1991, 4,001,527 people jammed the Skydome, and with yet another post-season collapse, you can imagine the media's take on our season. "Bigger, Better, Same Old Jays" was the take, and once again, Toronto brass went out of their way to keep the Canucks focused on baseball. With a ton of ticket-sales cash bursting the seams of the team's war chest, Minnesota's Jack Morris, who'd beaten us like a rug (*twice*) in the '91 ALCS, switched allegiances, pissed off the entire "Land of a Thousand Lakes," and became a no-good, stinkin', turncoat Blue Jay. Gifted with a whopping $10 million payday, there was simply no way the thirty-seven-year-old righty could have said no.

One day later, a similarly enormous payday lured the similarly middle-aged Dave Winfield north of the border and away from his archenemy, George Steinbrenner. With the Christmas Club funds now depleted, the Jays rang in the new year with more good cheer than ever before. This year's fall fix-up had been even more impressive (not to mention more expensive) than last. Having lost nothing but money, the Jays had now added one of the game's best pitchers and one of the game's best bats to our already impressive lineup. This time around, they were taking no chances.

Heading back into Dunedin with veteran status fast approaching, I was nonetheless faced with the most uncertain spring training of my career. I had started inconsistently for the Jays over the past two years. I had relieved VERY well, both at the end of last season and in 1989. Coming into the brand-new supercharged Jays season, I had no idea on which side of the fence I'd fall.

With '91 numbers a notch below the phenomenal Juan Guzman's stats, but comparable to both Jimmy Key's and Todd Stottlemyre's, and better than Tom Candiotti's (who'd now moved on to Los Angeles), I knew I deserved a legitimate shot at getting back into the rotation. At the same time, with Jack Morris now serving as king of the hill, Dave Stieb due back from the DL at any minute, and a young kid named Pat Hentgen showing early flashes of brilliance, we were twelve pounds of bologna in a ten-pound bag. The Jays were gonna be the best rotation in baseball, no matter *how* things shook out. It's an intimidating spring, but six weeks later, I'm walking on air.

Showing off terrific spring stats, and an uneventfully civil relationship with Cito, I headed north as the Blue Jays' fifth starter. Morris, Guzman, Key, Stottlemyre, Wells—that was our lineup, and barring absolute disaster, we were guaranteed to kick serious ass. Sure, Dave Stieb would ultimately bump *somebody* out of the rotation, but for now I was back on top, and hell-bent on making the best of my assignment . . . which lasted all of two starts.

Dave Stieb rejoined the Jays on April 19, and yours truly was once again shipped out to the pen. It wasn't a surprise. It wasn't a shock, but I have to admit, it *really* pissed me off this time. Yes, we had a great staff. And yes, I knew I could help this team from the pen, but at this point, my frustration level was skyrocketing. I'd been a very successful starter, but once again, with absolutely no faith shown in my ability to pitch, Cito, his coaches, the Jays' front office—all these idiots just heaved me back into the bullpen without any explanation or guarantees about what my role was gonna be on this team. It makes you wanna scream "Fuck you!! You can't keep messing with me! Make me a starter or make me a reliever! Just make a fucking decision! It's one or the other, I'm not doing both!"

In my mind, I'd become a puppet—tossed back and forth from rotation to pen, with no regard whatsoever for the royal mindfucking I'd now been enduring for the better part of three years. Never quite allowed to get comfortable as either a starter *or* a reliever, I was under the microscope at *both* positions. "Disgusted" might be the best way to describe my feelings, with "disillusioned" and "depressed" thrown in for good measure.

And then the scale came back. Ever since the minors, the Jays would sporadically drag the old scale out of the trainer's room and cordially request that I weigh in. With major-league scales impossible to jimmy, I was forced to cooperate. Anything under 230 pounds got me a pat on the back and a shit-eating grin from our trainers. Above 230, I'd be fined $100. You can imagine how well that kind of bullshit sat with me this year. At that point, I just shut down.

No yelling, no fighting, I never so much as kicked a locker. It would have been pointless. Bounced one more time into an undetermined stretch in the pen, I'd finally reached my point of no return. Clearly I was an afterthought to the Blue Jays, and barring some unforeseen miracle, the situation was never gonna change. That kind of bullshit can drive a guy crazy. It gets into your head. It gnaws at you. You read the sports pages and daydream about where you might fit into other franchises. You look at other staff rotations and plot yourself as a number three, maybe even a number two starter. You actually have to force yourself to go numb.

Burning in the pen, I slowly began realizing the *only* recourse I had against these dumb Torontonian fucks was to go out and do my job, and do it well. With that in mind, I went out to that mound every time I was asked, and just plain pitched my ass off—hoping to help my team while simultaneously hoping that somebody, *somewhere,* would notice my performance and give me a real shot somewhere else. It's a hell of a way to win a pennant.

Oddly, that chip on my shoulder paid off big-time, and for a solid month, from mid-May to mid-June, I threw *nothing* but shutout innings. At about the same time, Dave Stieb came up gimpy again. Guess who Cito punted back into the rotation.

For the next two months, with my brain now officially scrambled, I struggled mightily to get my game and my head back into a positive starting groove. It took a while. But except for one absolutely horrible start where the Brewers beat my ass to the tune of 13 earned runs in 4⅔ innings, I held my own, managing to go 6–6 by late August. And while those numbers are hardly *impressive*, keep in mind that at the same time, Jimmy Key, Todd Stottlemyre, and even Dave Stieb had all spent their seasons flirting with the .500 mark as well.

Still, with September and the postseason fast approaching, *my* .500 was ultimately deemed unacceptable to the Canadian baseball brain trust. With Cito and company huddling once more, I got bitch-slapped back to the pen one last time. In a last-ditch effort to "upgrade the rotation," the Jays sent two great prospects (Jeff Kent and Ryan Thompson) to the Mets, in exchange for free-agent-to-be David Cone. I knew Coney was great, but I have to admit, I wanted to hate him immediately.

But, of course, that didn't happen. You can't hate Coney. It's impossible; he's too cool, too funny, too much fun to goof with, and even in those few final weeks of the '92 season, we quickly laid the groundwork for a great, solid, enduring friendship. Meanwhile, I rode out the most schizophrenic month of my entire career.

The Jays were now rolling toward yet another postseason appearance, and for that reason, I tried my level best to make a painless slide back into the pen. With teammates I genuinely liked, and a really good chance for us to win it all this year, there was no way in hell I was gonna let my own personal bullshit ruin this experience. With a big, fake, locker room smile glued squarely on my face, I trudged through September pitching solid ball whenever asked. Watching my team win from a bullpen perch, three hundred feet down the right-field line, I was equal parts pumped and jealous. I'd never been on a team this good. I'd never felt this confident about our postseason chances. I'd never felt this left out.

After six years as a Blue Jay, I was thrilled with our success in '92. Thrilled for the guys, thrilled for the fans, and honest to God, beneath all the mismanagement bullshit, I was thrilled for myself too. Just being part of such a special season was a genuine thrill. And when you consider that a lot of guys ride out whole careers without *ever* approaching postseason play, I knew exactly how lucky I was. All things considered, it really wasn't all that hard to squash my own frustration back under the surface, at least 'til after the season.

Running through the playoffs, we went head to head with the same Oakland A's who'd manhandled us back in '89. Rickey, McGwire, Canseco, they were all back, with Harold Baines now handling the team's DH duties. In short, they were a powerhouse, rolling through the AL West with the same 96–66 record we'd racked up in the East. This year, however, with a little more experience, a little more speed, and a lot more power at the plate, we Jays turned the tables, and took the A's apart, 4 games to 2. Now it was time to beat up on the NL's best—the Braves.

Fulton County Stadium. With the standard World Series hype, and hoopla and bullshit and ass-kissing running amock at all corners of the stadium, Jack Morris and Tom Glavine kicked off the series with an ass-kicker of a pitcher's duel. Both guys were sharp, but with Atlanta's fans launching into a forty-five-minute version of their thoroughly obnoxious, thoroughly idiotic *"WOHHH-Wo-WO-Wo-Wo-Wo"* tomahawk-chop schtick (message to Braves fans: "Shut the hell up! You sound like morons"), Glavine was just unstoppable, tossing a complete game five-hitter, and walking away with an easy 3–1 victory.

One quick side note: in a pleasant, totally unexpected surprise, with his team down 3–1 in the eighth, Cito gave me the ball. My eyes went wide. David Wells, the kid from Ocean Beach who used to live in a Chevy, pushing shopping carts around a parking lot for a living, was now standing on the mound, pitching in the World Series of baseball. Lingering a moment at the top of the inning, I scanned the (hostile) crowd one time, soaking in every bit of the atmosphere, history, and excitement the moment could offer. I knew there was a very good chance I might never get back to this position again, and if that was the case, I wanted as clear a mental memory as humanly possible. Finally, with a little prodding from the home plate umpire, I settled in to pitch. An easy 1-2-3 inning followed, and though we went back to the hotel as losers that night, I knew the day would officially go down as one of the greatest in my life. Little did I know I'd be back on the mound less than twenty-four hours later.

Game 2. Coney's on the mound, struggling, with the Braves pounding out four runs in four innings. In the top of the fifth, with Coney in trouble again, Cito calls to the pen . . . for me. Apparently yesterday's outing got noticed. Working fast, my stuff's on fire here in the postseason, and I get out of the fifth without much trouble at all. I'll work a 1-2-3 sixth before Todd Stottlemyre takes over for me in the seventh.

Down 4–2 in the top of the eighth, three singles in a row chase Atlanta starter John Smoltz from the game, while cutting the Braves lead to 4–3. One inning later, with Jeff Reardon throwing smoke for Atlanta, the tomahawk choppers start moaning again. To their astonishment, Reardon gives up a walk to Derek Bell, and at that point, pinch hitter/unlikely hero Ed Sprague steps to the plate. A .234 hitter, Sprague's appearance immediately cranks up the volume on the gloating, overconfident Braves chant. The choppers are in for a nasty surprise. Our pinch hitter's got inside information.

Sprague is helped enormously at the plate this afternoon by a guy who's done nothing more than sit on his ass and pay attention. Rance Mulliniks, our part-time DH, part-time first baseman, part-time outfielder, has been watching Reardon very closely since he first came into the game. With a gleam in his eyes, he grabs hold of Sprague in the dugout and tells him, "Listen, dude. I'm not promising anything, but if this guy holds true to form, you're gonna see a first pitch fastball, low and away. Keep your eyes open for it."

Sprague goes to the plate now, settles in, and gets his pitch. Exactly as

Mulliniks predicted, it's a fastball, low, away, and hittable. Sprague swings, connects, and launches a tape-measure home run. It's just the second long ball of Sprague's *career*. We Jays take a 5–4 lead before dog-piling Ed Sprague into the shape of a pancake. Meanwhile, the tomahawk choppers shut down in mid "Wo-Wo." Two minutes later, the vast majority of them start leaving the game early.

In the bottom of the ninth, Tom Henke's perfect as always, and we Jays go home to Skydome with the series knotted at one apiece.

Game 3. With Juan Guzman on the hill facing off against Steve Avery, it's no surprise that the game stayed quiet through the early innings. That would all change in the fourth. With Deion Sanders at second base, and Terry Pendleton at first, Guzman's got David Justice at the plate. Connecting with a hard fastball, Justice sends a *long* fly ball into *deep* left-center. Devon White immediately bolts toward the wall. Running at speeds that'd make gazelles jealous, Devo flies to the warning track, leaps, hits the wall, and somehow breaking every known law of both aerodynamics *and* human physiology, he makes the catch. It's impossible, but he's done it.

Landing hard, Devo nonetheless shoots a terrific relay throw back toward Robby Alomar at second. Stunned, Deion Sanders stops dead in his tracks as his third-base coach jumps up and down, frantically waving him back toward second. Sixty feet back, with no coach directing traffic, Terry Pendleton has no idea the ball's actually been caught. He's motoring past second, looking to score, when he passes right by Deion. Pendleton's out.

Meanwhile, Deion's reversed direction and he's hauling ass, trying to beat the throw back to second base. He ends up caught in a rundown, jockeying back and forth as Robby Alomar and Manny Lee close in from both sides. Amazingly, with his own immense speed blazing, Deion makes a close play of it at second base. Robby Alomar swipes a tag at his ankles, nailing him by maybe three inches. It's close, but clear. We Jays have pulled off the first triple play in World Series history! Or not.

Second-base umpire Bob Davidson calls Deion safe. Cito argues the call, Robby argues the call, but it does no good. Meanwhile, on network television, nineteen different replays make it crystal clear that Davidson's blown it. The following afternoon, having seen the replays for himself, even Davidson will admit his mistake.

Bottom of the ninth. With the game knotted at 2–2, Mark Wohlers comes on to pitch for Atlanta. Robby Alomar steps in, and after looking at one nasty slider, he belts a letter-high fastball into right for a single. Two pitches later, with

Joe Carter at the plate, Robby steals second, and the drumroll begins. At that point, Carter's given the intentional pass, and Dave Winfield steps up, lofting a sweet sac fly to left that moves up both runners.

Second and third now, with one out. John Olerud's due up next, but when lefty Mike Stanton is brought in from the pen, Cito subs yesterday's hero, Ed Sprague, into Olerud's spot. An intentional walk to Sprague follows, loading the bases for Candy Maldonado. Jeff Reardon comes in from the Braves' pen to face him. Strike one blows by Candy at almost 100 miles per hour. Strike two follows. Reardon winds up again now, and he launches another bullet, which Candy promptly dekes into short left for a single. We Jays take the game 3-2, and go up in the series by two games to one.

Game 4's simple. Tom Glavine's awesome for Atlanta. Jimmy Key's awesome for Toronto. Pat Borders (who's lava hot these days) cracks a solo shot in the third that stakes us Jays to a 1–0 lead. Devo's RBI double in the seventh makes it 2–0. In between, we do nothing. Glavine's just too good.

On our side, Jimmy Key's even better, going a full eight innings while giving up just one scratched-out run. We go home with a 2–1 victory under our belts and a commanding 3–1 lead in the series. Premature victory celebrations are hard to suppress now—but a nasty Game 5 will shut 'em down fast.

With Jack Morris back on the mound against John Smoltz, the game is tied at 2–2 going into the fifth. That's when all hell breaks loose. The Braves' Otis Nixon leads off the inning with a bloop hit, and a steal of second base. Deion Sanders smacks an RBI single. Terry Pendleton doubles, sending Neon Deion to third. David Justice takes an intentional pass to first, and at that point, Lonnie Smith caps the slaughter with a massive grand slam into the right-field stands. Down 7–2, Cito calls me into the game once more, and at the risk of sounding less than humble, I throw a *great* two innings. Having now pitched in three of our five World Series games, I've come away with more confidence than ever before, giving up just one hit over 3⅓ innings.

Game 6. With David Cone back on the mound again, this time facing Steve Avery, both guys throw killer games, and we end up heading into extra innings with the score locked at 2. I need Maalox.

The mush-heads with the foam fingers once again launch into a rousing rendition of their stupid-ass Indian call as Charlie Leibrandt pitches a perfect tenth inning for the Braves. They shut up when Jimmy Key returns the favor. Leibrandt returns for the eleventh, and he gets one quick out before plunking Devon White with a pitch. From there, Robby Alomar singles Devo to third, Joe

Carter pops out to shallow center, and Dave Winfield, at the ripe old age of 167, gets all over a change-up and raps a two-out double down the line, scoring both Robby and Devo. A half inning later, Mike Timlin pounces on an Otis Nixon bunt, flips it to Joe Carter at first, and officially puts the Braves out of their misery. We Toronto Blue Jays are World Champions.

We hit the field, flying, soaring, diving onto one another with pure, unbridled, childlike joy. From there, with champagne flowing, and laughter and tears, and hugs all around, it's easy to live in the moment, forgetting all about my own frustration, and battles with management. Right now, none of that stuff matters. None of that stuff even exists. There will be plenty of time for reality once this fairy tale finally ends.

Back in Toronto, a parade through the city caps off our team victory celebration, with fans cheering us on as we pass. Later, back at Skydome, as we all empty our blue Formica lockers and start heading for home, *everybody* says their good-byes the same way—"See you next year, so we can do it all over again." We shake hands, slap backs. "Time to repeat the feat!"

"I hope so," I reply, having absolutely *no* idea what my future holds. I've been productive. I've been cooperative. But at the same time, I've made absolutely no pretense at being happy with my situation. I've been at odds with Cito for years, and my sour relationship with Pat Gillick goes back more than a decade. I expect no favors from either of those guys, especially with Guzman, Morris, and Stottlemyre all locks to be back next season, free agents Coney and Key probable, and young phenom Pat Hentgen being rapidly groomed as a starter as well. Closing out my locker, I'm convinced the Jays' long-term plans will undoubtedly find me locked in the pen. Heading home, I had no idea that my theory was wildly, naïvely, insanely optimistic.

Cito and Pat had already decided to dump me.

TEN

Detroit, Rocked City

Giving me a
briefcase is like putting
earrings on a hot dog.

—*Sparky Anderson*

1993: TIGER STADIUM

Metallica's *Black Album* is wailing from my boom box, eight D cells churning out a nice, bass-heavy, eardrum-rattling decibel level that rolls throughout the team locker room. My head's banging. My heart's pumping. My blood's flowing. My teammates, whether they're laughing at my music, grooving, or wincing, all throw thumbs-up my way, and high fives and "Good luck" wishes. My manager called me into his office this afternoon just to talk, to make sure my head was on straight, to make sure I was focused, feeling strong and ready to pitch. He's an amazing man, and I trust him implicitly. I just plain *like* him too. I'm on top of the world. I'm starting tonight. I'm a Detroit Tiger.

One week ago, I was out of baseball.

Within weeks of winning the Series, both Coney and Jimmy Key broke free of Toronto, working free agency to secure brand-new, long-term contracts south of the border. Coney went back to his roots in Kansas City, while Jimmy Key, royally pissed off at the fact Cito gave him only one start in last year's postseason, moved on too, becoming the ace of the still-lowly New York Yankees.

With all that in mind, I took a realistic survey of the situation and came to the conclusion that even with those defections, I was *still* going back to the bullpen. Here's why. Just days after Coney and Key jumped ship, Pat Gillick, giddy with success, and coming off yet another season where four million fans showed up at the Skydome,* reached into the vaults and hired himself another ex-enemy. Like Jack Morris before him, Dave Stewart of the A's quickly shifted alliances, and followed the Canadian dollars to Toronto.

From there, with Stewart and Morris at the top of the rotation, and the blazing-hot Juan Guzman behind them, I knew there'd be just two starting spots up for grabs. Todd Stottlemyre, coming off a terrific postseason, was a shoo-in for one spot, and I'd now been around the Jays' decision makers long enough to know that coming off their success with young Juan Guzman, fellow baby-phenom Pat Hentgen was a virtual lock to snare the five spot. Clearly, I'd be odd man out yet again.

And while the idea of another season out in the Jays' bullpen/dog kennel was by no means thrilling, at least (it seemed) I'd be going into the new season with a clear, solid sense of where I'd fit in. Y'know after years of yo-yoing around the staff, I'd know my place. With that in mind, the frustrations and uncertainty and aggravations of seasons past would melt away this year, allowing me to focus, work on my game, and make the best of an imperfect situation. With a long, deep breath, I'd talked myself into approaching the new season with a positive, flexible,

---

* Oddly, in a bizarre statement at a post–World Series victory celebration, Toronto management actually claimed (with a straight face) that despite winning the World Series, and luring more than four million fans to the park, the Blue Jays had *lost* money in 1992. Keep that in mind the next time you hear owners' numbers that cry poverty in the midst of team success.

optimistic attitude. With the additions of Dave Stewart and a nifty little Hall of Fame slugger by the name of Paul Molitor, the '93 Jays looked to be even better than last year's lineup of champions. Great things might be in store yet again.

As it turned out, great things *were* in store for the Jays, and for me too, only not in Toronto.

I saw it coming from a mile away. Heading into Dunedin, I pitched just once with the big-league squad before sliding across the complex to the poor side of town and working out with the minor-league guys. The party line had me "just getting some extra work in"—but the message couldn't have been more obvious. The handwriting was on the wall. Honestly, hiring skywriter planes to scroll YOU'RE FIRED, ASSHOLE! across the blue would have been more subtle.

"I'm outta here, dude," I say to Dave Stewart. "They're gonna waste my ass and release me."

"You're crazy. There's no way they're gonna release you, man," Stewart replies. "They're not that stupid."

Using every ounce of my self-control to keep from laughing out loud, I just said, "Watch, you'll see."

Weeks pass, I don't get released, I start pitching with the big club again, and we're now just four days away from the season opener. Confused, I pitch five innings with the big club against St. Louis, and while my stuff's not great, it's by no means a bad outing. With opening day now just ninety-six hours away, I go back to the hotel feeling like I've dodged the bullet.

The following morning I go to Grant Field, I work out with the team, and at that point the majority of the guys start getting ready to bus over to Clearwater for an exhibition contest against the Phillies. Adhering to time-honored spring training tradition, the fact that I pitched yesterday means that I won't be expected to make this trip. I'm done for the day, with plans to drive out to the beach for one last day in the sand before starting the regular season. Sitting at my locker, I'm already in my street clothes when Cito taps my shoulder.

"Suit up," he tells me. "You're going with the team over to the Phillies camp."

"Oh no I'm not."

"Oh yes you are." Mind you, this is already one of the longest, deepest chats I've ever had with the man.

"Cito," I say, pissed off now, "I just pitched five fucking innings yesterday. I'm spent. I can't even wipe my ass right now, and you want me to suit up and sit through an exhibition game? That's bullshit. I ain't doing it."

Cito sighs, then says, "Well then, go in your street clothes, but you're going."

Now I'm totally confused, and totally pissed off, but this being spring training, Gord Ash is in the clubhouse, and he's just heard my whole exchange with Cito. With that in mind, I know going AWOL will probably just get me fined bigtime. With one loud "What the fuck?" aimed at the locker room ceiling, I know I'm Clearwater bound.

Too pissed to sit on any fucking team bus, I get into my car and drive myself over to the Phillies complex. Now while the other guys are taking batting practice and shagging flies, I'm sitting around a locker room doing absolutely nothing, getting more and more pissed with every passing moment.

Forty-five minutes pass. And I'm literally jingling my car keys in my hand weighing the pros and cons of bolting when Cito approaches. "Pat Gillick's here," he tells me, staring at the floor. "He and Gord wanna see you."

Now the situation *almost* made sense. While the scenario unfolding before me was just screaming "YOU'RE RELEASED!!" it *couldn't* be that, because *no* front office would ever have its head far enough up its own ass to be releasing a veteran *this* late in the spring. It's just not done. It's not cool, and it's not at all in the best interest of your exiting player. This close to the season, with all twenty-six major-league franchises now down to the final tweaking and juggling of their opening day rosters, a flat-out release could be flat-out disastrous. It'd handcuff a player's options in terms of catching on with another club, and at the same time, it'd put the poor bastard into an almost impossible negotiating position should any new team show interest. Basically, unless you really don't mind kicking your man in the balls, you release him as early in the spring as you possibly can.

The Blue Jays didn't mind.

Heading into the manager's office, I found Gillick and Ash waiting for me with the same fascination for the floor tiles that Cito had shown, and at that point, there was a silence so long I nearly laughed. Finally, Gord Ash says, "Well, David, we came to a decision. It's a tough decision, but we have to release you."

I didn't say a word—I just nodded.

Now Pat Gillick says, "We tried to trade you, but nobody wanted you. We talked to a number of teams, but there was no interest, nothing."

I'm still sitting there, fuming, confused. "No interest, my ass." Maybe if these jugheads hadn't spent the past five years running my career into the ground they wouldn't have had that problem. I'm silent.

Gord Ash says, "Don't you have anything to say?"

I said, "Yeah, I do actually—I just want you guys to know that I'm totally fucking pissed off I didn't get a gold watch for my ten years of service." Their mouths dropped. I signed my release papers and left. I never looked back.

And there, with one last, lovely "fuck you" of a parting gift, the Jays had simultaneously fired my ass and *guaranteed* me a rocky, unsure slide into 1993. Walking back to my car (thank GOD I hadn't taken that bus), I burned rubber out of the lot, hit the U.S. 19 traffic, and dialed Gregg Clifton.

"Hey, buddy," I shout into the phone. "Guess what! I just got released!"

"Get outta here. No way."

"I kid you not."

"Okay, don't worry. Let me do my job and find you some work."

Within twenty-four hours, Clifton had come through big-time, and it seemed like every team in the majors wanted me. There was just one catch: nobody but nobody wanted to pay me the two-million-dollar salary Gregg had negotiated for me with the free-spending Jays. Quickly it became clear that with the late-spring dumping working against our bargaining power, I was gonna take at least a 50 percent pay cut. Oddly enough, that pay cut, and my unceremonious boning from the Jays, may have been the two best things that ever happened to my career.

Now the phone's ringing. Mel Stottlemyre (Todd's dad/current Yankees pitching coach) was with the Mets back then, and he and Mets' manager Jeff Torborg were first in line. They were trying to get me over there as a reliever, maybe with a spot start here and there, and they're both stand-up, solid guys, so I think they were being totally honest when they said things like, "Y'know, if all goes well, maybe we can think about moving you into the rotation."

I said, "No. Sorry. Not interested." They were offering like $600K for the year, and my thinking was that if I was gonna take a low salary, I was at *least* gonna try and find myself a guaranteed opportunity to start. St. Louis gave me a call about relieving at $800K, and I turned that down too. I almost buckled when Tommy Lasorda dangled a million at me as a lefty setup man, but with fingers crossed, I had Gregg keep the Dodgers at bay while we waited for a starter's spot. It came less than twenty-four hours later.

My phone rings. It's Cecil Fielder, who's now become a bona fide home-run-hitting beast. Having grown completely frustrated with his perennial bench-warming in Toronto, Cecil made one of the boldest career moves in the history of baseball, by taking his big-ass bat to Hanshin, Japan. There, throughout the 1989 season, my old friend made like Godzilla, crushing the ball all over the Nipponese countryside. These weren't so much tape-measure shots as they were odometer shots. Needless to say, even two thousand miles removed from the nearest major-league franchise, Cecil suddenly found himself very popular among MLB execs. He ultimately signed a big, multiyear deal with Detroit at the start of the 1990 season, and since that time, he'd blasted 130 homers out of Tiger Stadium, becoming a huge Motown hero in the process. Now he's calling me.

"Congratulations," Cecil tells me. "You finally escaped Toronto."

"Thanks a lot."

"Now listen to me," he continues. "What you ARE gonna do is sign with Detroit. I tell you this, because if you *don't* sign with us, I will personally come to your house, grab you by the face, drag you out your front door and down your front steps, and then I will beat your ass all over your front yard while your friends and neighbors watch."

Now, normally if a guy were to say something like that to me, I'd laugh, secure in the knowledge that (a) he's kidding, and (b) he couldn't make good on that threat even if he wanted to. However, in dealing with Cecil, neither one of those calming possibilities worked. With that in mind I just kind of laughed nervously into my phone.

"Here's the deal," Cecil tells me. "Sparky Anderson's gonna call you. He's a good guy, and a great manager, and you *can* trust him to be honest with you. Talk to him. Tell him what you're looking for and see what happens. Cool?"

"Cool." Sparky called me just about an hour later, which was thrilling even in and of itself. I mean, the guy's a legend. This is the guy who drove Cincinatti's Big Red Machine. This is the guy who won 104 games and a World Series with the Tigers in 1984. The man's one of the greatest managers in the history of the game.

"Hey, David, Sparky Anderson," he begins.

"Hi, uh, Sparky," I answer, fighting off the urge to call him "Mr. Anderson." "Thanks for calling."

Ten minutes pass, during which Sparky tells me he's liked my stuff for a long time. He thinks I have real potential, and he's prepared to flat out make me the Tigers' fifth starter.

"Guaranteed?" I ask him.

"You have my word," he replies.

"Done." At $900K, no human being has ever been so happy to take a 55 percent pay cut.* "Great!" I told Sparky, "I'll see you in Oakland."

With the Tigers starting their 1993 campaign on the road against the A's, I flew directly to the Oakland Alameda County Coliseum, where I pitched in just one quick, intra-squad scrimmage before starting and winning my first regular season game just four days later. At the same time, I began settling happily into my new surroundings.

With Cecil making the introductions, I quickly realized the Tigers' locker room was gonna be almost nothing like the Blue Jays'. Here, there were no cliques, no weigh-ins, no clubhouse politicians, and there sure as hell wasn't any second-guessing of the manager. The guys shaking hands with me here in the Detroit dugout all seemed to be having fun, playing hard, with a real sense of how they fit into Sparky's "big picture." Their welcoming gestures seemed genuine and warm. Best of all, when I asked Cecil why one enormous boom box is currently blaring great, old-school George Jones through the entire Tigers' locker room, he tells me that with Mike Moore on the mound today *he* gets to pick the pregame music.

"Wait a minute!" I practically shout. "You mean that whoever gets the start gets to play whatever music they want?"

"Exactly."

"All day?"

"All day, no matter how redneck corny it is."

I had a smile beaming from one ear clear across to the other. That night I made myself my first mix tape—AC/DC, Nugent, Sammy Hagar, Van Halen, Black Sabbath ("Iron Man" makes a GREAT pregame anthem, by the way). This mother-effing tape was a masterpiece. I'm literally halfway through recording it when my phone rings. It's Jason Scheff, former Ocean Beach troll, now lead singer for the band Chicago. He congratulates me on the move to Detroit, and when I tell him about the Tigers' great new "starter picks the music" rule, I launch into my whole audiocassette playlist.

"No Chicago, huh?" he asks me.

"Oh . . . uhhhhhh." I'm still stammering when he cracks up.

---

* Truth be told, when you add the severance pay owed to me by the Blue Jays (about 25 percent of my annual salary) to the Tigers' bargain-basement deal, and the incentive clauses Sparky threw at me (all of which I'd end up hitting), I actually came away from the 1993 season taking home a very modest raise. Not bad for an unemployable "attitude problem."

"Dude, I understand." He tells me, "Nobody's ever gotten pumped listening to 'Colour My World.' Listen to *that* and you'll end up slow-dancing with your catcher." Before we hang up, I promise to make Chicago my official postgame band, and Jason seems more than satisfied.

The following afternoon, with me getting the start against Seattle, I've got paint chips leaping off the walls with my head-banging anthems. I've also got teammates running for cover, laughing, hands over their ears as they all get their first taste of "the new guy." To his credit, when Sparky Anderson bolts out of his office, looking like a dad who's about to spank me with his slipper, he gets one look at my air-guitaring little pep rally, laughs, and just kind of heads back into his office, shaking his head with a poorly hidden grin. I was really gonna like it here—even if our team wasn't as good as the Jays.

Don't get me wrong—the '93 Tigers were a solid, respectable team. We just weren't a juggernaut, or a squad that was gonna come close to winning 100 games. Still, with Sparky on the bench, we did manage to raise a few eyebrows and hang near the top of the old AL East.

With a ton of power, and no speed at all, we Tigers were a big-swinging, big-whiffing bunch. With guys like Cecil and Rob Deer and Mickey Tettleton and Travis Fryman all hacking away with gigantic breeze-blowing at bats, we racked up more than our fair share of both Ks and three-run homers. With guys like Alan Trammell, Tony Phillips, and our gimpy-limpy captain, the fantastic future Hall of Famer Kirk Gibson, setting the table, we busted out with a *ton* of big innings. Down 7–2 in the eighth, we'd still have a fifty-fifty shot of catching your ass—as long as our pitching held out.

Mike Moore, the fireballing Oakland expatriate, pitched solid, steady ball throughout the season, and he was followed to the mound by veteran Bill Gullickson, a righty named John Doherty, Mark Leiter (Al's older brother), and me. We were hardly the staff of dreams, and when Leiter ultimately hit the DL, he was replaced in the rotation by such legendary temp arms as Sean "Ingmar" Bergman, Bill "Freddy" Krueger, and Buddy "Bride and" Groom. You've never seen more 12–11 losses in your life.

Out in the pen, Mike Henneman was the team's *very* solid closer, but his *real* claim to fame, at least as far as I'm concerned, has nothing to do with baseball. Y'see, very early in that 1993 season, Henneman's the guy who pulled me aside, reached into his jacket, and slipped me my first Metallica tape. "Put it on, dude," he told me. "These new guys are like nothing you've ever heard before." Mike was a rare bird in baseball, a head banger more devoted and extreme than me. Slipping the tape into the boom box and cranking the volume high, the man changed my life. My eyes went wide. My head bobbed uncontrollably. Bass-heavy rhythms coursed through my body like megavitamins. I'd never felt so up, so powerful, so flat-out ready to pitch. Over the course of my next fifteen starts, that music would pump me toward a 9–1 record with an earned run average in the middle twos. Needless to say, nobody in the locker room *ever* told us to turn it down.

As simple as this statement sounds, it was truly amazing to me that life as a major-league baseball player could be so much damn fun. After spending a full decade dealing with the daily headaches of Canadian travel, fighting with management, hiding from weigh-ins, all while choking to death from inside my team-mandated suits and ties, the relative calm, logic, and laid-back professionalism of the Tigers just thrilled me to the bone. Here, for the first time in my professional career, I was free to be me. Free to have a personality. Free to be an honest-to-God human being, as opposed to a bland, robotic "representative of the franchise." I could not have been happier.

But that's not to say things were always perfect. My relationship with Kirk Gibson began as a disaster. When we met for the first time on opening day in Oakland, Kirk was shagging a few pregame fly balls out in left field. Eager to become better acquainted, I joined him out there. At that point, our first annual butting of heads was just seconds away. Gibby explains it himself:

> I was in left, shagging flies, but I wasn't just killing time. I really needed the practice. I was never a very good defensive player. Now here comes David, and he's pounding his mitt, and kind of sliding up near me, hoping to catch a few too. I said to him, "Listen, Dave, maybe you should move over into center." Well, he just kind of looked at me, angry, like I had two heads. I said to him, "Think of it this way, if *you* were pitching, you wouldn't want me to drop a fly ball, would you?" And Dave kind of blows up and he says, "Wait, are you saying you'd just bag me?" He actually thought I was threatening to drop one on him in a game situation. It knocked me for a loop.
>
> And I told Dave, "That's not what I said at all. Let's you and me go up into the tunnel and settle this right now and clear the air and have an understanding." And that started us talking, and there was a real curiosity about each other. I could see how David's experiences in Toronto had left him almost shell-shocked. He was very defensive. Y'know, he seemed like he expected the worst in the people around him.

I think Dave was confused, and he was angry, and there was good reason for that. But as we got to know each other better, I think I was able to help David learn how to play the game of life a little better. Y'know, we talked about how there's always accountability on both sides of a disagreement, and that sometimes, especially in situations with teammates and coaches and front-office types, it's best to keep a handle on your gut reaction and to look for solutions rather than conflict. From Sparky on down, everybody on this team tried to be honest, and open, and helpful with each other. Once that reality sunk in, David really seemed to enjoy himself.

In time, Kirk would become my best friend on the team, and one of my very best friends in life as well. And while I spent the early part of that '93 season talking shop with Mike Moore and Bill Gullickson, it was Kirk and Alan Trammell who finally sat me down and made me a *much* better pitcher. Sitting with those guys in the dugout, and more often than that on barstools, we'd talk endlessly about how hitters think. Professor Gibson recalls his lesson plans:

Me and Alan Trammell, we'd sit with Dave and have a few pops and we'd just beat pitching smarts into his rock head. For example, a lot of pitchers won't throw inside very much, because they worry that if they leave a ball out over the plate, it's gonna get blasted five hundred feet out into the parking lot. But that's negative thinking. David has always had great location on his stuff, and so we'd tell him *you* won't leave the ball over the plate, *you'll* get it where you want it just about every time, and being able to come inside consistently could really make your *good* stuff great.

It works like this. Hitters *hate* the ball inside, because it's hard to get any kind of power going in that zone. At the same time, a lot of pitchers are so afraid of making that "big mistake" they won't throw there. A guy like David, who could pound these guys inside and get the ball in there for strikes all night long, becomes a *lot* more successful. With that extra tool in his arsenal, he can use both sides of the plate, he can mess with a guy's head. Not all pitchers have the control to do that, but David has the gift of aim. Me and Alan just beat that kind of stuff into Dave's big head for the whole season, and I think it helped him. Y'know, it was always: "Don't pitch scared. You're too good for that."

Kirk's not telling the whole story, because a huge part of what they taught me had nothing to do with pitch location; it had to do with hitters' brains.

Y'know, for years now, I'd been talking to the Stiebs and Flanagans and Keys and Moores and Gullicksons of the world about pitching, but when Kirk and Trammy became good friends, I suddenly found myself getting the firsthand inside skinny on exactly how great batters think. With the floodgates open, I'd grill these guys endlessly, digging for information on what *they'd* be looking for in specific game situations. What pitches were they sitting on? What were they hoping to see?

Like a power hitter, for example. I'd ask, "What's a power hitter looking for at the plate if I'm ahead 2–0?" Obviously, at that point he's looking dead-red. He's sitting on my fastball hoping to jack. He's hoping for something safe, fastball down the middle; something he can get a solid swing at. Fool him with a ball that breaks, and you may get yourself a fast 2–1. NOW what's he looking for? The guy *knows* you don't want to go 3–1, so he *may* still be looking fastball, but now you've shown him you're not afraid to throw a surprise at him. He may start thinking about a change-up or a curve. That little bit of indecision makes *whatever* you throw more effective.

Taking the Gibson/Trammell advice to heart, I started pitching inside with a lot more confidence and regularity. You know, big hitters all want to extend their arms so they can use their whole body in driving the ball to Pluto. Conventional wisdom finds guys pitching away, away, away, nipping the outside corner of the plate, just beyond the batter's reach, in a spot where a small mistake will more than likely just get fouled off, or cost you ball one. Assuming that's your plan, batters are forever crowding the dish . . . which of course makes well-placed inside stuff even more effective.

When a batter's looking away, and all of a sudden you come up into his kitchen, backing him up, you can *really* mess with his head. Three innings later, he's back at the plate thinking, This guy's coming in, and you start him off with a curveball, outside corner. At that point he's thinking, Okay fine. NOW he's coming in. You stay outside, 0–2. Now he's thinking, Oh shit—he's coming with the curve, and *there* you bust his hands in. He's done. Now you've got the guy completely screwed up. He's off balance. He's yours. That's how you work a hitter.

Still, even though Kirk and Trammy were nice enough to spend their evenings shooting me full of fantastic batting intelligence, I was by no means immune to their heartless, cruel, and immature pranks. In fact, one story Kirk has personally *insisted* I include in this book is just so juvenile, silly, and beneath my dignity, that well . . . I'm just gonna let him tell it. For those of you too mature to indulge in such childish ramblings, I suggest you flip ahead. My continued baseball insights and well-reasoned editorial opinions will reconvene in just a few pages. Thank you.

Kirk Gibson's Hunting Story

Early in the season in 1993, I was sitting in the Detroit locker room before a game, reading through a hunting magazine. Dave saw me sitting quietly, sort of peacefully enjoying myself, and y'know, that's not something he can tolerate. So he comes bounding over, saying, "Hey, Gibby, what are you doing?" And because I really didn't know him that well yet, I gave him the whole story.

I said, "Well, I'm really into the environment, and ecology, and managing our renewable resources, and y'know, I grew up here in Michigan, so I care about our water here, and our air, and our forests, and I also like to be a resource manager." Now Dave looks at me like I'm speaking Chinese. He used to do that a lot actually.

"I like to go hunting," I explain. And then I showed Dave the magazine I was reading, and when he saw that I was ordering some supplies out of it, he asked, "What do you need all that for?" And I told him, "I'm going on a deer hunting trip." His eyes light up, and he gets excited, and he says, "I'll go!" I barely even knew the guy at this point, but that's Dave. He invited himself.

So I said sure, and I got him the gear he needed, and we took him out, and he didn't know ANYTHING. Y'know, here's this kid from California whose idea of being part of nature is to visit the San Diego Zoo, and now we've dragged him out into the middle of nowhere in Michigan. And Dave's petrified. He's just sure that a bear's gonna attack him. He's carrying extra guns, and a radio communicator unit; it's like *Rambo Goes to the Woods* out there. Dave's got two shotguns and a pistol hanging off him, and the whole time we're in the woods he's waiting to be mauled. So y'know, in that situation, there's really only one thing a fellow hunter can do. We set Dave up.

We're out in the woods, and at eleven o'clock at night it was about fifty-five degrees out. We get up the following morning at four-thirty, and there's eight inches of new snow on the ground. So there in the dark, we showed Dave a deer trail that was almost entirely snowed over. We told him to follow it, and not wanting to look like he didn't know what the hell he was doing, he agreed.

So now Dave goes off wandering through the snow, lost, and worried that a bear, or a deer, or a raccoon, or a bunny, or a something is gonna come diving out of the underbrush to attack him, and he's hating life.

Finally, we took pity on him and told him we'd actually set him up. That trail was all but impossible to follow. I laughed, and apologized, and Dave took it well, and then I told him that to make it up to him, we'd take him a little deeper into the woods and find him a really *big* trophy buck for himself.

Of course we set him up again.

While we were eating lunch, I had my friends get hold of a really big, stuffed and mounted buck. And I told the guys to take the head out to the woods near the blind where Dave had been hunting. They did that, and when they got there, they got a whole bunch of branches and brush and sticks and they sort of dug this stuffed buck into a position so that it looked like a deer just hovering at the edge of Dave's clearing. It wasn't really noticeable at first glance, but it was positioned so that sooner or later, Dave was gonna have to find it.

So now we're done with lunch, and we're heading back to our blinds, and I'm telling Dave, "Now, when you get into your blind, really take your time, because some of these deer actually know the blinds are there, and they'll sit off at the edge of the woods for a long time before they come into clear range." We split up, and now Dave turns his anti-attack radio on, and I'm talking him into position. I say to him, "Take your time; be very quiet. What you want to do is just kind of sneak into your blind, and then very carefully sort of scan the area around your blind to see if there's any buck activity."

Like twenty seconds later he's yelling into his radio, "Oh my GOD, Gibby! There's a MONSTER out here!"

So now I'm just trying not to laugh. I tell Dave, "Give him hell! Give him hell!" And by now, everybody in the whole place knows what's going on except Dave. And all of a sudden we hear BOOM!

I get on the radio now. "Did you get him? Did you get him?!"

BOOM! BOOM! BOOM!

Boomer practically screams into his radio, "I MISSED HIM!!!!!!!"

I yell, "Reload! Reload! Quick, before he runs away." Y'know, like any deer on earth is gonna hang around while some guy in a blind reloads two shotguns.

BOOM! BOOOOOOOOM! BOOOOOOOOOM!

Dave keeps shooting 'til he's out of ammo. He has no shells left and this stuffed deer's still sitting there, staring at him from the edge of the woods. "What do I do now?!" Boomer asks over his radio.

"Well," I said, "if he's still standing in the same spot, you MUST have wounded him. Maybe he's paralyzed or something. Why don't you take your bear pistol, walk over there real slow, get as close as you can, and see if you can't take him down."

Boomer leaves his radio on as he's walking and we can hear him crunching through the snow. Then there's silence, and a long pause, followed by Dave yelling, "All right, WHO's the asshole?!?!?"

It was great!

MOVING ON.

Back in the locker room, while I was thoroughly enjoying my best season ever, I was also getting a crash course in Sparky 101. Sparky was God with the Tigers, the kind of manager who'd literally stand in the middle of the locker room and tell you "It's my way or the highway, people." Get on his bad side, and there was no escaping his wrath. Worst of all would be to have the man decide you were soft.

Tiger with a mullet
(AP Photo/Roberto Borea)

More than anything else, Sparky hated pussies. If you were out there moping on the field, or whining, or finger-pointing, or trying to milk an injury, or playing it safe, or not running hard, or not diving after a ball, you were done. Sparky had no time for you. Your ass would be nailed to the bench, and you wouldn't see any daylight for a long while. It didn't matter if you were a third-string catcher or the starting left fielder, he treated everybody the same. Pussies got benched. Perennial pussies got shipped out of town, fast. Sparky rubbed a lot of people the wrong way, but I loved the guy. He was blunt. He spoke his mind. He didn't pull punches, and you always knew exactly what he was thinking.

Sparky would give speeches where he'd put his ratty old slippers in the middle of the locker room floor and say, "See those shoes down there? Those are Cinderella's slippers. Try 'em on. If they fit, there's a horse and carriage outside that'll take your sorry, princess ass right out of town, and I promise nobody'll miss ya." You'd hear him say that and you knew *somebody* was in deep shit.

Or he'd say, "Guys, this clubhouse is like a garden, and I love my garden. I like the vegetables. I like the flowers. I like the little bees. But you know what's really bad for my garden? Weeds. And lemme tell you, when I see a weed in my garden, I pluck it right out and get rid of it." The next day somebody would be gone. Traded, released, whatever. The weed had been plucked, and every guy on the team learned a lesson in unity. That's how Sparky worked. He was unique. He was cool. He taught me a lot.

Sparky was a great guy. You played by his rules, but he had an even keel, and you really got the feeling he was happy to see you every day. He'd talk to you like a person, like a friend, like a man. He was honest. He was genuine. He'd catch you in the morning and ask how you were doing. He cared about his players, and we really liked him back. Y'know, Sparky may have been the first friend I ever had with liver spots and wrinkles. At the same time, the guy was a baseball genius. He was a student of the game, and by 1993, he'd been studying a long time. I think that man may actually have known *everything* about baseball. *Every* fucking thing. You couldn't throw him if you tried. "Hey, Skip—how many stitches in a baseball?"

"Six hundred and sixty-seven."

"Hey, Skip, how many feet down the left-field line at the old Ebbets Field?"

"Three hundred and seventeen."

"Hey, Skip—bottom of the eighth, runners on second and third, Carl Yastrzemski's at the plate. You're pitching. What's the plan?"

Answer: Drill that Polish son of a bitch, and strike out the bastard on deck.

Over the course of that '93 season, Sparky really took me under his wing. He taught me about baseball, and he taught me how to behave like a man. We talked all the time about how to best handle different situations on *and off* the field. He got me to stop moping around if I was getting hit. He taught me to focus, to be aggressive, to be confident. In a very real sense, he taught me how to pitch like David Wells. "PITCH your game," he'd tell me. "Don't pitch around. Don't get cute. Don't walk people. Don't be timid. Throw YOUR pitch, your way. Make the bastards play your game. You've got the stuff to be great." Coming from such an unimpeachable source, that kind of praise goes to a guy's head pretty quickly. Especially when he's having more success on the field than ever before.

With Gibby and Trammy and Sparky all bouncing around inside my head, I hit the All-Star break at 9–2, with the Tigers running a handful of games over .500. At the same time, I'll spend that half season in the very best shape of my career, thanks in large part to a gung-ho sadist named Brad Andress. As the Tigers' strength coach, this ripped, six foot three, 225-pound moose takes his job very, *very* seriously, kicking our Tiger asses with calisthenics from hell on a daily basis. While we do sit-ups, and stretch, and grunt, and moan, and crack, and swear, Brad and Sparky drink coffee and laugh. We're whipped into better collective shape than any team I've ever been on, and oddly enough, it's smack in the middle of all this healthy activity that I first notice a twinge of pain and a bit of postworkout stiffness in my back. It's nothing like the lightning bolts of agony that'll be shooting up my spine in a few years, but the fuse has officially been lit. At the same time, in a much more aggravating development, my elbow is fucking killing me.

From late June forward, I've got pain and inflammation with every start. I gag down the glorified aspirins trainers wishfully call anti-inflammatories, and I'm iced up like a penguin for *long* stretches of time, but nothing helps. Pitching through the pain, I spiral quickly downhill, losing five in a row, stinking up the field right through the bottom half of July. By August 1, Sparky's shut me down, urging me to rest up, rehab, and let myself heal before we open up a bigger can of worms. Three weeks later, bored to death and dying to get back on the mound, I ignore a tiny bit of residual pain, get my official clearance to pitch, and charge back into action a happy man.

Easing back into the rotation with a couple of short, solid relief outings, I'm back on the starter's hill by August 31. My arm, however, still seems to think we're on the DL. With a couple of no-decisions, a couple of losses, and a couple of outings that raised my season ERA to 4.19, I stumbled, disappointed, through the last part of my inaugural season as a Tiger. Though we ultimately closed out the year at 85–77, a solid ten games back of the front-running/league-smokin' Blue Jays,* and way out of contention, I still wished I could have done more in helping us Tigers win a few September ball games. I'd learned a lot this year, and

---

* Well on their way to becoming World Champions for the second year in a row.

I was genuinely proud of this third-place team. I was fond of my teammates, happy with my manager, and with those things in mind, my own crappy finish felt entirely unacceptable. "Wait'll next year"—easily the lamest rallying cry ever written—was nonetheless repeated ad nauseam as we Tigers all made our getaways for the winter. Oddly, I found myself wishing I could stay.

I loved Detroit. I loved the people, I loved the area, I loved the climate, and to me, Tiger Stadium was just gorgeous. Full of charm, and history, and thick, green turf and style, this magical old place was as far removed from the cold, plastic ugliness of Skydome as a building could get. Walking through the same hallways Ty Cobb called home was about as thrilling as it got. Only Yankee Stadium would ever rank higher with me in terms of sheer, goose-bump-raising thrills. All in all, it should come as no surprise that as the springtime of 1994 rolled in, I was already thinking seriously about buying a house and settling in for the long haul in Motown.

Coming into the 1994 season, I'm feeling great. The elbow's pain free, my adrenaline's running, and with the Tigers making a handful of positive lineup changes, I'm actually kind of optimistic about our chances. Dan Gladden and Rob Deer have both followed up disappointing '93 seasons with '94 retirements, and taking their places are .306-hitting, ex-Torontonian Junior Felix, and any combination of Kirk Gibson, Eric Davis, Milt Cuyler, and Juan Samuel. Each of those solid part-timers will play about thirty-five games in the outfield while Gibby, of course, spends the lion's share of his "off" days at DH. On paper, we look pretty good, and with the solid veteran Tim Belcher now shoring up our fifth-starter spot, I've talked myself into believing we Tigers stand a decent chance of taking our division, or at least sliding into the postseason as the American League's first-ever Wild Card team. But, of course, this being 1994, pettiness, greed, inflexibility, and a seemingly insane work stoppage would soon render all those rose-colored predictions irrelevant.

Still, fully assuming that all the crazy talk about an upcoming strike would just fade away, I was focused once more on enjoying my time in Detroit. Sadly though, very shortly into the season, the same elbow pain that nagged at me through the second half of last season came roaring back, this time bigger and more bad-assed than before. I'd swell up badly after pitching now, getting hammered pretty badly in the process. With that in mind, just three outings into the '94 season, a series of X rays and MRIs reveal a little squadron of bone chips floating around near my elbow. Believe it or not, this is good news.

After surviving one badly blown-out elbow in the minors, any problem this small, this easily detected, and this easily fixable seemed like a gift-wrapped birthday present. I hit the DL smiling this time, and four days later, my old buddy Dr. James Andrews once again slices, dices, and saves my career. Undergoing a routine little operation this genius could have performed standing on his head, I was off the table in what seemed like two minutes. Even more amazing, within two weeks' time, I was ready to throw. The only problem was Sparky wouldn't let me. With my arm and my future at stake, and the Tigers already flopping into the '94 season as a soggy, punchless, pitching-poor mess, Sparky refused to rush me back. Finally, right around Memorial Day, the old man caved, shipping me down to Class A Lakeland, where I could get an inning or two of rehab work under my belt before rejoining the team on June 4.

Back on the mound, though our team was in free fall, I did manage to remain pain free and have some fun. Over the following ten weeks, I tossed five complete games. I picked up my first shutout, and I walked almost *nobody* (at one stretch facing 156 batters without a single free pass). By mid-August, though our team had fallen into the basement, and fans had begun avoiding Tiger Stadium like the plague, our Tigers' locker room was still a supportive, positive, upbeat place. In fact, in its own backward way, that summertime swoon of 1994 was as inspiring a stretch as I'd ever encountered. We Tigers may have been old, and strikeout prone, and broken down with injuries, and saddled with the highest team ERA in baseball, and doomed to finish dead last this year, but with Sparky driving, there would be *no* finger-pointing, *no* self-pity, and no giving up. In fact, by the time the strike hit, we'd even begun a modest winning streak.

But then it was over. With owners and the players' union exhibiting *none* of the guts, teamwork, or character we had flowing all over our last-place Tigers' locker room, major-league baseball shut down for the season in a sea of red tape, injunctions, double-dog dares, and inflexible macho posturing. Don't get me wrong, I completely understood the issues, I sympathized with my union, but I could not for the life of me figure out how anything this stupid could possibly be in the oft-mentioned "best interests of baseball." I was disgusted by the whole mess and thoroughly embarrassed. When the insanity ultimately escalated to the point of cancelling the '94 World Series, I couldn't even *imagine* fans coming back anytime soon. When the replacement players rolled in during the spring of 1995, I was afraid you guys were gone forever.

Pissed off at the whole situation, I spent the first part of that '94 off-season forgetting about baseball entirely while wobbling from *Brauhaus* to *Brauhaus* through a long, fuzzy Oktoberfest tour of Germany. From there, however, back home on my couch, I spent the rest of that winter nestled, depressed and lethargic, beneath a mountain of beer cans and fast-food wrappers. In my mind, baseball was dying, and with that in mind, I didn't exercise at all. Hell, I barely moved. And by the time the assholes at the top finally made peace (sort of) and returned us to work, I was fatter than ever, wheezing, and huffing my way through '95's abbreviated spring training. From day one, my back hurt again— not enough to slow me down too badly, not enough to get me on the table for my first cortisone shot, but that day was now unstoppably approaching.

At the same time, still perfectly happy with my tenure in Detroit, I'd just bought myself a beautiful new house, out in a lush, green suburb of the city. With a big yard and a pool and two fireplaces and a huge, high-tech, dream kitchen, I unpacked with the firm belief that I'd be here for decades. Pitching well, with a team that really seemed to need me, I went into the season secure in my position while cautiously optimistic about our team.

With new president/CEO John McHale at the helm after last season's disappointment, I'd hoped better times were in store for Sparky and crew. Instead, very shortly after being hired, McHale openly began dismantling his team of aging veterans, in favor of fielding a squad of younger, home-grown, significantly cheaper players and "grooming those young men for future greatness." With that in mind, Eric Davis and Kirk Gibson lost their outfield time to twenty-four-year-old Bobby Higginson (season average .224), and twenty-three-year-old Danny Bautista (.203). Starters Tim Belcher and Bill Gullickson were shipped out to make room for twenty-three-year-olds Sean Bergman (7–10, 5.12 ERA) and Felipe Lira (9–13, 4.31 ERA). Thirty-seven-year-old Alan Trammell got benched in favor of twenty-four-year-old Chris Gomez (.223). Later in the season, struggling vet Mike Moore made way for new and improved prospect Jose Lima (3–9, 6.11 ERA). And while some of those guys would go on to have solid major-league careers, it was stunningly, immediately obvious they'd all been rushed, way too fast, to the bigs. As a result, we '95 Tigers flat-out sucked while a bench full of miserable, decommissioned vets quietly sat, counting down the days 'til October. Even Sparky Anderson seemed like somebody'd knocked the wind out of him.

Oddly, even amid the executive-assisted franchise suicide, my own game was booming. With maturity, and experience, and pitching smarts, and good health all finally on my side, I overcame a slow April to ring up a *very* strong first half, which culminated in my first invitation to an All-Star Game. Granted, I was the one mercy pick afforded the league's worst team, but still, just to be on the same field with a lineup packed with guys like Cal Ripken Jr., Randy Johnson, Ken Griffey Jr., Frank Thomas, Kirby Puckett, and legendary closer Lee Smith was a thrilling, truly humbling experience. To paraphrase Groucho, it was hard to buy into any All-Star club that would have someone like me for a member.

Four days later, back in Detroit still riding high on my All-Star cloud, I began a scorching 5–0 streak that would close out my days as a Tiger. At thirty-two years old, with a contract rising above the two million mark, there was no way I was going to fit into Detroit's dirt-cheap, baby-faced future. With that in mind, the team began quietly shopping me to playoff contenders, and when the Cincinnati Reds came calling, offering two very young pitching prospects (C.J. Nitkowski and Dave Tuttle) for one David Wells, the Tigers bit hard. I never even saw it coming.

We'd had an off day, and I was at home, watching *Baseball Tonight,* when all of a sudden I see my name and picture on ESPN in a video-doctored Cincinnati Reds hat. Peter Gammons is telling America that I'd just been traded. I actually remember punching Gammons's face on the screen, just for being the messenger.

"What the fuck is going on here?" I shout at him, royally pissed. For all of the reasons you've been reading about in this chapter, I did *NOT* want to leave Detroit—not at all. I was so bummed that I'd been traded, I literally sat there in my house crying, "You've gotta be kidding me."

But they weren't kidding. Before I'd even unpacked all the moving boxes in the garage of my new Detroit dream house, I was taping them back up and shipping my stuff to Cincinnati, where Davey Johnson and his very good team were rapidly closing in on the postseason. And while I have to admit that the idea of getting myself back into the playoffs was exciting, it didn't make my Detroit good-byes any easier. Sparky, Cecil, Kirk, Trammy, Henneman, Mike Moore, Travis Fryman, Lou Whitaker, every one of those guys wished me good luck the rest of the way, and to a man they all added something along the lines of "I wish I was going with you." An era was ending in Motown. The following season's Tigers would lose an astounding 109 games, and both Kirk Gibson and Sparky Anderson would opt for early retirement. So much for happy endings.

Meanwhile, with the lure of the playoffs calling, and some very good reports on Davey Johnson, I moved on to Cincinnati, hoping to find a clubhouse as comfortable, professional, and supportive as I'd found in Detroit. At the same time, I'm hoping the rumors I've been told about Reds owner Marge Schott will turn out to be untrue. I keep hearing she's cheap, and obnoxious, and overbearing, and bigoted, and drunk, and absolutely clueless about the game of baseball. Heading off to Cincy, I don't believe the hype, opting instead to believe that the stories I've been handed are at best exaggerations of the truth. *Nobody* could be *that* clueless.

Shows you what I know.

ELEVEN

Better Dead Than Reds

The thing I don't like
is when Schottzie II takes a crap
at shortstop, because I might
have to dive in that shit.

—*Barry Larkin*

MIDSUMMER 1995: MARGE SCHOTT'S HOUSE

This woman is killing me. Coming off a ten-game road trip, with one day to rest before starting a twelve-game home stand, the entire Cincinnati Reds roster has been commanded to attend a "team party" thrown at Marge Schott's estate. Nobody wants to go, mostly because none of us can actually stomach the nutty old turd. She *has* to have seen that coming, because right from the beginning, Marge has guaranteed her team's cooperation by threatening to fine any player who no-shows with a $1,000 fine. Suits and ties are required, and that dress code's cursed big-time as the day "off" dawns bright and hot and humid as hell. The cursing intensifies when we actually show up at Marge's place and find out the party's taking place in an outdoor, non-air-conditioned tent.

Nestled on seventy acres, smack in the middle of Cincinnati's way-swanky Indian Hill suburb, Marge's forty-room mansion rises up out of the landscape like some evil queen's fairy-tale castle. Large and dark, a little bit creepy, and bearing some obvious signs of neglect, the place seems like a perfect home for your friendly neighborhood poltergeist. We players aren't allowed inside. Instead, sweating right through our suits inside a plastic tent where it's easily 110 degrees, we're trotted out like prize heifers to meet the Reds' sponsors, suppliers, service providers, media people, and ad sales types. I'd rather be anywhere else on earth.

Giant fans and outdoor air-conditioning units are clearly in place at both ends of the tent, but even with her guests sweltering, Marge never turns them on. Normally, that'd just seem insane, but here it makes perfect sense. Marge Schott and electric bills are a volatile combination. This is a woman who actually shut down Riverfront Stadium's out-of-town scoreboard because the bulbs that light it up waste power, and the service that provides the scores cost her a whopping 350 clams a month.

Meanwhile, sopping and surly, we Reds greet an endless stream of invited guests, fake smiling, photo posing, and ball signing 'til it feels like we're gonna pass out. Outside the tent, one skinny elephant runs endless, miserable laps around the lawn while loaded up with an ever-changing array of kid commuters. Farther out on the grass, a flock of baby goats, sheep, calves, ponies, and llamas lay panting amid the confines of their traveling petting zoo. Inside the tent, their stink is just faintly noticeable above the hors d'oeuvres and human body sweat. I can't take any more. Luckily, teammate Dave Burba's as big a party pooper as me.

Dave's wife, Star, is pregnant, and very quickly, the two of us decide to make her our ticket outta Dodge. Coming up with a foolproof escape plan, the three of us approach the Reds' owner as if she might actually bite us at any moment.

"Hey, Mrs. Schott," Dave says.

"What is it, honey?" Cincinnati Reds fact of life number one: Marge Schott calls *everybody* "honey," or "doll," or "sweets," or "baby." That way she never has to actually remember your name.

"Well, see, my wife, Star, is pregnant, and she's not actually feeling all that well today. So, y'know, we hate to leave your lovely party, but I think we should probably head home and get her into bed. You don't mind, do you?"

"Course not, darlin'."

Star's now doing her best to look believably nauseated, and sensing the opening, I leap. "Yeah, and see, I actually drove Dave and Star here today," I say, lying right through my teeth, "so I'm gonna give them a lift home, then come back here right after that." Two believable lies in one sentence—pretty good batting average.

Marge jiggles the vodka rocks in her glass while taking a big deep drag on her 988th Carlton 120 of the day. "All righty then," she scratches out. "See you back here in a little bit."

"You got it."

Dave and Star and I now literally run to our cars, diving in, and immediately cranking the AC to meat-packing, bronchitis-inducing levels of cool. Together, we tear off her property like Bo and Luke and Daisy Duke in a pair of "General Lees," thrilled with the fact we've beaten her system, at least for today.

Coming into Cincinnati, right at the trading deadline, I'd heard *all* the standard Marge Schott horror stories. The racial slurs, the bizarre behavior, those stories had been around forever, and I just didn't believe 'em. Tall tales, I assumed, urban legends. There's no way in hell that stuff could be true. I mean come on now, would the owner of a major-league baseball franchise actually walk around using the N-word? Could anybody in that position get away with quotes about Hitler like "He was good in the beginning, he just took things too far"? *Nobody* could be *that* offensive. In less than a week, Marge had me rethinking my position.

Right from the start, this woman struck me as unbalanced, often intoxicated, and thoroughly obnoxious. She threw ethnic insults around like they were the most natural thing in the world. Her breath was constantly fragrant with the springtime freshness of tobacco and cheap booze. And as far as I could tell, the woman had absolutely no interest in baseball. Still, through some sort of clouded, impaired, ego-driven judgment, this woman also believed she was absolutely beloved, not only by her players, but also by every single human being in Cincinnati.

Waddling out onto the Astroturf before each home game, Marge would often be clutching a wrinkled plastic Baggie full of the "lucky hair" she'd shaved off her dead dog, Schottzie. She'd then begin accosting her players in mid-warm-up. Halfway through stretching, they'd look up to find Marge standing over them saying, "C'mon, honey, let Schottzie bring you luck," at which point, she'd waggle a big handful of ratty, nasty dead-dog hair all over their uniform. Guys used to hide whenever they saw her coming—except for John Smiley.

"Hi, honeyyyyyyyy," she'd squawk at him. "Come let Schottzie bring you some luck."

"Get . . . the FUCK . . . away from me . . . with that DISGUSTING . . . filthy . . . shit!" John would say it slowly, and carefully, taking great care to make sure each word was filtering completely inside Marge's head.

With Brandon, the little Red machine

"Awww, honey," she'd whine. "Don't be like that. It's just a little hair from my baby. The hair can't bite ya." And with that, she'd let out a phlegmy, rattling, low-octave laugh that would carry all the way to deep center field and instantly just make your skin crawl. It actually sounded a lot like a garbage disposal.

While that kind of stuff should give you *some* idea of just exactly how that Cincinnati Reds franchise went from "classy front-running dynasty" to "laughingstock" during that woman's twelve-year ownership run, it is by no means the whole story. For that we've gotta talk nickels and dimes.

This woman pinched pennies so hard she gave Abe Lincoln headaches. Need a couple of extra Reds caps, or socks, or T-shirts, or wristbands? The old broad would charge you for them. Honest to God. She didn't even let the equipment managers stockpile them in the locker room. Y'know, you'd ask for like six hats, and these guys would have to go up to Marge's office, get her okay, then get the hats, then hand them over while Marge wrote out a bill for you. It was unheard of. It was insane. It was Marge. Even worse, we 1995 Reds were the only team in baseball that traveled on commercial flights.

Remember all that good stuff I was telling you about the charter jets, and the comfortable seats, and the good food, and the new movies? Well, forget it all. Here in 1995, *this* team flies Pan Am, or United, or whatever airline offers the old woman the cheapest group discount. On Schott-approved getaway days, our entire Reds team would pack up, leave the ballpark, get on a bus, drive out to the airport, lug our bags through check-in, then sit around the airport for an hour or two (or more) waiting to board a plane. Madness. It was enough to make me miss the "good old days" at Canadian customs.

We '95 Reds were the only team in baseball without video equipment to use in monitoring our pitching mechanics, or our swings at the plate. Too expensive. Our locker room exercise equipment was ridiculously antiquated, like something out of an old Vic Tanny salon. Marge actually complained out loud about her team using too many balls in a game. She routinely gathered up the Reds' broken, game-used bats and had them sold as souvenirs. Just as routinely, the woman's photo had a place of honor in the Reds' locker room urinals.

This was a woman who didn't trust players' accountants to take the taxes out of their checks, so she did it herself. She taxed our meal money too. Even worse, this woman had her underlings keep a detailed record of every single phone call that went into or out of the Reds' locker room. She hated the idea of paying for her players' long-distance calls. Personal calls ranked even higher on her shit list, but worst of all, she hated when *women* got on the phone with her players.

"Cutesy-poos" is what she called 'em. Groupies, blind dates, casual friends, girlfriends, even live-ins. It drove that woman nuts to think that her players might actually have normal (and/or not-so-normal) adult sexual relations outside the formal confines of marriage. Guys tell me stories about how she had the team videotaped getting on and off planes to make sure there was no "monkey business" going on. They tell me (though I'm not sure I believe them) that every call to the dugout was recorded, its subject matter logged by Schott spies. When they warn me to expect that a lot of my fan mail will arrive mysteriously pre-opened, sure enough, a solid percentage shows up in just that condition.

Can I *prove* this woman was behind *all* of that? Of course not. Honestly, most of my time in that town was spent avoiding the old bag, so I never got all that up close and personal with her everyday habits (thank Christ). Still, if it walks like a duck, and quacks like a duck . . . it seems logical to go with the "it's a duck" hypothesis. To me, the woman always just seemed like ten pounds of cuckoo in a four-pound clock.

On the other side of the coin, Reds' general manager Jim Bowden was a rare bird in baseball, a straight-shooting, honest, top executive with a real love of the game. He did a good job too. Even smack in the middle of the day-to-day chaos Marge wrought, and handcuffed by the old woman's woefully, laughably, ridiculously underfunded and underloved minor-league system, Bowden *somehow* managed to build a winner for Cincinnati. In total, the Reds payroll for that 1995 season rang in at just $37 million, but we still played .590 ball, taking the NL Central by nine games. Now *that's* cost effective.

Only two guys on this team would hit more than twenty home runs for the season. Only one would hit .300. We'd have no twenty-game winners. None of that mattered. None of us cared. Without big names or a lot of press, we '95 Reds won our games as a band of hard-playing, dirt-eating, overachieving hard-asses. We never gave up. We played as a team. We battled relentlessly. We gave 110 percent every single day. And while I *know* I just spit out four of the most overused clichés in the history of baseball, they're nonetheless accurate in painting a picture of this tough, driven, undeniably blue-collar team.

With Benito Santiago behind the plate, Hal Morris at first, Bret Boone at second, Jeff Branson at third, and an outfield made up of Ron Gant, Jerome Walton, and Reggie Sanders, we were *very* solid, if not flashy, or handsome, or dripping with celebrity. Our one bona fide superstar was Barry Larkin. Rolling like a freight train through the finest year of his career, Barry hit .319. He stole 51 bases, and in the field he was a human vacuum cleaner, just sucking up ground balls on either side with superhuman dives and picks and impossible fireballing rockets to first that routinely broke the lacing in Hal Morris's glove. At season's end the man will win the Gold Glove at short, and he'll be named the National League MVP to boot. He'll deserve 'em both.

On the mound, Jose Rijo had been solidly labeled the Reds' ace until his arm exploded in July, but in his absence, lefty Pete Schourek (another career-year guy) clearly deserved to inherit that crown. After four soggy seasons with the

New York Mets, and one here in Ohio, Pete's turned his stuff around this year to become nearly unhittable. He'll be 18–7 by season's end, with a 3.22 ERA. Behind him, John Smiley's throwing yet another of his standard terrific seasons, and behind Smiley, Mark Portugal's tossing a little better than .500. Kevin Jarvis and Tim Pugh both spot start through the season as our number five guys, going a combined 9–9 for the year. Again, we're a reliable, respectable, nonglittering bunch. We're Ford trucks as opposed to Ferraris. As for my own performance, it seems that this *particular* pickup somehow made a wrong turn on the way to Cincinnati and wound up back on the "roller coaster" exit.

Sliding into a brand-new league, full of brand-new batters, and a brand-new strike zone that seems to run smaller and tighter than the AL umpires' version, I follow up my scorching 11–3 Detroit record with a couple of wobbly, unsure outings against the Mets and Florida Marlins. By "start three," though, I've adjusted, I'm comfortable, and I'm back with guns blazing, winning three in a row, with complete game victories a couple of times over. That's when my back started hurting . . . bad.

I wince through four innings against the Pirates, getting lit up for eight hits and four runs. I then spend the next five days stretching, twisting, and getting massaged. Feeling *much* better, I go back to the mound against the Colorado Rockies, where I stiffen up again, almost immediately. I've got the needle inside me twenty-four hours later—and after the sting, my back works great. My next start rolls in as a complete-game four-hitter against the Padres, and I won't throw another flat-out bad outing all season. Cortisone becomes my new best friend.

Meanwhile, tucked away in the corner of our dugout, one huge reason for the Reds' playoff run sits alone, like some middle-aged, computer nerd, gleefully poking through a pile of game-specific cyber-analysis while simultaneously plotting double and triple lineup switches, and calculating the statistical percentages of today's lefty-righty matchups in his head. You can hear the gears turning in there. Smoke billows from his ears. He's Davey Johnson, and despite the fact the man gives off the laid-back, easy-going demeanor of any main character at Disneyland's Country Bears Jamboree, make no mistake—inside that skull, Davey's a type A superachiever roaring through every game with his accelerator floored. He just makes it *look* easy.

Davey plays a lot of golf, and by that I mean a LOT of golf. At home, on road trips, if it's not pouring, Davey's gonna get in a solid nine, or twelve, or eighteen holes. At the same time, in major-league ballparks all over the country, other managers are suited up, wandering around their locker rooms, tinkering with lineup possibilities, chatting up beat writers, drinking seven or eight gallons of coffee, reading the local papers, poking around the bat racks, and in general *looking* busy. Davey don't play that. To Davey, results are a lot more important than appearances, and *nobody* wins more ball games than Mr. Johnson.

Got a 7:35 night game at home? Davey might roll in somewhere around 5:00, just in time to review the mountains of stats and analysis he's got clogging the arteries of his computer. At that point, confident and secure about the night's game plan, he hits the field to watch a little batting practice. Shaking hands, slapping backs, giving encouraging, positive messages to all his players (both slumping and streaking), it's easy to see how this guy took a very young, very green, very talented bunch of New York Mets and turned them into the juggernaut of 1986. He builds confidence. He instills pride. He monitors his players closely, huddling with them whenever and wherever he feels their concentration might be slipping. He allows pitchers to work through their own jams. He's not a yeller. He's not a disciplinarian. He simply trusts his players to care about winning every bit as much as he does.

Marge Schott can't stand him.

With typically demented logic, Marge has pissed and moaned and disliked Davey ever since she hired him in 1994, in large part because that sinful heathen, Davey, actually chose to live with his girlfriend before marrying her. I kid you not. I'm told Marge also hates Davey's golf-friendly work ethic, and his supposedly arrogant, egotistical demeanor. The fact that this man took her underfunded, mediocre Reds to the top of the standings in 1994 makes no difference to Marge. She wants Davey out, and in one of the most bizarre front-office moves in baseball history, she's not only told Davey he won't be back in 1996, but she's also asked him to spend the 1995 season grooming bench coach Ray Knight for the job next year.

How nutty is that?

People wonder how Davey could stay with the team after essentially being fired on the layaway plan, but his attitude was always: "Why quit? Why not stick it out? The Reds have a chance to take the NL Central this year. Why bail?" Sitting at the end of our bench like some big, superintelligent basset hound, Davey quietly goes about the business of winning while simultaneously making his disapproving team owner look dumber with each successive W.

Still, even with all the success, there are those days where Davey's relentless player moves, lefty-righty switches, and lineup shuffling can make you absolutely nuts. Worst for me was September 24, 1995, during a day game in

Philadelphia against the Phillies. I'm on the mound, and though I'm generally a lot sharper during night games than afternooners, my stuff today is unbelievably sharp. The sweeping curve seems bigger and more accurate than usual. The pop on the fastball's surprising even me, and by the time we're five innings into this sucker, it's clear that I may even be flirting with a no-no. I'm perfect through five, then six, at which point, though the Reds are riding a five-run lead, Davey begins totally fucking with the players behind me—and my head.

You don't mess with a no-hitter. You don't talk about it, you don't joke about it, and you never *ever* do *anything* on the field that could conceivably put the whammy on whatever cosmic good vibes may be shepherding your pitcher toward perfection.* Again, Davey don't play that. During the fifth and sixth innings, with pinch hitters, pinch runners, and sweeping positional rearrangements flying off his manager's clipboard, five of the eight position players behind me end up getting shifted around the field and/or benched in favor of subs. This is unheard of. This is nuts.

Charlie Hayes singles off me almost immediately. Fuming on the mound now, I point the finger of blame directly at Davey (as opposed to my own distracted/crappy curve), and I end up losing focus just long enough to give up two more hits, and one run. Running back to the dugout, I'm wild-eyed now. Fire may actually have been leaping out of my nose. Finding Davey at the bottom step of the dugout, I'm plagued by temporary insanity. Tossing my hat to the floor, I head-butt that guy as hard as I possibly can. And right away, I see stars. I know the man's got a reputation for being hardheaded, but I swear to God, Davey Johnson's skull may actually be made of granite. Post-butt, I'm wobbling, shaky, scared that I may actually pass out.

"What the fuck are you doin'?" Davey asks, seeming not the least bit phased by the onslaught of bone on his rock hard melon.

"You don't EVER mess with the lineup during a no-hitter! That's a cardinal rule, dude! You don't do it!"

"Whatever . . . ," Davey says back, laughing now. "You okay?"

"Yeah, I think so," I reply, smiling at the middle Davey of three while silently making a mental note never to head-butt that man again. It's actually a pretty good testament to Davey's temperament that he was able to laugh off what could easily have gone down as the beginning of a *really* bad relationship.

---

* Even Tommy Kamphonik knows better than that.

Laughing over that story, and the subsequent lump on my forehead, for weeks after the fact, Davey and I actually grew closer than ever.

By the time the 1995 regular season is over, we Reds have run away with the NL Central, leaving the Houston Astros sucking our dust, nine games back. The division title sends us to Los Angeles, where we'll square off against the heavily favored Dodgers in the NLDS. With Ramon Martinez, Ismael Valdes, and Rookie-of-the-Year-to-be Hideo Nomo, at the top of L.A.'s rotation, every baseball writer in the country predicts that our Reds' bats are about to go limp. They're all wrong. First inning, first game, we Reds explode for four runs on our way to an easy 7–2 victory.

Pete Schourek is fantastic for us, scattering just five hits over seven innings, while *our* hitters run amok. All through Chavez Ravine, the silence is deafening, with "die-hard" Dodger fans packing up their cell phones and crudités, and heading for the freeway by the top of the fifth. Whatever psychological edge the Dodgers may have had coming into this thing gets wiped out in less than an hour.

Twenty-four hours later, though John Smiley's struggling, working his "B–" stuff against Ismael Valdes, we Reds steal another quick victory and fly out of town. Now down two games to zip, the Dodgers join us back to Riverfront looking listless and flat. Smelling blood, we Reds have no mercy, opening up a Game 3 can of whup-ass while flat-out destroying that team 10–1.

On the mound, your author is having the time of his life. With our team confidence sky-high, and my stuff stronger than ever, I'm flying. I've got my big game. I've got my start. I even get a hit. My chronic case of "gimmetheballitis" has *never* been this joyfully treated. Another round of champagne-squirting target practice follows. This time Dave Burba takes it in the gut.

One day later, when the Braves take a 10–4 victory over the Rockies, we've got ourselves a Championship Series opponent. Once again, we're the underdogs, but though the Braves' bats are on fire right now, our Reds lineup is even hotter. This series is gonna be a real slobber-knocker, one of those classic situations where good pitching is gonna have to rise to the occasion and cancel out good hitting. Over the course of the next week, that's exactly what happens. There's just one problem: it's the Braves' good pitching that flattens the Reds' good hitting. With Tom Glavine, John Smoltz, Greg Maddux, and Steve Avery lined up back-to-back-to-back-to-back, we Reds are just plain overmatched.

Coming into Game 1, at home in Riverfront, before an astonishingly small crowd of thirty-six thousand and change, Pete Schourek goes to the mound against Tom Glavine, and while both guys toss absolute gems, we end up losing a 2–1, 11-inning heartbreaker.

One day later, we dive into extra innings again, this time locked up at 2–2. John Smoltz and John Smiley have both been removed, and as we go to the tenth, regular-season-starter Mark Portugal is on in relief. Pitching out of the pen for the first time in his career, Mark warms up quickly, then looks uncomfortable on the mound as the Braves quickly load up the bases. He stays in the game. Far *FAR* removed from the Captain Hooking style of Williams, Gaston, and Anderson, Davey's "lingering at the dance" is now driving me every bit as crazy.

I can feel my teeth gritting as Portugal's 0–2 curve skitters past Santiago's glove, and the Braves take a 3–2 lead. Javy Lopez comes to the plate. Portugal stays in the game. Lopez drills a fastball straight down the left-field line. Please go foul, I'm thinking. Please go foul.

But it doesn't. Javy's fly ball stays fair by maybe three inches and flops down into the bullpen for a three-run homer. We're fucked. Mark Wohlers shuts us down in the bottom of the tenth, and we head for Atlanta down two games to squat. After a travel day off, it's my turn in the barrel.

Fulton County Stadium: they're at it already. Even as the opening lineups are being announced, the tomahawk choppers are "Wo-Wo-Wo-ing" at full force. With their team halfway to another National League Championship, they're smelling blood. It's my job to shut them up, which I do, by shutting their team *out*, through the first five innings of play. Unfortunately, Greg Maddux does the same to us Reds, and that makes my one big mistake of the game all the more glaring.

Bottom of the sixth, with one out, Fred McGriff tags me for a double, and I follow that up with a semi-intentional walk to the blazing hot Mike Devereaux. With two men on base, I've now got the Braves backup catcher Charlie O'Brien at the plate. A notoriously lousy hitter, O'Brien has long stretches where he can't hit a beach ball with a tree trunk. With that in mind, I'm confident I can beat him for a nice, inning-ending grounder, or maybe a sweet little K. I pitch him in, I fire smoke at him, I get ahead in the count, and yet somehow I can't quite swat this gnat. O'Brien fouls off pitch after pitch, keeping himself alive at the plate for the better part of a month. Finally, with one last blast of heat, I launch the pitch I'm sure will put this guy to bed once and for all.

The guy hits it 440 feet. Standing there on the mound like Charlie Brown, it's all I can do not to shout Good grief! One of the worst hitters in the National

League has now just beaten me, on *my* big game stage, in front of a national TV audience. Pissed as I am, I've got to hand it to the man. He got me fair and square. Down 3–0 now, we'll go on to lose this sucker 5–2. Shuffling back to our locker room, it's time to start praying for a miracle.

No dice. Steve Avery starts Game 4 for the Braves, and though he's been struggling all season long, today he's on top of the world, ultimately tossing six innings and allowing just two Reds hits. And though on our side, Pete Schourek pitches yet another great game, giving up just one run over six strong innings of work, it's just not good enough to counter Avery's classic. Though the Braves ultimately added another five runs to their slaughter in the seventh, that offensive landslide was entirely unnecessary. We lose big, 6–1. Season over. *Never* before had that goddamned "tomahawk chop" been quite so maddening.

Closing out the season, manager-in-waiting Ray Knight pulls me aside to talk contract. With one year left on my current deal, Ray's looking to get a handle on what it might take to keep me in Cincinnati for the long haul. Moving and talking at roughly six times the speed of Davey, Ray's positive and upbeat, and he talks about how he's "committed as hell" to keeping me as part of his rotation. He asks what I think is a fair price for extending my deal, and I tell him flat-out. I wanted three years at $15 million. With my current salary still bearing the damage of being dumped by Toronto (I stood at just over $2 million in 1995), the numbers I laid out would put me in the neighborhood of guys like John Smiley, Ken Hill, Doug Drabek, Jimmy Key, and Tom Glavine. Far from reaching for the stars, I'm really just looking for a fair deal.

"No problem!" Ray chirps. "That should be just fine. Looks like we're gonna be in business for a long time." We shake hands, smiling. "Looking forward to it," I reply.

Ain't gonna happen.

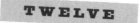
Baltimore Chops

I've got it!
I've got it! I've . . . oops.

—*Jeffrey Maier, rotten twelve-year-old
kid from New Jersey*

CHRISTMAS 1995: WAIMEA BAY, HAWAII

Steeped in sunshine, roast pig, and lots and lots of mai tais, I lounge through late December enjoying the good life and a *very Mele Kalikimaka* on Oahu's gorgeous north shore. With me is my girlfriend (and future wife), Nina, my old Ocean Beach buddy/Chicago front man Jason Scheff, his wife, and their two kids. Playing on the beach for two weeks straight, every single one of us is now blissfully sunburned, waterlogged, and hula trained (you'd be amazed how good I am). With no phones at the resort, and our cells back home on the mainland, we're also completely, consciously, and joyfully out of touch with the real world back home.

Sitting down to a post-Christmas breakfast buffet where it seems like all the fruit and flowers on earth have been miraculously dumped into this one dining room, I'm scarfing through a mango while Jason flips through the first newspaper either one of us has picked up in a week. Moments later, I'm face first in a pineapple boat when I hear him shout, "Oh my God!"

"What?" I shout back, sticky-faced.

"Dude!" Jason says. "You got traded!"

I look at Jason, quickly decide he's yanking my chain, and with one curt "Yeah, right" I'm back in my fruit boat.

"No, dude. I'm not kidding," he says, handing me the paper.

I roll my eyes at him and take the bait—but Jason's not kidding. There, right in the middle of *USA Today*, is my picture. I *have* been traded, this time to the Baltimore Orioles, where Davey Johnson's been hired as manager for the 1996 season. Somehow, over the course of the past three months, Ray Knight's "No problem . . . looks like we're gonna be in business for a long time" has been bitch-slapped by Marge Schott's "Sorry, honey, he's not worth that kind of money." Clearly, with no *real* intention of signing me to any sort of contract extension, the Reds have decided to punt, trading my ass out of town while they still have a chance to get something back.

Scanning the article, I'm quickly aggravated to find that on the open market, David Wells is apparently worth just one journeyman outfielder and an iffy, low-level, minor-league prospect. It's a head scratcher. Even when you factor in Marge Schott's shortsighted salary dumping, this deal makes no sense. I mean, my God, the woman's Saint Bernard would have shit on this one. That's when the lightbulb goes on over my head. That's when I realized that even though it takes a very special man to screw Marge Schott, the Orioles now had two guys up to the task.

First, there's Davey Johnson. Scooped up by Baltimore just days after the Reds were dumb enough to let him go, Davey's always been a straight shooter, and a David Wells fan, and it makes perfect sense that he'd be pulling strings to get me back onto his mound. Second, Pat Gillick's now GM in Baltimore, and despite having the sincerity and fashion sense of your average television evangelist, the man is a *remarkably* talented dealmaker. The man could sell ice cubes to Eskimos. With those factors in place, and those two guys conniving to back door me out of Cincinnati, the Reds' monumentally bad trade suddenly makes a lot more sense.

Still, with Gillick grandstanding in the press about how *he's* the man responsible for bringing me to the Orioles (as opposed to Davey), the aroma of his bullshit wafts all the way to Hawaii. Quickly I recall just how easily this man gets on my last nerve, even at a distance of 4,850 miles. Honestly, though I'm happy to be heading for Baltimore, and thrilled with the idea of reuniting with Davey, I know for a fact that I'm gonna have trouble being anywhere near Pat Gillick. Repeatedly jerking me into and out of his bullpen, showing no faith, and no loyalty, and no interest in me for six years in Toronto, this guy very nearly managed to run me out of baseball. By late 1995, I'd survived nine seasons in the big leagues, and flourished and succeeded in *spite* of this guy . . . not *because* of him. With that in mind, you can understand how his showboating over my trade gets my blood boiling fast. Heading into Baltimore, it is my solemn vow that should the man even come close to uttering the prase "weigh-in" within two hundred feet of me, I *am* gonna shove a medical scale right up his ass.

Still, GM notwithstanding, the Orioles are shaping up to be one helluva team, thanks in large part to the no-holds-barred pissing contest currently being waged between Orioles' zillionaire owner Peter Angelos, and the Yankees' zillionaire owner George Steinbrenner. With off-season trades and free-agent signings, and payrolls skyrocketing past the (then unheard of) $50 million mark, the Orioles and Yankees are each hell-bent on becoming alpha dog in the 1996 American League East. All moves considered, Baltimore's taken the preseason lead.

Since November, the Yankees have added David Cone, Tino Martinez, Jeff Nelson, Tim Raines, Joe Girardi, Mariano Duncan, and Kenny Rogers to their already impressive roster. On the flip side, they've also hired a new manager, who immediately starts the local media predicting gloom and doom and the end of the world as the Yankees know it. With a lifetime managerial record of 894–1003, Joe Torre comes home to New York amid a tidal wave of negative press. Branded as "Clueless Joe" by a local tabloid, Joe's labeled the one "clear mistake" of an otherwise awesome Yankees off-season. It gets me excited. If Joe's really *that* bad, the Birds have got the division all but locked. Obviously that wasn't the case.

Meanwhile, three hundred miles down the road, the Orioles have countered, matched, and even outdone the Yankees, move for move, by consciously pulling in a truckload of proven winners from all over the major leagues. Davey Johnson (with a World Series victory, an NL pennant, and a lifetime managerial record of 799–589 under his belt) arrives to manage the team; Roberto Alomar takes over at second base; Randy Myers and Roger McDowell (both hand plucked from Davey's mid-1980s Mets dynasty) move into the bullpen. B.J. Surhoff comes to town off a .320 season in Milwaukee. Former Braves Mike Deveraux and Kent Mercker are both used to winning division titles every single year. And that leaves me. With a World Series ring on one finger, an All-Star appearance, and solid performances in last year's NL playoffs, I'm slowly but surely gaining a reputation as your "go-to guy" in big-game situations. Together, along with lock Hall of Famers Rafael Palmeiro at first, and Cal Ripken Jr. at shortstop, we O's seem fully capable of stomping a mud hole in those '96 Yankees and any other team stupid enough to get in our way.

Getting things backward as usual (© *1966 Tadder/Baltimore*)

Right out of the gate, we Birds start the season 11–2, and with the wind filling our sails, our chests puffed, and our egos soaring, we quickly lose ten of our next twelve. "Shake it off!" we shout to one another. "We just have to go out there every day and play the way we know we're capable of playing." We're lying. We have absolutely *no* idea what the hell's gone wrong, and with no idea how to right the ship, we've been reduced to shooting empty, asinine, meaningless clichés across the locker room at one another. Up in the owner's box, Peter Angelos is fuming already. There are rumors he feels the team's undisciplined, unfocused, and sloppy; and that he thinks Davey's too soft. Angelos is a disciplinary stickler, micromanaging to the point of having his sons scout batting practice prior to home games, just to make sure everyone's game socks and the T-shirts under our jerseys are all regulation black. Y'know, we've got limp bats, and a pitching staff that's stumbling big-time, but this guy's worried that our socks and underwear don't match. It's amazing to think that someone so rich can't buy himself a clue. Note to team owner: (1) open legs; (2) remove head from own ass.

Personally, my 1996 gets under way just fine, with two victories, a solid no-decision, and a complete game in my first three starts. Feeling great on the mound, I give up just four earned runs over my first twenty-four innings pitched . . . and that's exactly when my big toe exploded. I had no idea what caused it, no recollection of having bumped or bruised or twisted the ugly-ass digit, but my GOD that little fucker hurt. I just kind of woke up one morning, stepped out of bed, took one stride toward the bathroom, and ended up giving a high, falsetto scream, like a six-year-old girl, flopping to the floor, grabbing my left big toe, and squeezing . . . which actually just made the pain about three times worse.

The toe wasn't swollen, there was no broken skin, but the whole thing was a sort of nasty, raspberry reddish purple mess. Gobbling Advil and hobbling off to the stadium, I showed it to a pair of Orioles' team trainers, one of whom actually said "Ewwwwwwwwwwwww!" "What the hell is that?" they wondered. "Did you maybe stub it on something?" At first glance, they were as clueless as I was. Prescribing rest, elevation, ice, and more Advil, these guys assured me that if I took it easy, and stayed off the aching dog, I'd more than likely be good as new in a day or two. With strict orders to lay in bed, eat room service, and do absolutely nothing, I bit the bullet and followed my doctors' couch-potato orders to the letter. Three days later I hit the mound at Arlington Stadium, with a toe that was *still* on fire, then limped (literally) through an absolutely horrendous start. Entirely incapable of getting comfortable on the mound, I ended up getting shelled for nine hits and six earned runs in just over four innings of work. Now I was pissed.

More ice. More elevation. More Advil. More room service. More assurances that this thing should blow over very soon. Five days later, now pitching off a cleat full of molten lava . . . I get clobbered even worse. Clearly unable to pitch in this condition, I now miss three starts, waiting for the toe to stop murdering me. Finally, when I can no longer even lay a bedsheet over the motherfucker without wincing in pain, my tiny sliver of patience gets tossed in favor of pure, unadulterated rage. It feels good. It feels right. I'm done with reasonable, rational behavior.

Blindsiding the trainers and doctors with an unscheduled visit/tirade, I bounce off their walls, demanding a *real* answer as to what the hell's wrong with my foot. Medical tests are run, we take an MRI and X rays, and the following morning I learn I have "the gout." The gout? What the hell? All I know about gout is that Benjamin Franklin had it during the Continental Congress of 1789. It's an antique disease, isn't it? Like dropsy, or the plague, or trouble with your lumbago. "What are you people smoking?" I remember asking the docs. And then I got the lecture.

"Gout is a painful inflammation of the joints, brought on by a failure of the metabolic process, which results in an excessive buildup of uric acid in the blood."

"In English, please?"

"Simple. If you're prone to this thing, eating or drinking too much of the wrong things can and will cause *exactly* the symptoms you're suffering now. Little needlelike crystals of uric acid can form in the joints and—"

"Exactly what 'wrong things' are we talking about here?"

"Foods high in purine, like dried beans and peas?"

"No."

"Sardines?"

"No."

"Liver?"

"Hell, no."

"Organ meats?"

"Fuck, no."

"And alcohol?"

"Hey! Look at the time! Why don't you just give me some pills, and we can all be on our way."

Two naproxen later, I'm actually feeling a little better. Muscle-bound little anti-inflammatories, these babies *work*. Within forty-eight hours, I'm feeling a lot better and tossing seven innings of four-hit ball against the California Angels, giving up just one earned run while leveling my record at 3–3. I'm back! From there, with the toe problem put behind me once and for all, I hit the mound feeling great and proceed to spend exactly one month rolling through a spectacular run of . . . flat-out ass-sucking. From May 25 to June 25, I go 1–4, with only a pair of lucky no-decisions keeping me away from 1–6. I lose to the A's 6–3. I lose to the Tigers 8–3. I lose to the Angels 10–3. I give up at least eight hits in every one of those outings. Why? What the hell are you asking *me* for?

Honestly, if there was *any* away to objectively and effectively scrape down to the root cause of a slump, we'd *all* be Hall of Famers. You too. Pitchers, batters, the bad times hit us all with equal mystery. We *try* to figure 'em out. We try to end the run early. We try consulting coaches and teammates, and even family members for their input, but in the end, ninety-nine times out of a hundred, the slump eventually just ends up rolling out as mysteriously as it rolled in. Could my toe problems have messed up my mechanics? Sure. Could my three missed starts have messed up my focus? Sure. Could an ex-girlfriend have slapped a voodoo curse on my ass? Your guess is as good as mine. All I knew was that as we approached July 1, one year removed from being knighted as an official major-league All-Star, I was now 4–7 with an ERA just shy of 6.00. Oddly enough, those stats fit right in with the rest of the Birds '96 pitching staff.

With Mike Mussina as resident ace, followed by Scotty Erickson, Rocky Coppinger, me, and Kent Mercker, there's not one of us with an ERA under five. Mussina's stuff is up, Scotty's walking guys around the bases, Coppinger's getting shelled, and Mercker's a flat-out bust. With a small muscle tear in his shoulder, he's become a fastball pitcher with the world's worst fastball. As a result, by late June, he's 3–6 with an ERA of almost 7.50. Pat Dobson, the hardest-working pitching coach in baseball this year, has been running around the clubhouse putting out fires for months. With disasters exploding from every starter in his rotation, and pea-soup-thick tension in the air, the man deserves a medal simply for not murdering any of us.

There was only one pitcher who seemed to be consistently on throughout the season, and he was in the bullpen: Randy Myers. Randy Myers wasn't a good closer . . . he was *great*, and like *all* great closers, he was also *completely* off his rocker. In fact, even by "crazy reliever" standards, Myers was cuckoo. Never settling for the simple, tried-and-true classics of deranged closer behavior, Randy blew off hot foots, and streaking, and shaving-cream attacks in favor of *much* weirder game. Stacked up in Randy's locker, and tucked away behind a stack of old *Soldier of Fortune* magazines, you'd generally find his cache of large, nasty-looking smoke grenades. Behind *them*, you'd find a collection of *very* large, *very* sharp machetes. Knives, bows, arrows, slingshots, M-80s—the man was very proudly loaded for bear . . . and/or teammates at all times.* And now, an electric cattle prod enters the story.

Receiving this sucker through the mail one afternoon, Randy danced around the Orioles' clubhouse like some *really* demented kid on Christmas morning. Giant smile beaming, Randy couldn't help but experiment with his brand-new toy. Repeatedly blasting a *really* nasty-looking blue flame from the end of the prod (while laughing maniacally), Randy ran around for the better part of an hour, shocking anything and everything that caught his eye. Doorknobs, urinal handles, towel racks, my keys, Scotty Erickson's bracelet, Davey Johnson's big metal desk, *everything* was fair game, including one slow-moving clubhouse kid who took a big blue *ZAP*, right in the ass. This was too crazy. This was too scary. This was a disaster waiting to happen.

It didn't wait long. All through that night's game, Randy sat on the bench, alone, wide-eyed, gears clearly turning inside his head. Three hours later, back in the locker room, while most guys were chowing down and shmoozing the press, Randy was at his locker, trying and failing to conceal a big, evil grin. My stomach tightened. My Spidey-sense tingled. Something was definitely up. Never before have I stripped down and run for the showers so quickly.

Five minutes later, lathered up and bullshitting at full speed with fellow pitcher/fellow sudser Alan Mills, I'm suddenly thrown face first into a scene from *Psycho*. From out of nowhere, a fully clothed Randy Myers leaps into the showers, cattle prod in hand, and lunges toward me.

"HAAAAAAAAAAAAAAAA!!!!!!" he screams.

"AAAAAAAAAUGHHHHHH!!!!!!" I scream back, diving for my life and eluding Randy's zapper.

"What the fuck is that?" asks Alan Mills, shampoo obscuring his ability to avoid his own impending doom. "I just—ARRRRRRRRRRGGGH!!!!!"

A GIANT blue flame shoots from Randy's zapper. Mills goes down hard, then gets up ready to kill. Myers runs back into the clubhouse now as a naked, wet, still half-soapy Millsy gives chase, vowing to kill Myers, then falling dead into the buffet table as an entire locker room full of Orioles laughs their asses off.

■ ■ ■ ■ ■

* Myers would ultimately lose his entire weapons stash on a night when President Bill Clinton decided to visit us Birds in the locker room. Sweeping into the clubhouse with a pair of highly trained police dogs, a large squad of black-suited Secret Service types were quickly dragged to Randy's locker. Everything was confiscated, and though Myers protested loudly about having his civil rights violated, he never did get most of his weird little arsenal back.

MANAGEMENT, HOWEVER, IS NOT LAUGHING. ANGELOS AND GILLICK are now grumbling loudly. Having spent $50 million on a ready-made, instant pennant winner, there was no way those guys were gonna suffer a flat, under-achieving ball club gracefully. With that in mind, Angelos fumes in the owner's box while Gillick is quoted in the press complaining, "We haven't played well all year. In fact, we've played terrible."* As much as it grates on me to see him venting, in public, in black and white, I can't help but agree with the guy on this one. From top to bottom, we Birds *have* been "terrible," and in time-honored baseball tradition, it's not long before the finger-pointing starts.

Slowly but surely, rumors start circulating through the clubhouse and then through the press that *my* problem is I'm not a gamer, that I give up on the mound, and that while I seem to care an awful lot about nightlife and drinking, I don't care enough about winning baseball games . . . my systolic rises fast. "What the hell?" NOTHING could be further from the truth. NOTHING could be quite so infuriating. I mean really, why not suggest that I'm struggling because I'm currently in the middle of sex-change hormone therapy? Or maybe I'm worn out from my secret romance with Janet Jackson. Either of those theories would be *at least* as plausible as the "Wells doesn't want to compete" bullshit.

When over the next few days Davey Johnson and Pat Dobson each pull me aside to "chat" about my "commitment on the mound," I smell a rat. Suppressing the immediate urge to gift Davey with another head butt, I instead begin speculating that the "message" Davey and Dobson were sending may in fact have filtered down from the top and my beloved GM, Pat Gillick. That conclusion saves Davey a lump but spurs a major flare-up just hours later.

Mussina, Erickson, Mercker, Coppinger, Myers, McDowell, and a handful of other bullpen guys are gathering with me in the Camden Yards clubhouse for a pitchers' meeting, and with the way things have been going this season, the mood is understandably tense. Though we're still a couple of games above .500 and holding down second place in the AL East, the Yankees are pulling away. Now, with a road trip looming and six games with the Bombers fast approaching, we're going over batters and tendencies with more than our usual share of intensity. That's when Pat Gillick walks in.

We go quiet as the man grabs a chair, slides it across the floor, and sits down smack in the middle of our meeting. That's all it took.

---

* Murray Chass, "Baseball Notebook: Oriole Starters' Horrendous Form Has Foes Smiling (and Hitting)." *New York Times,* June 23, 1996.

"What are you doing?" I asked him, veins more than likely throbbing in my neck. Steam more than likely spouting from my nostrils.

"What I'm doing," he said, smirking, "is sitting in on a meeting of my pitchers."

I said, "No you're not. Get the fuck out of here!"

"Now, wait . . . see."

"Shhh! I don't wanna hear that. *You're* not in here. *You* don't belong in here. Get out! We don't want you in here!"

Gillick can't believe it. His eyes go wide. His face goes bright red. His mouth hangs open. He slides his chair back across the floor, exiting in silence as fifteen pitchers and one pitching coach all bite the insides of their mouths in a desperate, doomed attempt not to laugh. "Now then, gentlemen," I say, "where were we before being so rudely interrupted?" Twenty minutes of giggling follows, wherein everybody does their own personal impersonation of Gillick, and none of us talk pitching at all.

Hours later, in a development that surprises absolutely no one, I hear that Gillick is once again looking to dump me. The only real shocker is that *this* time around, Pat apparently wants Bobby Bonilla run out of town on the same rail. Bobby Bo's been hassling with Davey all season long, and my best guess is that Pat simply wants his two biggest "assholes" out of the Orioles' locker room . . . now.

Here's the deal. All over baseball, you'll find guys who've spent the better parts of their careers being falsely portrayed by the media as complete and total rectums. Me, Bobby Bonilla, Barry Bonds, Albert Belle, Carl Everett, John Rocker, the list goes on forever. It's long, and ugly, and not *entirely* without merit. But at the same time, whether we've been labeled surly,* or selfish, or publicly struggled through domestic trouble, or said stupid things, or chased trick-or-treaters off our lawns from behind the wheel of a speeding SUV, there's not a guy on that list I wouldn't want on my team. At the same time, based on limited, mostly *on*-the-field interactions, I have to say I really *like* a lot of those alleged supervillains. Do I dig deep? No. Do I care *at all* about their supposedly shaky moral fiber or ethics? *Hell* no. I want to win. *Everything* else is secondary. You play hard? You play well? You want a ring? You're in. It's that simple. Honestly, I'd be roommates with Charles Manson if the crazy little shit could pull an outside curve.

---

* Most likely for keeping our distance from the press.

Trust me. *NONE* of baseball's ever-changing cast of whipping boys are *ever* as bad as they seem, and truth be told, a solid handful of this sport's "golden boys" are a lot nastier . . . they just play nicer with the media. With all that said, almost *nothing* that occurs *away* from the stadium will *ever* brand a fellow player an asshole in the eyes of this peer. However, out on the grass, there are a million ways you can earn yourself that scarlet *A*. Here's a couple of the most effective:

■ Cover your arms with seventeen pieces of Kevlar padding and then have the balls to stand on top of home plate. If ever there was reason to plant a baseball-size bruise on a guy's ass, this is it. The only problem is: even if you're begging for a beanball, even if you're waggling your dick over the outside corner of my dish, if I so much as brush you back, I'm gonna draw a warning from the home plate umpire. Do it again and I'm gone. With that injustice in mind, look for half the Oakland A's to start wearing suits of armor to the plate by early 2004.

■ Beat me for a home run, then stand at the plate, watching it fly out, before taking a slow walk around the bases. Immediately and irrevocably, you're now a jackass for life. I *will* throw at you ("Whoopsy, sorry about that, pal."). I *will* pitch you up and in for the rest of your life. I *will* pump my fist in the air every time I make you whiff, and I *will* do whatever I can to make every one of our future encounters a thoroughly miserable experience for you. I will also get in your face, right on the field, as guys like Bobby Higginson, Jim Thome, and Carlos Delgado can attest. Best of all was the day Geronimo Berroa rocked me for a 400-footer, then practically crawled toward first base.

"You better run, asshole!" I shouted at him as he trotted along, smiling.

"What'd you say?" he shouted back, still smiling. "I can't hear you over all these home run cheers!"

"I SAID 'You better RUN, asshole!' and I said that because if you don't pick up your pace, right *now*, the *next* time you come up to bat I AM gonna break one of your ribs. Got me, cha-cha?"

I swear to God, the dude triple-timed it from second base to home.

And while as far as I'm concerned, those are far and away the two *best* ways to earn your asshole stripes, there are a lot more routes to take. You can refuse to play hurt. You can care more about your personal stats (or your contract) than your team's won/loss record. You can choke in the clutch over and over and over again. Batters can take themselves out of the lineup whenever a particularly tough pitcher comes to town. Pitchers can maneuver their starts to miss Arizona and Atlanta, and pitch to Florida and Pittsburgh. You can smell bad. You can whine. You can openly rag on your manager. You can mistreat your clubhouse attendants. You can steal from your teammates. You can visit the clubhouse buffet table naked.* You can try and sell me unwanted real estate. You can try and sell me unwanted cocaine. You can push your born-again stuff to an outfield full of happy heathens. You can be a big fan of John Tesh . . . *that* one will buy you a lifetime membership.

In short, no matter what the media has to say, it's not all that easy for a player to achieve true "asshole" status. Like everything else in baseball, it takes hard work, endless dedication, and a whole lot of natural ability.

ANYWAY, BACK TO THE RUMORS OF ME AND BOBBY BO BEING TRADED. Three days pass. Nothing happens, and that's when I hear Gillick's plan has been squashed. Peter Angelos has loudly and angrily vetoed Pat's proposed double dump. Standing at my locker, I have to laugh, wondering if maybe Pat will shift gears now and just drop me from his roster three days before the end of spring training '97. Oh, to be a fly on *that* office wall.

I'm gonna take some liberties here and buzz forward through a lot of the 1996 regular season because, quite frankly, we Birds never really got the machine oiled up and purring until August. With that in mind, there's not a whole lot of excitement to be had in spelling out the intricate, everyday details of a hundred games spent stuck in the mud. There were some bright spots: Brady Anderson was smack in the middle of his insane 50-homer season. Robby Alomar was batting .325 or better throughout the summer. And I got to watch Cal Ripken Jr., still in his prime, who was flat-out awesome.

Without any doubt at *all*, the single greatest clubhouse leader I ever played with was Cal Ripken Jr. Standing regally at his locker, baldy head shining like a crown, the Ancient One presided over the Birds' '96 clubhouse with quiet but unchallenged top-dog status. Teammates willingly bowed to Cal's authority, respecting his reign for three very good reasons. First, the man was a living legend, having achieved more prominence in the game of baseball than any of us could ever *hope* to match. Second, despite being a first-ballot Hall of Famer, the

---

* I once saw a guy come away from the spread with potato salad on his cock. I pray it was accidental.

Brandon at the plate. We could have used his bat.

dude never rested on his laurels, always playing at the cliché of 110 percent, always tits deep in his game. Third, and probably most important of all, we O's kneeled before Cal because he was absolutely and inarguably capable of kicking every one of our asses. Ripken was a stud, and even as his Social Security checks were beginning to roll in, the man made a regular habit of joyfully wrestling his much younger teammates into twisted masses of whining, crying, "UNCLE"-screaming submission. Depending on your outlook, "the great one" could also be a genuine pain in the ass.

But that's baseball . . . or at least the locker room. Sure, man's evolved a lot over the past two million years, but out on that playing field, and/or squirreled away beneath the stadium in our team locker rooms, all major leaguers quickly revert back to knuckle-dragging, mouth-breathing Neanderthal status. Ultimately, there's not a whole lot of manners swirling around our Ben-Gay-scented jungles, and with that in mind, the rest of us never looked twice when Cal would leap into action and wrap a headlock on Rocky Coppinger, or a figure-four leg-lock on Jeffrey Hammonds. Those guys had made the mistake of messing with our pack's alpha wolf, and now they were simply paying the price. It was nature's way. Scotty Erickson, Tony Tarasco, Brent Bowers, Robby Alomar, Esteban Yan, me, anyone dumb enough to mix it up with Grandpappy Ripken ultimately took a spanking, endured a lot of pain, treated his teammates to a public display of humiliating (and in their eyes hilarious) defeat, and finally got banished from the clubhouse nursing a bruised ego and licking a whole lot of wounds. Like rutting apatosauruses, or those rams you always see butting heads on the Discovery Channel, our species had once again seen its fittest survive.

Best of all was the night Arthur Rhodes and Alan Mills, fed up with Cal's bullying, decided to launch a surprise double-team attack. This was it. They were finally gonna pair up to give Ripken a taste of his own medicine. Squatting on opposite sides of a row of lockers, they waited in silence to leap, which they did, the second Cal walked out of the weight room. Pouncing like a pair of wild-eyed hyenas, Mills and Rhodes got the early upper hand, but within seconds, Hulk Ripken had an ankle lock on Rhodes, with another big foot stomped all over Millsy's Adam's apple. Their cries were pitiful, but since nature knows no pity, the rest of us were forced to laugh our asses off at their misfortune, hooting and hollering and begging for more. That's how baseball works.

Oddly enough, even after all the pain he's dished out, even after all the twisted arms, the pink bellies, the bent-back thumbs, the atomic wedgies and merciless Indian burns, the general public *still* thinks of Cal Ripken Jr. as a sweet, mild-mannered Prince Charming. To you civilians, the man's a cross between Jimmy Stewart and God. Well now you know the truth, people. The bubble's busted. The cover's blown. Cal Ripken Jr. is *really* . . . mean . . . sometimes . . . at least if you're dumb enough to get in his face and challenge him to a wrestling match.

BY JULY 27, WE BIRDS ARE RIGHT BACK AT THAT GODDAMNED .500 mark, and eleven full games back of the Yankees. With the *division* title now an *extreme* long shot, we're fourth in line for a Wild Card berth, behind the Mariners, A's, and White Sox. Sweating through the soupy humidity of summertime in Baltimore, we're now officially facing a long, hot, thoroughly unpleasant stretch drive. With guts tight, and frustration levels skyrocketing, the team desperately needs a shot in the arm—which we get in the form of future Hall of Famer Eddie Murray.

Kent Mercker, who's had a really hard time as our fifth starter (3–6, 7.76 ERA) gets dispatched to Cleveland, and we Birds get Eddie Murray in return. Eddie slides into the DH hole immediately, and in one of those weird, inexplicable baseball phenomenons, we start winning. Our pitchers seem to get sharper, we score more runs, strand fewer runners, and before you know it, we're on a roll. Call it character, call it leadership, call it karma, call it luck, call it chemistry, I have *no* idea how the hell it worked. All I know was that almost as soon as Eddie Murray "came home" to Baltimore, the gods chose to smile upon us, and we started winning . . . a lot. Rolling through August at 19–11 we're right back in the thick of the Wild Card chase by Labor Day. And when Todd Zeile arrives just in time to make our playoff roster at third base, we Birds roar through September at 16–11, rising from the midsummer ashes to lock up an unexpected visit to postseason play.

Honestly, this team was so fucking hot through the final two months of the season, that anything and *everything* seemed possible. Wild Card? No problem. Eight wins in a row? Piece of cake. Knock those goddamned Yankees out of first place in the AL East? Sure! Why not? But time's running out. We may need to do something drastic.

A big, fat, 200-watt lightbulb clicks on over Davey Johnson's head.

Let me explain. Even though we Birds are currently blazing toward September on a *ridiculous* hot streak, we're nonetheless saddled with the same "fifth-starter" problems we've been fighting all year. With Mercker exiled to the craplands of Cleveland, righty Jimmy Haynes and lefty Rick Krivda have both filled in with mediocre-to-lousy results. A combined 6–11, they're workmanlike starters, but they're now also speed bumps in this team's unexpected drive toward October. With that in mind, Davey's lightbulb is all about moving to a four-man rotation through the rest of the season.

I *love* the idea, as do Scotty Erickson and Rocky Coppinger, who's a gen-yoo-ine tough guy—but we hit the wall though when it comes to Mussina. The Moose, our ace, doesn't want any part of the situation. No way, no-how. It's a real monkey wrench. Time to start nagging.

I say to Mike, "Dude, a four-man staff is gonna give us *all* more innings. It's gonna give each of us four more starts. And you know as well as I do that by October, it's *absolutely* gonna give this team a handful of extra wins. First place? Home field advantage? A postseason edge?" No luck. The Moose ain't biting. He's worried about pitching on short rest, worried that both his game and his arm will suffer. They're legitimate concerns, but I *still* can't help thinking, Fuck that stuff, Moose. Let's just do whatever it takes to win it all! My gut feeling was if my left arm falls off in November, who cares? I'll wear my World Series ring on the right. But that brand of kamikaze logic ain't easy to sell, and despite our finest collective whining, Mike just wouldn't budge. I was *more* than a little bit pissed, but that's when the Moose surprised everybody.

Days pass, and as we Birds continue burning through August, the Moose finally snaps, catching us all by surprise, performing a screeching 180 that would have left thick, black skid marks across any eight-lane superhighway. "You remember that four-man rotation we talked about?" he asks Davey one afternoon. "Let's do it." Davey beams. The Yankees are now officially within striking distance. Risking his game, his health, his arm, and a whole lot of future seven- and eight-figure contracts, the Moose puts *everything* on the line for this team. He's come through for us big time. We plow through September like a team possessed.

Sadly, however, despite our finely crafted Cinderella story, the Yankees refuse to collapse. After a sub .500 August, the pinstriped bums go absolutely nuts, burning even hotter than us Birds. When we go 11–4 through the middle of September, they go 12–3. When we win three out of four on the road, they grab four in a row at home. I hate 'em. We're winning big. We're playing great ball. We're roaring through a four-man rotation that's just about untouchable, and yet despite every one of our best efforts, we *always* seem to be four games back. Doesn't this Joe Torre guy know 1996 is *our* year? Don't the Yankees know a team of destiny when they see one? By late September, still trailing the bastard Bombers, it's time to revise the game plan. As of right now, we Birds officially set our sights on destroying New York in the postseason, with a more immediate goal of locking up the Wild Card as quickly and as painlessly as possible.

But even *that* won't be easy.

September 27. We're in Toronto with a magic number of just one, but we're not gonna get it tonight. We ARE, however, gonna witness one of the weirdest moments in modern baseball history. Roberto Alomar's at the plate, and umpire John Hirschbeck, whom I actually like for his dependable, steady, large strike zone, is behind the plate. Robby looks at a curve that's just barely outside.

"Strike three!" Hirschbeck shouts.

"You're killing me with that pitch!" Robby shouts back.

"Well, then I guess you're gonna have to *swing* at the ball," Hirschbeck barks. The crowd gets loud now, sensing trouble.

Robby's heading toward the dugout, still yelling, "If it's a strike, I'll swing . . . but that wasn't a strike!"

"I'm warning you now. You better not say another word."

Rafael Palmeiro settles into the batter's box. He takes a ball, and from the dugout, Robby yells something along the lines of: "Yeah, why don't you just pay attention and get on with the game?!"

Here comes Hirschbeck. Walking toward the visitors' dugout, he shouts, "That's it, he's outta here!"

Here comes Davey. Up out of the dugout with surprising speed, Davey runs to Hirschbeck, shouting, "Jesus Christ! You can't do that. This is a big game!"

"Yeah, well, you better tell *him* that!" replies Hirschbeck, pointing at Robby, who's now barreling across foul territory toward the ump. Robby and Hirschbeck go nose-to-nose, chest-to-chest, belly-to-belly.

Now the "motherfuckers" fly. Now the "son of a bitches" and "who the fuck do you think you ares" and "goddamnits" fill the air so fast you can't even tell whose curses are whose. The crowd goes nuts. Davey makes a bad moving pick, and that's when it happens. Robby Alomar uncorks a large, well-horked loogey at Hirschbeck, and all hell breaks loose. "He spit in my face!" shouts Hirschbeck as Davey gets help dragging Robby away from what's become a manslaughter-inducing situation.

The dilemma: while the above couple of paragraphs spell out the way *I* experienced "the incident," I *have* heard alternate takes. For example, I've been told that Robby charged Hirschbeck only after Hirschbeck called Robby a "spic motherfucker," however, amid the roar of the crowd and the confusion of the moment, I have to say I never heard that slur get thrown.

Pressed for quotes after the game, Davey Johnson played it smart by saying only "they're both guilty," and then slipping away from the clutches of the press. Robby Alomar wasn't that smart. Arriving for the following night's game, Robby's surrounded by the press and asked yet again about the previous night's flare-up with Hirschbeck. His reply is a monumentally bad choice. "I used to respect him a lot," Robby says. "He had a problem with his family when his son died—I know that's something real tough in life—but after that he just changed, personality-wise. He just got real bitter." You can see the reporters' eyebrows rising in midbyte. It's insensitive. It's inexcusable. It's insane. Hirschbeck has recently lost a son to a rare brain disease, and though he doesn't know it yet, Robby's quote is about to get him crucified unless Hirschbeck finds him first. If that's the case, he won't be so lucky.

The media circles now, clucking away until Hirschbeck arrives, at which point they descend like vultures, gleefully tattling about Robby's quote while stirring up a nice hot batch of instant controversy. Hirschbeck (rightly) freaks, heading straight to the Orioles' clubhouse, hoping to break our second baseman's neck. "Where IS the motherfucker!" he screams, plowing through the lockers. "I'll KILL HIM!"

A high-pitched "Yeeeeeeeeeeaaaaaaaugh!!!" pierces the locker room. It's my four-year-old, Brandon. Hanging with me for today's game, the little guy's been happily running through the Orioles' locker room, only to end up two feet away from the raging, roaring, bloodthirsty Mr. Hirschbeck. Seeing the guy as some combination of Big Bad Wolf and Jack's Giant, Brandon streaks through the room and leaps into my arms. It actually stops the tirade for a moment.

"Oops. Sorry, Boomer," Hirschbeck whispers. "But *where the* HELL IS THAT &;mC%$ %$#;mC#&$$ (())(&;mCer?!!!"

Hirschbeck storms off through the showers now, as if Alomar might be dumb enough to hide in there. No luck. Mercifully, the Orioles public relations types have already spirited Robby away from the area, knowing full well they've got to come up with a public apology and some *serious* spin doctoring. With that in mind, Hirschbeck's assault never gets off the ground, and the frustrated ump is wisely sent home from the ballpark. Alomar sneaks back in just prior to game time.

Booed louder than I've ever heard a human being booed before, Robby nonetheless tunes out the Canadian crowd, plays his standard stellar game, and in the bottom of the tenth, he breaks a 2–2 tie with a home run that clinches our postseason Wild Card spot. The Blue Jays crowd hates us for winning, they hate Robby for his home run, and on some profound level, they hate the fact that this spitting, supposedly evil symbol of everything that's wrong with baseball can still be so motherfucking good. This time, like it or not, the villain wins in the end.

At any rate, with a lousy first half behind us, an "ugly incident" survived, and a Wild Card spot locked up, my champagne-snipering skills prove as sharp as ever. On the night we clinch, Davey Johnson takes a nostrilful of Asti Spumante in mid-TV interview, Rafael Palmeiro gets blasted with a graceful, arcing shot right over the top of our lockers, and I even manage to make like William Tell, shooting Cal Ripken's hat right off his head. I swear to God, NOBODY's as lethal as me shooting booze. At the same time, in a frenzy of high spirits and really bad taste, teammates are running rampant through the clubhouse now, spitting mouthfuls of beer and champagne at one another while playfully "ejecting" their teammates from the locker room. Even *I'm* a little offended by that one.

In the end, spit boy gets off lucky, eating a five-day suspension that won't go into effect until the start of the '97 campaign. Incensed MLB umpires immediately threaten to boycott the playoffs unless Alomar's suspension is rewritten and restructured to take place right away. Within days, however, they've folded like a two-dollar suitcase. Robby's *in* for the playoffs, and despite the noise and chaos and wind of the past couple of days, we Orioles survive the hurricane unharmed . . . except maybe for me.

This time around, I head into the postseason fighting off yet another round of "back spasms," which is really just a baseball euphemism for "this dude's fucked up." Back on August 18, coming off a shaky, uncomfortable outing against the Brewers, I lasted just one inning against the A's, giving up 8 hits, 2 home runs, and 7 earned runs in just under 25 pitches. Wincing with each windup, I battled through the humiliating inning, but something was clearly wrong. All I knew was that with the postseason in sight, there was no way in hell I'd bench myself now. Shot up with cortisone right after the game, I was temporarily good as new, happily ignoring my spinal column through five great starts in a row. Start six, however, on September 14, against the suck-ass Tigers, is a nightmare. Barely surviving four innings against the worst team in baseball, I shake off the disaster, chalking up the shelling to simple fatigue, assuming that there's no way a cortisone shot could have worn off so quickly. With 200 innings already under my belt this season, it's an entirely plausible lie.

Five days of rest and massage follow before I get mugged in Yankee Stadium, lasting just three innings, giving up six runs and eight hits to the league-leading Bombers. Cecil Fielder hits two absolutely ridiculous home runs off me, causing me to seriously weigh the option of plunking him in his next at bat, against the probable ass-whupping I'd have to endure. Either way, as Davey mercifully yanks me away from the carnage, one thing's for sure. Fuck massage, fuck stretching: I need another shot.

However, with the playoffs now a sure thing, and only one more start before the postseason, I decide to hold off shooting up as long as possible. The end result finds my last start of the season a 5-inning, 9-run catastrophe, where the Angels' Mo Vaughn homers off me in three separate at bats. After the game, I act like every bad "junkie" you ever saw wander through an episode of *T.J. Hooker*, skulking through the clubhouse desperately seeking my fix. I get it a half hour later, and with a full week off between this start and the first game of the Divisional Playoffs against Cleveland, I've got time to rest, relax, rest, relax, and rest some more. By game time, I feel nothing short of great.

Scheduled to start in Game 1, at Camden Yards, I can feel the old postseason adrenaline rushing through me for days ahead of the start. And while the local papers openly wonder why Davey's going into Game 1 with a guy who's sub-.500 season was capped with three diseased performances, we both know that with my back medicated, and my heart pumping for the playoffs, the Indians are in big trouble. It's my game, in my house, at my time of the year. You just don't beat me now.

October 1, 1996. Cleveland comes into town having won 99 games in the regular season. Charles Nagy, with 17 Ws racked up all by himself, seems a clear-cut favorite over me, a guy who wobbled to 11–14, with an ERA over 5. The media idiots surround me with "How does it feel to be the underdog?" questions for hours before the game, and it's all I can do not to smack them. Metallica blaring, they have no idea how unbeatable I'm feeling. Later, I walk through the Indians lineup with Pat Dobson, knowing I'm gonna own these guys tonight. I'm more than ready, and

Postseason form, circa 1996
(© Mitchell Layton/Newsport)

when Brady Anderson leads off the game for us with a gigantic home run out onto Eutaw Street, I'm practically ready to pop.

Feeling great at the rubber, I'm tits deep in adrenaline battling this *very* good Cleveland lineup, but that doesn't mean I'm perfect. In the second, Manny Ramirez beats me on a 1–1 fastball, launching it just inside the left-field foul pole, maybe four rows back in the cheap seats, to even the score at one. Pissed, I get through the inning without any further damage, then watch B.J. Surhoff put us back on top with a solo shot into right. An inning later, Cal Ripken muscles one off his hands and drives in Rafael Palmeiro to buy us a 3–1 insurance run.

In the fourth, still feeling strong, I get beat *again* by Manny Ramirez, this time for a single that bounces off the mound and skitters into center field. Pissed at Ramirez, and distractedly keeping one eye on his lead at first base, I let a 1–1 fastball sit too fat over the plate, and Jeff Kent practically drools at it as he swings. He lines a shot down the left-field line into the corner for a double.

Ramirez stops at third. Sandy Alomar comes to the plate now, and though I smoke him with a nasty fastball inside, the guy inside outs me and rips a single over his brother Robby's head. Ramirez scores. Finally, Omar Vizquel plays small ball, drinking a little looping sac fly into right that brings Kent home too. From there, I wriggle out of the inning without further damage but kicking myself for that one obese pitch to Kent. We're now tied up at 3–3.

Back at square one, I maintain my focus, bear down even harder, and I'm flat-out awesome through the fifth and sixth (he said, modestly). Working one, two, three in both innings, I get through the sixth with just six pitches thrown. Thoroughly enjoying every moment of this tense, tied-up contest, I hop over the right-field line (note to aspiring pitchers: NEVER *step* on the right-field line—it rings up *seriously* bad juju), plopping down into the dugout, where I'm immediately treated to a mother lode of run support.

Nagy struggles, and he walks the bases full just in time to be yanked by Indians manager Mike Hargrove. Alan Embree relieves, and one pitch later, Robby Alomar brings a run home with a long sac fly. Three pitches later, Rafael Palmeiro takes one off the shoulder, and that's enough for Hargrove. With the bases loaded, Paul Shuey relieves Embree as Bobby Bonilla comes to the plate.

The count runs to 3–2. Bonilla steps out. Camden Yards is louder than I've ever heard it. Shuey steps off. The tension rises beautifully. Bonilla steps back in, and the two guys lock eyes. Shuey delivers at 93 miles per hour. Even as he releases I can see that the pitch is seriously low. Bonilla swings anyway. I wince. Bonilla golfs the sucker almost out of the dirt and crushes it WAY back into the right-field seats for a grand slam. The place goes nuts. As he's cheered by the fans and squashed by his teammates, we shove Bobby out of the dugout for a curtain call then pull him back in to answer the bullpen phone—the guys down there wanted to congratulate him too.

Heading into the seventh with a 9–3 lead, I'm having more fun than any human being should be allowed to have. Staked with a huge cushion, with a back that feels great, and stuff that seems to be getting stronger inning by inning, I consciously pause to enjoy the moment, and the crowd, and the fact that I've once again got the ball in a big-game situation. It doesn't get any better than this—a fact that's proven quickly, when Kevin Seitzer busts a one-hopper off my left foot.

I'm leaping in pain, then limping in pain. Davey jogs out, takes the ball, and ships me off to the showers before I can even complain. With a six-run lead, he's taking no chances on me getting hurt. The crowd stands now, applauding as I tip my cap and disappear into the dugout, my outing complete. And though each team will score one more run before this game's over . . . this game's over.

Up one game to zip, Scotty Erickson doubles that lead with a sweet 7–4 victory over Cleveland's Orel "Bulldog" Hershiser. With that one in the books, we're off to Jacobs Field on a roll.

Game 3 would pit Jack McDowell versus Mike Mussina. With one more victory between us and the ALCS, this one was gonna be good. Rolling out onto the field before the game, the boos were monumental, and while Cleveland's always harvested a bumper crop of loud, ignorant yahoos, tonight's crowd, zeroing in on Robby Alomar, is even louder than normal.

They get worse when Kenny Lofton starts the game with a liner to left . . . which Bobby Bonilla misplays into a two-base error, and by the time Lofton's stolen third, the momos are at full shriek. When Kevin Seitzer's dribbly little squibbler to first brings Lofton home, they're so obnoxious I'd have given anything for a nice cold fire hose that I could have used to shut them up.

Six innings later, with the game tied at 4–4, Jesse Orosco has his bases full of Indians when he's relieved by Armando Benitez, who in a big-game situation is about as reliable as a schizophrenic on crack. Crumbling in the first of a career-long series of big-game collapses, Armando presents Albert Belle with a gift-wrapped, basketball-size 1–2 fastball, which Belle happily deposits eight miles away over the left-center-field fence. The Indians take the lead 8–4, and they add one more in the bottom of the eighth. We lose the game 9–4, which means Game 4, tomorrow night, is gonna be mine. I can't wait.

The biggest game of my career is staring me in the face, and it's all I can do not to laugh. *This* is fun. *This* is exciting. *This* has got me pumped like never before. I pace. I crank my boom box. I air-guitar like Eddie Van Halen to "Panama." I bounce. I drum on the furniture. I leave the hotel and simply walk around Cleveland. And with hours to kill before tonight's first pitch, I hit Jacobs Field unbelievably early. AC/DC, Metallica, Megadeth, Slayer, everybody gets a run through the stereo today.

By game time, I'm stoked up big-time, and I fly through the first three innings untouched. Staked to a 2–0 lead by back-to-back homers from Palmeiro and Murray, I am thoroughly disgusted when I manage to give the lead right back in the fourth. Heading back to the bench at 2–2, I beat the hell out of a couple of dugout garbage pails, then sucker punch a Gatorade cooler. I know it's pointless, and childish, and not the least bit productive, but right about now, it feels *really* good.

One inning later, I let Jose Vizcaino's leadoff single get followed by a solid Kenny Lofton sacrifice, and an Omar Vizquel single. Just that quickly, my 2–0 lead has become a 3–2 deficit. After the inning, I kick *serious* garbage pail ass. Seldom in the history of our species has an inanimate object taken such a thorough beating from a human being. This time around, on the losing end of the box score, the release is a lot less satisfying.

Meanwhile, across the diamond, Charles Nagy is pitching a helluva game and striking out a *lot* of Orioles. In six innings of work, Nagy whiffs twelve of us. When he's relieved by Alan Embree, Embree strikes out the side to put that number at 15. On my side, I manage to get through the sixth and seventh unscathed before Davey sits me in favor of righty Terry Matthews. On the bench now, with the Gatorade tub begging for another ass-whupping, my solid outing isn't nearly enough to make me happy. To me, leaving on the short end of a 3–2 playoff game is *completely* unacceptable. Thankfully, with a couple of big singles from B.J. Surhoff and Robby Alomar, we're able to bounce back to 3–3 in the top of the ninth. The Jacobs Field crowd, which hates Robby Alomar with a passion right now, goes dead silent. The biggest villain in all of baseball has just been rewarded with yet another super-size hit. If *that* won't take the wind out of their sails, nothing will.

Tied at 3–3, we head into extra innings, and after a scoreless tenth and eleventh, Robby Alomar comes back to the plate to lead off the top half of the twelfth. The roar is deafening. Hitler pinch-hitting for Mussolini would have been greeted more warmly. Twenty-two different Orioles have struck out today, and yet, thanks to this umpire-wetting monster, we're still tied up at 3–3. The fans are indignant when Robby steps into the batter's box, and they practically have a stroke when Robby takes a first pitch strike. They roar in disapproval as Jose Mesa throws an 0–1 pitch low and away for a ball. And they nearly drop dead when Robby takes Mesa's next pitch (also low) and cranks it 406 feet over the right-center-field fence. Robby rounds the bases to dead, stunned, defeated silence. Meanwhile, in our visitors dugout, we Orioles make like feeding time at the monkey house. We're jumping up and down, screaming, climbing the walls; it's all we can do not to cartwheel across the infield.

Cleveland's pitchers ultimately strike out twenty-three Orioles that day, but it just doesn't matter. When Randy Myers works a 1, 2, 3 ninth, we move on to the ALCS, having disposed of one juggernaut, just in time to face another . . . the New York Yankees. Heading into Yankee Stadium under a steady game-day downpour, I feel the pinstriped ghosts more keenly than ever. It's October, in the postseason, in Yankee Stadium, and as I stand in the dugout alone, watching rain drip off the upper deck, my heart is soaring. Scotty Erickson's scheduled to take the ball tonight for Game 1, and I can't help feeling jealous. Mike Mussina will take the hill tomorrow. I'm penciled into Game 3, the first start back home in Camden Yards, which is nice, but it ain't Yankee Stadium. Beyond that, with a lifetime 9–1 record at the house that Ruth built, I can't help thinking I could really help us out up here in New York. Apparently, just about a hundred feet away from me, Davey Johnson agrees wholeheartedly.

When Game 1 ultimately gets washed away by a Big Apple monsoon, Davey uses the excuse to juggle his rotation. The extra day of rest allows him to swap starts between me and the Moose. I'm now ball-pointed into Game 2, while Mike gets Game 3 at home. Yes, he's pissed. Yes, at 19–11 he *deserves* to be pissed, but quite frankly, right now I couldn't care less. I've got Game 2 in the Bronx, and I'm the happiest boy on earth. Mussina's uncharacteristic 0–2 record in Yankee Stadium this year, with a Bronx ERA of nearly eight, has forced Davey's hand. Since we're a heavy underdog in the series (again), Johnson's pulling out all the stops in ensuring at least a split before going home to Baltimore. If that ruffles some feathers, so be it. As it turns out, Davey's strategy pays off, but while we Birds *do* gain a split in the Bronx, we *should* have gone home up 2 games to zip. You know this story.

Game 1 finds Scotty Erickson facing Andy Pettitte, and tossing a solid six innings for us Birds, allowing the Yankees to score just twice on five scattered hits. Coming into the seventh, Scotty takes the mound with a 4–2 lead, but after getting Tim Raines to fly out, he quickly gets into trouble. Wade Boggs walks. Bernie Williams doubles. Out comes Davey. Out comes Scotty, replaced by Ol' Man Orosco, who makes short work of Tino Martinez, handcuffing the Yankees' first baseman with a gorgeous 2–2 slider.

Now Cecil Fielder comes to the plate, and with the words *three-run homer* dancing through his head, Davey has Jesse walk the big man intentionally, loading the bases in the hope of grabbing a quick force out from on-deck batter Paul O'Neill. When Charlie Hayes gets announced as a pinch hitter for O'Neill, Davey lifts Jesse in favor of the right-handed Armando Benitez. Now *Joe Torre* gets tricky, swapping Darryl Strawberry into the lineup in place of Hayes. Bases are loaded in a big game, with a lot on the line, and with all that in mind, it should come as no surprise that out on the mound, Benitez once again chokes, walking in a run to cut our lead to 4–3. The score stays there, right up until baseball history gets made in the bottom of the eighth . . . by a twelve-year-old.

You've seen the tape. You know what happened. With one out, Derek Jeter comes to the plate and drives an 0–1 fastball to right. Tony Tarasco sprints to the wall, where he's camped out just below Yankee Stadium's right-field seats, waiting to make the catch. At that point, from out of nowhere, a trivia question is born. Q: What's the name of the rotten little twelve-year-old kid from New Jersey who royally fucked the Orioles in the 1996 ALCS? A: Jeffrey Maier.

He's twelve years old, he's wearing his baseball mitt to the game, and he needs a *lot* of work on his fundamentals. Reaching out over the top of the wall, Jeffrey grabs the ball out from over Tarasco's head, but it pops from his glove, bouncing back behind him into the stands. (Note: kids should always use *two* hands when destroying a major-league team's entire season.) Umpire Rich Garcia immediately signals for a homer, and that's when all hell breaks loose.

Davey has a conniption. The whole Orioles bench empties out onto the field. Yankees fans are cheering. Tony Tarasco looks like a balloon inflated to the point of exploding. Davey gets ejected, and after a long, long argument, play *finally* resumes with the score tied at 4–4. It's unbelievable. It's maddening. It's infuriating, but the play stands. All we can do now is go out on the field and take the game back. Three innings later, we're still trying.

With the score knotted at four through the eighth, ninth, and tenth, Mariano Rivera shuts us down in the eleventh, at which point Randy Myers goes to the mound and gets spanked by leadoff hitter Bernie Williams, who smashes a high 1–1 slider deep into the left-field seats. Game over. O's lose. It's as aggravating a defeat as I've ever endured.

Sitting silent in the locker room now, while the local press momos repeatedly ask "How do you feel about the boy?" (A: While I hate that he fucked us, you have to admit the kid's got balls.), I know as of right now, I'm face-to-face with the single biggest challenge of my career. If we Orioles are gonna have ANY chance of winning this thing, it's up to me to stop the bleeding, fast. And while a victory tomorrow won't guarantee *anything*, a loss will all but send us home for the winter. In a strange, almost masochistic way, I *love* the tension. It's *my* game, *my* challenge and in a very real sense *my* season hanging in the balance. Too excited to sleep, I lay awake all night striking out phantom Yankees in my head, focusing on the task at hand, and thanking whatever being controls the universe for the chance to be in exactly this spot. Me versus Coney, how cool is that?

From my hotel room I watch the sun rise over the East River. By 5:45 A.M. Metallica's blaring. I take the world's longest shower. I read all four New York papers. I call friends. I call room service. I wander Manhattan. I hit F.A.O.

Schwarz. I hit Central Park, and *still* I've got eight hours to kill before game time. By two o'clock I'm once again wandering a deserted Yankee Stadium, with the ghosts, and the history, and today's game plan all running simultaneously through my head. At the same time, I've got Sparky Anderson wandering through there too, hovering in my brain like a leather-faced Obi-Wan Kenobi. I walk through the Yankees lineup with him like we used to do in Detroit wishing he were here to teach, and focus, and make fun of me, and swear at me in person. Finally, after one last stroll through Monument Park, where I get to spend a little quality time with the Babe, it's time to get busy.

Heart racing, adrenaline flowing, I'm pleased to find my stuff behaving very well. The curve is sweeping, the four-seamer's popping, and my location is solid on just about everything. Now more than ever I'm anxious to pitch . . . as it turns out *over*anxious. With Coney walking the bases full and throwing more than thirty pitches before finally weaseling out of the first inning unharmed, I sit on the bench watching, waiting, stewing, obsessing, while desperately awaiting my turn on the mound. By the time I get there, my eyeballs are ready to pop out of my head I'm so excited. It shows.

With my head and my control both adrenaline-addled, Derek Jeter singles, hard. Then, Tim Raines singles, hard. Then, Bernie Williams singles, *really* hard, scoring both Yankees on base. In a span of ten pitches, I'm already down 2–0 and facing disaster. Sparky Anderson yells at me in my head. Pat Dobson yells at me from the dugout. Catcher Chris Hoiles calls time and pays me a social call at the mound where I swear a lot and he talks me down. With the tangible mess at hand quickly sweeping aside the legend, and the grandeur, and the dozens of Yankee ghosts in my head, I'm slapped out of my distracted, overexcited funk pretty damn fast. As my mom used to say, "You can't worry about world peace when the kitchen's on fire." Right now, I've got work to do.

Locking in almost immediately, I get down to business, and with some smarter pitching, I settle down fast, ultimately steering clear of disaster when Cecil Fielder hits a sharp grounder right at Robby Alomar, who flips to Cal Ripken, who flips to Raffy for a classic 4-6-3 DP. Cecil, who generally times his sprints to first base with a calendar, is out by fifteen feet and looks decidedly pissed with his at bat. Inning over, I jog back to the dugout, leaping over the foul line, secure in the knowledge that I'm now prepared to kick *serious* ass.

Todd Zeile ties up the game for us with a two-run homer that just barely pokes its way over the left-field wall, but from there, both Coney and I settle in for a run of *really* nasty hurling. Coney holds us O's to just two runs over six innings of work, during which he throws roughly 9,642 pitches. Over on the other side of the box score I match him frame for frame (*mostly because there's no way in hell I'm letting Coney beat me—I'd be hearing about it for decades*). Finally, when Joe Torre yanks Coney at the top of the seventh, replacing him with Jeff Nelson, my Birds strike back.

With a Robby Alomar double, followed by a Raffy Palmeiro homer, the scoreboard quickly racks up a 4–2 Orioles lead. In the dugout now, you can literally feel the momentum shifting our way. Fuck Jeffrey Maier. Fuck our underdog status, we're going home to Camden Yards 1–1 with the wind at our backs. Finally, with the Yankees threatening one last time in the bottom of the ninth, Armando Benitez relieves Randy Myers. An immediate knot forms in my gut. Big game, pressure spot, I'm seeing giant red flags. I cross my fingers and toes, I say two Hail Marys, and apparently my strategy works. Armando comes through big-time, getting Cecil Fielder to foul out, and Tino Martinez to pop up into shallow right. Now it's official: *this* series is ours.

Or not. Heading home to Camden Yards with confidence building, Mike Mussina takes on Jimmy Key in Game 3, and when Brady Anderson singles in front of another Todd Zeile dinger, we Orioles are staked to a fast 2–0 first-inning lead. The score holds tight until the top of the fourth, as a Bernie Williams walk, a Tino Martinez single, and a dribbly little Cecil Fielder ground-out combine to manufacture a run for the Yankees. With Mussina throwing bombs on the mound today, the homer-happy Yankees have got to be happy with whatever small-ball runs they can scrape out.

At the same time, on the opposite side of the box score, Jimmy Key's tossing his standard great game too, and with that in mind, the fifth, sixth, and seventh innings pass *really* fast. Batters on both teams just kind of scratch and spit, while hacking cluelessly at the plate. In the eighth though, having thrown a *ton* of pitches, the Moose is fading fast. Davey hangs with him. He gets Joe Girardi after a warning track heart attack, but then Derek Jeter belts a 1–1 fastball into the right-field corner for a double. Davey stays with Mussina. Bernie Williams smacks a first-pitch curve into left for another single, this time scoring Jeter. I'm looking to the bullpen for signs of life. Davey stays with Moose. It's now 1–1 to Tino Martinez, and Tino connects straight down the left-field line. Is it foul? Is it fair? It's a double. Action now in the bullpen, but still Davey hangs in there with Mussina. If I had any hair I'd be pulling it out now. Come ON already! I'm shouting inside my head. Cecil Fielder steps in, takes a fastball high, then punches a 1–0 curve into the seats in left. It takes fourteen months for Big

Daddy to complete his victory lap. *NOW* Davey relieves Mussina. I get a lump on my head from banging it against the side of the dugout. Yankees lead 5–2, and that's how it ends.

Down two games to one, we're still full of piss and vinegar in the Orioles clubhouse. *Everybody's* talking about how *we'd* be up 2–1 right now if it weren't for one rotten twelve-year-old kid, and one blind forty-six-year-old umpire. By game time, we hit the field loaded for bear, as confident as ever, and it takes all of one half inning before the Yankees manage to spank us down. With Rocky Coppinger on the mound today against Kenny Rogers, Derek Jeter's leadoff double is followed by a Bernie Williams homer that sails right up and over the out-of-town scoreboard. The Yankees are up 2–0 before we Orioles even get to bat.

Though we O's manage to scrape out a run in our half of the first, Darryl Strawberry leads off the second by hammering a 0–1 changeup over the out-of-town scoreboard with even more altitude and velocity than Bernie Williams's first-inning shot. Less than ten minutes after cutting the Yankees' lead in half, we're back down by two—and right here, even in the middle of hating their guts, I find myself admiring just how hard and relentlessly and powerfully these Yankees play the game of baseball. Honest to God, look around the major leagues and you'll find players who are more talented than these guys at every single position, but almost none of those guys play as hard, as smart, or as gutty as the Bombers. Is it tradition at work? Is it Joe? Is it really good scouting? At this point I have no idea. All I know is they're a helluva team.

But so are we, and in the bottom of the third, a Chris Hoiles homer brings us back to 3–2. A half inning later, Paul O'Neill returns the favor, with a two-run shot that extends the Yanks lead to 5–2. Bottom of the fourth, heads still very much in this game, we O's battle back hard, knocking Kenny Rogers out of the game while scratching out two runs on a Cal Ripken walk, a wild pitch, a Pete Incaviglia single, and another jack by B.J. Surhoff. It's 5–4 Yankees, and that's where we stay, all the way into the eighth.

There, with righty Alan Mills on the mound, Bernie Williams connects for what seems like his 400th big hit of the series. It's a ground-rule double that one-hops the fence in right-center-field. Jesse Orosco relieves Mills and promptly surrenders a little dink single to Tino Martinez that sends Williams to third. As Cecil Fielder comes to the plate, Benitez comes in to relieve Jesse. I've got agita. Benitez goes to 0–2 on Fielder before Cecil connects with a Baltimore chop to Zeile at third base. Zeile makes the throw to beat Cecil at first, but Bernie

(© Mitchell Layton/Newsport)

Williams scores, and Tino goes to second without a throw. Here comes Darryl Strawberry, and smack in the middle of yet another pressure cooker, Armando goes to 3–1 on Darryl, at which point Strawberry uncorks a two-run shot that just barely clears the fence in left. Yankees lead 8–4, and with an awful, "punched-in-the-stomach" gloom settling in fast, we Orioles head for the showers down three games to one.

October 13, 1996. Camden Yards is packed with diehards hoping their Birds may still have a miracle or two tucked under their caps, but with a six-run rally in the third, the Yankees quickly follow up yesterday's jab in the gut with a bolo punch to the heart. We're cooked, but there's not a guy on the bench who quits. Scotty Erickson settles down and holds the Yankees scoreless through the fifth, and Arthur Rhodes, Alan Mills, and Randy Myers do the same through the sixth, seventh, eighth, and ninth.

Meanwhile, though Todd Zeile and Eddie Murray each belt solo homers, we O's head into our last licks down 6–2, and though Bobby Bonilla manages to swat us a beautiful two-out, two-run desperation homer, it's too little, too late. Cal Ripken grounds into a 6–3 putout to end the game, the series, the season, and my Orioles career.

Today, for the first time ever, I'm a free agent, and right from the start, my objective is clear—*Get the Yankees on the Hook*. With that in mind, even as the New York beat writers are wandering through our "losers' locker room," pressing us defeated Orioles for parting quotes, I'm already hard at work. With cameras, and microphones, and tape recorders pushed at me from all sides, I stand tall, in my underwear, endlessly praising the Bombers and their fans while simultaneously chattering about how great it must be to play in New York City. In a perfect world, I'm hoping the Yankees' brass will see those quotes, read *between* those lines, and soak up my obvious hint.

The plan works beautifully, and exactly one month later, the Yankees make contact. That's where my future goes bust.

The Yankees' GM, Bob Watson, rings Gregg Clifton, and just seconds into their phone call, Watson blindsides my agent with the question "Exactly what kind of deal is it gonna take to make David Wells a Yankee?" Reeling, Gregg asks for some time to consider that question, and three days later, after conferring with me and doing a bit of research, he gets back to Watson with a proposal of three years at $17 million. Hearing those numbers, Watson literally coughs into the phone, stifles a laugh, and responds with "Wow . . . uhhhhhh, that's a *lotta* money." There's no counteroffer. There are no follow-up calls. We're dead in the water.

Heading into December, with the Thanksgiving doldrums behind us, the Orioles, Indians, and Jays all start sniffing. Each team expresses interest in signing me, but each of those prospects gives me a headache. Though it's clear now that the Yankees have ditched me, I'm *still* carrying a bonfire-size torch. It's like having a crush on Cinderella, but dating her ugly stepsisters. I'm surly. I'm close-minded. I'm hoping for a miracle . . . which I get within hours.

On December 8, 1996, Jimmy Key is responsible for one of the single greatest moments of my baseball career . . . he quits the Yankees, abruptly heading off to Baltimore, where a brand-new $35 million, free-agent contract awaits him. George Steinbrenner is said to be *furious*. With Key gone, his Yankees' rotation now consists of a damaged David Cone, a fantastic Andy Pettitte, an aging Doc Gooden, and an unreliable Kenny Rogers. It's a very good sign. There's just no *way* George is gonna tolerate heading into the spring with a staff full of question marks and holes, and there's no way in *hell* he's gonna let Peter Angelos steal Jimmy Key without retaliating. As of right now, the Yankees actually *need* me. My heart races. My eyebrows rise. Gregg Clifton gets a call the next morning.

"Hi, Gregg, Bob Watson here. Just wanted to let you know that we're all still *very* interested in bringing David Wells to the Bronx." This time around, it's Clifton who's stifling the laugh. After gagging on our first proposal, and weeks of laying low, the Jimmy Key–less Yankees have suddenly fallen in love with me. And while I'm *more* than ready to sign whatever deal Watson may toss my way, Gregg wisely counsels me to move slowly, for one very good reason. His name is Roger Clemens.

As a free agent out of Boston, Clemens has blown off the Red Sox, and he's now officially testing the waters as a rocket-for-hire. He has been hunted by every team in baseball, and the Yankees, Blue Jays, and Indians have quickly risen to the top of the pack. With the same three clubs courting us both, Clifton knows there's no need for speed. First, no matter *where* Roger signs, his new deal will no doubt break records while immediately raising the going rate on *all* solid, veteran pitchers. At the same time, while *one* of those three teams *will* be lucky enough to sign Mr. Clemens, two *won't*, and those jilted suitors will suddenly find *me* at the top of their shopping lists. With all that in mind, though I'm dying to sign on Watson's line, Gregg and I play it cool, telling the Jays, Indians, and Yankees that we're just gonna sit this dance out, keeping our options open, and getting back on the floor only *after* Roger Clemens has been signed. It turns out to be a very smart move.

In the days to come, the Clemens numbers get real crazy, real fast. Toronto dives in at nearly $25 million over three years. Cleveland ups the ante to $28 million, and when George Steinbrenner visits Roger's home in Texas, the rumor mill *swears* the Boss is now ready to offer the Rocket *$32 million* over *four* years. That news catches even Yankees GM Bob Watson off guard. "It wouldn't surprise *me*," he grumbles to the press, rolling his eyes. "*Nothing* surprises me anymore." Meanwhile, another Yankee official, under a cloak of anonymity, says "George wants to get Clemens. . . . He's not listening to anybody about this. It's his money and his deal."* Translate that to mean: "Yep, the $32 million's on the table, and we all think the Boss is nuts."

Friday the thirteenth. Roger Clemens stuns the Yankees by rejecting George's $32 million in favor of Gord Ash's *$24.75 million*. Speaking to the press right after his announcement, Roger explains his decision by citing "Toronto's superior quality of life," its polite fans, and the fact that he'll be allowed to dink fungoes to his boys on the field at the Skydome. Back home in Florida, I think Roger needs a straitjacket.** Forget about the money. Here's a guy with a chance to become the ace of the World Champion Yankees, and he chucks that opportunity for nice

* Jack Curry, "Yanks Pitch to Clemens as Texas Woos Wetteland." *New York Time*s, Dec. 13, 1996.
** Did Roger simply use George's wallet to wring more cake out of the Jays? God bless him.

playgrounds, docile crowds, and the ability to smack a few Wiffle balls across some Canadian AstroTurf? Nuts! Hours later, in a development that shocks absolutely *no one*, Bob Watson's back on the phone with Gregg Clifton.

Watson's ready to deal. Clifton's now ready to oblige, and together those guys bat around a tentative deal worth $15 million over the next three years. Everybody's happy, everybody's positive, but that's where the monkey wrench hits. Watson explains that based on my less-than-spotless reputation, George Steinbrenner is now refusing to dive into any Wells deal without testing the water first. "I know this is strange," Watson tells Clifton, "but before we can make any of this official, Mr. Steinbrenner would like to have a face-to-face meeting with David. No agent, no GM, just the two of them." Clifton's caught off guard.

"Uhhhhhhhhhh . . . well . . ."

"Mr. Steinbrenner would like to take David out for dinner and get to know him, one on one . . . man to man."

"Uhhhhhhhhhh . . . lemme call David, and get right back to you."

Now *my* phone rings, and together, over the course of the next ten minutes, Gregg and I decide to turn *down* George's invitation. We've got a better idea. Forget the stuffy restaurant, forget the chitchat and small talk. If George Steinbrenner *really* wants to find out if I'm "Yankee material" the two of us should hook up right here in Tampa, at the Yankees Spring Training Complex. Legends Field is crammed to the cheap seats with Bombers' memorabilia, and there, amid the retired numbers, and signed game balls, and team photos, and plaques, I can knock the man's socks off with a full-on blast of Yankee-mania.

We hook up the following morning, and though I'm *incredibly* nervous, the mood lightens almost immediately. Wandering through the monuments, and the green grass, and the history of Legends Field, the Boss and I hit it off. We talk Rizzuto, and Whitey, and Billy Martin, and Reggie, and Catfish, and Munson, and Guidry, and Horace Clarke, and Roy White, and the Babe, and Jeffrey Maier, and at *least* seven or eight hundred other Yankee topics. We make each other laugh. We enjoy each other's company, and right through the meeting, I'm working hard to impress George with *exactly* how badly I want this gig. In the end, though our ballpark meet-and-greet has been scheduled to run just fifteen minutes, the Boss ends up hanging with me for an hour and a half. It's still the best "first date" I ever had.

That afternoon, Steinbrenner punts Watson out of the negotiations and calls Gregg Clifton personally, raving about our meeting and making it clear that he *himself* will now be negotiating my deal. Believe it or not, that's a bad thing. Clearly impressed with my desire to be a Yankee, George now *also* knows that I do *not*, under any circumstances, want to be an Oriole, Indian, or Blue Jay. My blood is pinstriped, and with that in mind, George (ever the businessman) backs away from the Watson numbers and lowballs me, offering a deal that plops onto the table as three years at $11,950,000. With a bunch of difficult incentive clauses sprinkled on top, the deal *could* ultimately (though improbably) be worth $14,650,000.

"I'll *take* it," I tell Clifton.

"Over my dead body!" he shouts back. With Steinbrenner closing in, Toronto's gotten serious too, blasting out an offer that would have *guaranteed* me $13.4 million, with incentives that could easily have taken the deal as high as *$17 million*. "As of right now," Gregg tells me, "it's gonna cost you two million dollars to play for the Yankees, but the way I see it, we've got three options. First, we can play it safe, suck it up, and take George's offer."

"Let's do *that*!" I shout at Gregg.

"Hear me out," he replies.

"Second, we can call George's bluff. We can say that if the Yankees don't match the Jays' offer, you'll go north. The only problem is, if George *doesn't* bite . . . you're a Blue Jay again."

"Ugh! Let's go with option one."

"Shut up and let me finish!" Gregg yells. "Third, the New York press guys have been calling my office all day looking for comments about this thing. Maybe we can use *them* to sort of unofficially reach out to George Steinbrenner's office one more time. Which option do you like, buddy?" Gregg asks, knowing full well that my answer's gonna be a no-brainer.

Yankee Killer Wells to Boss: BRING ME TO THE BRONX!

That was the back-page headline in the December 16 *New York Post,* and with every square inch of smudgy, black ink, I'm turning up the heat under George Steinbrenner. I tell the whole city:

I've loved the Yankees all my life, and pitching in pinstripes would be a dream come true. . . . I can't describe what a thrill it would be to pitch for the New York Yankees. . . . Bob Watson talked about how bringing Roger Clemens to the Yankees would be the biggest deal since signing Babe Ruth. Well if they get me, they practically get the Babe. . . . George wanted a gamer, and I'm his guy. I'd pitch on three days' rest for that team. I really hope George makes it happen.

Bingo! Our bargaining power's now skyrocketing.

Having been publicly spurned by Clemens, and Key, and also John Wetteland (who's just signed a deal down in Texas), George is now duty bound to sign me. Anything less would have been a public relations disaster. By lunchtime, with the *Post* on the streets, Steinbrenner and Clifton are at it again, proposing and counterproposing over the course of a day-long (and then evening-long) haggling session. At 2 A.M., with Steinbrenner now occasionally snoring between volleys, the deal *finally* gets done. I'm a New York Yankee. And though incentive clauses ultimately made the Yankees' offer even sweeter than the Jays',* I couldn't care less. Honestly, though Clifton would have murdered me, to play for the Yankees, I would have happily agreed to *whatever* George offered.** My fondest childhood dream had really come true. How many people on this planet *ever* get to say that? How many get to be Yankees?

Back home in Tampa, I'm walking on air, once again marveling over the cold, hard fact that I am, without a doubt, the single luckiest human being on this planet. Right then and there, with my dream finally achieved, I stare into the mirror, vowing to make *every* second of my Yankee career perfect. Over the next few days, with talk radio and the New York tabloids all chanting that I'm no Jimmy Key, and swearing that my "loose cannon" status will ultimately doom my career in New York, à la Ed Whitson, I'm all the more determined to succeed. I want to hit Legends Field and toss a few dozen fastballs right now. I publicly vow to work out at the Yankees' training facilities all winter long, and time and again, I promise the press that David Wells *will* hit spring training 1997 hard and fast, taking no prisoners, and making the Yankees proud from day one.

Falser words have never been spoken.

---

* As written, with incentives met, the deal could have been worth $18,550,000 over four years.
** Y'know, "$400 a week and all the hot dogs I can eat?" I'm there, baby!

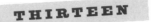

THIRTEEN

Bronx Busting

I worry when things are too calm.
I picture a ship in the ocean with no wind and the sails all up.
If there's no wind, then it doesn't go anywhere.

—*George Steinbrenner*

We have the potential for a lot of controversy,
which we're looking forward to.

—*Joe Torre*

SATURDAY, JANUARY 4, 1997, 10:15 A.M.:
PUBLIX SUPERMARKET CHIPS AND DIP AISLE

Packers versus 49ers, Jaguars versus Broncos, the NFL playoffs are in full swing, and my house is just hours away from being invaded by a dozen cordially invited animals. Together, we're gonna watch some football, and drink some beer, and shout at the TV screen, and jump up and down on my furniture, and chow through a mountain of junk food, and drink some more beer, and swear, and root, and scratch, and fart, and laugh until a lot of us end up falling asleep on my couch. I can't wait. Even at this early hour, I'm bounding through Publix, tossing salsa and industrial-size bags of tortilla chips into my wagon. Slim Jims, hot dogs, popcorn, peanuts, Ritz crackers, pretzels, BBQ chips, Fritos, and three different kinds of aerosol cheese get tossed in too. I hope it'll tide the beasts over until the six-foot heroes and pizzas and chicken wings get laid out. Smiling, I can feel my arteries clogging just thinking about that spread.

With my shopping cart bulging, I'm working the aisles, when without warning, and from out of the nowhere, I'm wracked with a sudden jolt of severe, almost unbearable, pain. It's like I've got a lightning bolt shooting through my stomach, punching up into my chest. My eyes go wide. My skin goes white. I'm gasping for air, and I go down hard, onto my knees. Scared to death, I have absolutely no idea what's happening.

I hang on tightly to my shopping cart now, working hard to avoid going facedown on the supermarket floor. I wonder if maybe my appendix is bursting. I wonder if maybe I've got some sort of kidney stone. I wonder if maybe I'm having a heart attack. I've never felt pain exactly *like* this before. Panic sets in, but then, just as quickly as the blinding pain came on, it passes . . . completely. In less than a minute, I'm fine. Honest to God. I'm freaked out, sweating, and shaken up, but I actually *feel* pretty damn good. With that in mind, I decide to be a tough guy, to ignore the whole episode, to whistle past the graveyard, and keep on shopping. Maybe it's something I ate.

Less than thirty minutes later, I'm tossing the last of the party chow into my wagon when my pager goes off, beeping me to call home. Figuring Nina must have a couple of last-minute additions for my shopping list, I leave my cart where it is and head toward the nearest pay phone, where I dial the house. "What's up, girl?" I ask as Nina answers.

"Hey, David," she begins, her voice cracking. "Can you, um . . . can you just kind of come home right away?" A knot forms in my stomach. Something's *very* wrong. Nina's clearly holding back tears, and even by the time I'm halfway through asking her "What's wrong?" she's flat-out crying. "I'm sorry . . . I'm sorry," she tells me as she hands the phone off to one of the football animals.

"Dave, just trust me," he says. "You need to get off the phone and come home, now. We'll fill you in when you get here."

"I'm on my way."

Leaving two overflowing shopping carts in midaisle, I bolt the market and race home, wondering what the hell is wrong. Screeching into the driveway, I run inside to find Nina sobbing and the football buddy trying hard not to. Though I stare at them both, nobody says a word. Finally, I just shout, "What?!"

Nina takes a breath. "We just got a call from San Diego," she tells me, "and, um, your mom had a heart attack. . . . She died just about an hour ago." My head drops. My heart sinks. The news hits hard, with waves of grief knocking the wind out of me. Falling into Nina's arms, I'm struck by a million memories, by the terrible loss, and finally, by the realization that back there in the supermarket, as that sudden, harsh, unexplainable pain was shooting through me, I was, without question, *feeling* my mother die. Even as the woman lay dying, even with a thousand miles between us, the *most* basic bond between my mother and me had *proven* itself unbreakable, and undeniable, and more powerful than I could ever *possibly* comprehend. As days pass, I'll find myself unexpectedly comforted by this tangible, physical proof of our everlasting connection. Until now, the old song and dance about deceased loved ones "living on inside our hearts" always seemed like mindless, fairy-tale bullshit. Now I know for a fact it's true.

Brandon and Attitude Annie quality time

My mom's funeral was spectacularly, almost shockingly, upbeat. Though dozens and dozens of red-eyed, misty Ocean Beachers, Hells Angels, friends, relatives, and acquaintances turned out to solemnly honor this unique woman, it took all of ten minutes before the first wave of "Attitude Annie" stories kicked in. Arms flailing, smiles wide, voices rising, it seemed like *everybody* in the place had their own personal tall tale to spin. Parties, biker rallies, good deeds, bad deeds, maybe even a fistfight or two, the stories about my mom were all over the board, but every single one of them was loving, and heartfelt, and joyful. The old girl would have loved it.

That evening, as family and friends gathered in a local bar to toast my mom's memory one last time, I somehow managed to draw the short straw and get myself saddled with the role of "designated driver." Nursing maybe three beers over the course of four or five hours while simultaneously watching my pals get happily, blissfully, thoroughly hammered, I was never so thrilled to hear a bartender yell "last call!" Still grieving, still sober, and exhausted both physically and mentally, I was *more* than ready to call it a night. At 1:55, I began rounding up my boozy, woozy human cargo, telling each of them that I was gonna run out to the parking lot and get my car. I'd be back to drag their tipsy asses home in two minutes flat. At that point I practically jogged to my rented Town Car.

Pulling up alongside the bar, I double-parked, left the car running, and ran inside to start shepherding people toward the door. "Let's go, people!" I shouted. "The bus is leaving!" at which point I buzzed back outside to my car. The whole process took ninety seconds . . . tops.

Approaching the rental, I notice that the engine's not running. I know for a fact I left it idling, so my first thought is that maybe the motor's stalled. I'm thinking, Fuck! If this thing's dead I'm gonna be here all night. I run around to the driver's side, praying I'll be able to restart the engine, and that's when I realize this car's not stalled at all . . . my keys are gone. It doesn't make sense. The door's unlocked, and I'm sure I left it running, but the keys are nowhere to be found. Could I be wrong? Did I bring the keys *inside*? I'm looking at the car seats, the mats, checking my pockets . . . no keys. Now, it's literally like 2:15 A.M. There's *nobody* on the street except me, and that's when, out of the corner of my eye, I see two guys on the corner, maybe a block away. *Now* it makes sense. Suddenly I've got a pretty good idea where my keys went.

Running down the street, I stop the two guys and say, "C'mon, let's go. Gimme the keys to my car. It's late, and I'm really just not in the mood for this right now."

"We didn't take 'em," they tell me, each of them trying and failing to hide a shit-eating grin.

"Look, I'm not kidding. Don't fuck with me right now. It's late," I tell them. "I want my keys, and this really isn't a good time to get on my bad side."

Something in my body language must have told them I meant business, because in no time at all their smirks disappeared, and the assholes got real cooperative, real fast. "Look," they tell me, "*we* didn't mess with your keys, *those* guys did!" And now they point toward *another* pair of guys walking away from us, maybe another 150 yards down the road. I take off after them.

I catch up about a block away, and despite the fact these guys are every bit as big as me, I confront them immediately. "Listen," I say, "just tell me the fucking truth. Did you take the keys out of my car?"

"Fuck off," says the bigger of the two. So now I turn to the other guy and I say, "C'mon, can I just have the keys to my—" And that's as far as I got.

BAM!

I take a solid right to the side of my face and get knocked down, at which point both of these guys start kicking me. I'm in big trouble. I cover up my face and my head with my hands, and I'm trying to roll away from them, trying to just keep myself from getting killed. That's when I snapped. Lying there on the street, taking boots to the ribs, and the legs and my stomach, something inside me exploded. Suddenly, all the events of this week, with the loss and the anger and the grief I'm still feeling about my mom, all of that stuff just bursts. I get up, and at full rage, I blast the guy who hit me with a full-on left. I smacked him square on the chin and knocked him on his ass.

Now I turn toward the other guy, but Dave Allen, one of my very best friends, has already leveled the playing field. Flying into action alongside me, he's already in the middle of flattening opponent number two with one awesome right.

It was beautiful. Dave clipped that asshole with a sweeping, nasty-assed/TV cop-show knockout haymaker. I'm like "Whooooooo! Damnnnnnnnnn, Dave!"—but because I'm just standing there like an idiot watching my friend go all *Starsky and Hutch* on this guy, I forget about the guy *I* knocked down. Two seconds later, he gets up and clocks me again. I see stars, but I'm able to shake it off. We go toe-to-toe, and I end up just beating the shit out of him, breaking my hand in the process.

With my fist throbbing badly, we left those guys lying and headed back toward the bar and my car. As we're leaving, one of the guys shouts, "Your keys are under your car seat, asshole! We hid them as a joke!"

I stop in my tracks and turn toward the idiot. "You dumb shit!" I shout at him. "After all that, you're just gonna tell me where my keys are?" I wobble toward my car, shaking my head. I look under the seat, and sure enough, there are my keys. The jackass wasn't kidding.

Keys in my good hand now, I go back into the bar, grab a case of beer and my human deliveries, and finally hit the road. I drop my sister, but by this time, my hand's really *really* killing me, and being the brilliant doctor that I am, I decide that I must have jammed my pinky. If that's the case, I know just how to fix it. All I've got to do is get one of my passengers to pull hard on the pinky and pop that little finger back into place. "C'mon, Jimmy," I told a friend. "Give it a real solid yank. It's gonna hurt like hell, but if you *really* pull this motherfucker it'll end up good as new."

Sometimes I'm an idiot. Trust me, if you learn NOTHING else from this book, learn this. Never . . . *ever* . . . ask *anybody* . . . to yank on the fingers of a broken hand. I count Jimmy down from three. He yanks for all he's worth, and I hit a screaming high C that would have made Pavarotti proud. I'm seeing little birdies now, and kings and queens, like I've just been hit on the head with an anvil in some old Bugs Bunny cartoon. So now, being a bona fide supergenius, I decide Jimmy must not have pulled hard enough to really fix this sucker. "Pull it again!" I tell him. "And this time, don't be such a pussy. Three, two, one . . ." Jimmy gives it his all this time, and as he pulls, I'm rattling windows all the way to Oregon. Quickly, I grab my case of beer and give up on the idea of designated-driving the rest of my passengers home.

Lesson number two: beer, even in mass quantities, makes a really lousy pain reliever. Though I'm going pop—glug glug glug, pop—glug glug glug, the pain in my hand just keeps getting worse. At 4 A.M. , with the moon setting, and the size of my hand still rising, I bum a ride back to my hotel. There, I find that Nina's already awake, looking beautiful, bright-eyed, and ready to hit the gym. I, on the other hand, look like I've just shuffled in off the set of *The Texas Chainsaw Massacre*. Nina freaks, perhaps due to the fact that I'm covered, head to toe, in blood.

"Don't worry, honey, it's not *my* blood," I say, sounding and looking exactly like an ax murderer. Clothes ripped, sweating, stinking, I'm now drunk off my ass, with *really* bad breath and a giant left hand that looks like it was drawn for Fred Flintstone. I'm a pretty bad-looking boyfriend right now. Promising to explain myself as soon as I grab a quick shower, I run into the bathroom as my horrified Nina immediately begins contemplating life in a nunnery.

Twenty minutes later, with my body boiled and my clothes thrown away, I tell Nina the whole story. The keys, the fight, the hand, the yanking, the screaming . . . and when it's all over, instead of running for the hills, Nina just holds me close and says, "C'mon, let's go home." With her words wrapping around me like a warm blanket, I couldn't possibly agree more.

Quickly we pack up our stuff and get the hell out of Dodge. Hitting the San Diego airport, we catch the first shuttle back to L.A., but we've got to wait out a ninety-minute layover before we can board the earliest flight back toward our home in Florida. Sitting together in the terminal at LAX, Nina watches over me as I finally hit the wall. Lying down "just for a second" with my head on a carry-on bag, and my back on the floor, I quickly pass out. Ninety minutes later, poking and cajoling with all her might, Nina fights hard to bring me back to life, then helps me to my feet and gets me onto the plane, where, seconds later, I pass out again, never opening my eyes until we bounce down onto the tarmac in Florida.

Pitchers and catchers report in a month—unless, of course, said pitcher is charged with felony assault and the Yankees front office exercises its right to walk away from said pitcher's brand-new contract, thus crushing said pitcher's lifelong dream of actually playing for the Bronx Bombers. I know it's far-fetched. I know that I did nothing wrong. I know that when pressed to comment on the situation, George Steinbrenner simply smiled and said, "I know if somebody stole my keys, I sure wouldn't kiss him." Still, when the San Diego Police Department calls to inform me they're investigating the case upon the formal complaint of my two "victims," I can't help but ponder the worst-case scenario. Meanwhile, with the hand still throbbing, yours truly gets examined by an orthopedic surgeon and a hand specialist who both agree I've got a fractured fifth metacarpal bone in my pitching hand. And while that *sounds* pretty damn bad, the news is actually pretty damn great. Fitted with a soft brace, I'm told that if all goes well, I should be throwing again right around the second week of spring training. I take my first deep breath in a *long* time.

With *that* bullet dodged, I'm halfway home, and ten days later, bullet number two is looking decidedly avoidable too. When one of my self-proclaimed victims describes me in his initial police report as "the baseball pitcher that makes $4.2 million a year,"[*] I'm told his credibility plummets fast. From there, as police investigations conclude that the two complainants really *did* take my keys and stash them under my seat, *my* side of the whole bizarre story suddenly seems remarkably plausible. By January 28, it's official. The San Diego County district

* Jack Curry, "Wells Won't Face Charges over Fight." *New York Times*, Jan. 29, 1997.

DAVID WELLS

attorney's office decides not to file charges. I can finally put all this behind me, wipe the slate clean, and hit spring training like gangbusters. Yeah, right.

Less than two days into spring training, I'm still playing long-toss and babying my cracked hand when out of the blue, I feel the gout coming back. Awww, shit! I'm thinking. Not this, not *now*. Having already made a bad *first* impression with the Yankees, I'm about to go two for two. Just like last year, the gout starts as an uncomfortable throbbing ache, and just like last year, over the course of just a few hours, that pain grows to become absolutely unbearable. The only difference in my condition *this* time around, is that the pain is in my *right* foot, not my left, and that makes the situation a whole lot worse. As a lefty, I need to plant my right foot hard when I throw, and until this thing's healed up entirely, that's gonna be impossible . . . unless, of course, Yankee fans don't mind seeing their starting pitcher rubbing his foot and crying like a baby after each and every pitch.

The Yankees take blood tests. And while I know full well what the results are gonna reveal, I keep my mouth shut, hoping for a miracle, and hoping to keep the beat writers at bay. Coming off the street fight, with the New York tabloids gleefully painting me as some drooling, free-agent mistake who lives in a cage, guzzles booze, and bites the heads off small animals for fun, the last thing in the world I need now is to let the beat guys blow this gout thing out of proportion. I can see the headlines now: WELLS'S 'GOUT' OF CONTROL or maybe WELLS'S TOE NAILED. I can imagine the articles too, running amok with the fact that this stupid little disease can be aggravated by overeating or alcohol. With my early spring gut and my barroom-busting reputation, I'll be a sitting duck. With all that in mind, it's time to start taking the old nonsteroidal anti-inflammatories, and lie to the press. With any luck at all, I'll be feeling better before they have time to turn this into a big deal.

On February 16, as reporters descend after watching me limp through an outfield jog, I slap on the old cheese-eating grin and tell them, "I've just got a little blister under my *left* big toe. It's nothing to worry about. Move it along, boys. Nothing to see here." Hauling the old "turf toe" euphemism out of mothballs, I buy myself twenty-four hours of peace. However, when the Yankees make it public that my blood tests have come back positive for gout, in my right foot . . . I'm suddenly public enemy number one. The writers surround me like a pack of hyenas, asking questions just this aggravating.

"Why lie about which foot was hurting you?" they inquire, their tone more suited to asking "Are you now, or have you ever been, a pitcher with an aching big toe on your fat right foot?"

"What? Look, it's always been the right foot that's hurting," I tell them. "Is this really a major story? Whoa! Jump back! Stop the presses!" Fuck this. I ain't playing.

"What medication are you taking?"

"Ancient Chinese secret!" They stare at me now. I stare back.

"Do you think your overeating had anything to do with the gout?"

"Jesus, do you know I overeat?"

"No."

"Then why bring it up. I mean really, are you also gonna ask me if I'm still beating my wife? Look, if I'm hungry, I'm going to eat. No matter what it is. That acceptable to you?"

"Do you consume . . . beer?"

"What about it? I'm an adult. I'm allowed. I like beer. It does a body good, and if beer's what's ailing me, I guess I'll have to go to whiskey. If that's bad too, I'll move on to vodka. If that's bad too, I guess I could try water, but you have to be careful there, *that* stuff'll kill ya." Looking back on the incident, maybe the next book I write should be called *How to Lose Friends and Infuriate People*.

For days after the fact, I take a beating in the media, and over the course of the next few months, "Wells versus the New York press" will become an ongoing soap opera. The tabloids will run pictures of me leaving bars late at night, with captions openly wondering if this is acceptable behavior for a highly paid major-league starter. Page Six will routinely run accounts of my barhopping and/or strip-club-crashing escapades. It gets to a point where I half expect the *Enquirer* to have me romantically linked with Bigfoot, or giving birth to an alien's baby. For now though, with an especially crazed spring training in full swing, my gouty big toe quickly becomes yesterday's news.

Coming off their first World Series victory in eighteen years, the Yankees spent the off-season losing their Series MVP and closer John Wetteland, and getting played, screwed, and dumped by Roger Clemens. On top of all that, they've now officially swapped Jimmy Key, a reliable, quiet, workmanlike starter, for me, a guy who's put a street fight, *and* a broken hand, *and* a disaster-plagued big toe under his belt before we've even come *close* to opening day.

Meanwhile, thankfully, I'm not the only problem child in Tampa this year. First, though Joe Torre's already stated that Cecil Fielder will more than likely get 500 at bats in 1997, Cecil remains at home, upset about his role with the club, and apparently still outraged over the fact Joe benched him in favor of Darryl

Strawberry in last season's ALDS. He's demanding a trade. At the same time, Wade Boggs and Charlie Hayes are *both* miserable about sharing third base, with each of them openly preferring a trade to any sort of platoon situation. And while Andy Pettitte seems a sure thing on the mound, starters David Cone, Dwight Gooden, and Kenny Rogers are all question marks. Coney and Rogers are both coming back from off-season arm surgery, and a dead-armed Gooden didn't even make the Yankees '96 postseason roster. Finally, although they would soon be proven wrong, baseball pundits were predicting a quick, ugly mental breakdown for the Bombers' new closer, Mariano Rivera.

"Mariano's too high-strung to be a closer," they pontificate. "He'll crack under pressure." Repeating as World Champions is by no means a sure thing. *Sports Illustrated* is a lot more blunt about our chances, saying, "All the money in the world won't buy this team a return date with destiny."

Back here in Tampa, sitting down with Joe Torre and the Yankees' minor-league trainers, I endure the single most humiliating "baseball" meeting of my life. Today's subject is "gout," and over the course of forty-five minutes, I'm told that eating right can help me feel better and play better . . . WOW! I'm given a dietary book to help me make better choices about what I eat. I'm told "fruit and soup" might make a lovely light lunch. I'm ready to bang my head off the table. Hitting the trainers with a quick fingers-crossed promise to "change my habits if that's what the Yankees want me to do," I'm able to slide away from the meeting and move on to less embarrassing, less brain-numbing affairs. Meanwhile, I'm already wondering if it'd be at all possible to stockpile nonsteroidal anti-inflammatories for future flare-ups. If only the dealers in Washington Square Park stocked them. "Loose nonsteroidal anti-inflammatories! Two dollah!" That'd be sweet.

Thankfully, mercifully, my medicine works wonders, and just a week after reporting to camp, I'm up on the mound for the first time. With Mel Stottlemyre at my back, I toss fifty fastballs in ten minutes, and in the first *good* news I've had in months. I feel *great*. The ball is popping. The toe is bearable. The hand feels fine. The back feels fine, and in no time at all, Mel and I are both smiling big-time. Let's face it, fifty fastballs thrown to some guy with a number 92 on his jersey isn't exactly world news, but for me, it's a real breakthrough. Physically, I've got my first real taste of being back at 100 percent, and mentally, after finally fulfilling a lifelong dream to *become* a Yankee, *this* marks my first even mildly positive moment. If my toe wouldn't fall off, I'd be popping champagne to celebrate.

On the road as a brand-new Yankee

The Florida weeks pass as slowly and pointlessly as ever, but little by little, as the preseason chaos fades, and the '97 Yankees start taking shape, I find myself October dreaming, even in March. Personally, I feel fantastic, thrilled to death to be working out every day and perspiring into regulation pinstripes. At the same time, though my cracked metacarpal hasn't healed, I blow off the doctors' advice to have a screw drilled into the bone, in favor of just a removable cloth splint. The hand doesn't hurt, and with my stuff moving nicely, I was like "the hell with the screw. I'll just pitch busted." Mechanically, the pinky's just a guiding finger, so I figured if it ain't broke, or in this case, even if it IS broke, don't fix it. With that in mind, I'd simply hit game day, take off my splint, and throw. Rolling through the latter half of what turns out to be a kick-ass spring, I make plans to take a mallet to my hand in January of '98.

Around me in the starting rotation, the guys who aren't lucky enough to have a busted hand are pitching pretty well too. Andy Pettitte's awesome, Coney seems entirely healed from 1996 aneurysm surgery deep within his right armpit, and while Kenny Rogers is feeling a little lingering pain from his preseason arm surgery, and Dwight Gooden's fighting off an abdominal pain, they both seem to be throwing really well from the mound. Behind them, the '97 Yankees look tough to beat.

Tino at first, Mariano Duncan at second, Jeter at short, and Wade Boggs, coming off a monster spring, swipes the third-base job right out from under Charlie Hayes. Joe Girardi's behind the plate, and with a resurgent Darryl Strawberry beating out a hammy-hobbled Tim Raines for the starter's job in left, Bernie Williams in center, and Paul O'Neill in right, we Yankees take the field as one nasty-assed franchise. On the bench, however, after a brief flirtation with AWOL status, a stewing, joyless, untraded Cecil Fielder begins going through the motions as the Yankees' "most-of-the-time" but not "all-of-the-time" DH. And while right now Cecil qualifies as the one real migraine on Joe Torre's agenda . . . that will change fast.

April 1, 1997: opening day. On the road in Seattle, we start the season as far away from Yankee Stadium as a team can get, but it just doesn't matter. With double-Babe on my back (33) and a Yankees cap on my head, I'm absolutely in heaven. Now it's for real. Now it's official, a fact I wish weren't quite so true when we take a quick 4–2 beating. With David Cone on the mound, this game packs even more emotion than most opening days.

With a vein graft hiding inside his armpit, David's confided in me that he's scared by the reality that every pitch he throws could now be his last. He wonders how much time he has left. He worries that the graft might tear. He worries with each and every windup.

Today though, while Coney throws a solid six innings and change, two off-speed, fat-plated mistakes to Junior Griffey let the kid go yard in his first two at bats. Another dinger to Russ Davis serves as Coney's only other breakdown. With that in mind, although it's impossible to get David to accept this fact, even in defeat, with just seven hits allowed over 6⅔ innings, he really did pitch well. But that's Coney.

One quick paragraph on David Cone. The guy's a monster. On the mound, off the mound, in the locker room, in the dugout, in my living room, in my swimming pool, he's a *lot* like me . . . he just gets way better press. Don't let the "smart guy" stuff fool you. Don't let the "silent, reserved competitor" angles pull the wool over your eyes. Don't let the "student of the game" stories turn your head. Coney is without question every bit the rabble-rousing, ball-busting, beer-drinking goofball that I am. Almost from day one, we're joined at the hip in the Yankees clubhouse, and bestowed with the nicknames "Scumbag and Scumbag" or sometimes "Silent Scumbag" and "Loud Scumbag." I'll leave it up to you to figure out who's who. David becomes my best friend on the team almost immediately, and we'll ultimately become just about inseparable. He's a great pitcher, a great man, and a great friend. It's just a shame he's so flat-out, double-bagger ugly.

Back in Seattle, with a nuclear-strength explosion at the plate, and Andy Pettitte tossing a gem on the mound, we split the Seattle series with a 16–2 romp. From there, after one day off and a puddle jumper ride down to Oakland, I make my first Yankees start, which oddly enough comes with equal parts exhilaration and sadness.

Traveling into California for the first time since my mom's funeral three months ago, it's hard to accept that she's not here. There's no way in hell "Attitude Annie" would have missed this game, screaming, and shouting, and punching the arms of the people next to her with every single pitch. She knew exactly how badly I wanted to be a Yankee, and with my first start closing in, I'm dying to call her. I want her to be in the best seats in the house. But that's obviously not possible. And while I *do* leave tickets in her name at the will-call window, I know they're gonna sit empty. A quick little conversation with the sky is as close as I'm gonna get to her today.

"Thanks for getting me here, Annie," I say from the mound just prior to the start of inning one. "Now what'ya say you help me kick ass?"

She's with me, and over the course of seven innings pitched, the Oakland A's scratch out just six hits and one run from our two-generation attack. Leaving the game with a 2–1 lead, I give the old girl a quick thumbs-up as I leave the field. And though Jason Giambi ultimately connects off the Yankee bullpen with a two-run shot that travels halfway to Mexico, and we lose the game 4–2, I stand in the showers feeling pretty good about my start, and my career, and my whole charmed life. Whitey Ford, Don Larsen, Ron Guidry, Catfish Hunter, Goose Gossage . . . me. Amazing.

Losing two of three to Oakland, we Yanks move down the coast to *take* two of three from Anaheim, where my second start of the season becomes a complete game 12–5 victory. It's a solid outing, wherein, except for a lousy five-hit, four-run fourth, I pretty much snowplow through the Angels' lineup. Leaving the field with my first Bombers W, I know that within an hour's time, I'll be charter-bound for New York City and Yankee Stadium. How cool is this?

Flying home 4–5 after our West Coast trip, we Yankees may not be setting the world on fire, but except for our bullpen, which is struggling mightily, we *have* played pretty solid baseball. With that in mind, none of us have any idea the wheels are about to fall off this wagon. We're about to lose six of our next seven at home. We're also just days away from losing Darryl Strawberry, whose knee suddenly swells to the size of three knees plus an elbow, *and* Dwight Gooden, whose preseason abdominal pain turns out to be a surgery-size hernia. Both guys go ballistic.

With double-decker comebacks at stake, Darryl tries hard to downplay his pain, while Doc is locker-kicking pissed that the Yankees trainers dropped the ball in spring training. Diagnosed early, Doctor K could have been stitched up in Tampa, rehabbed, and be back tossing at 100 percent by now. Fake smiles screwed on tight, both guys give positive statements to the press saying they hope to be back soon. They won't be. In their absence, Tim Raines and jumpy journeyman Mark Whiten will share time in left, while Ramiro Mendoza comes out of the pen to become our number-five starter.

Meanwhile, with his $65 million team at 5–11, the end of Boss Steinbrenner's patience has quickly been reached. Exploding in his office, George rails about the team's listless, lazy, lame-assed play. He threatens wholesale personnel changes. He rips into the bullpen. He laces into Bob Watson, demanding that the GM make alterations to the roster, and in the most frightening sound byte of all, George says, "If we slip much more, I may have to get personally involved." Three hundred miles down the Atlantic seaboard, Peter Angelos and his Baltimore Orioles have made matters exponentially more irritating for the Boss by leaping out of the gate at 12–4. Worst of all, just across town, the overachieving Mets are beginning to steal tabloid headlines right out from under us underachieving Bombers. We're in big trouble.

Coming home for quick sets against the A's and Angels, we'll lose four out of five, with my own Yankee Stadium debut stinking up the Bronx worse than a Hudson River garbage barge. Stepping out onto that diamond, pinstriped, double-Babe on my back, the ghosts of that building all around me. I'm thrilled beyond words. The crowd cheering, Eddie Layton on the organ, Bob Sheppard on the P.A., Phil Rizzuto and his cannolis tucked away somewhere in a broadcast booth, I'm literally near tears. At the same time, however, I'm *really* ticked off.

My stuff won't stay down. Warming up, the fastball, the curve, the slider, everything's coming up in the strike zone today. I make adjustments, I focus, I bear down, but still I'm just a little bit "off." And while I'm dying for my Yankee Stadium debut to be perfect, the Angels have other plans. We lose an ugly one, 6–5, on a day where a few scattered boos usher me off the field that Ruth mowed.

Booed at home in April . . . Welcome to New York.

I go home nursing my wounds, but thankfully, Dorian's Red Hand and a pint or two of Dr. Heineken's miracle cure-all are just a two-minute walk away.

Taking a fantastic apartment on the Upper East Side of Manhattan (a feat made possible *only* if you've just signed a new three-year deal with the Yankees), I quickly find that I'm less than a block away from a great little old-school, low-key, hassle-free, keg-tapping watering hole called Dorian's Red Hand. Within a week, I've been there three times, and within a *month*, it's become a poststart tradition for me, and Graeme Lloyd and Coney, and Tino, and a whole lot of other guys on the Yankees roster. We get treated well at Dorian's, and the whole place just has the sort of casual, private, laid-back atmosphere that's nearly impossible to find in an island crammed with ten zillion loud, trendy, obnoxious, poser-packed clubs. You know the places: where clowns with receding hairlines and ponytails wear leather pants and chat into cell phones, while across the floor, frowning women smoke clove cigarettes, sneer at the wait staff, and try their hardest to look bored by it all. Dorian's doesn't play that. Dorian's has more of a best-pal's-rec-room feel, and when you've just spent the last three hours getting shelled by the White Sox, that's a very good thing.

April 30. Two weeks after the boos and the booze, I'm back in the Bronx and back on the mound, this time against the Mariners, and right from my first warm-up toss, I know today's outing's gonna kick ass. The four seamer sizzles and pops. The curve sweeps. The off-speed stuff appears to be in slow motion, and with all that going for me, I spend the next two hours spanking 9 strikeouts, 7 hits, and 1 earned run over 7⅔ innings of work. Jeff Nelson and Mariano Rivera relieve, and while Rivera gets beat for a left-center moon shot by Jay Buhner, we hang on to win 3–2. It's taken a month, but I've finally snagged my first Yankee Stadium W. As an added bonus, the victory marks the 1,000th win in Joe Torre's managerial career. Maybe that buys me some brownie points. Maybe now Joe won't wince like I'm driving a nail through his head during my pregame *Black Album* ritual.

Getting the hell out of an ugly April at 14–13, we Yankees roll through the better part of May struggling just to stay near the .500 mark while melodrama unfolds all over the map. By midmonth, a slumping Wade Boggs (batting .143 in May) loses third base to the younger, more powerful, slicker fielding Charlie Hayes. Responding to the move by telling the press "it's fine. When you're stinking up the joint, you should sit," Boggs is lying. This thing's killing him. Now officially branded "a legend in decline" and chasing after a 3,000th career hit that (thanks to Hayes) may never come, at thirty-nine years old the man stews as a second stringer, sometimes distracted, sometimes detached. It's impossible to miss the suffering in Boggs's face, and there's not a guy in the clubhouse who doesn't feel for him. The situation will grow ever more uncomfortable as the next few weeks unroll.

Meanwhile, as Dwight Gooden begins a minor-league rehab assignment, Darryl Strawberry's knee, which originally appeared to be just a mild case of tendinitis, has flat-out refused to heal. Wearing a brace now, the Straw's had to put off beginning his *own* rehab assignment several times due to persistent pain. In midmonth, when Darryl finally *does* report to Norwich, the leg lasts all of five innings before he's forced to shut it down again. With Straw's setback, you can't help but worry about the guy. Fingers crossed, a clubhouse full of Yankees pray he'll stay strong and beat the demons this time around.

Back on the field, this team finally gets hot. Taking ten of thirteen from K.C., Minnesota, and Texas, Tino's on a tear, Bernie's on a tear, Paul O'Neill's on a tear, and I'm not doing too badly myself. Notching a complete game W against the Twins, and a 5-hit, 2-run, 8⅓-inning victory over the Royals, I'm 4–1 by the time we head for Arlington, which is precisely where this team once again starts crashing and burning . . . big-time. Guess who gets the downward spiral started.

May 16. For the second time in my career, I've got a legitimate shot at a no-hitter. Fifteen Rangers up, fifteen mowed down, and heading into the sixth inning with an armful of great stuff, knocking off a dozen more seems a genuine possibility. And then I fuck up. Laying a 1–0 fastball over the fat part of home plate, Billy Ripken clocks a double down the left-field line and immediately downgrades my no/no dreams down into a legitimate chance to lose this 0–0 game. Swearing on the mound, furious at myself for that one mistake, I lose focus and quickly make another. Falling behind Damon Buford 2–0, I hang a slider that your grandmother could have cracked into the parking lot at Arlington. Buford connects, and in two seconds flat, we're down 2–0. I need to kill something. Heading back to the dugout after *finally* escaping the inning from hell, I've got obscenities flying at Rangers fans, at myself, and at the dugout wall. I heave my glove. I kick the shit out of a team cooler. I KO a case of sunflower seeds. Meanwhile, Joe Torre's frowning at my fit from the end of the bench. To Joe, getting beat's acceptable. Beating *yourself* isn't. Raging through the dugout now, Joe knows I'm well on my way to doing just that.

Top of the seventh. One pitch. Will Clark cracks a shot that's still rising as it hits the right-field foul pole. Three nothing, Rangers. One *more* pitch and Juan Gonzalez doubles hard into the deepest part of right center. I'm fuming. I'm roaring. I'm boiling. I'm gone. Joe's had enough, and he practically sprints to the mound to get me the fuck out of his lineup. "That's enough, David," he grumbles, taking my ball. "Let's go." Jim Mecir comes on to relieve, but the floodgates are open, and we go on to lose the game 6–0. From there, in no time at all, we'll go on to lose eight of our next ten games. But wait . . . there's more.

After getting hit pretty hard in the first of his minor-league rehab starts at Columbus, Doc Gooden has joined the team in Arlington. Here, under the watchful eye of Mel Stottlemyre, Doc goes through a few minutes of wild, slow, unimpressive bullpen work before going out to a local strip club called the Fantasy Ranch. In the process, he misses team curfew and beats the bejesus out of a local cabdriver over a disputed $4.20 fare. It's fucking insane. Returning to the team hotel, Gooden maintains he became incensed when the driver made an unscheduled stop along the way to pick up a stripper from yet another club. The detour causes Doc to miss the Yankees' 2 A.M. curfew, and he knows full well that with his history, the wrath of George will be upon his ass fast. As legend has it, the furious Doc storms up to his room, refusing to pay his $4.20 fare. The cabby gives chase. "You sonofabitch! You gimme MONEY!" the guy allegedly screams through the halls, pushing Dwight from behind.

Gooden opens up an economy-size can of whup-ass.

Doc's in trouble. Steinbrenner throws a fit. The driver's side of this already embarrassing story gets even more upsetting when the cabby says Doc bolted the cab without paying only after the stripper refused to come back to his room and party.* Though Doc maintains he was stone cold sober, accusations and counteraccusations fly. Steinbrenner bans Dwight from traveling with the team 'til the end of his rehab assignment, and rumor has it Doc's Yankee career is hanging by a thread. Overnight, one more pothole hits this team's road to post-season play.

And now, on top of everything else, we're sneezing. Honest to God, just when things seem bleakest, a flu rises up out of nowhere and spreads like well . . . the flu, through a huge portion of the team. Losing through Texas, Toronto, and Boston, our headaches aren't entirely baseball based. Achy, sleepy, phlegmy, and weak, the snot rags fly as we Yankees try our best to make

* Bullshit . . . in my humble opinion.

it through defensive half innings without boogering up our uniform sleeves. Bernie, O'Neill, Mariano Duncan, Charlie Hayes, we're all pretty much miserable, while Joe Girardi's got it even worse, dealing with the same batch of symptoms, all from inside the unscratchable, unwipeable nose-cage known as the catcher's mask. At this precise moment in time, sick and tired and smack in the middle of a suck-ass losing streak, we Yankees pack up our things and head home to the Stadium for a pair against the front-running O's.

Already 6½ games back in the AL East, we're playing "must-win" games even before the end of May, and now, faced with our biggest team challenge of the season, we sniffly Yankees pull together, focus, and fall flat on our faces. With Andy Pettitte enduring a rare off night, we lose the first game 8–6, and when Kenny Rogers takes the mound at the start of Game 2, there's not an unclenched ass on the bench. Rogers has been struggling with bad luck, blown leads, inconsistency, and high-profile losses all season long. Already, Yankee fans hate the guy with a real Ed-Whitson-style mania, and their boos and abuse only seem to make Rogers's problems worse. On the mound against the Birds, in what's clearly the biggest game of our season, Rogers collapses again, this time getting hammered for 9 runs over 4 innings while the KICK ME sign on his back grows to mammoth proportions. Even as the Orioles are tap-dancing over Rogers on the field, up in the owner's box, George Steinbrenner is eagerly pursuing the sad-sack pitcher's replacement. Hideki Irabu is his name.

Endlessly, not to mention *annoyingly*, referred to in print as the "Nolan Ryan of Japan," he's been the object of the Yankees' lust forever, and apparently, the feeling is entirely mutual. With the American rights to Irabu originally gobbled up by the San Diego Padres, the Japanese legend has repeatedly spurned that team's offers, insisting that he's only interested in playing American ball for the New York Yankees. Six months of negotiations later, with the Yankees greasing the Pods to the tune of two great prospects and three million bucks, the Boss has finally gotten his man.

Traveling to Tampa to watch Irabu pitch, George comes home glowing, thrilled to death with his high-priced new import. Since George is shelling out $12.8 million to Irabu over the next four years, it's clear that somewhere in this team's starting staff, *somebody's* days are numbered. Is it Rogers? Probably, though there's always the chance that a resurgence by Rogers will make the rapidly rehabbing/doghouse-dwelling Gooden the odd man out. As Charlie Hayes is always saying, "Every day's a soap opera in *this* clubhouse," and with that in mind, this particular chapter will remain a cliffhanger, at least until Irabu finishes his month-long "mini-spring training" in the minor leagues.

Now eight games back of the O's, it's time for the Boss to start yelling. Working the local papers like a master puppeteer, George fumes about how this team's got a World Series hangover. He calls us undisciplined. He calls us unfocused and lazy and soft. He rails about how the bullpen's in "complete disarray." He complains that he has no gutsy, ballsy leaders among his relievers and openly wonders if losing John Wetteland was a mistake of cataclysmic proportions.

From there, he slams Dwight Gooden for the fight in Arlington, and he flat-out clobbers Mariano Duncan, saying that the slumping infielder should no longer be considered the Yankees second baseman. He's no longer the starter, no longer a reserve, and from this date forward, he should be classified only as a backup, utility outfielder. The man's on a frothy, fuming roll now, and that's when he gets to me, beating me up for not currently having a won-loss record as good as last year's lefty, Jimmy Key.

"So far," he says, "the difference between Wells and Key is significant. I think Key is 8–1 and Wells is 4–3. I think it's about time Wells stepped it up too. I like him. I like his bluster. I just want him to pitch better. I want him to use that bluster with his curveball and his fastball and his slider."* Laughing out loud in my locker, I actually get a pretty big kick out of the big man's talking grapefruits. Sure his comments are pretty much nuts. Sure he's off base, but we're his team, he's signing the checks, and you have to admit he's got a right to complain. Hell, if I paid $65 million for a 26–24 team I'd probably shoot somebody.

With the venting complete, the carnival continues. Wade Boggs starts pushing for a trade, while Andy Pettitte, who's normally as quiet and well mannered as a Sunday school teacher (probably because he *is* a Sunday school teacher), has a meltdown when he learns of Irabu's salary. With a Yankees record of 39–20, and a Yankees *salary* of just $600,000, there's no way in hell Andy can justify seeing a man who's never pitched in the major leagues make five times his cheese. It's a sentiment echoed all over the clubhouse, most vocally by Mariano Rivera, whose Spanish-language tirades are liberally peppered with the phrase *dinero mal!* (sick money).

Meanwhile, Mariano Duncan, dissed big-time in the Boss's tirade, fires back by angrily demanding a trade. "There's no reason anybody should have to play for someone who doesn't appreciate them," he says. "Send me the hell out of

* *New York Times,* May 3, 1997.

here or release me!" Ahh, the Bronx Zoo. I love the smell of conflict in the morning. If only Billy Martin were here, maybe we could go out, get hammered together, and punch out some salesmen.

June. Believe it or not, after all the chaos, all the infighting, all the ugliness, and all the flat-out shitty baseball, we Yankees have hit bottom and begun rebounding big time. Taking three of four at Fenway, we start the month on a roll, and though we drop another pair to Baltimore at Camden Yards, we then bounce back to win five in a row against Milwaukee and Chicago, and fifteen of twenty-one through the rest of the month. Yours truly starts the month in high gear too, racking up back-to-back Ws while allowing just two runs over fifteen innings of work. At that point, traveling to Florida under stormy dark skies, I bear-hug a returning Dwight Gooden,* then hit the field for one of the weirdest starts of my career.

First of all, let me just say that as far as I'm concerned, the Marlins have no right to exist. It rains every fucking day in their piece-of-shit Pro-Player Stadium, and the local population is made up almost entirely of retirees who'd rather hit the early-bird special at Red Lobster than risk breaking a hip at any damp, ugly baseball stadium. Forget Minnesota and Montreal, the *real* franchise that oughta get axed is Florida. That said, you can safely assume I hit the drizzly, muddy mound in Miami with a large chip already weighing down one shoulder. From there, I'm immediately confronted with Greg Bonin, an umpire whose strike zone tonight seems about the same size as your average slice of toast. Standing in the rain, miserable, wet, and forced to throw fat, midplate gimme-balls in order not to walk every player in the Marlins lineup, I get in trouble fast.

Bases loaded with a hit batter, a walk, and a cheap bunt single, I toss five straight strikes at Gary Sheffield and come away with a 3–2 count for my trouble. Mr. Sheffield launches pitch six 450 feet toward downtown Miami. From there, losing my composure fast, another phantom walk and a gimme-ball double put the damage at five. And though I get out of the inning without further disaster, I'm now officially hot enough to turn the raindrops falling on my head instantly into steam. I lead off the next inning at the plate.

Stepping into the batter's box with a borrowed bat in hand, I politely quiz Mr. Bonin on his strike zone, his eyesight, his sanity, and his sobriety. That's it.

---

* Dwight ultimately settles out of court with the Texas cabby for just about $100K, end-running both an ugly court case and the lingering fury of the Boss.

I'm tossed. Expletives flying, fingers pointing, nostrils flaring, we jaw at each other for a solid minute and a half before Joe Torre and Mel Stottlemyre drag me away like Jake La Motta at the Copa. Jim Mecir relieves me, tossing three more innings before the game's finally called on account of typhoon.

For days after the ejection, Joe Torre doesn't speak to me. Mel Stottlemyre doesn't speak to me, and I hang around the clubhouse privately stewing over the fact that after the game Joe laid into me with the press. "Were you aggravated by Wells's behavior?" the reporters ask. "Hell yeah," Joe replies. "I was a lot more than aggravated. There's no excuse for that kind of behavior. It's unprofessional, it's selfish, and he really left us hanging." Rumors float through the dugout that my skip's got a hair up his ass about my "concentration lapses." At that point, with cold shoulders aimed squarely at me, and my own pissed-off stubbornness aimed back, we're at an impasse.

Back at home, I'm scheduled to pitch tonight against the Mets, and with no end to the cold war in sight, I hit Joe's office to clear the air. Tail between my legs, I apologize to Joe about getting tossed in Florida, while making it clear that in the future, I'd like to hear his complaints about me face-to-face, as opposed to reading them on the back page of the New York Post. We shake, and with the air cleared, Joe wants me to know he never holds a grudge. "If a manager does that," he tells me, "he runs out of players pretty damn quick." That night I beat the Mets 6–3, and smiles quickly return to all the residents of the kingdom. Almost.

First it was Boggs, then it was Hayes, and now for the first time since Abbott and Costello dropped dead, I Don't Know really is on third. With Charlie Hayes slumping, and Wade Boggs showing flashes of brilliance in spot starts and pinch-hitting duties, Joe Torre once again declares third base up for grabs. A platoon is now officially in place, and it's gonna remain in effect until one of these guys steps up to the plate (literally) and earns a full-time spot. With both candidates still insisting the job should be theirs, Joe's platoon meets with Bronx cheers from both sides of the clubhouse. Boggs in particular seems unhappy with Joe's resurrected audition process.

Meanwhile, Hideki Irabu's now on track to start the first game back after the All-Star break. Our joy knows no bounds.

June 28. At home in the Bronx, we are today's nationally televised game on the Fox network, and with that in mind, I've decided to pay tribute to my biggest, brightest, most beloved Yankee hero, by wearing one of Babe Ruth's own caps back onto the field in the house that "he" built. It's a beautiful hat, stitched inside with "G. Ruth" spelled out across its leather band. The Babe wore this thing through the better part of his 1934 season. Overpaying for the hat ($35,000) while enduring our god-awful mid-May road trip through Arlington, I've been dreaming about this moment ever since. Today, a tangible piece of Babe Ruth's legend returns to the field at Yankee Stadium . . . thanks to me. Is this gonna be awesome or what?

As I walk into the game with a gigantic smile, the ghosts of Yankee Stadium have never been more vibrant, more alive, or more real, and the sense of history attached to this cap is nothing less than mind-blowing. Honestly, I'm so honored and awestruck to be wearing this thing that it's all I can do not to cry like a baby. Meanwhile, back in the dugout, my skipper is pissed.

Way back in May, I told Joe that I planned to wear the hat in a game sometime at the Stadium, and he responded with a big smile and a solid thumbs-up. Here and now, however, he's bent out of shape because I sprung this thing on him as a surprise, which didn't allow him to clear things with the front office prior to the game. Coming back to the dugout after a scoreless first inning, Joe tells me to take it off.

"Why?" I ask him.

"Because it's not a standard uniform."

"Are you kidding?"

He's not kidding. "Rules are rules. You can't wear something like that without giving me some advance warning, so I can check it first with the organization," Joe says with a furrowed forehead.

"Oh, come on," I reply, just dumbfounded at the idea that *anybody* working for the Yankees front office could, even at their *most* anal retentive, have any problem at all with my wearing this historic cap. I sigh now, fists clenching, biting my lip hard. "Fine." To me, there's nothing on this earth more aggravating than a pointless, arbitrary, blindly respected rule. However, knowing full well I'm not gonna win this battle, and with last week's cold shoulder still fresh in my brain, I keep the peace by playing the good soldier.

I swap hats with my usual 1997 model while my insides turn somersaults. It's just a hat, I chant in my head, while simultaneously trying to drown out a chorus of, Bullshit! Ten minutes later, with the Yanks going down one, two, three, I'm back on the mound, with my entire game out of whack. Clearly I'm distracted. Clearly I'm pissed, but just as clearly I'm getting my ass kicked. If Joe and Mel thought I had "concentration lapses" before, they ain't seen nuthin' yet. With my location shot, four runs cross the plate in the second, and another one scores in the third. Lost on the mound now, and completely unable to get my game back on track, I hit the showers as Kenny Rogers (who got demoted to the bullpen when Doc Gooden came home) takes over in the fourth. He fares no better than me, and by game's end, we've lost this sucker 12–8. And though I'll spend the next day or two stomping stone-faced through the Yankee clubhouse, I am by no means this team's unhappiest camper.

"I've conceded the job," Wade Boggs says in formally requesting a trade. "Mentally I'm shot. The bottom line is I stink right now, and Charlie is swinging the bat well and it'll help the team more if he plays and I don't." Maybe so, but as unhappy as Boggs may be, he's got to know there's a limited market for slumping thirty-nine-year-old former All-Stars with $2 million contracts. Bob Watson's unable to find a taker. Boggsie's going nowhere, fast.

Meanwhile, down in Florida, a depressed Darryl Strawberry finally opts to undergo knee surgery, which will get him back to 100 percent but keep him out of the lineup until at *least* August. And back in the Bronx, one month after his Mariano Duncan tirade, the Boss quietly tosses a halfhearted apology to Duncan's agent. Duncan just as halfheartedly tosses back one of his own. But the bad blood's still hemorrhaging between them.

Days later, with the Boss pulling the strings, Duncan and whipping boy/pitcher Kenny Rogers get packaged up and sent to San Diego in exchange for the Pods power-hitting outfielder Greg Vaughn. With Vaughn slumping of late, George's "baseball people" decide a change of address might be just the thing to kick-start the slugger's production. At the same time, nobody argues that a one-way ticket out of town might really help Rogers and Duncan return to form. With the deal all set, everybody's happy. Everybody's relieved, except perhaps for the Yankees' team doctor.

Vaughn fails his routine physical. Simple tests reveal that the real source of Vaughn's slump wasn't his dissatisfaction with the Padres, but a rather nasty tear of his rotator cuff. The deal's off, and less than twenty-four hours after Torre's said his good-byes to his two biggest headaches, they're back, like a recurrent yeast infection. And while Rogers is actually pleased with the chance to right his own ship in New York, Duncan needs a straitjacket. A week later, when the Boss makes a grandstanding effort to welcome Duncan back from the All-Star break with a hearty, locker-room handshake in front of the press, Duncan flat out ignores him, leaving George spanked and hanging in front of the media.

As for me, though I'm still pissed off through the days following "the great hat massacre," I go into the break righting last week's disaster with 7⅓ innings of five-hit, one-run ball against the Jays. Heading home now for seventy-two hours of quality Dad-time, I've got a huge smile plastered from one ear to the next. Three days of Power Rangers, Marco Polo, and Hot Wheels follow, during which I think about baseball *maybe* twice. Finally, heading back into La Guardia with the team at 48–37, I'm starting to feel pretty good about our second-half chances. Though there's still seven games between us Yankees and the 55 30 Orioles, one side-by-side glance at our team rosters screams that those guys can't *possibly* keep up the pace. Our pitching's better, our position guys are better, and while Davey Johnson's awesome, unless he's sold his soul to Satan, there's no *way* that team can keep up their .647 pace.

Step one toward catching the Birds comes tonight, when the "Japanese Nolan Ryan" takes the mound for the first time as a New York Yankee. Entering the clubhouse with his interpreter, Irabu's already working a tough room. His credentials questioned, his salary envied, his right to even step foot in a major-league clubhouse doubted severely, a large percentage of this roster would be perfectly happy to FedEx the big righty back to Nagasaki.

First thought: WOW this guy has a big double chin. Second thought: WOW this guy looks happy to be here. "Pee-no-sto-ripe-oo!! Ya!!!" He beams, taking hold of his new uniform. "Pee-no-sto-ripe-oo!! Nice!" Working the room now, shaking hands with whatever teammates aren't openly avoiding his one-man show, Irabu says the same thing at each stop. "Nice-ah to meetchu!" he says with a little bow to Coney.

"Nice to meet you too. Welcome. If there's anything I can do to help you get settled, just lemme know."

"Tank you, tank you." He moves on to Paul O'Neill.

"Nice-ah to meetchu!" he says with the same little bow.

"Yeah. You too," says O'Neill with a little thumbs-up.

"Tank you, tank you."

"Nice-ah to meetchu." My turn, with the little bow now.

"Thanks. I'm glad you're here," I say, smiling warmly. "There's a badger on your face and your dick is on fire."

"Tank you, tank you." He moves on with a smile.

On the mound that night, the man with the 100-mile-per-hour fastball and the 90-mile-per-hour dipping, diving, dropping splitter makes an entire squad of doubters wonder if maybe we *should* believe the hype. Giving up just two runs on five hits while striking out nine Tigers in 6⅔ innings of work, Irabu looks great on the mound, even amid the absolute circus that *is* Yankee Stadium.

Tonight 52,000 fans are packed up into the nosebleeds for Irabu, which is even *more* impressive when you consider this team's been averaging just 23,000 per game. Four *hundred* reporters cram the press box. Thirty-five *million* Japanese are watching the game back in the land of the rising sun. For this guy, in his first game, in a brand-new league, in a brand-new country, to look that kind of pressure in the face and kick ass is really something special. Honestly, faced with the same situation, Kenny Rogers might have burst into flames.

Suddenly, Baltimore's seven game lead looks a whole lot shakier.

And here we go. Coming back from the break taking three in a row from Detroit, we knock the O's lead in the East down from seven games to four and a half. Momentum building, we even manage to survive back-to-back catastrophes. First, Bernie Williams takes an unscheduled trip to the DL with a badly pulled hammy. And less than a week later, when Cecil Fielder tries scoring all the way from first on a Mark Whiten double, he makes a headfirst dive into home plate that registers as a 6.7 on the Richter scale. No lives are lost, but the impact turns Big Daddy's thumb into a piece of rotini. And while Bernie will be back in just about three weeks, Cecil's break puts him out for two months. In his absence, Wade Boggs and a returning Tim Raines will ultimately take turns as our DH du jour. Still, even with our big bats biting the turf, this team just keeps on winning, except maybe for Hideki.

Coming off that first big win in the Stadium, Irabu's back on the fifteenth, a sweaty, sticky, steamy, suffocating mess of a day. Though it's ninety-three degrees at game time, the guy's nonetheless wearing a long-sleeve shirt under his jersey in an effort to hide the weird little batches of therapeutic magnets he's got glued all over his body. "They relieve tension," his interpreter tells me. "They promote healthy blood flow. You try some please?"

"Uhhhhhhh, maybe later," I spout back. "I've got this uhhhh . . . *thing* I've gotta do . . . like . . . over there." Different strokes for different folks I guess, but long sleeves on a day like this seems flat-out suicidal. Somebody probably should have warned him. Somebody probably should have tried to explain how hot it was gonna be for him out there on the mound this disgusting afternoon. Nobody does. Ninety minutes later, having given up five runs and nine hits and three home runs in just five innings of work, a drained, dehydrated, disgusted Irabu soaks his head under a cold, ego-deflating early shower. Five days later, in Milwaukee, against a lousy Brewers team, the man will fall apart completely.

Lasting 6⅔ innings, Irabu gets beat for 6 earned runs, and 7 hits on a day where his best pitch clocks in at 91 miles per hour. At the same time, out on the mound in front of a crowd that chants "OVERRR-RATED! OVERRR-RATED!" at him for two hours straight, Irabu has a meltdown. Giving up the first two runs of the day, Hideki yanks off his mitt and comes justthisclose to slamming it onto the turf. Getting beat for a homer when he's up in the count, Irabu stomps laps around the pitcher's mound while scowling, teeth clenched at the sky. Struggling with his control, Irabu literally kicks the resin bag right to the edge of the infield grass. At the end of the bench, Joe's disgusted while Don Zimmer's entire head turns red.

Taking the ball after Irabu's 108th pitch, Joe looks ready to slug Steinbrenner's pet project right in the mouth. Leaving the field, Irabu bids farewell to the Milwaukee faithful by looking directly into the stands and launching a symbolic loogey half the size of Tokyo. He denies it after the game, but trust me on this one—that was a purpose-hork if ever I saw one. Freak-out complete, Joe and George and the big man's interpreter spend the better part of a week discussing acceptable Yankee behavior. The noose is tightening.

July 26. Another outing, another disaster, and this time, with 54,000 Yankee faithful booing the Nipponese Nolan relentlessly, you can't help but feel sorry for Irabu. Lost on the mound, a lack of confidence just beams from the man's face. As he faces the Seattle Mariners, one great hitter after another gets into the batter's box, smiling broadly and showing no mercy. Have you ever seen that old Bugs Bunny cartoon where Bugs pitches against the Gashouse Gorillas and they hit him so hard the batters just form a conga line around the base paths? That's how this felt. Griffey, A-Rod, Jose Cruz Jr. One after another the line drives shot away from home plate, with six runs allowed in just two innings pitched. Joe finally has no choice but to euthanize this outing. The crowd screaming for his head, Irabu appears zombified as he heads for yet another early shower. "I don't know when he's going to start again," a beaten Joe Torre informs the press. Two days later, Hideki's demoted to Columbus, becoming the first $12.8 million pitcher in the history of the minors. "I told you so" rings out from every corner of the clubhouse.

Thankfully, with Pettitte and Coney pitching beautiful baseball, and Doc hanging tough right around the .500 mark, I run through the rest of July with mostly solid stuff. On July 14, I'm back on the mound at prebreak form, chasing after my 100th career victory. Facing Cleveland, I toss 7⅓ innings, giving up just one run in the second and another in the eighth. Still strong on the mound, I'm mad as hell when Joe comes to yank me with the score tied up at 2–2. Exiting the

Midseason form, 1997
(© Mitchell Layton/Newsport)

game, I pause for a moment to reflect on my performance and beat the snot out of the bullpen phone. I then go on to murder a light fixture, a water cooler, and a big chunk of the Indians' clubhouse wall. I don't want to sit. I *want* my "100."

Heading into Milwaukee, I follow up an unusually hot warm-up with one of the very best starts of my career. A complete game, 99-pitch, 3-hitter, I shut out the Brewers and snag W number 100. Maybe it's the milestone. Maybe it's the weather. Maybe it's the extra bowl of Cap'n Crunch I gobbled down this morning, but whatever the reason, every one of my pitches seems extra sharp today. My velocity's up, my curve is gigantic, and my location is practically dead-on. I pitch with the lead throughout the game, my teammates making it easy for me by gifting their pitcher with an 8-run cushion. You can't have more fun than that, at least not with your pants on.

Coming off my best performance of the year, my worst follows—9 hits, 8 runs, 2 home runs, all given up in just 3⅓ innings of butt-ugly baseball. The Mariners pound me like a piñata. My stuff's flat. Everything's up. My location's off. My velocity's saggy, and the worst part of the whole thing is I've got no idea why. My back feels fine. My arm, my shoulder, my mechanics? Fine, fine, fine. I spend the next five days hoping it's just a fluke, which it is . . . sorta.

Facing Oakland at home at the tail end of the month, I'm right back on track with another complete game, 3-hit shutout, only *this* time, the outing comes with a whopping 16 strikeouts attached. With John Hirschbeck behind the plate, working the same screen-door-size strike zone that got him loogied by Robby Alomar, the combination of great stuff and "called third strikes" pays gigantic dividends. By the time I sit down for the home half of the sixth, I've already put 10 Ks in the books. That's when Coney runs over and drags me off to the corner of the dugout.

"What the hell are you doing, Scumbag?" I ask him.

"Look up there, Scumbag."

Coney points up to the upper deck facade behind third base. I fall down laughing. Up there, a bunch of twisted, rebel fans have built me my own customized "K" corner, with ten huge, home-drawn beer mugs plastered up to mark my progress. I *love* that, largely because in a very real way, it proves once and for all that the fans in this town are taking to me every bit as hard as I've fallen for them. Smart and sharp, attentive, vocal, and opinionated, there's no other city in the league where fans hang so hard on every pitch of the game. Wander through Dodger Stadium, and you'll find twice as many cell phones as scorecards. Wander through Jacobs Field, and you'll find 80 percent of the attendees chewing on their own toenails. Here in New York, it's a whole different story, and with beer steins hoisted high, I've never felt so at home.

With my son Brandon now spending big chunks of his summer vacation with me in the city, we're forever exploring the Big Apple together, finding something new and exciting and amazing almost every single day. We hit Central Park every morning, racing our little remote control cars through footpaths and over rocks and into the ankles of old people. Together we'll visit the dinosaur bones at the Museum of Natural History, where we get into a raging debate over just how bad tyrannosaurus farts would smell. Other days, we might hang at the planetarium, or the zoo, or the Empire State Building, or the Statue of Liberty, or Chinatown or Times Square, where we practically *live* at the All Star Café. Going head to head in the joint's humongous video arcade, I have to cheat just to stay close in "Street Fighter II." With a playground like New York City to wander through, my time spent with Brandon is magical, though it does make me miss him even more when he's gone. Coach Zimmer plays a lousy game of "freeze tag."

August 1. At seventeen games over .500, with a nice head of steam driving us into the month, our situation gets even brighter when Bernie Williams returns from the DL. Immediately he's back to form, making spectacular catches, hitting multiple homers, and sparking our offense toward an 11–4 jump on the month. Meanwhile, with Wade Boggs hitting .358 since the All-Star break, mostly as a designated hitter, and Tim Raines on fire in left, we've got guns blazing from one hole to nine. This is great news, because after a brief flirtation with vulnerability, the Orioles are once again running amok, playing .650 ball for the month of August. And while we Yankees are now way out front in the AL Wild Card race, only a *total* pussy could find comfort in that.

In Kansas City on the fourth, I flirt with throwing my third shutout in four games, before running out of gas in the ninth and getting tagged for three runs. Still, I record my twelfth victory of the season. Wins thirteen and fourteen follow, with a 4–1 smoosh of the Twins in Minnesota, and a less impressive 10–5 slugfest at home. On a roll now, I'm less than five days away from having the wheels fall completely off my season. Coney is just *three* days away from the same fate.

August 17. At home against the Rangers, Coney works just one uncomfortable inning before pulling himself out of the game with shoulder soreness and an inability to get loose. With a year-old vein graft buried deep within that arm, Coney's taking no chances. A rupture in that graft would end his career. A *severely* ruptured graft could bleed out badly enough to cost him his arm. Brave face screwed on tight, Coney heads for the hospital immediately while everybody in the dugout looks upstairs and attempts to call in a favor. Hours later, when we're told Coney's suffering from a simple (if painful) case of tendinitis, this team breathes a huge sigh of relief. If all goes well, we're told, Coney may miss just one start. In a surprise move, two days later, he goes on the fifteen-day DL.

"It's just a precaution," affirms Bob Watson. "We just want to make sure David won't be rushed back into action." Sound thinking, especially when it becomes obvious that David's soreness isn't quite as "minor" as we'd all hoped. Late August and early September workouts find Coney tentative and still hurting, and with those setbacks posted, Joe Torre rolls his eyes, crosses his fingers, and starts juggling a ragtag starting rotation through a nerve-wracking, late-summer swoon.

While Andy Pettitte remains a shining bright spot in what's now become the shakiest rotation in baseball, we go downhill fast from there. Dwight Gooden's 3–2 August puts him at the top of the food chain, while Hideki Irabu returns from exile, tossing just one solid outing against the Royals (5⅓ IP, 3 ER, 5K) before imploding on the mound yet again.

This time around, we're in Anaheim, where "old Jonathan Winters face" (as Irabu's been nicknamed by bullpen coach Billy Connors) gets upset with umpire John Hirschbeck. Called for balks twice in the same game, Irabu begins stomping around the pitcher's mound, grumbling loudly while kicking dirt in Hirschbeck's direction. Hirschbeck immediately takes a little stroll to the mound, where he and Irabu end up nose-to-nose. At that point, at least according to one Yankee infielder, Hirschbeck peppers a string of more generic epithets with the phrase "you Japanese motherfucker." And while Hirschbeck's alleged language has no bearing whatsoever on the game (largely because Irabu has no idea what he's saying), a lot of Yankees quickly begin reconsidering Robby Alomar's side of *last* year's Hirschbeck showdown.

One week later, in Oakland, Irabu is still free-falling, getting rocked for 5 runs and 8 hits in just 3⅓ innings of work. With his season ERA now at 7.07 and rising, Irabu is bullpen bound. Meanwhile, trading roles with Irabu, Kenny Rogers will spot start through August, going 2–0 before back trouble and a shellacking by the Seattle Mariners bring the black cloud right back over his head. Still, as shabbily as our starters have tossed, nobody, but *nobody*, goes into a tailspin like me.

At 14–5, I sail into mid-August on an ego-puffing roll. From there, I'll spend the next month unable to even *buy* myself an out. In Anaheim, I get *killed* for 10 hits and 11 runs in just 3 innings pitched. In Seattle, an oatmeal-mushy curve and piss-poor location lead to *ridiculously* long home runs by Jay Buhner and Dan Wilson and another butt-ugly loss. Back home in the Bronx, the streak hits three as the Montreal Expos hang me out to dry with yet another egg-sucking performance. This time around I'm not *quite* so bad, getting beat for 6 runs and 8 hits over 8 innings pitched, but the long ball kills me again, and *this* time it nearly causes me to punch George Steinbrenner in the face. Lemme explain.

Second inning. Waffling through my third straight lousy-stuff-start, I kick off the inning by getting spanked for hard singles by both David Segui and Rondell White. Darrin Fletcher comes to the plate now, and with a breadbasket fastball delivered to him snail mail, he uncorks a fly ball toward the right-field seats.

Damn! I'm thinking. I can hear John Sterling now. "IT is HIGHHHHHH-HHH! IT is FARRRRRRRR! IT is . . . hey, wait a minute." Paul O'Neill's camped out at the warning track now, heels against the fence, and from where I'm standing, it looks like this ball's gonna be caught. I go thumbs-up on the mound, only to watch yet another Yankee fan make like Jeffrey Maier and turn a routine fly-ball-out into a home run. This time it's even more obvious than in last year's playoffs.

O'Neill makes a jump at the fence. The bleacher creature leans out and literally smacks mitts with Paulie. Fletcher's ball bounces out of O'Neill's mitt, off the fan's hand, and over the wall for what "Blind" Mike Reilly (at first base no less) rules a home run. Paulie goes ballistic. "YOU DON'T DO THAT TO THE FUCKING HOME TEAM!!!" he screams from right field. "HE HIT THE BALL! HE HIT MY GLOVE!" Choruses of "BULLSHIT" echo through the house that Ruth built for a solid ten minutes. Up in the owner's box, the veins in George Steinbrenner's forehead are visibly throbbing.

Middle of the eighth. Joe tells me I'm done. Down 6–2 with Pedro Martinez on fire, I've got a pretty good idea this ain't gonna end pretty. I head for the showers, still muttering under my breath about the bleacher boob. Shuffling into the clubhouse, I'm surprised to find George Steinbrenner already inside. "David," he grumbles in lieu of a friendlier greeting.

"Hey, Boss," I reply. "Listen, I think you're gonna have to put more security out there in right field, or a higher fence, so that nobody can lean in and do that shit anymore."

"Yeah, well, I think *you* oughta worry more about winning ball games, and less about my security staff. 'Cuz right now, you ain't no pitcher."

"What?"

"You . . . ain't . . . no . . . pitcher! At least not the kind of pitcher I thought I was getting when you came over!"

There's a tense silence now. People are scattering out of the room like it's an Old West saloon just prior to a shootout. I try to stay cool. I fail.

"Listen, old man," I growl. "If you don't think I'm a fucking pitcher, why don't you trade me?"

"Trust me," George says, "I've *tried* to trade you, but nobody wants your fat ass. I'm stuck with you."

"Motherrrrrrrrrrrrrrrrrrfucker!" I shout, getting into George's face now. "Let me tell you something. I *never* give up. I take pride in what I do when I go out there, and don't you *ever* doubt my fucking ability as a pitcher. That's the worst thing you could possibly do." We're nose-to-nose at this point. "So fuck off! In fact, I think you'd better just get out of my face, go back to your box, and watch the rest of the game on TV. 'Cuz if you hang around here much longer I'm gonna beat your ass." That's it. It's go time.

"Go ahead! Do it!" George orders. "Try me. You think I'm afraid of you?" George has a sort of modified Charles Bronson face working now. "Come on!"

"One more word, and I'm gonna break your fucking jaw!" I warn him. "I ain't kidding." I'm really not.

But George isn't backing down. Cue the theme from *The Good, the Bad, and the Ugly*.

A staring contest follows. Nobody budges until finally a pair of suits who'd been chatting with George earlier swoop in and lock elbows with the Boss, ushering him away, while supplying him with a clean, face-saving exit.

Meanwhile I storm into the lounge, where I pound a couple of Buds. Ten minutes later, I head back to the showers, still steaming, only to find George right back in the same spot as before. Now he's talking with Billy Connors, and this is where I admit I kinda took things too far.

"Are you still in here?" I spout off, pointing. "Get your fucking ass out of here right now, and go up to your box and watch the game like I told you! I'm serious." George exits grumbling. Two minutes later, when I'm lathered up and cooled down, the magnitude of this altercation sinks in fast. Mariano Duncan never came anywhere near this kind of insubordination, and George shipped *his* ass to Canada for just a crappy minor leaguer and $50,000 cash. With that precedent set, I'm liable to end up drawn and quartered somewhere out near center field. Either that or playing for the Marlins. I shudder at *both* possibilities.

Twenty-four hours pass. No death, no trade, and I'm actually feeling pretty good. Fooling around in the clubhouse, I'm trying to get Bernie Williams to quit playing Andres Segovia on his guitar in favor of a little Bachman Turner Overdrive. That's when the phone rings and I answer it, and because I was in a goofy mood that day, I say, "Hello, Yankee Stadium, second base."

An angry voice on the other end of the phone goes "WHO IS THIS?!" and at that point, I laugh and say, "Well, I don't know . . . who is THIS?"

"It's GEORGE!"

D'oh!!! "Uh, hi, George," I mumble. "This is Boomer."

George goes, "Boomer . . . Hrmph."

I bend. "Listen, George, I just want to clear the air. I want to apologize for the way things came bursting out the other day."

George says, "Well, I want to apologize too. I shouldn't have laid into you that way. You just keep doing what you're doing because you're a hell of a pitcher. You showed me something special yesterday."

And there it was. George had slipped. I'd gotten a peek at his cards, and suddenly our whole locker-room lockup made a little more sense. *Sure* George was pissed about my lousy performance. Sure he was hot under the collar over the fact that his big-budget team was now playing like a blue-light special. But with all that in mind, by no means was George *just* venting at me the other day. He was testing me too. He was trying to see for himself what I was made of. George is a guy who wants warriors on his team. He wants fighters, guys who stick up for themselves, guys who defend themselves. He doesn't want players who can be intimidated, or cowed in the face of adversity, or conflict, or tension. And despite the fact that our confrontation really did get pretty ugly, some part of George must've been thrilled with my aggressively antisocial behavior.

After the game that night, George came down to the clubhouse, and we shook hands and shared a couple of beers and ended up laughing like hell over the whole thing. In an odd, backward, just slightly twisted way, nearly ripping out each other's throats actually bonded us pretty well. And when news of the showdown hit the local tabloids, it also made me a hero to nine zillion Yankees fans. Still, despite the happy endings and good press, my current slump was about to get even worse. So was the Yankees'.

September. We lose three in a row in Philly, where Kenny Rogers and Dwight Gooden come up short in decent outings and a spot-starting Hideki Irabu earns himself a 3-inning, 9-hit pass right back to the bullpen. From there, six games back, we head home for the first of eight September matchups against the front-running Orioles.

Big game situation. The blood's boiling. The heart's pounding. The Stadium's full. This is my kind of game. I lose it, 5–2. Trying to hit corners I'm literally three feet off target. Trying to put fastballs at the O's knees, I come away tossing letter-high Christmas presents. I'm walking leadoff batters. I forget to cover first on a routine grounder to Tino. And with Joe Girardi calling for a sinker, a mix-up in our signals gets him a cut fastball instead. It clips the tip of his glove, fracturing his finger in the process. Losses just don't come any uglier than this one. Back in the dugout, Joe's frowning at me again. Honestly, there are whole long chunks of this season where my relationship with Joe Torre is a lot like the one Dennis the Menace has with Mr. Wilson.

Four consecutive starts have now brought on four consecutive losses, during which time I've been tagged for 26 runs and 38 hits over 25⅔ innings. With my location a mess, and almost everything I throw sitting fat and juicy at belt high or better, it's time to pull over and ask for directions. I corner Mel Stottlemyre after the game and we make plans to watch tape of my recent starts to see if we can't pick out where the hell this train went off the tracks.

Mel's great at this. Honestly, I know it sounds like I'm blowing smoke to flatter my current pitching coach, but this guy really is a cut above the rest. Got a hitch in your delivery? He'll find it. Is the opposing pitcher tipping his pitches? Mel knows. Is your body language screaming that you're running on fumes even if your mouth protests that you're fine? You won't fool *this* guy. With that in mind, remote control in hand, we frame-by-frame our way through hours of Wells tape, and come up empty. Sure there's a little hiccup here and there that I can try to smooth over, but the simple quick-fix, easily corrected mechanics problem I was hoping might jolt me out of the doldrums simply does not exist. We're losing. I'm back at square one, but believe it or not, this team has yet to hit bottom.

One day later. When Andy Pettitte gets hit in the face with a first-inning drive from Cal Ripken, it's a very bad omen. Leaving the game with one huge Angelina Jolie lip sticking out of his face, Andy heads out for X rays while Hideki Irabu heads in from the pen and quickly gives up 9 runs en route to a humiliating 13–9 loss. One day later, with Ramiro Mendoza on the hill, we drop another one, running our losing streak to six in a row, and nine of our last ten.

The August/September meltdown (*AP Photo/Ann Heisenfelt*)

Now trailing the O's by a full nine games, it's time to start seriously thinking Wild Card.

With the White Sox and Angels both wobbly, fading, and currently running five games behind us, the AL Wild Card is clearly ours for the taking. And while getting into the playoffs through the doggy door isn't exactly the picture-perfect Yankees ending, I'll sure as hell take it in a pinch. Apparently I'm not alone in that sentiment, because somehow, even at our lowest, even with our impossible first-place dream now officially slipping from our grasp, this entire team starts smiling. Honest to God, with that great, unreachable goal off our backs, it's almost as if we're all finally free to shift gears, focus on the positive, and roar toward a date with the postseason. We'll go 17–5 the rest of the way.

Meanwhile, though the rest of the team may be taking it up a notch, I'm still a mess on the mound. On September 10, Boston clubs me for 5 runs and 12 hits over 7 innings of work, and on September 15, they beat me up again, this time for 6 runs and 12 hits over 5 innings of work. At this point I'm wondering if I can squeeze in a visit to Lourdes between starts.

September 20. Having finally rested, and rehabbed, and iced, and cortisone-shotted himself back into pitching shape, David Cone returns to Yankee Stadium for his first pain-free start in five weeks. Going a decent five innings against Toronto, Coney strikes out five while surrendering two squibby little runs. The entire Yankees roster breathes a huge sigh of relief. For us to have any chance at all of thriving in the postseason, Coney's gonna have to be . . . well, Coney.

September 21. I'm playing long-toss in the outfield at the stadium when Mel Stottlemyre jogs up and casually drops a bomb.

Catching up to me out in the grass, Mel asks if we can talk for a minute. "Sure," I tell him. "What's up?" With that, Mel ushers me deeper into right and away from the long-tossers, which automatically stamps our upcoming conversation with big red warning stickers reading PRIVATE and BAD NEWS. "Listen," he tells me, "I want you to know you might be in the bullpen for the playoffs."

"What the fuck?!!!" I *totally* lose it. I *totally* go off on him. I shout, "Aw, you're full of shit, Mel! There's no way! This is crazy! I'm fourteen and ten. I've *earned* that spot! Jesus tap-dancing Christ! This is bullshit!" My relentless rampage is now echoing through all of Yankee Stadium and half of the Bronx. To his credit, Mel just kinda listens to me scream myself out, calm and cool until finally he just quietly, rationally, replies, "Look, I'm not saying you *won't* be part of the postseason rotation, but you've had five *really* bad starts in a row. I want you to understand it's an option we're looking at."

I can't believe it. Sure I've hit a rough patch. Sure I'm struggling. But Mel knows as well as I do, it's a *temporary* funk. Is he testing me? Maybe. Is he hoping the veiled threat of a postseason on the bench will slap me out of my slump? Absolutely. Would he really start Dwight Gooden or Kenny Rogers ahead of me in the ALDS? I don't know, and that's what drives me nuts. It's a good thing too . . . I always pitch better when I'm suppressing the urge to kill.

September 22. Silence. In my last six starts, I've been tagged for 34 runs, and 62 hits in 38 innings. Opposing batters are hitting me at a .360 clip, and my ERA during the slump now stands at a ridiculous 8.05. My manager's lost faith in me. My pitching coach has too. The press monkeys have been running around my locker all week, screeching and scratching and spreading the news that tonight's "audition" is a "make or break moment" for me. Time to "show what I'm made of" they write, time to "rise to the occasion," time to "put up or shut up." Fuck that. As far as I'm concerned I "showed what I'm made of" the night sixteen hand-drawn beers were hung up in the left-field stands. I "rose to the occasion" by winning ball games, week in and week out, with shutouts and strikeouts and complete games and 14 victories so far this season. Sorry, guys. Want me to play nice on this one? Want me to spit out some cute sound byte about how I've got my fingers crossed and I'm gonna go out to the mound and give my coaches and my team 110 percent? Fuck you.

No Metallica tonight. No noise. No goofing around. No laughter. I just don't feel like it. In his office now, Joe Torre's talking to the press, saying things like "any time you send a pitcher out there who's pitching for a spot in the rotation, you get a better idea about him." Excuse me? Joe continues about me with "I'd like to see him get into trouble and get out of trouble. I'd like to see him maybe give up a couple of runs and get back up." Please understand me on this one. Joe Torre is a tremendous manager, and a wonderful man, but right about now, with the guy showing *absolutely* no confidence in my abilities, I'm ready to smack him.

This is humiliating. This is insulting. This is a conscious attempt to jump-start my stalled season . . . and it totally works. Stepping onto the mound with everything to lose, I'm simply too pissed off to suck. Pitching with a mission, and a fury, and a fastball that's popping for the first time in weeks, I stay eight innings at the dance, giving up just seven hits and one eighth-inning run. Postgame beer in hand, I'm told Joe's response to my start went: "He pitched very well. Hopefully, he can repeat that or be close to it, and we'll have a race going."

"What!"

Repeat it, Joe says, "and we'll have a race going." How maddening is that? I'm 15–10 now, solid in my last outing, and *still* I don't get Joe's blessing. With Cleveland now looking like our probable first-round opponent, I take the bull-shit by the horns, cornering Mel and Joe, in an attempt to clear the air once and for all. With the sales pitch flying, I flat-out begged them to start me in the playoffs, for their own good. Pressing harder I even tried to sell those guys on starting me in Game 1. Honestly, I had a *great* track record against Cleveland. I'd stuck it up their butts twice in the 1996 playoffs. And with Coney's arm still hurting, and the Indians riding as the one team that owns Andy Pettitte (they've blown him out twice this season), I said flat out to Joe, "You want to win, put me in!"

"Lemme get back to you on that," he replies, making a beeline to . . . well, just about anywhere else on the planet. Too bad. I *still* say we would have taken that series if he'd listened to me.

September 27. Last start of the season. On the mound in Detroit, facing a truly sorry excuse for a lineup, I'm rocking and rolling my way through 7 innings of 5-hit, 1-run ball. Yanks win 6–1. At the same time, out in the visitors' bullpen, David Cone throws ten minutes of pain-free, three-quarter-speed fastballs. That's it. Lock it up. Coney, Pettitte, Wells. I'm pitching in the playoffs. Joe's gotta formally announce it to the press any minute . . . doesn't he?

Nothing. An hour passes. Still nothing. Damn! I storm out of the clubhouse now, twelve-pack in tow, knowing full well that a homicide may go down if I stay. "Elvis has left the building!" Coney tells the flock of reporters looking to grill me.

Twenty-four hours later, with our last regular season game about to unroll, there's *still* no news, and once again, my blood is boiling. Helloooo, a little vote of confidence over here for your 16–10 third starter please? I mean, I under-stand you want to keep Dwight Gooden motivated as long as possible (just in case Coney's arm falls off during Game 1), but this is ridiculous. I'm dying to punch a wall. I doubt any third starter has ever gone into a postseason so thor-oughly disturbed.

Game 1. In Yankee Stadium 57,398 maniacs cram into the rafters, setting a new all-time attendance record at the Stadium. Stepping onto that grass, in that building, with the fans roaring, and the atmosphere at two million kilowatts, it's impossible *not* to get crazy. One more Yankee milestone. One more raging adrenaline rush. Coney's back, I've finally gotten my Game 3 start confirmed, the universe has realigned itself in a positive configuration, and all is right with the world. This series is ours for the taking. The overconfident posturing lasts all of twenty minutes.

Out on the mound, it's clear from pitch one that Coney's in big trouble. His location is shaky, his velocity's down, and while he still ranks as a bona fide Einstein on the rubber, tonight the bad shoulder overrides the super-size brain. Coney's down 5–0 by the end of the first. At this point, normal teams would be making early dinner reservations off the bullpen phone, but if you've learned anything so far in this chapter, it's that we Yankees ain't normal. Four innings later, we'll have this sucker tied up at 6–6.

Bottom of the fifth. Derek Jeter comes to the plate, and like clockwork, every fifteen-year-old girl in the house screams like a banshee for the "dreamiest Yankee." They scream even louder when Derek takes an 0–2 fastball and deposits the sucker into the first row of seats in left, just barely clearing the fence. Derek laughs as he trots back into the dugout, swearing that the only reason that ball got out was that every fan down the left-field line must've inhaled at the same time. It's now 7–6. Yankees lead. Paul O'Neill steps in and follows Derek's minihomer with a 408-foot monster of his own. Up 8–6, we hang right there to take a quick lead in the series. After an off day tomorrow, we'll pick up with Andy Pettitte taking the hill against twenty-one-year-old rookie Jaret Wright in what *should* be a squash. Meanwhile, Coney's season is hanging by a thread.

By the time we gear up for Game 2, Coney's already back at Columbia-Presbyterian. Tossing softly in an attempt to shake off yesterday's disaster, David's now battling renewed shoulder pain. He immediately undergoes yet another MRI, after which David's doctors report a lot of "routine wear and tear" but no major structural damage. That's the good news. The *bad* news is, though he won't in a million years admit it, David's shoulder now hurts like a motherfucker. And while Joe Torre wisely refuses to tip the press as to whether or not David will make his scheduled start if we play a Game 4, Coney already knows it won't happen. Sitting alone in the clubhouse, head in his hands, my friend is sobbing. He's probably gonna pound me for spilling that secret, but I think it's a great illustration of just how gutsy, and competitive, and flat-out tough the man really is. Even at this stage of the game, Coney refuses to say "uncle," pronouncing himself "day-to-day" while his shoulder burns.

Game 2. Moments after Andy Pettitte's cruised through *his* half of the first, Jaret Wright takes the mound, looking understandably intimidated. The kid stares up into the stands as the Yankee Stadium faithful explode. He takes deep, calming, cleansing breaths between each and every warm-up toss. He's stretching. He's overthrowing. He's distracted. He's tentative. He's snakebit. He's ours.

Wide-eyed, clearly intimidated, and struggling mightily with his control, the kid's got our batters smelling blood. They roll through a first inning that finds Wright throwing thirty-five pitches, the vast majority of them outside the strike zone. Walking the bases full, the kid ultimately gets smacked around pretty good, and by the time the carnage is over, we Yankees are the proud owners of a handsome, early 3–0 lead. But that's where Mr. Wright shuts the door.

Showing a lot more composure than his years should allow, Wright bounces back from his first-inning jitters to hold the Yankee bats scoreless through his next six innings of work, ultimately scattering just three hits over the remainder of his outing. At the same time, Andy Pettitte, fighting through a rapidly stiffening back, crashes and burns. This one was weird.

Rolling through his first three innings of work, Andy's looking as dominant as ever, and with two quick outs in the fourth, he seems well on his way to another 1-2-3-inning. But that doesn't happen. Instead, Pettitte walks Matt Williams, and at that point, while 57,000 ball-busting Yankee fans chant "HALLLLL-LE! BERRRRR-RYY!" at the top of their lungs, David Justice comes to the plate with a high-volume reminder of the gorgeous ex-wife who now hates his guts. One pitch later, Justice shuts up the crowd with a sharp single into right. From there, Pettitte's day goes downhill fast. Sandy Alomar singles. Jim Thome singles. Tony Fernandez doubles, and by the time Andy's inning from hell is finally over, the Indians are up 5–3. Tagged for two more with a Matt Williams homer in the fifth, Pettitte heads for the showers, repeatedly beating himself up with the phrase "I blew it." We head to Jacobs Field with the series knotted at one apiece. Now it's my turn.

Got a house? Bet it on me, because there's no way I'm losing this game. Coming off the slump, I'm sharp as a tack. Surviving my manager's late-season heat, I'm *dying* to prove Joe was wrong. It's October. It's the postseason. It's party time, and I flat-out *own* this Indians team. I may be the first ironclad "sure thing" in the history of sports-wagering.

These are the numbers that earn me a sentence or two of bragging: 9 innings, 105 pitches, 74 strikes, 5 hits, no walks, 1 earned run. Feeling fantastic on the mound, every one of my pitches is effective tonight. At the same time, for absolutely *no* apparent reason, these Indians spend the entire evening swinging at first pitch, after first pitch, after first pitch. I mean, really, could you make it any *easier* for me? Was there a team meeting that said "let's be ridiculously aggressive out there"? I have no idea. All I know is that high and inside, they're first-pitch swinging. Two feet off the plate, they're swinging. Tossing first-pitch garbage right through that lineup, I'm ahead in the count all night long. You just can't give me that kind of advantage . . . at least not in October. We take this sucker by a score of 6–1.

Up two games to one now, we need just one more W to move on. And while that would have been a "gimme" with Coney's arm at full strength, right now, right here, there's not a cocky soul in the clubhouse. Shortly after the end of Game 3, Joe Torre finds Dwight Gooden and says, "You've got the ball tomorrow, Doc. You're pitching Game Four." When Doc looks equal parts excited and pissed at the news, I can't say that I blame him.

Carried on the roster as a long-relief insurance policy, Doc was overlooked entirely when Coney went down in Game 1. The same thing happened when Andy Pettitte fell apart in Game 2. Now, having not pitched a live baseball in a solid week and a half, Doc finds himself tossed, totally unprepared, into the single biggest game of the Yankees '97 season. Pitch well, and we clinch. Suck gas, and the series gets evened up at 2–2, with the momentum clearly shifting Cleveland's way. Going back to the hotel, I know for a fact Doc felt primed and ready for a serious ass-whupping. He was nervous. He was negative. He was about to surprise all of us.

Game 4. In a rematch of their Game 1 showdown from the 1988 NLCS, Dwight Gooden and Orel Hershiser are back on opposite mounds. Older now, and wiser, with a lot less velocity and a lot more ball control, both guys turn back the clock to lock up in an unexpectedly solid pitchers' duel. Hershiser gives up two quick first-inning runs, but from there, the Bulldog's in ass-chomping form, shutting out the Yankees right into the eighth.

Meanwhile, across the board, though Doc Gooden's making like the Doc Gooden of old, Joe Torre's got the man on a *very* short leash. Giving up a solo home run to David Justice in the second inning, and then a double to Matt Williams, the bullpen's up and throwing in a flash. On the mound, Doc's visibly seething, clearly angered by Torre's quick-triggered call to the pen. Pounding through the next two batters, Doc's on a mission, and he gets out of the inning without further damage. From there, Doc cruises into the sixth before leaving the game with a well-earned 2–1 lead. Backslapped, high-fived, hugged, kissed, and complimented into submission as he hits the Yankee bench, Doc's come through for this team yet again.

But it's not to be.

Eighth inning. Mariano Rivera's on the mound, untouchable as ever, when Sandy Alomar steps in, works the count to 2–2, then takes a hacking, windmilling swing at a ball up and out of the strike zone, and deposits that ball up and out of Jacobs Field. Tied up at two, we go to the ninth.

Ramiro Mendoza's on the mound now, and his stuff looks nasty as ever. Marquis Grissom leading off, and the little bugger dinks a little bloop single into right. No big deal. Bip Roberts follows the bloop with a sac fly that puts Grissom at second, and that brings Omar Vizquel to the dish. With yet another solid pitch served up by Mendoza, Vizquel connects with an ordinary drive back toward the mound. Mendoza takes a stab, but it deflects off his glove and sails past a crossed-up Derek Jeter into left. Grissom scores and the Jacobs Field crows go insane. "Ah, fuck you all!" I shout up toward the pandemonium. "We'll kick your ass tomorrow!"

Game 5. Right from the beginning, this one's looking like another pitchers' duel. Jaret Wright's throwing smoke from the get-go, and in our half of the inning, despite some lingering stiffness in his back, Andy Pettitte looks flat-out awesome. Everything's working, everything's solid, but just like in Game 2, one inning's meltdown will cost Andy dearly.

With two men on base in the third, Manny Ramirez steps up to the plate and smacks a ground-rule double. From there, Matt Williams (who never seems to make an out through this whole series) clocks a sharp single to right, and when the smoke clears, the damage stands at 3–zip. One inning later, even as Cleveland is adding another run with a Sandy Alomar double, a groundout, and a sac fly from Tony Fernandez, you can't help but see Andy returning to form.

It makes Pettitte nuts. From domination on the mound, through a rough patch of *maybe* six batters, and back to domination, Andy's nonetheless stepped into a 4–0 hole. And though this team will *never* say die, and we end up scoring two in the fifth, and one more in the sixth, that's as close as we get. Paul Assenmacher and Jose Mesa stomp our bats flat through the seventh, eighth, and ninth, and just like that, eight months of work becomes toast. By the time the Jacobs Field fireworks are booming over the outfield grass, I'm already three beers into a twelve-pack, and thinking 1998.

Having finally become a Yankee, having survived, thrived, nose-dived, and rebounded in the Bronx Zoo, there's now just one unfulfilled dream left in my vast Yankee stockpile. Come hell or high water, I ain't leaving this town without my ring.

No off-season has ever seemed this long.

FOURTEEN

Bronx Booming

> Yesterday, the Yankees'
> David Wells pitched a perfect
> game by retiring twenty-seven straight
> Minnesota Twins. After the game, he
> celebrated by retiring twenty-
> seven straight Heinekens.
>
> —*David Letterman*

DECEMBER 1997: MIDDLE OF NOWHERE

I'm cold. I'm ankle deep in mud. I'm flat-out lost in some godforsaken stretch of garbage-strewn Michigan woods. I need coffee. I need blankets. I need a couch and a TV. I get none. Instead, I get frostbitten toes and a low-flying bird that poo-bombs my hat. I'm not a happy camper. Meanwhile, bounding through the brambles with a giant smile on his face, praising the weeds and practically salivating over a trail full of deer tracks, is Kirk Gibson. Sounding a lot like the Crocodile Hunter, Kirk whoops, "Is this place fantastic, or what?!"

"If this is *fantastic*," I shout back, "I'd hate to see your idea of 'pretty good'!"

"Hey, just remember this was your idea, pal!" Kirk yells at me as he scurries up a tree for an aerial view of the place.

Gibby's right. I've got no one to blame for this mess but myself. Kirk explains:

In the fall of '96, some people I know opened up a really beautiful game ranch enclosure in Michigan, and they invited me to be the first hunter up there. I invited David to come with me, and we ended up having a really fantastic time. Dave shot his first deer there, with a bow, and that lit the lightbulb. Dave's like "This place is awesome, dude. Why don't *we* start up a game ranch of our own?" That's how Dave is. Y'know he thinks, Hey, I liked this new experience. Now I wanna do it every day.

But I actually loved David's idea, and I ultimately had a long chat with a Realtor who went out and found us 1,300 wooded acres in Michigan. But y'know, when I first showed the land to David, it was nothing like that really nice ranch we'd been to. Our place was ugly. The fields were all weedy, and there was garbage all over. Lemme tell you, Dave wasn't too thrilled. But see, I'm a visionary guy, and I knew this land had good, healthy clay soil, and there was limestone all over the place that I knew I could excavate, and crush, and lay out to make roads. I knew we could make good fishing ponds there. And there was a lot of open space too, that I knew we could farm to help feed whatever animals we'd bring in. There was a ton of work to be done, but the place was really perfect.

And that was it. Kirk made like Grizzly Adams. I made like a stereotypical city slicker. We had the paperwork thrown on the front burner, and in no time at all, the Kirk Gibson/David Wells Buck Falls Ranch was born. At that point we fenced-in the property, bought ourselves about three dozen deer, set 'em loose, and let nature take its course. Right now, that same herd stands at just about 225.

In the meantime, with a retired, flannel-clad, facially stubbled Gibby managing the place, our land started taking shape fast. Roads went in, fields got

With Gibby, at the ranch

plowed, and by the following spring, we'd have corn, and soybeans, alfalfa and clover, on the buffet for one very happy group of big, beefy, plus-size bucks. In no time at all, Kirk's vision and enthusiasm and talent will combine with my, uh, cheerleading, to begin turning our wasteland into a woodland paradise. In years to come, the ranch will become a huge part of my life, as well as an eagerly anticipated part of my postseason ritual. For now though, Kirk and I will spend the better part of this winter playing with our sprawling, new, wildlife-stocked toy.*

Springtime for Hitters

January 1998. Almost a year removed from my mom's passing and the street fight in San Diego, and the broken hand, and the gout attack that sent me to spring training '97 as a walking disaster, I slide toward "pitchers and catchers '98" without bumping into even the tiniest catastrophe. No trades, no battles with management, not a single incident that requires a police report; by Boomer's standards, I've become boring, with my only real antisocial behavior coming as part of my son Brandon's marathon, no-holds-barred, backyard ses-

---

* I should also mention Lee Holberton, who puts up with both me AND Gibby, and keeps the ranch in amazing, tip-top shape. Thanks, Lee.

sions of "kill the guy with the ball." It's a very good sign—one of many in this long, hungry, championship-deprived Yankees' winter.

First, there's Coney. Fresh off an October date with an arthroscopic surgeon, David Cone spends his off-season wiping the bad taste of the playoffs from his mouth by rehabbing like a madman and throwing regularly, right from the start of December. In mid-January, while the Yankees suits and the New York tabloids are openly referring to Coney as "a raging question mark" and ever-so-gently targeting mid-May as a "possible" return date, Ol' Aches and Pains sits at my kitchen table, laughing and flipping those articles the bird. Feeling strong and confident and irrationally guilty for having to shut it down last October, Coney's on a mission, swearing he'll be ready for opening day. I know better than to doubt the guy.

Meanwhile, on the day after Christmas, another huge part of the Yankees' 1998 success jumps onto a makeshift raft, catches a current, and begins bobbing all over the Caribbean Sea. With his common-law wife and six other defectors in tow, Orlando Hernández leaves Cuba behind, taking to the sea in a desperate attempt to find freedom, prosperity, and the chance to actively pursue his life-long dream of becoming a major-league ballplayer.

With a 129–47 lifetime record for the Cuban national team, the man comes with outstanding credentials and a well-known, deep-seated desire to take the field as a New York Yankee. For years, while pitching for Cuba, Hernández would regularly incur the wrath of management by working out with a beat-up, sun-faded Yankees cap on his head. And while two and a half months of contract negotiations, legal red tape, and some unexpectedly strong competition from the Seattle Mariners will slow down the process, Hernández will ultimately be signed, sealed, pinstriped, and high-kicking by the first weekend of March. Talk about a "team of destiny," we Yankees are about to pluck a 12–4 pitcher right out of the ocean.

But wait, there's more (he said, doing a solid Ron Popeil). With Charlie Hayes and Wade Boggs *both* leaving the Bronx, the Yankees fill their brand-new hole at third base by diving headfirst into a "flop swap" that quickly makes *two* teams ecstatic. Kenny Rogers gets shipped off to Oakland, taking his great arm and his bad luck with him. In exchange, we Yankees haul in the A's biggest underachiever, third baseman Scott Brosius. Having hit a truly rotten .203 for the '97 season, Brosius has plummeted 101 points from his 1996 batting average of .304. However, with baseball genius/superscout Gene Michael sticking his neck out to declare Brosius an easily repaired fixer-upper, the Yanks pull the trigger, coming away with a guy who's gonna spend the '98 season hitting .300 for this team out of the *number nine* slot in the batting order. It just doesn't get any better that that.*

Meanwhile, Cecil Fielder moves on to California, still grumbling about how George Steinbrenner mysteriously disappeared last season after personally calling Big Daddy's cell phone to guarantee him a long-term contract extension. Truth be told, George never called Cecil at all. It was Dwight Gooden on the other end of the cell that day, working his pitch-perfect Steinbrenner impersonation to play a practical joke on Mr. Fielder. When Cecil took the bait, bit hard, and even talked about the "positive phone call" to the press, Dwight simply spent the remainder of the '97 season too scared to fess up. As a result, Fielder grinds through 1997 stewing, wondering why the hell "George" would back away from his own self-proposed big deal.

At any rate, the truth of the matter says that even though Cecil's gonna spend the '98 season a continent removed from us Yanks, we probably won't ever miss him. Coming into spring training, both Tim Raines and Darryl Strawberry are back at 100 percent, and piling on the power. At the same time, switch-hitting veteran slugger Chili Davis joins the team. And with Chad Curtis coming back off a very solid '97, Joe Torre's immediately gifted with a wonderful left-field/DH, preseason logjam.

And finally, just a week before we pitchers are due to report at camp, the Yankees pack four minor-league prospects off to Minnesota in exchange for Chuck Knoblauch, a guy who's arguably the best leadoff hitter in the majors. ESPN and the New York tabloids immediately brand the deal an unfair, unbelievable, flat-out steal for us Bombers, while the Minnesota papers piss and moan about unfair competition while letting fly with a collective whine of "We wuz robbed!" Still, love the deal or hate it, Knoblauch's signing stands as the final installment in what's now become a vast Yankee stockpile of talent.

As Knobby moves in at the top of the order, this very good lineup becomes flat-out bulletproof. We've got .300 hitters with power up and down the dial. We've got *no* guys who swing for the moon and whiff 150 times a season. There's a great balance between righties and lefties. *Every* hitter's smart. *Every* hitter's a veteran. *Every* hitter's proven, and heading into Tampa, the only *real* question mark on this year's roster has to do with us starters. Cue the cheesy soap opera organ.

* Kenny Rogers will spend 1998 going 16–8 as the ace of the Oakland A's staff.

Will David Cone's shoulder bounce back? Will Andy Pettitte return to form after fighting through back pain last October? Can David Wells rack up two good years in a row?* And with Kenny Rogers exiled to Oakland, and Doc Gooden insanely *choosing* to play for Cleveland, will Hideki Irabu and Ramiro Mendoza prove up to the task? And what about Señor Hernández? Will the Yankees risk repeating last year's Irabu-llshit by rushing their new find to the bigs? For the answers to these and other burning Yankee questions ("Will Derek Jeter and Mariah Carey ever find *true* happiness?") tune in next week to Yankees spring training '98.

February. One by one we return to Legends Field. One by one we're slapped in the face by our first-look, firsthand evidence of how great this team really is. Knoblauch, Jeter, O'Neill, Williams, Martinez, Davis, Strawberry, Posada, Brosius; spend fifteen minutes watching this lineup take BP and your jaw *will* hang open. And while everybody in camp works hard to keep their bland, faux-humble, press clichés in tact ("Y'know, guys, it's a long season and we're just gonna have to take it one day at a time and give 110 percent"), there's not a guy in the clubhouse who's not secretly thinking ticker tape.

Out on the mound, though El Niño keeps postponing our games, and minor injuries keep slowing our progress, we Yankee starters come around pretty convincingly too. Coney looks solid, as does Andy Pettitte, and though I somehow manage to pull a muscle in my rib cage, I'm feeling opening-day ready before I've even downed my first green St. Patty's Day beer. And while Ramiro Mendoza is surprisingly wobbly (6.92 ERA for the spring), Hideki Irabu is surprisingly great, tossing thirteen straight innings of scoreless ball in his last two spring starts, even while fighting off some mild tendinitis in his elbow. At the same time, this year's high-profile Yankee import, Orlando Hernández, is putting on a mitt-busting, leg-kicking show that practically screams "Take me north!"

However, still licking their wounds after last year's Hideki disaster, Yankee brass decide to proceed with the utmost caution on El Duque. With that in mind, Hernández is Columbus bound, where he'll go 6–0 before getting hoisted up to the bigs during the first few days of June.

---

* Apparently Joe Torre was pondering the same question. On January 17, he sent me a short, handwritten note that was equal parts pep talk and preaching. It read (in part): "Boomer— You had a good year in '97, but your stuff says you should have *great* years. . . . Being a great pitcher or player is all about responsibility." I read it three times and still came away confused. Was that a compliment or a complaint? It felt kinda like bringing home a hard-earned B+ on your algebra mid-term and hearing your dad say, "That's nice, son, but y'know, if you'd studied harder, that B+ could have been an A."

Meanwhile, steamrollering our way through spring training as a businesslike swarm of attack Huns, I've never been on a squad so anxious to get the regular season started. "It's just *sickening* how good this team is," Andy Pettitte keeps saying, his steadfast Christian morals of "fairness" and "equality" effectively stomping his ability to enjoy our big-doggy, powerhouse status. At the same time, Chuck Knoblauch, released from years of ninety-loss seasons in Minnesota, sees no ethical problem at all in rolling over the competition, and *he* rolls through the spring looking a *lot* like that little yellow "Have a Nice Day" smiley face guy. Oddly though, Knobby's grin is *not* the biggest in camp. That one sits on the face of Derek Jeter, a shortstop who's now got his own personal celebrity cheerleader.

Sitting there in the sunshine, hair flowing, tan skin glowing, smiling constantly, Mariah Carey obviously knows absolutely nothing about the game of baseball . . . but nobody cares. Every time Derek steps into the batter's box, Mariah cheers, Derek smiles, and the rest of us sigh. Of *course* we're jealous. At one point, Coach Zimmer actually uses the phrase "hubba hubba" in describing "Derek's cute little singin' gal." He then takes endless abuse as we all gather at one end of the dugout, point up into the stands, and announce that Connie Francis has just entered the loge section wearing an "I Love Don Zimmer" T-shirt. There's a flat-out, forty-man crush going on through that spring, and it's a testament to Derek's character that we don't just instantly hate the poor guy for having it all. I mean, really, he's young, rich, handsome, talented, up-close-and-personal with Mariah Carey. . . . I've had teammates who would have been strung up for less.

With the team starting the season on an eight-game West Coast swing, the Yankees' suits have booked us two final exhibition warm-ups against the Padres, *in* San Diego. I get the Saturday night game, and as a Yankee, pitching in San Diego, in the exact same stadium where I used to buy $1.50 nosebleed seats, I'm having the time of my life. So are my buddies. Leaving nearly fifty comps at the gate, I've now got a horde of raucous old pals in the stands. And with rain delays pushing back the start of the game for nearly an hour, every one of them's drunk, and loud, and rowdy by the time I throw pitch one. They're hooting. They're screaming. They cheer wildly every time I adjust my crotch. Out on the mound, I'm literally giggling between pitches. Needless to say, right through that start, I'm working as fast as I can, hell-bent on joining the party ASAP.

The rain, however, has other plans, and when play is stopped in the fourth, I'm equal parts mortified and tickled to find a couple of my most . . . uh, "mellowed" pals hanging upside down over the dugout roof and chatting with Joe Torre.

"Hey, Mr. Torrrrrrman, Reeee, Torre," they shout. "Since it's raining, does that mean Boomer's done for the night? Let us know, 'cuz he said we should meet him at the bar exactly one hour after he throws his last pitch, okay?"

"He's not done yet," Joe replies, actually smiling.

"Awwwww, mannnnn," they moan back. "Ya sure?"

"I'm very sure," Joe says, laughing and rolling his eyes now.

Meanwhile, I'm busting a gut down at the other end of the bench, and with my mind focused much more intensely on the party than on the Padres, my final outing goes by in one big crappy, soggy flash. Six runs, five innings, poor mechanics, I couldn't care less, bolting from Jack Murphy Stadium to spend a little hometown quality time with a pack of my closest personal degenerates.

We start things for real April 1, in the rain, in Anaheim, with a flat-footed, slow-moving, constipated loss that surprises us all. Three more butt-ugly losses follow, and by the time we're a week into the brand-new season, the newspaper guys are *already* wondering "How long will George Steinbrenner allow this to go on?" and "Is this all you get for $72 million?" At 1–4, this team's already being portrayed as a bloated, big-budget *Bad News Bears*. I have to laugh, because aside from Joe Torre's dead-on Walter Matthau face, that's an *entirely* groundless comparison. Packed with talent, there's no doubt that any minute now this team is gonna wake up and start kicking some serious ass. It finally happens during my next start.

Inside, at the Kingdome, I'm *truly* lousy, but with the Yankees bats emerging from their hibernation, we hand the Mariners a humongous 13–6, 18-hit smackdown. The floodgates are now officially open. The swagger is back.

We'll go 16–2 through the rest of the month.

Coming home to the stadium, with Joe DiMaggio throwing out the ceremonial first pitch, I stand in the dugout with tears in my eyes. This is magic. This is what being a Yankee is all about. This man is a tangible, genuine link to everything that's made this franchise special. DiMaggio walks slowly to the mound now as 56,000 people jump to their feet, roaring with an ovation as big as any I've ever heard this stadium produce. Up and down the dugout now, nobody blinks. Nobody moves. Nobody breathes. Paul O'Neill stares intently. Zimmer tears up. Derek Jeter wraps an arm around Zim's shoulder. On the field now, Joltin' Joe rears back and tosses a passable eighty-four-year-old strike to Joe Girardi. Flashbulbs pop. The crowd roars again, and seconds later, Girardi

Legends Field, with Whitey Ford and "Louisiana Lightning" *(AP Photo/Kathy Willens)*

returns to the dugout, where he immediately steals my Kleenex. Inspired, excited, proud, and grateful just to be here, this team scores 17 runs that day.

Winning our first three at home, the team is rolling at 6–4 by the time I'm due back on the mound, and that's when the roof falls in. No, really, I'm serious. The actual roof falls in. At just about two in the afternoon, with the park empty, a 500-pound support beam falls from the underside of the upper deck, down into the front row of the loge section right about midway between third base and the left-field wall. Section 22, Row A, Seat 7 . . . demolished. All that's left is a four-inch hole in the concrete.

Repair teams race to the scene. Engineers scramble to make sure the stadium's not in danger of immediate collapse. PR people run amok. George Steinbrenner immediately cranks up the heat under his (wrongheaded) bid to get the Yankees a new stadium. Mayor Giuliani rushes to the scene and works the media hard, praising the "fine workers" who are "quickly and efficiently taking steps to preserve this fine New York City landmark." With chaos swirling and hidden agendas being milked like Guernsey heifers, we Yankees are told to stay home.

Two days later, with Yankee Stadium still undergoing a series of structural inspections, the team meets in the clubhouse at 6:30 A.M., gets dressed, then gets bused over to Shea Stadium in time to work out before our noon start against

Anaheim. Ever seen me at 6:30 A.M.? You probably shouldn't. Even worse, having spent the better part of last night at Irving Plaza watching a band called Sister Hazel, I'm now officially a mess. Grumbling and swearing, I sleepwalk onto the team bus, flopping into the last seat in the last row, before prepping for my start with an intense forty-minute nap session. By the time we hit Shea, with forty winks behind me and five cups of coffee poured down my gullet, I'm *almost* halfway to human. Surprisingly though, even amid these odd, sleepy, totally uncomfortable surroundings, I'm on fire.

Four or five times this season I'm gonna go to the mound with an arsenal that's inexplicably stronger than anything I've ever thrown at opposing batters before. I can't explain it. I can't understand it and sure as hell got no control at all over when and where this superstuff decides to show up. All I can tell you is that right now, here in the ugly blue and orange confines of Shea Stadium, with bags under my eyes, and a pair of Egg McMuffins sitting like rocks in midgut, I'm struck by my first minimiracle of the year.

From out of nowhere and for absolutely no apparent reason, I hit the mound with stuff that's almost entirely unhittable. Every pitch feels sharp and accurate. Every pitch feels like it's got a couple of extra miles per hour behind it. Every curve sweeps. Everything close gets racked up as a strike. Giving up just one hit over my first eighteen batters faced, I head into the seventh feeling great, but my untouchable status is about to wear off. Darin Erstad homers to lead off the seventh. Three easy outs follow. Phil Nevin does the same in the eighth. Three easy outs follow. Gary DiSarcina makes it a hat trick in the ninth. Joe Torre comes to get me. I head back to the bus with a 6–3 victory, having given up just 4 hits (3 of them homers) in 8 innings pitched. A bus full of sweaty Yankees congratulates me all the way back to the Bronx.

We head into May at 17–6. On top of the world now, this team's now losing ball games about once every week and a half. And while my own stuff has been solid, and my run-support has been huge, I'd be lying to you now if I didn't explain that Joe Torre is driving me absolutely nuts.

Joe's a fantastic team leader, and a whiz with the press, and a good guy, and a great tactician on the field, but the man seems to think I'm constantly wobbling at the brink of a breakdown. Big trouble, small trouble, early in the game, late in the game, if I'm on the mound, showing any small sign of trouble, you can rest assured there'll be a pitcher or two warming up in the pen. On April 20, after holding the Jays scoreless through five, I get touched for a leadoff double. Bang! There's Jeff Nelson and Mike Buddie warming up in the pen.

D A V I D   W E L L S

On April 25, with the Tigers lying down nicely through 4⅓, I hit a rough patch, getting touched for three singles and a double while making an ugly throwing error in the field. Get 'em up now? That'd be fine. That'd make sense, but that wasn't the case. Facing this lousy Tigers team, Joe's got action running in the pen by the time those guys have gotten their second hit. And while I ultimately survive that inning, and three more sharp, scoreless frames, Joe's postgame quotes are a lot less than thrilling. Talking about how great it was that I didn't get "unraveled" in today's rough inning, Joe looks forward to more of the same. "Now, it's a question of mental toughness," he says.

I got your "mental toughness" right here, buddy.

Five days later, having given up 3 runs over 6 innings to the Mariners, I head into the seventh nursing a 7–3 lead, feeling pretty good on the mound. Still, when David Segui leads off with a single, there's Jeff Nelson and Mike Stanton up and throwing in the pen. I'm out of the game two batters later. Nelson and Stanton then combine to bring home six more Seattle runs by the time we're out of the eighth. Now I'm pissed. And with a chip on my shoulder ever since Joe's playoff-bound second thoughts about me in '97, I'm ready to bust a gasket. Who would have guessed Joe would beat me to it.

Midsummer heat
(© *Mitchell Layton/Newsport*)

May 6. With the team now riding a ridiculous 20–2 hot streak, I take the hill in Arlington, where it's 94 degrees at game time and *at least* 110 on the field. The sun broiling, the clay infield baking, I hit the mound, and I melt. It's *Texas* hot out there. Go sit on your toaster and you'll get some idea what that's like. At any rate, with the Yanks quickly taking a 9–zip, second-inning lead, I head to the mound to start my third inning of Kentucky Fried pitching, at which point I explode.

The nightmare goes like this. Kevin Elster flies out to Paulie O'Neill. Fernando Tatis drops a single in front of Chad Curtis in left. Tom Goodwin singles into right, moving Tatis to second. Mark McLemore walks, and the bases are full. Rusty Greer grounds out to Tino at first, unassisted, while Tatis scores, Goodwin goes to third, and McLemore hits second. Juan Gonzalez comes to the plate now, and he smacks one off the tip of Knobby's glove into center while Goodwin and McLemore score. The official scorer calls an error on Knoblauch, and with that, I immediately pitch a fit in my head.

With the Gonzalez shot flying past me like a bullet, I never got to see what a monumental effort it took for Knobby to even come *close* to that sucker. Seconds later, with three runs in, and the scorer's big E showing up, big and ugly, on the scoreboard in right, I quickly assume the worst. At that point, I get stupid and blow a gasket.

FUCK! I'm thinking to myself. I could have been out of this disaster with just one run scored! God-DAMNIT, Knobby! More curses chase after those. My brain is baking. I'm *totally* distracted, *completely* unfocused, and still *thoroughly* unwilling to believe that my own lousy pitching is what's really behind this inning from hell. Standing on the mound, it's a whole lot easier to get pissed off at Knoblauch.

From there, taking deep desperate breaths on the mound, I look into home plate as Will Clark steps in. I might as well set up a tee for the guy. Jumping all over a half-rotten pitch, Clark doubles as Gonzalez motors over to third. Three balls later, Ivan Rodriguez smacks another distracted pitch into left, singling home *both* runners. I'm reeling. Mike Simms is at the plate now, and with my temperature soaring and my entire head swimming, this little piss-ant of a hitter plants one *way* over the right-field fence, bringing home the Rangers sixth and seventh runs of the inning. He also ends my *really* bad day.

Joe's out to the mound by the time Simms completes his lap of the bases. And somehow, with the Yankees still up 9–7, amid my rage and frustration and the ignorant, wrong-assed belief that I would have been *out* of this thing if not for Knoblauch's error, I'm actually equal parts humiliated and furious at being yanked so early in the game.

"Let's go, David, that's gonna be all for today."

I throw up my arms in disgust. I grunt, loudly. I refuse to look Joe in the eye. I refuse to hand over the ball. Storming off the mound, I take three giant steps before casually flipping the ball backward into Joe's general direction. I've lost my cool, entirely. I'm mortified. I'm shamed, and at least in *this* case, I'm 100 percent wrong. Three more days of the cold shoulder follow, during which time Mel and Joe avoid me like the plague. At the same time, knowing full well it'll drive me crazy, Joe turns the screws by mentioning time and again to the press that one very plausible explanation for my Arlington meltdown could be the fact that I'm "out of shape." Once again, the double standard thrives. Win and you're "burly" or "barrel-chested." Lose, and you're "fat."

At the same time, three days removed from "the incident," with my body back at room temperature, and my television set broadcasting endless replays of the Texas Tirade, I'm now starting to feel like a genuine horse's ass. It gets even worse when I learn that over in the official scorer's booth, on Joe Torre's advice, Chuck Knoblauch's "error" behind me has now been *officially* reclassified a hit. I need a meeting.

That afternoon, Stottlemyre, Torre, and Wells sit down in Joe's office to once and for all clear the air. Quickly I apologize for my behavior on the mound back in Arlington, and just as quickly, Joe accepts. Done deal. From there, however, the bigger issues fly.

"You guys can agree with me, or you can tell me I'm crazy," I say, "but there's something I've gotta get off my chest."

"Go ahead," Joe says.

"It's simple," I tell them. "My job is to go out on that mound every day, and pitch as well as I possibly can. I think I do that pretty well, and my record last year backs that up big-time. But I have to say, from where I'm sitting, it really seems like you two guys have no faith at all in my ability."

"That's not true at all," Joe tells me, big eyebrows high.

"I don't agree with that statement either," Mel adds, "and I think you've really—"

"Hear me out," I interrupt. "Ever since the bad starts last August, it feels like you guys have been pulling me out of games earlier than the rest of the rotation. Coney gets in trouble, he works through it. Andy, same thing, but with me, you've got guys working in the pen from the first *possible* sign of trouble. You *know* I hate it when you get guys up and throwing, especially early in the game. I mean, how the hell do you expect me to get better, and learn how to pitch, and play tough, and work through trouble, if you never let me get out of my own jams?"

And at this point, Joe leans forward, looks me square in the eye, and says, "Listen to me. I believe in you. I believe in your abilities. Don't ever doubt that."

"Same here," says Stottlemyre.

"But now let's talk pitching," Joe continues, and that opens the door to a wide-ranging conversation that spills around the office for almost exactly an hour. Joe talks about character and heart. He explains that while he loves the way I fight, and scratch, and challenge individual batters on the mound, he *also* believes I can lose focus, and get flustered and disgusted and sometimes even quit on myself in bad outings. He tells me that when the going gets rough, his perception is that I stop thinking, stop pitching, and just start throwing. If that means he's gotta keep me on a shorter leash than the other guys, so be it. Nostrils flaring, we argue *those* points for a while.

"Honestly, Joe," I tell him, "in *my* mind, I *never* give up. I *never* give in, and I *never* resort to the sort of gutless, sackless, corner-nibbling junkballs that might actually get me out of a bad inning with less damage. You stand at *my* plate, I'm gonna challenge your ass. You beat me? Fine. I'd rather get beat with a double than a walk. That may not always be the *smartest* way to work on the mound, but it sure as *hell* ain't quitting."

From there, with Joe cracking a smile, the ice is officially broken. "Fair enough," he tells me. "Now how 'bout this. How about if I promise to stop getting guys up early when you're pitching, and *you* promise to work your ass off for nine innings every start, with good stuff or bad." The ice is gone. The deal is set.

Sitting together in Joe's office, horrible coffee in hand, the three of us now slide into a long, animated conversation about strategy, and specific situations at the plate, and toward the end of the hour, we all just start bragging about how Jorge Posada's fast becoming the world's greatest catcher. Honestly, though none of us pulls any punches, this whole meeting is inclusive, and friendly, and warm, and in retrospect *brilliantly* played on Joe's part.

Calm and honest, and completely nonconfrontational, Joe's listened to me, responded man to man, and sent me back to the clubhouse feeling strong and motivated, and a whole lot better about our relationship. And while the two of us will probably *never* choose to share a hotel room (can you imagine?), I think we each came away with some pretty good insight into the other guy's head. My season swings uphill immediately.

May 12. With K.C. in the Bronx, I hit that mound with something to prove, and eight innings later, having given Mr. Torre absolutely *no* reason to get *anybody* off their folding chairs in the pen, I return to the dugout with a great weight lifted from my shoulders. Five hits, two runs, solid stuff, one shaky inning that I work through without any melodrama, and when Mariano slams the door shut in the ninth, I can sing through my shower with renewed confidence, restored juju, and a sweet 3–2 victory. It's good to finally relax. Thank God the distractions are over, I'm thinking as I shave. Maybe *now* I can stay out of the headlines for a while.

Not gonna happen.

Perfect

As of this writing, fifteen men in the history of organized baseball have ever thrown a perfect game. Only ONE of those men did it half-drunk, with bloodshot eyes, monster breath, and a raging, skull-rattling hangover. That would be me. *Never* in the history of professional sports has a feat so difficult been accomplished by an athlete so *thoroughly* shot. I'm gonna need to backtrack for this one.

By now, you've undoubtedly figured out that I tend to view New York City as a gigantic, personal playground, customized to my own twisted standards of satisfaction. Here in Manhattan we've got sports bars, cigar bars, sushi bars, and titty bars, and music, and theater, and Letterman, and Howard Stern, and Ten's, and Papaya Kings, and Veruka, and the China Club, and ten million *other* distractions that'll keep a boy smiling 'til dawn. By May of '98, I'm nose deep in them all.

I'm going to concerts, I'm going to clubs, I've met Creed for the first time, I'm weaseling my way into movie premieres and show openings, and at *least* once a month, I'm now hanging at *SNL*. It's always a great time. The excitement, the chaos, the electricity, the panic, the pressure to perform, all of that stuff's familiar and comfortable and appealing to me. And from the relative safety of my perch just next to the studio bleachers, I stand with Lorne Michaels as the magic, and the comedy, and the laughter of his show all come together, thrilling millions of people across the country—or they don't, with sketches bombing as flop sweats and the smell of death roll in fast. Either way it's fun to watch.

Now comes the most unbelievable part of this whole story. Lorne Michaels *likes* me. Honest to God, we're really good, compatible friends. And though we take endless ribbing for resembling Jethro Bodine and Dick Cavett together, there really is a strange, positive chemistry at work. Long story short, we enjoy each other's company, and with that in mind, it should come as no surprise that on Saturday, May 16, with the '97–98 season of *SNL* completed last week, I get a call from the show's production office inviting me to their unofficial season-ending wrap party. This is a big one.

Honestly, as I explained at the top, *SNL*'s *weekly* wrap parties are always monster-size blowouts, often raging 'til long after the cows have come home. Do the math, and you can imagine the immense, raucous, roof-raising, steam-blowing, liver-damaging intensity of their season ender. I know *I* was. There's just one problem.

"DAMN!" I shout as I listen to my voice mail about the party. I've gotta pitch on Sunday, in a *day* game, at Yankee Stadium! If I go to the *SNL* party, I *will* end up fried. I'll eat too much. I'll drink too much. I may smoke myself a Cuban or two, I'll stay out WAY too late, and by game time, they'll have to cart me to the mound in a wheelbarrow. Somehow, I don't think that'll help the newly negotiated peace accord between me and my manager. I call Marci Klein to RSVP myself off the list. That's when she blindsides me.

Giving Marci the whole song and dance about how I've gotta pitch on Sunday, I thank her for the invite, but she won't let me off the hook. "Y'know," she tells me, "Dennis Rodman came to one of our cast parties about a year ago, and he had a fantastic time. He danced, he ate, he drank, and he ended up staying out with us until nine in the morning. At that point, he never went back to his hotel. He never went to bed. He just went straight uptown to Madison Square Garden, played a one o'clock game against the Knicks, and had himself the very best outing of his career. He scored like thirty points that day with a boatload of rebounds. I just thought you should know that."

"Marci," I tell her, "I'll see you Saturday night."

I know it's nuts. I know I'll probably regret it in the morning, but this is just too good to pass up, and what the hell, if Dennis Rodman could survive it, I sure as hell can too . . . I hope. What the hell, I tell myself, there's no reason on earth I have to stay out all *that* late.

Wrong.

This party is too much fun to even *consider* leaving at a reasonable hour. The music's loud. The food is great. The drinks are strong, and top shelf, and flowing *way* too fast for my own good. Holding court at the bar, Will Ferrell and Chris Kattan and Molly Shannon are all funny as hell. Meanwhile, Colin Quinn, who may be the one sober guy in the place, is nonetheless pitching a fit. Pushing me into a corner, he pokes a finger into my ribs, railing, "Listen, cocksucker, let me tell you something . . . " From there, he's off, biting his knuckles while ranting and raving about the sorry state of his love life, and his career, and his Irish penis, all while relentlessly referring to himself as "the lonely, *lonely* prince." With tears in my eyes, and my face sore from laughing, there's no way in hell I'm going home early.

5:00 A.M. Drunk, exhausted, reeking, reeling, I flop into bed in a comatose heap. Brandon dive-bombs me at 8:30. He's staying with me this week, and with rooster blood coursing through his veins, he's now wide awake, and ready to play. He's loud. He wants breakfast. I want to die. With a freight train roaring through my brain right now, I wobble to the kitchen.

"What do you want to eat?" I whisper, nursing half-closed eyelids and a cotton mouth. "I think there's cereal. *That's* nice and easy."

"I want *pancakes*!!!" The kid beams.

"Ughhhhhhhhhhhh. No, wait. Brandon, you're killing me here." Even the mental image of pancakes is making me ill. "You sure you don't want like Cheerios or something?"

"PANCAKES!!!"

"Hrmph." That kid's loud.

"And BACON!!!"

"Bleeeaugh." That one sends me to the sink . . . false alarm.

"And CHOCOLATE MILK!!!"

"AAAAUGH!"

I don't know if any of you have ever *tried* cooking pancakes and bacon when you're semidrunk *and* hungover *and* queasy, but let me tell you, it ain't fun. Pork fat and blood alcohol is a nasty, *nasty* combination.

My dad gets up now, asking if I'd gotten the number of the truck that ran me over. He's with me these days, living with me, helping me with Brandon, lending a hand, and I'm thrilled that he's here . . . but right now, I'd be the happiest man in the world if I could just be alone, in the dark, and the floor would stop moving. None of those wishes are about to come true. I can't even go back to bed.

Brandon and my dad are both flying back to Tampa this morning, and they're due at the airport by ten. I'm due at Yankee Stadium at the same time. With that in mind, once the pancakes are gobbled, I've gotta toss the kid in the shower, get him dressed, get him packed, get him kissed, get him hugged, then buckled in next to my dad in a Town Car bound for La Guardia. From there, I'll have just enough time to make a mad dash toward sobriety and a pain-free head. I hit the shower. I brush my teeth four times. I guzzle coffee. And when all's said and done, I head off to the stadium feeling like . . . shit. I'm gonna get shelled.

In the clubhouse now, there's a half-pot of coffee already brewed. I drink it all. In the trainer's room, there's an unopened bottle of Excedrin. I take a fistful. In my locker, there's a full aerosol can of Right Guard. I spray myself bigtime, hoping to mask the alcohol fog that's currently wafting up out of my pores. In my pocket, there's a full box of Tic Tacs. I chew them up in one giant mouthful, swishing them around in my cheeks, hoping to achieve maximum mintiness. Keep it together, I'm thinking. Don't let 'em see how you're hurting.

It's time. With Mel Stottlemyre already waiting for me in right field, I walk the last mile toward what I'm sure will be the worst warm-up of my life. Still, with the chemical effects of my caffeine and aspirin megadosing finally kicking in, Mel registers only minor horror as he gets his first good look at my big, hungover, Fred Flinstone face. "Feeling strong?" he asks me, with a pretty good idea that I don't.

"You *know* it!" I lie, launching into a painstakingly awful take on my standard twelve-minute, forty-pitch warm-up. Long-toss comes first, during which I feel like I'm shot-putting with every heave of the baseball. "Let's GO, baby! Feeling GOOD!" Mel shouts, his voice going right through my head like a drill bit. I want to lay down in a fetal position.

"Let's move on to the stretch," Mel chirps, *way* too chipper. "Time to turn up the heat."

"You got it!" I reply, skull-cracking, big cheesy grin stapled firmly in place. I trudge toward the bullpen mound now, promising God that if he'll just get me through this one measly start, my lips will never touch alcohol again.

God's not buying. He's been burnt by this lie too many times. As a result, I'm condemned to suffer my own consequences, beginning with a body that flat-out refuses to obey my commands. Step one in my warm-up is to throw maybe fifteen or sixteen fastballs, just enough to get comfortable and loose, while gaining a feel for the mound, and the ball, and my mechanics, and home plate. Step one *today* has me feeling like all the bones in my body have been mysteriously rearranged overnight. My velocity's solid, but my *delivery* feels off. Looser than usual, floppier, more fluid. I'm Jell-O in spikes. Is it the alcohol? The caffeine? The complete lack of sleep? The answer is "D: All of the Above."

Curveballs come next, and my first comes up short, sailing a solid three feet out of the strike zone, and sweeping with bigger, sharper movement than anything I've ever tossed from a mound in my life. Three more do the same.

"MOTHERFUCKER!" I shout, turning, and heaving one sacrificial baseball as far as I can, right out over the center-field wall.

"No, Boomer, your stuff looks good. You're having a good warm-up," Mel assures me. I don't believe him, and right now, I'm more certain than ever this day's gonna suck. Working through the rest of my arsenal, I find myself wrestling with the same kind of exaggerated movement on *everything* I throw. Balls that sink, sink lower. Balls that hop, pole-vault through the zone. I'm gonna walk twenty batters today, I'm thinking on the mound.

As ritual and superstition dictate, having completed my stretch work, I now have to grab a bottle of water, take three big sips, spit, then get back on the mound and go through that same series of pitches, this time from a full windup. And while some minor adjustments start bringing my control back into semi-reasonable shape, I'm *still* feeling doomed. At this exact moment, I could not *possibly* have my head any farther up my own ass.

Joe Torre glides into the pen now, asking Mel, "How we lookin' down here?" I prepare for the worst. Maybe I can just sprint to the D train and make a pregame escape.

"WOW!" Stottlemyre shouts, to my absolute amazement. "It's *scary,* how good this guy's throwing!" His eyes are huge, both thumbs *way* up, a look of genuine excitement on his face. I've *never* seen Mel this happy. He's not a cheerleader. He's not a phony. Mel's a flat-out, no-bullshit, straight shooter. Could I *really* be throwing good stuff?

I never saw it coming. Hungover, and queasy, and desperately sleep-deprived, I was blind to my own unbe-lievable luck. Out there in the pen,

The ritual: three big sips and spit
(*AP Photo/Kathy Willens*)

with my mind set on merely *surviving* this start, I was completely missing the bigger picture. Bigger movement, heightened velocity, an extrasharp, last-second pop, who cares if my stuff's weird this morning; *these* abnormalities kick ass. Mel praises my warm-up all the way back to the clubhouse, where ten minutes later, with Metallica blaring and the caffeine and aspirin now coursing through me at full throttle, I'm bouncing off the walls, 180 degrees removed from my early-morning stupor. I'm *more* than ready to take on the Twins.

It goes by in a flash. Three up, three down. Three up, three down. Locked in tight at the mound now, I'm tunnel-visioned, looking toward home. *Every* pitch is working. *Every* call goes my way, and by the end of the fifth, with a huge Beanie Baby Day crowd of 49,820 beginning to cheer with every single pitch, the Yankee clubhouse has already become a *very* superstitious place.

I'm at the head of the list. Leaving the mound after each 1-2-3 inning, I work the *exact* same routine. In order to keep the baseball gods happy, I know

I've got to hop over the first-base line, then jog toward the extreme home plate side of the dugout. Once there, Mel Stottlemyre will greet me with the exact same "Way to GO, Boom-ER!" It's *gotta* be that inflection. It's *gotta* be delivered in the same tone each time, or this whole perfect game thing could come tumbling down like some cheap house of cards. Mel knows that's true, and with the big one at stake, he plays his part perfectly, inning after inning after inning.

Passing Mel, I must now walk silently *through* the Yankees dugout and into the clubhouse, where I'll sit in the same crappy beige folding chair, sip from the same bottle of water, and watch my team bat on TV. However, once our first out gets recorded, I've immediately got to stand, turn, and head back down the same exact path to the dugout, ultimately sitting down in the same exact spot on the bench. No one dares park their ass on my magic spot. No one talks to me either, except for Luis Sojo, who just *never* shuts up . . . *ever*. We couldn't stop him from chattering if we tried.

Seventh inning. Matt Lawton flies out to Bernie Williams in shallow center. The crowd's really getting crazy now, and for the first time in my career, I find myself wishing they'd just shut up. They're making me nervous, and I'm trying like hell to keep myself from getting caught up in that. You find your knees shaking, and the next thing you know, you're gonna get beat. You're gonna start thinking too much about what you're throwing, and that's exactly where you're gonna hang a pitch and get killed. Guaranteed. Over and over again, I catch myself slipping. Over and over again I force myself to change subjects in my head.

Hey, look at the time, I'm thinking. Brandon's probably just about home by now. I wonder if he's watching the game. Oh, fuck! Bad move. Forget Brandon's watching. Think of something else, fast!

Hey, look. It's a hot dog guy. I *like* hot dogs. Hot dogs are *good*. Yep, get some ketchup on there. Mmmmmmm, hot dogs. I'm trying anything. Meanwhile Jorge Posada and the home plate umpire are staring at me, wondering why the hell I'm in space.

Feeling the pressure now, I hit my first full count of the game, falling to 3–2 on second baseman Brent Gates, who ultimately cracks a sharp grounder right at Tino. Two down. The crowd goes nuts. I take a series of long, deep breaths while trying my best to look totally cool. It's not helping. One batter later, I fall behind 3–1 to Paul Molitor of all people. Great. Down in the count, and I've got a Hall of Famer at the plate. Fastball, in. Paul swings and misses. The crowd roars. Sinker now, and it's a good one, one of the best I'll throw all day. Molitor swings over the top for strike three. The crowd goes totally mental. Three up, three down, the perfect game stands, but this time, it wasn't easy. It's ritual time again.

I hop. I see Mel. "Way to GO, Boom-ER!" And I once again disappear into the clubhouse 'til my team makes an out. Once that's happened, I'm back on the magic seat, alone, but then Coney shows up. He stares at me, then talks, breaking the worldwide "silence is golden" rule of perfect-games-in-progress. He could take a head butt at any time.

"Guess it's time to break out your knuckleball," he says, straight-faced.

And with that, I let out a roar that blew bottled water right out my nose. How can you not love that guy? Coney had my back. He'd seen me tensing up on the mound through the seventh, and with that, he broke an unwritten law of the dugout, got into my face, and busted me right back to earth. It makes a huge difference. "Knuckleball!" Coney yells at me through the rest of the game.

"You got it, Scumbag!" I'll shout back.

Eighth inning. Relaxed on the mound now, it's groundout, groundout, pop-up to Tino. Piece of cake. Hop, "Way to GO, Boo-MER!," clubhouse, magic seat, you know the drill. Now Coney's back again, this time with a big fake sneer in place. "You showed me *nothing* out there, Scumbag. *Nothing!* NOTHING! Where was the knuckler, you big pussy?!" We're laughing right into the ninth.

Ninth inning. I walk to the mound with a huge, standing ovation already in progress. I'm gonna hyperventilate if I take any more deep breaths. You couldn't get a greased needle up my ass right now. Third baseman Jon Shave is at the plate. Seven guys behind me all start praying that *anything* hit goes toward somebody else. *Nobody* wants to mess this up. *Nobody* wants me to blow it. "Let's do this, Annie," I say to the sky, and with that, there's nothing left to do but pitch. On the radio, John Sterling and Michael Kay call it like this:

Sterling: *David Wells, three outs away . . . Now the windup, low, the count 2 and 2 . . .*

Kay: *Wells with the top two buttons of his uniform shirt open. You can see underneath the sweaty, gray, New York Yankees T-shirt. Blousy shirt, everything hangs over the belt. He's unbelievable.*

Sterling: *Wells now is ready, and deals 2–2. Swung on and popped up to shallow right. Knoblauch out, O'Neill in. O'Neill makes the catch. One away.*

Stay with your game. Don't get crazy, now, I'm thinking. Just another inning. Just another batter. There's a long, loud, drumroll playing in my head.

Kay: *Every one of the 49,820 standing now at the stadium.*
Sterling: *Now David Wells is two outs away . . . Here's the catcher, Javier Valentin, and there's the curve. Low, 1 and 0.*

Now the crowd boos, and boos, and boos, not caring at all that my last pitch missed the corner by a solid six inches. Coolest fans in baseball. I love these guys. I try not to laugh on the mound.

Sterling: *Wells deals 1–0. Fastball. Strike, outside corner. That's been a key pitch for Wells all day long. . . . Now Wells rocks and the 1–1; breaking ball, grounded foul behind the plate. Big, slow breaking ball, down to the ankles of Valentin, and he got a piece and fouled it back.*
Kay: *I wonder if any player wants the ball hit to him. They're all rooting for strikeouts I think, no matter how sure-handed they are.*
Sterling: *And it'll be a 1–2. Wells ready . . . the pitch . . . he struck him out! Two outs.*
Kay: *Imagine the pressure. One out away from immortality!*

I've got a heartbeat like a hamster. All I can see is Jorge's glove. Honest to God, I'm tunnel-visioned now like some cheesy movie-theater special effect. I decide to throw fastballs, as hard as I can, and just hope for the best.

Sterling: *Here's Pat Meares, the pitch. Swung on and fouled back. Meares is a very good hitter, so if Wells is going to get it, he's going to earn it. The 0–1.*

The ball leaves my hand, heavy, and I swear to God, it takes forever to reach the plate. I'm watching the pitch in slow motion. Solid toss, up and in, Meares swings underneath it, popping it up toward the right-field boxes. It's out of play . . . or wait, no, maybe, maybe.

Paul O'Neill's sprinting toward the wall as fast as his gimpy, grandpa legs will take him. He's under it! Oh my God!

Sterling: *He's gonna get it! O'Neill near the line . . . he makes the catch! David Wells! David Wells has pitched a perfect game! Twenty-seven up,*

twenty-seven down. Baseball immortality for David Wells, and thuhhhhhhh
Yankees win! THUH-UHH-UHHHHH-UHHHHHH YANKEES WIN!!!

I go nuts. Nuts! The team swarms. I look for Jorge over the mob. "Jorge!" I'm yelling. "Jorge!" From nowhere, Luis Sojo streaks in and tackles me with a giant smile and high-volume Spanish-language congratulations. "Get away from me, man, I want Jorge!" I shout, but by then it's too late. I'm dog-piled. I'm backslapped. I'm gang-bear-hugged. I crush Knobby's ribs. I make Derek Jeter's eyes bug out. I *finally* get to squeeze the life out of Jorge Posada.

Now the Yankees relievers sprint in from the pen. Graeme Lloyd grabs me hard by the shoulders and screams into my face, "Dude! You just pitched a perfect game for the *New York Yankees!!!*"

Now I'm hoisted up onto the shoulders of Darryl Strawberry, Willie Banks, and Bernie Williams while the stadium goes double live gonzo. "Yeahhhhh!!!" I'm pumping my fist in the air all the way to the dugout.

They dump me. And while the stadium maniacs refuse to let their ovation die down, I sit on the bench next to Coney. Putting an arm around my shoulder, the quiet Scumbag points at the scoreboard, saying, "Why don't you just stare at it for a while, 'cuz you earned it, you deserved it, and it's something you're never gonna forget."

We sit together now, silently, dugout emptying, crowd still crazy until finally I turn to Coney and say, "This is some good shit, now isn't it?"

Coney just grins. "Wait 'til tonight!" he beams. "I'm going inside. Don't forget your curtain call." He disappears down the runway, and the dugout is mine. My eyes run back to the board. My hands are shaking. My heart is pounding. The satisfaction is overwhelming. Nobody can *ever* take this away from me.

Finally, with one last lingering look at that long line of zeroes, I hop up the

(© Photo File, Inc.)

dugout steps and onto the field as every corner of Yankee Stadium roars at me. The moment explodes inside my head. I tip my cap in two directions, but I disappear fast. I've got to. One second longer and I'd have been standing in front of 49,000 fans just bawling like a baby.

Inside the clubhouse, Joe Torre grabs me tight and shoves an expensive Monte Cristo cigar in my mouth. Don Larsen, who threw the last Yankees perfect game, back in 1956, phones with congratulations ("I hear *you're* goofy too," he tells me). Steinbrenner's next on the line, from Tampa. "Tell me something," he begins, "now that you've pitched a no-hitter for the Yankees, and you've reached 'immortal' status, will you at least tuck in your goddamned shirt?"

"No chance, Boss."

"I didn't think so," he replies.

Meanwhile, the whole locker room's gone nuts. Don Zimmer's bouncing up and down like a roly-poly kid on Christmas morning. Mel Stottlemyre gloats and bullshits that he knew my perfect game was in the bag right from today's warm-up session. Mayor Giuliani calls to offer me the key to the city. Billy Crystal runs into the room now from his seats near the dugout. "Hi, everybody," he says. "I got to the stadium a little late. Did I miss anything good?"

There are reporters everywhere. *Everywhere*. Flashbulbs are popping, microphones are pushed a half-inch under my nose, and for the bulk of the next forty minutes, I *try* to answer the obligatory "How do you feel?" questions, but that's an impossible task. It's too big a moment. I'm awestruck. I'm tongue-tied. I'm humbled. Honestly, for the first time in my life I'm at a *complete* loss for words.

Finally, with the reporters shooed, it's time to do some *serious* celebrating. Step one finds all of us Yankees having a quick glass or nine of the Dom Pérignon Boss Steinbrenner's been kind enough to supply. Step two finds Coney, Graeme Lloyd, Dale Sveum, Chili Davis, and me heading across the street, where a badge-wearing, nightstick-toting surprise party sneaks up on us, fast.

Right across the street from Yankee Stadium there's a little parking area where we players leave our cars before each game. It's Cyclone-fenced, and gated, and it's always patrolled by the same handful of cops. Great guys, all of 'em, they're nearly as thrilled with my perfect game as me. And because we stragglers have taken a lot longer than usual in returning to our cars today, these cops are now officially off duty, ready to celebrate, and waiting for me with open arms, gigantic smiles, and a *whole lot* of beer. With about twenty patrolmen in there, I'm not going anywhere. Who am I to disappoint New York's finest?

"BOOMER!!!" the men in blue shout as they see us approaching. "Get in here, baby!" And with that, not wanting to risk resisting an officer, the five of us jog inside the lot, laughing like hell. Tall boys at the ready, the men in pinstripes and the men in blue now combine to enjoy one hell of a party. Sitting on car hoods, six-packs in hand, we swap baseball war stories for *police* war stories, shooting the shit 'til the last of the Heineys are gone. Two hours into the party, we're still having a *great* time inside that lot, and that's when I notice there's *still* a solid three hundred fans nutty enough, and loyal enough, and hard-core enough, to be waiting for me just outside the fence. That's impressive. I can't disappoint *them*.

The cops open the gates, and at that point, Sharpie in hand, I spend the better part of an hour being congratulated by fans while signing their programs, and ticket stubs, and hats, and Beanie Babies, and at least one boob. At that point, it's time to *really* start painting the town.

With Coney navigating, we booze-cruise through Dorian's. We hit the China Club and Veruka. We hit Chinatown to scarf down a gigantic, hot-sauce-covered Szechuan feast. We wobble up and down Manhattan, East Side and West Side, in an endless, blurry haze of barhopping, and by the time it's all done, for the second night in a row, I flop into bed about halfway through the Big Apple's morning rush hour.

Eight hours later, still too wired to sleep, I head for the Ed Sullivan Theater. David Letterman's waiting for me.

Matthew Broderick, then me. That's tonight's *Late Show* lineup, and I'm nervous as hell. Forget standing in front of 50,000 fans at the stadium, *this* is scary. Have you ever seen that episode of the *Brady Bunch* where Cindy goes on

On the *Letterman* set with Nina . . .

... and Dave (© *Alan F. Singer*)

a quiz show and freezes up on camera? That was me on *Letterman*. "Take me through the last out," Dave commands.

"Uhhh . . . . Um . . . . you'll get me all nervous again," I whisper.

"Well, which Twin was it?" Dave asks, carrying me.

"Heh . . . heh heh, Pat, uhhhhh Meares, I think."

Talk about Stupid Human Tricks. I'm out onstage for all of four minutes, and it seems like an hour. But the audience is kind, Dave does his best to keep me from vomiting all over the set, and I ultimately survive my stage fright unscarred. I'll do better over the next twenty-four hours, with Regis and Kathie Lee, and Conan, and Howard Stern, and Mayor Giuliani as he hands me the key to the city. "Careful, mayor," I tell him, "there are a lot of doors you don't want a guy like me opening."

"Yeah, you're probably right." He laughs. "I can envision the keg party at Gracie Mansion now. Why don't you give that key back and let me give you the key to Jersey City, instead."

May 19. Just about fifty hours after Paulie put away the last out in my perfect game, things are *finally* beginning to get back to normal around the clubhouse. Bernie's playing some classical mumbo-jumbo on his guitar. Tim Raines is telling bad jokes and laughing at his own punch lines. Luis Sojo continues his season-long, never-ending, locker-room monologue, and off in a corner, relatively unrushed by reporters, I'm free to once again sit around in my favorite ratty T-shirt, decompressing from the events of the past two days while slowly beginning to look ahead to my next start. With the craziness of the perfect game now officially behind me, I'm looking forward to a few days of sweet, simple, maybe even slightly boring baseball. I don't get it.

Eight innings into a home game against the big-spending, bottom-dwelling Orioles, we're down 5–4 with Armando Benitez on the mound, and two runners on base. Bernie Williams is at the plate, and with another high-pressure moment in front of him, Armando blows it *again*. This time he feeds Bernie a letter-high cantaloupe of a pitch that practically explodes when Bernie connects. Three seconds later we Yankees are up 7–5, with Tino at the plate.

Key to the city (*Courtesy of the Mayor's Office, New York City/Diane Bondareff*)

First pitch from Benitez. Neck high and way inside. Tino bails but ends up taking the pitch right between the shoulder blades. He goes down, hard. "Aw, FUCK YOU!" Darryl Strawberry yells from the dugout, and he sprints for the mound with Chad Curtis in tow. Benitez drops his glove and gets ready to rummmmmm-bullllllllllll. The benches empty, and just like that we've got a slobberknocker at the pitcher's mound. Darryl dives in. Paul O'Neill roars. Benitez charges at Straw, and now it's time for yours truly to teach this Jabroni a lesson. At the edge of the infield grass, I intercept Armando's attack, grabbing Benitez by the neck and squeezing just hard enough to make reliever-juice. Eyeballs bugged out, Armando ain't going anywhere.

"Lemme GO!!" he's screaming at me. "Lemme GO!!" I fail to honor that request.

Meanwhile, with Benitez out of action, Orioles pitcher Alan Mills weasels his way into the pile and punches Darryl in the face. Sticking and moving, Mills is heading for the hills long before Darryl has any chance to return the favor.

In the end, Benitez gets a fat, eight-game suspension and a $2,000 fine. Darryl and Graeme Lloyd each get clipped for three games and a grand, while Jeff Nelson and Alan Mills each take two-game beatings and $500 fines. The "perfect-game" era is officially wiped off the map, and in its place, a whole new wave of postbrawl team unity comes sweeping into the Yankees' clubhouse. And while this team was close-knit even before beating the crap out of the Orioles (which we did, you big bunch of Marys), *now* we're bonded like brothers.

I've never seen anything like it. We go out to dinner as a twenty-five-man group. We hit hotel bars as a twenty-five-man group. In Boston, in our hotel corridor at 2 A.M., we New York Yankees stumble upon the sounds of a *very* loud, ridiculously and *hilariously* foul-mouthed couple doing the nasty* in their room. (*"AIEEEEE! Slap that ass, you monster man!"*) Together we gather at their doorway for the better part of twenty minutes, giggling and joking as a twenty-five-man group. We do everything together. There are no cliques. There are no petty rivalries or jealousies. All of that falls away with the fight. And while we've been the best team in baseball since opening day, starting right now, we're flat-out unbeatable. We'll be 61–20 by the All-Star break.

It's not hard to keep my *own* hot streak cooking as well. With my won/loss record standing at 4–1 on that hot, hungover morning of the perfect game, I've been gaining momentum ever since. Combining a surprisingly long streak of solid, dependable, extrapop pitching, with a tidal wave of Yankee run support, I surf toward the break at 11–2.

With those numbers on the table, Joe Torre starts talking in the papers about how he believes my whole perspective on baseball has changed since the perfect game. I don't buy it. Instead, I believe Joe's whole perception on *me* has changed since that game. I'm the same guy I've always been. I approach the game the same way. I'm just enjoying a bit of a hot streak. If I've changed at *all*,

* Make that *"very* nasty."

somebody forgot to send me the press release. At the same time, spouting as much flowery new-age psycho-mumbo jumbo as your average *Oprah* show, the New York press suddenly begins praising my "new sophistication" on the mound, and my "mental maturity," and even my "rapidly emerging leadership potential." Huh? Me? Yeah, right! It's bullshit. All *I* can figure is that one prolonged stretch of really good pitching has *finally* distracted the world's attention away from my gut, and my personality, and my behavior off the field. I'm not complaining. What the hell, it's nice to be seen as "Gallant" instead of "Goofus" for a change, especially in Joe Torre's office.

Ever since our long, great, closed-door meeting in May, there really *has* been a more comfortable, less chlorine-and-ammonia vibe growing between my manager and me. We respect each other. We talk a lot more. We're on the same team. And while Joe *still* winces and grimaces and runs for his office at the first strains of my boom-boxed heavy-metal tapes, he can't help but love the noise I've been making on the mound. *That* kind of success could make a mongoose hug a cobra.

July. Heading into the All-Star break, with *all* the chips falling my way, Cleveland manager Mike Hargrove hits me with yet another great, unexpected, 1998 surprise. Hargrove asks me to join his 1998 All-Star pitching staff, and not only that, he wants me to start. I fall on the floor. How cool is that? Can I *be* any luckier? Can my life *possibly* get any better? I'm on fire. I swear to God, if I went to the Quickie Mart right now and bought you a lottery ticket, you'd stand at *least* a fifty-fifty shot of winning it all.

Coors Field. On national TV, in a ballpark where my son Brandon could hit thirty-five home runs in a season, I'm facing a lineup that includes Barry Bonds, Mark McGwire, Mike Piazza, Andres Galarraga, and five more guys who can take any pitch I deliver and deposit that sucker 600 feet away. It's *fantastic* fun. Facing this modern-day Murderers' Row, I'm not the least bit nervous. Instead, once again mining my own, peculiar, big-game psychosis, the challenge and the excitement and the butterflies of the occasion all somehow end up getting metabolized in my body as positive energy and optimism and confidence. I hit the mound with a smile.

And while I end up throwing two innings of no-hit, no-run ball at the top of a 13–8 AL slaughter, you know as well as I do that *nobody* cares about the score in this game. It's more about pomp, and circumstance, and TV ratings, and for a lot of players, the collection of their All-Star incentive bonuses. As for me, while playing in that game was a thrill and an honor and a blast, the *real* highlight of my All-Star performance comes after the game. Cornering Billy Crystal, I actually manage to swap him one baseball signed by me, and Don Larsen, for a pair of his first-row, center-court, New York Knicks floor seats. Now *that's* a steal. I fly home feeling like I've just mugged an Oscar host.*

Second half: what can I tell you? Right through July, and through August, we Yankees just plain win. We're relentless. Fans all over the country hate us. Editorials in every major sports publication start raging about the "lack of parity in major-league baseball" and how George Steinbrenner's unfair brand of "checkbook baseball" has bought his Yankees the pennant. The Yankees' response? Screw you! We're flipping the bird to all who complain. Mooning the whiners, and the losers, and the also-rans, and the bush leaguers, we step on the gas, hauling ass toward October. We win with the long ball. We win with the bunt. We'll beat you with a shutout on Monday and a 15–14 pileup on Tuesday. It's ugly. It's almost embarrassing. It's the single greatest season of my life.

I won't lose a game through July and August, but Coney's the one having the really awesome summer. Conserving pitches, meticulously monitoring his own reinvented, postsurgery mechanics, I've never seen him look so intense on the mound. His game face is red. He sweats more than me. When David's personal catcher, Joe Girardi, makes the mistake of visiting the mound uninvited, he'll more than likely get bounced back toward home with a long string of curses ringing in his ears. You don't mess with Coney on game day. Not this year. The guy's 15–3 by the first of August. At seventy-eight years old, the gimpy old man's well on his way to yet another 20-game season.

On off days, I'll often take Brandon up to Coney's humongous *Beverly Hillbillies*–style mansion in Greenwich, Connecticut, mostly because Coney's indoor swimming pool allows us to rack up some hotly contested cannonball contests (I'm the reigning World's Champion), but also I just plain enjoy the guy's company. In our two years together in the Bronx, Coney and I have become great friends, sharing ups and downs, and bad plane trips, and bad road meals, and a bunch of butt-ugly bar closings, and through all that time, not once have I wanted to kill him. That's top-notch compatibility in my book. With all that in mind, the two of us will spend the '98 season as road roomies.

Roommates? Didn't that tradition leave baseball right around the time the million-dollar salary rolled in? Yes. But with the Yankees of '98 rolling into most

---

* I don't want to mention any names here, but *somebody* never paid up, and if you were to analyze this, you might be able to figure out just exactly who that city slicker is.

major-league towns as the single biggest attraction of the year, the carnival atmosphere borders on ridiculous. Every hotel lobby is crammed. Every hotel bar is impassible. Just getting through the lobby door can take an hour of autographs and disposable Kodak moments. Don't get me wrong. I really *like* meeting fans, and it's *great* to play for a team that inspires such loyalty and excitement, but when it's 1:30 A.M., and you've just pitched eight innings, and your bed's upstairs waiting, there's not an athlete on earth who's *that* eager to be loved. Well, maybe Knoblauch.

In the dugout, doing my best Coney impression
(© *Reuters 1998/Ray Stubblebine*)

Sure there's back entrances. Sure there's freight elevators. Sure there are security guys who can block for you as you rush past the crowd and behave like a complete asshole, but why live like that? We've got money. We've got connections. Why not end-run the whole thing? With that logic percolating, Coney and I began phoning Four Seasons and Peninsula-level hotels from coast to coast, booking ourselves into their finest two-bedroom suites through every Yankee road trip of the season. Sure we're away from the team's "official" hotel, but who cares? We'll get to the park on time. We'll still show up to pitch. And as for me, the better mattresses at the five-star joints really do seem to help keep my back from stiffening up after starts. That *alone* seems cause enough for the revised living arrangements.

Best of all, with the Yankees' hotel bar inevitably packed with gawkers and groupies and autograph hounds, the rest of the Yankees are now free to come hang at "Scumbag & Scumbag's," a fine pub and party joint open twenty-four hours a day, with good food and drink, and questionable clientele. Coney and I quickly begin providing a home away from home to many of the Yankees' younger players. Homer Bush, Mariano, Shane Spencer, Ricky Ledee, Jorge— sooner or later *everybody* will show up at our door. We're relaxed, we're low-key, we're free, and we're private. Hangouts don't come any cooler than that.

Catch the midnight *SportsCenter*? Have a few beers? Order some wings or a pizza from room service? No problem. We're like one big converted-basement rec room on the road. If Coney and I could have just slapped up some ugly wood paneling all over the fancy hotel walls, the effect would have been perfect.

August 1. This team is insane. FIFTY games over .500. FIFTY! Taking the mound against Seattle, I nearly blow the milestone by sucking my way through the first half inning. Four pitches into the game, with a single surrendered to Joey Cora and an A-Rod home run, I'm in the hole 2–zip. From there though, I settle in for a solid, complete-game outing, while my team comes from behind to erase my mistakes. A hundred and sixteen pitches later, I'm gifted with a 5–2 W, and a season record that now stands at 13–2. Fifty games over? That's nothing. Two weeks from now we'll be 94–32. This team now stands a really good chance of blowing right past the 116 wins of the 1906 Chicago Cubs and racking up the greatest single season in baseball history.

Q: *Is it October yet?*
A: *It's not even September.*

Oddly though, with a ridiculous sixteen-game lead in the division, and a solid six weeks to endure 'til the playoffs, we Yankees slowly but surely start proving we're human. We get lazy. We get flat. We lose six of eight to the Angels and Twins in mid-month. And when this team clinches a postseason berth on the insanely early date of August 29, things get even worse. With nothing at stake, and no life in our bats, we Yankees crawl into September on an 8–11 run. Granted, when you close out a crap-stretch like that with a record of 102–64, the idea of wholesale panic is nothing short of laughable. Still, the seeds of doubt have been planted, and there's not a guy on the bench who's not starting to press.

September. First day of the month and yours truly tosses another gem . . . he wrote, modestly. With Oakland in town, I'm a monster on the mound, feeling better and sharper and stronger than I have all season long. Good fastball, very sharp curveball, cut fastball, the sinker, the change, everything's cooking tonight. Once again though, this weird, unexpectedly great stuff sneaks up on me after a *really* terrible warm-up. Honestly, out in the pen tonight, I felt like I'd be lucky to last four innings. They've got the World Champion Toms River Little Leaguers on the field with us tonight for "The Star-Spangled Banner," and a kid-pitcher named Casey Gaynor stands next to me on the mound.

"Hey, Casey," I whisper as Robert Merrill sings.

"What?"

"How you feeling?"

"Great!"

"Your arm's okay?"

"Yeah!"

"Good, because I stink tonight, and you may have to come in and bail me out." I'm only half-kidding.

But then it came back. From completely out of the blue, I'm throwing rockets, feeling better than I did back at Shea. Better than the day of the perfect game. Better than *ever*. Better than you can possibly imagine. Jorge notices immediately, as does Coney, and even by the third inning, with nine up and nine down, my stomach's in knots. "This can't be happening!" I tell him. "Not again. Somebody out there better get a hit off me soon, or I'm gonna puke all over the rubber." With umpire Jim McKean running a strike zone about the size of a refrigerator tonight, the possibility of another no-no is genuine, and thrilling, and scary as hell.

Seventh inning. Joe Torre inserts Chad Curtis into left field, swapping out Tim Raines, and my brain explodes. For the second time in my career, a manager's dicked around with the lineup while I've got a no-hitter on the line. My teeth are grinding.

Rickey Henderson flies out to left. So far so good. Ryan Christenson racks up a whiff. Twenty up, twenty down, and with that, human moose-boy Jason Giambi comes to the plate. Fastball in, strike one. Fastball in, strike two. Jorge calls for a curve, and with an imperfect grip on the ball, I get the sucker just a little bit up, at which point Giambi dinks it just over Knobby's glove for a single. The crowd stands and cheers. I breathe a huge sigh of relief, then get back to the business at hand. One out later, I head for the dugout, passing Giambi on the infield grass. "Thanks, buddy," I tell him. "You took a lot of pressure off my ass."

"No problem, dude. Anytime," Jason says with a laugh.

Back in the dugout now, I corner Joe Torre. "You made the switch and you jinxed me. You absolutely *jinxed* me. You know what that means?"

"Wait now—" He *knows* what it means.

"Davey Johnson's not gonna be the only manager to earn himself a head butt, now is he?" Eyes wide, I smoke Joe as long as I can without laughing. Meanwhile, Zimmer's closing in behind me, ready to crack me in the snout with a Louisville Slugger.

This team will win its 100th game of the year on September 4, on the road, in Chicago, and it means absolutely *nothing*. Knocked down from "Invincible" to "Ordinary" status over the course of the last three weeks, the team's milestone met with more urgent pep talks than gloating. "A hundred means nothing if we don't go home with a ring," Derek Jeter keeps saying. At the same time, Darryl Strawberry talks about how the '88 Mets won 100 games easily, but they ended the season fat and lazy and overconfident, ultimately getting knocked out of the playoffs by the tougher, smarter, and hotter Los Angeles Dodgers. Everybody in the clubhouse gets hot under the collar. Everybody gets pumped. There's no way in *hell* that can happen to *us*.

We lose eight of our next twelve.

September 7. Fenway. I'm 5–10 here for my career, over twenty-one starts, and tonight the Red Sox get lucky again. Tonight, two terrible umpires and one bean-eating fan combine to give me an acid reflux that practically incinerates my esophagus. Rolling through six innings of two-hit, shutout baseball, I enter the seventh to find that all of a sudden, for no reason at all, home plate umpire Larry McCoy has apparently shrunken his strike zone by half. Inside corner? That's now a ball. Right down the middle? That's now "Ball two!" It's maddening.

Jorge calls for breaking stuff. I can't throw it. I know it'll just be called a ball. I shake him off and throw fastballs, getting clipped for a single, and another, and a double, and another double. For the first time in a *long* time, I'm flustered on the mound. Angry and distracted, I get ripped for three runs before escaping the inning with the score tied 3–3.

"You're crazy, Larry. Fucking crazy!" I shout as I exit, because y'know, when an umpire's being a dick, it's always a really good idea to curse him out in public. In the dugout, Joe's stewing. I haven't seen *that* for a while. One inning later, things get even worse.

John Valentin hits a deep fly ball to center. Bernie camps under it, and at that point, some Boston-baked boob goes all Jeffrey Maier on me, leaning over the fence to swipe the ball away from Bernie's glove. "Home run!" shouts second-base ump Chuck Meriwether.

"What the fuck?!" shouts David Wells. I lose the game 4–3. It's nuts. I'm raging, but since this is the same *exact* scenario that got me into hot water with Steinbrenner last season, I ditch Fenway and hightail it to Cheers real fast. The September slide of the Yankees continues without a hitch.

September 8. Quick footnote. Mark McGwire hits number 62 tonight, smacking a low line drive just over the left-field fence in Busch Stadium. First thought: thank *GOD* I wasn't pitching. Second thought: where will it end? The man's at 62 with a solid three weeks left to play. We Yankees watch McGwire's shot a million times over in clubhouse replays at Fenway. Closest to the screen is Darryl, who stands smiling, staring, never once averting his gaze. He's been following the homer chase for months, talking about it incessantly, and now he's flat-out riveted by the grand finale. Watching Darryl, you can't help but wonder if some part of him is dying, feeling the effects of time lost, and a body abused, and talents disrespected, and things that might have been.

September 9. Orlando Hernández is on the mound, and though he's won just one of his last five starts, and he ultimately blows a 5-zip lead in this one, Ramiro Mendoza bails him out. We Yankees take a 7–5 victory over the Red Sox, and we clinch the AL East. "We needed this!" is the dominant cry amid the champagne and high fives of the clubhouse. "It don't mean a thing if you ain't got that ring!" Stuck in this goddamned rut, the champagne sniping feels unjustified tonight, and there's an undeniably weird, uneasy, negative under-current to this team victory celebration. Playing sub-.500 ball for the better part of a month now, it's hard not to wonder if we're sliding toward major disap-pointment.

September 11. The Yankees are fighting again, this time at home, against Toronto, because Roger Clemens is head-hunting. Third inning, the Rocket snags a Joe Girardi grounder, bare-handed, to turn a pretty double play. He shakes his hand after the fact. One batter later, he's at it again, this time making a lunging, bare-handed grab at a liner from Knobby. No dice. *This* time the hard shot ricochets off his hand and leaves Roger's palm aching. He gets through the inning, but it'll come back to haunt him in the fourth.

Clearly uncomfortable as he returns to the mound, Roger's tagged for a Paul O'Neill single, a Bernie Williams single, and a Tino Martinez double that scores O'Neill. Scowling on the mound now, Roger gets Jorge to ground out, but the hard-hit ball sends Tino to third while Bernie Williams scores. Ricky Ledee comes to the plate now, and when this rookie has the audacity to actually smack a long sac fly to center, Tino scores too. Bases empty, game tied at three, Scott Brosius comes to the plate and takes Roger's first pitch in the top of his back. This is classic Clemens.

I'm not gonna make judgments, and the first thing you need to know is that *every* pitcher will occasionally flatten a guy who's been crowding his plate. Some guys will get you in the ass, others go up high and scare the hell out of you. In 1998, Roger's reputation said that if you got him good and flustered, sooner or later he'd lose his cool, and *somebody* was gonna get his bell rung.* Rumor also held that as a bona fide superstar, Roger would seldom, if *ever*, get knocked by the umps for his beanballing ways. With the bases now cleared of Yankees, and a picture-perfect brushback scenario in place, you can readily understand how we Yankees exploded with Scotty's brand-new, perfectly round bruise. And though Roger denies he was head-hunting that day, purpose pitches don't come any more perfect that that.

Brosius stares down Clemens. Clemens stares back. Brosius slowly walks to first base. Everybody in the Yankee dugout is on the top step. The theme from *Rocky* plays in our heads. At this point the home plate umpire, Mike Reilly, does absolutely nothing. No ejection. No warning. *Nothing.* Joe Torre goes ballistic. He shoots to home plate, veins throbbing from all sides of his neck.

Joe screams that any other pitcher would get tossed for such obvious bean-balling. Reilly doesn't agree. Joe gets personal. Joe gets ejected.

Top of the fifth. Hideki on the mound with Shannon Stewart at the plate, and Stewart takes a first pitch to the ass. Stewart glares and moves toward the mound. Irabu charges home. Joe Girardi gets between them. Super-Darryl's back in action in a flash. So's Graeme Lloyd. So's Homer Bush, who lands a sweet uppercut to Jose Canseco. Chugging toward home, Don Zimmer gets in Reilly's face and quickly joins Joe in the clubhouse. The baseball teams ulti-mately make like hockey teams for the better part of five minutes before order is restored and our gentlemanly round of America's pastime continues.

We'll lose that game 5–4, when Shannon Stewart goes yard on Irabu and practically walks around the bases, smirking at us all. It's impossible to watch. Infuriating. Aggravating. And it serves as a picture-perfect wake-up call for this mediocre, funk-flattened Yankee September. Problem is, we never bothered answering that call. We just rolled back over, pulled up the blankets, and went back to sleep. We'll lose 5 of our next 6, the last one a sloppy, lazy 7–0 shutout at the hands of a horrible Tampa Bay team. At this point, Joe Torre's had enough.

Joe calls a team meeting, which is rare. Joe's visibly angry, which is even more rare. Joe proceeds to rip us all new ones, which is flat-out unheard of. "Lis-ten up, guys," he begins. "Today is September sixteenth, and the postseason starts in less than two weeks. You want to be embarrassed? You want to watch the World Series with your asses parked on your sofas at home? Keep playing like you are right now." An entire team looks at the floor.

* See also: Mike Piazza.

For the next fifteen minutes, Joe rakes us over the coals about "going through the motions on the field" and "embarrassing ourselves, and the Yankees, and the fans." Joe rails that we're not prepared on the field. We're not focused. We're not playing hard. We're not intense. Joe makes it clear that he doesn't give a rat's ass that we're now 64 games over .500. In his opinion, though we played great ball through the first five months of the season, right now we're a soft, lazy mess, "deluding ourselves into thinking that we can turn our game on or off at a moment's notice." That ain't gonna fly. Closing out the session, Joe makes it clear that unless this team wakes up soon, we're about to get blindsided by the single greatest postseason collapse in the history of baseball.

The room stays silent for a long, *long* time.

The rooster finally crows.

With Joe's words lighting a fire under all our asses, the sleeping giant of the Bronx finally awakens. We Yankees roar through the end of the September winning 10 of our last 12, and 7 in a row to close out the regular season. Of course, being "the Boomer," I can't let things end without getting into Joe Torre's doghouse at least once more. This time around, even *I* have to admit, I *totally* deserve it. This time around, I win Asshole of the Week honors, pretty much hands down.

September 18. Facing Baltimore, and staked to a 6–2 lead, I've had decent stuff on the mound, but the Birds have been squibbing little bloop singles and infield hits, and broken-bat drop-ins off me all night long. I *hate* that crap. Honestly, it makes me nuts. I'd much rather see you beat me fair and square with a 300-foot double than some little garbage-ball that just barely rolls to the outfield grass. I'm aggravated on the mound now, and it comes back to bite me in the sixth.

Up by six runs, Joe Torre wisely decides to give his playoff-bound outfielders the rest of the night off. Tim Raines comes out of left, Bernie comes out of center, Paulie comes out of right, and we start off the sixth with Ricky Ledee, Chad Curtis, and Shane Spencer taking their places. Cal Ripken grounds out to start off the inning, and that brings a September call-up named Lyle Mouton to the plate. Mouton gets under a pretty good cut fastball, and squibs it through the hole into shallow right for a single. "What the hell?" I shout. I've *gotta* be setting a new world's record for most crap singles allowed in one game. Left fielder Danny Clyburn steps in now, and two pitches later, it happens again. Clyburn dinks a catchable little squibbler into shallow left. Jeter runs out. Chad Curtis and Ricky Ledee both come in, but *nobody* calls for the ball. It ends up dropping between everybody for yet *another* pissy little single. *Now* I lose my composure completely.

"Fuck!" I yell on the mound. "Not another one!" I throw my arms into the air. I stand on the infield grass. I glare at all three fielders. I stomp around behind the mound, showing them up as I whine and moan and behave like an ass as the stadium crowd boos loudly.

And that's it. I'm off my game. Distracted and confused I now give up three straight singles and three straight runs before manager Torre comes out to yank me off his field. I slap the ball into his hand as he approaches, stomping off the field like an eight-year-old kid demanding a do-over. Ramiro Mendoza relieves, and by the time he's finished his warm-ups, Joe's already cornered me in the clubhouse.

"Your behavior on the mound tonight was mopey, and selfish, and unprofessional," he tells me. "I thought we were done with that stuff." Ow. "You know those guys in the field have been making plays behind you all year. You know they deserve better. Sure, they blew one tonight, but you just can't show your teammates up like that. I expect you to find them after the game, and apologize, and set things right."

"You got it." Joe's absolutely right on this one and I know it. With that in mind, Jeter, Curtis, and Ledee each get their own private apology right after the game, and all three accept in a heartbeat. We're cool. The water's under the bridge. I've learned a lesson, and it's time to move on . . . this time, toward October.

Coming home for one last home stand before the postseason wars begin, this hot Yankees team sends a nasty-assed message by taking three out of four from the AL Central Champion Indians, then sweeps four in a row from the cellar-dweller Devil Rays. Biggest moment of the week: there's no question, it's Coney's 20th victory.

Tossing 101 pitches over 7 shutout innings, the quiet Scumbag closes out his season at 20–7. It's been exactly a decade since Coney's *last* 20-win season, and when you stop and remember just how badly the '97 season ended for this man, with shoulder pain, and surgery, and the very real chance that his career might have been over, Coney's 20-game feat seems all the more amazing. You can't help but love this guy. Presented with the game ball by Joe Girardi, Coney falls apart, and I have to tell you a good-size chunk of the Yankee dugout follows suit.

September 27. Another day, another victory, and this one's number 114. With a clean, simple 8–3 shellacking of the Devil Rays, this team passes right by the 1954 Cleveland Indians to become the winningest American League franchise ever,* but everybody here knows that milestone means nothing. This team may have spent the past six months racking up a .704 winning percentage, and a 114–78 record, but as of right now, none of that matters. As of right now, we're 0–0, with 11 victories standing between us and a ring. It's crunch time. I'm smiling. We're ready for war.

With Cleveland going into a first-round battle against the Wild Card Red Sox (who finished 22 games behind us in the East), we Yankees get set to face the AL West Champs, Texas. This year, Joe gets the postseason rotation right. He gives me the ball for Game 1, at home, where I'll be taking the hill against my old minor-league running buddy/bar-fight instigator, Todd Stottlemyre. I'm thrilled with Joe's vote of confidence. I'm pumped with the big-game opportunity. Hero or goat, I thrive on this stuff.

Game 1. Somewhere, Eddie Van Halen is wearing my jersey and playing guitar. Months ago, having seen the band from backstage and hung out for a few waters and coffees after the show, I managed to swap with Eddie one Boomer-worn Yankees jersey for one concert-played Eddie Van Halen axe. (Can you believe I get away with these lopsided deals?) When Eddie calls to wish me luck on the afternoon of Game 1, I twist his arm into promising he'll wear that jersey and send me good vibes tonight from the stage. He makes good on the offer, and I take the mound feeling fantastic.

With Eddie Van Halen, after a show

With the single greatest regular season of my life now behind me, and the psychic best wishes of a guitar god filling my sails, I've never been more confident, or relaxed, or just plain happy entering a big-game situation. My stuff is moving. My fastball is popping, and by game time I know the Rangers are gonna spend the night looking at a whole lotta top-shelf heat. There's just one problem: Todd Stottlemyre's brought his A game with him as well.

---

* Obviously, our September sleepwalking kept us from matching the '06 Cubs for best-ever status. We did, however, beat out the legendary 1927 Yankees for the best *Yankee* season of all time. That's a *much* cooler accomplishment as far as I'm concerned.

Bottom of the eighth. Having thrown 120 pitches, I'm desperately hanging on to a scratched-out 2–0 lead and fading fast. With one out, Rangers' second baseman Mark McLemore doubles over the head of Chad Curtis. Joe Torre sprints to the mound.

"How are you feeling, Boomer?"

"I'm okay," I mutter back like I always do.

"No . . . ," says Joe, pulling me closer to him, eyes locked on mine, "tell me how you're feeling."

"I really feel okay," I tell him. "Y'know, it's not like the first four innings or anything, but I can go."

Joe stares. The gears are turning. The relievers are warming. Jorge dives in. "Listen, Joe, he's still good to go. He's really got it!"

"Good enough," Joe says. "I'll see ya after the third out."

"You got it, Skip."

Joe pats my right shoulder and he's gone.

I stare down at Roberto Kelly in the batter's box now, and over the next three minutes, the two of us will battle through an endless, hard-fought, nine-pitch at bat. Finally, after Roberto's fouled off at *least* three "ball fours," I get lucky. One sweet little fastball nicks the inside corner of the plate, and I win this duel. Roberto takes a big, fat K, looking. From there, Rusty Greer busts a slow-roller to Derek, and one gorgeous toss to first later, I'm back in the dugout and done for the night. Joe and I exchange well-earned thumbs-ups as we pass. It's been a big night for us both. And when Mariano Rivera makes like . . . well, Mariano Rivera, and slams the door shut in the ninth, we Yanks grab a quick series lead at 1–zip.

Mobbed in the locker room after the game, I am surrounded by a sea of reporters that parts down the middle when George Steinbrenner roars in. He grabs me . . . by the face. Big hands pinching me hard at both cheeks, the Boss is grinning from ear to ear. "You're a fucking warrior, baby! A fucking warrior! Jesus Christ, I could kiss ya!"

"Please don't," I reply, laughing, face still squashed in his clutches.

From there, having greased Smashing Pumpkins' lead singer, Billy Corgan, with a couple of great seats to tonight's game (which I'll later use as leverage in weaseling a signed guitar out of him), I'm out of the clubhouse and out on the town in twenty minutes flat. With my Game 1 start now behind me, my *only* responsibility is to relax, have a good time, and show up tomorrow in time to watch this team win Game 2. It's just that simple.

Game 2. Andy Pettitte's on the mound, performing multiple exorcisms. First, this man's been haunted all season by the ghosts of his double losses to Cleveland in last year's ALDS. Second, having struggled through most of the second half, and losing five of his last seven starts, Andy's got demons up the ying-yang tonight. Can he rise to the occasion? Can he wipe the slate clean? Can he erase his own bad karma?

Yep.

Andy's flat-out awesome. His change-up is ridiculous, practically stopping in midair before it reaches the plate. His two-seamer is *killing* the Ranger righties, and best of all, for the first time in a long time, Andy's consistently throwing his curveball for strikes. He allows just one run over seven innings pitched, and when Jeff Nelson and Mariano Rivera start turning the screws through another pair of nasty, unhittable relief innings, you can see our opponents deflating. Stick a fork in these Rangers, son. They're cooked. Heads down, shoulders slumped, those guys head home to Arlington with their backs to the wall.

Meanwhile, amid all the postgame excitement of our raucous Yankees' clubhouse, there *is* one piece of sad news. Darryl Strawberry isn't with us tonight. He's at Columbia Presbyterian Hospital. Suffering from relentless stomach pain throughout the last few weeks of the regular season, Darryl simply toughed it out and kept playing. Last night, that pain was back, with cramping much more severe than *anything* Darryl had previously endured. It just didn't matter.

Refusing to abandon his team, or his responsibilities for anything so trivial as his own well-being, Darryl once again remained silent, vowing to delay medical treatment "until the day after this team wins the World Series." He won't make it.

This morning, with his pain worsening, Darryl finally caved and grudgingly went to the hospital. And while clubhouse rumors have already saddled Darryl with everything from an ulcer, to appendicitis, to *really* bad gas, preliminary doctors' reports are leaning toward an infection of the colon. A frightening prognosis, but with the Yankees' own press corps talking about a Game 3 return for the Straw Man, in Texas, this team hits the road with a large, collective sigh of relief.

October 1, Arlington, Texas, 8:30 A.M. With a morning workout planned, this team's not even dressed yet when a pale-faced, wet-eyed Joe Torre calls for our attention. "Guys," he tells us, "I'm sorry to tell you that the doctors back in New York have run a series of tests, and uh . . . it looks like Darryl Strawberry has colon cancer."

Silence, minutes of dead silence. Then the sobs can be heard. Joe tells us that Darryl will undergo surgery as early as Saturday, and the news just punches through us all. Everybody's quiet. Everybody's wrecked. Everybody says their own kind of prayer. Later, we head out to the field, hiding behind our sunglasses, silently going through the motions of a lackluster workout. Game 3 suddenly feels like nothing more than a silly, unimportant distraction. That will change.

Game 3. With everybody on the team now sporting a big, fat, Strawberry-inspired #39 on their caps, we're glued to the clubhouse TV watching Darryl's surprise, videotaped message of inspiration. "I want you to know," Darryl says over the TV screen, "that my heart is with you, regardless of what

Champagne snipering in Arlington *(© Reuters 1998/STR)*

I'm going through . . ." Darryl then points at the lens and says, "Go get 'em." That's it. Bet the farm, mortgage your house, sell off your stocks, and visit your bookie. This team's a lock. There's no way on earth we're gonna let Darryl down. Hours later, when Coney takes the mound with a roaring fire in his eye and the Laredo slider at full-bore, lethal intensity, I almost feel sorry for Texas . . . almost.

Aaron Sele's on the mound for Texas, and on any other night he might have beaten us. Good location, nice movement, this kid throws himself one hell of a game. But tonight, that's just not good enough. Tonight this team's on a mission, and though both Coney and Sele are shut-out-magnificent through the first five innings, Sele's luck is about to run out. With a solo home run from Paul O'Neill and a three-run monster from Shane Spencer, we Yankees take a quick 4–0 lead in the sixth. That's more than enough, but that's also when the sky falls in.

With two outs in our half of the sixth, a Texas-sized monsoon rolls in. Buckets of rain are falling. Sheets. A half hour later, the delay's still going strong. One hour, two hours, three, still the old man is snoring. The umpires hold out, refusing to throw in the towel, and finally, their determination pays off. The rain slows down to a drizzle, and both teams hit the field at 1:24 A.M., and by 2:26, it's official—4-zip, Yankees. We move on to the ALCS.

After the game as the inevitable wave of reporters shuttles through the clubhouse, Tim Raines jumps up onto a table, holding a bottle of champagne, and immediately shuts the room down. "Excuse me!" he shouts. "As everybody knows, Darryl wanted us to win this one for him." Tears in his eyes now, Raines holds his bottle high and shouts, "Well, this is for you, D. Strawberry!"

All over the room, champagne glasses and beer cans are raised high. "STRAWWWWWWWWWW!!!!!" gets shouted at roof-raising volume. This one's for you, buddy.

Saturday, October 3. Darryl Strawberry undergoes 3½ hours of surgery, and though doctors remove a 2½-inch tumor from his colon along with 16 inches of intestine, the news is fantastic. There are no complications, and no signs at all that the cancer has spread. With Darryl now resting comfortably, giving his nurses a hard time, and whining for cheesecake, doctors are predicting he'll make a complete, no-strings-attached recovery. Huge sighs of relief explode from the clubhouse. Huge smiles stay in place through our workout. Twelve hours later, when the Indians bump off the Red Sox to become our ALCS opponents, those same smiles will turn just a bit evil.

Cleveland! *This* is the team that knocked us out of '97. *This* is gonna be a steel-cage, no-holds-barred grudge match. Adding gasoline to the fire, the Indians are sending Jaret Wright to the hill for Game 1. Wright's the pitcher who shut us down *twice* in last season's playoffs. Revenge is being served cold this fall.

I've got the ball for Game 1.

October 6, 3:30 P.M. I hit Yankee Stadium feeling strong, and excited, and proud as hell that Joe's handed me this start. The mix tape goes in. The volume gets cranked. Don Zimmer runs away with his hands over his ears. I'm more than ready.

One by one, we Yankees get introduced to the crowd, taking the field in front of almost 58,000 screaming, devoted, wild-eyed fanatics. Their cheers are enormous, but when Bob Sheppard surprises this crowd (and us Yankees) by solemnly announcing "Number thirty-nine, Darryl Strawberry!" in his usual spot, the whole place flat-out explodes. With Darryl's picture smiling down at the crowd from the scoreboard, chills run through the stadium. "Dar-RYL!, Dar-RYL!, Dar-RYL!" they shout, and though Straw's still bedridden, just about a mile and a half away in Columbia Presbyterian, those cheers have *got* to be rattling his windows.

Moments later, as Darryl's wife, Charisse, throws out our first pitch, the whole place freaks out all over again. Inspired? You could say that. My heart's pounding. The adrenaline's up. And when it's finally time to play ball, I sprint to the mound, where my 1, 2, 3 half-inning feels thirty seconds long. Jaret Wright won't be that lucky.

He's shook. Mel sees it. I can see it. And over at home plate, smiling like the Chesire Cat, Chuck Knoblauch sees it too. Jaret's tight. He's nervous. He's rushing his pitches. He's not following through, and that's leaving his fastball up in the zone. You just can't do that against a lineup as good as this one. We're up 5–zip by the end of the first. Question: how great is *this*?

Answer: pretty damn great. Staked to *that* big a lead, I'm having the time of my life out there on the mound. I'm loose. I'm aggressive. I'm challenging hitters, and my stuff is popping, and breaking, and blowing by guys, right into the ninth. This one goes into the books as a sweet, uncomplicated, 7–2 W.

It won't be nearly this easy tomorrow.

Game 2. Back in the Bronx, back on my ass, I sit on the bench, watching David Cone mow through the Indians lineup like a John Deere tractor. Everything's working. His pitch count is tiny, and except for one fluttering 0–1 change-up that David Justice smacks over the right-field fence, Coney's fantastic through eight innings pitched. Tonight, however, there's just one problem. Charles Nagy's just as good. Eleven innings later, *long* after both starters have called it a night, we head into the twelfth all tied up at one. That's where this contest comes completely unhinged.

Jeff Nelson's on the mound. Jim Thome's at the plate, and he smacks a lead-off single. Enrique Wilson sprints on to pinch run for the bear-size Thome. Travis Fryman's at the plate, and with the Indians clawing for whatever runs they can get, there's not a Yankee on the field who's not thinking "bunt." With that in mind, the entire infield is already shifting as Fryman squares, and connects, and dinks a beauty of a slow roller right up along the first-base line. Wilson takes off for second. Tino charges. Knobby covers first. Fryman sprints up the infield grass toward first, blatantly outside the base paths.

Tino fires to Knoblauch. Fryman gets in the way. The ball hits Fryman square in the back and bounces off his numbers to the edge of the right-field grass. Knobby throws a fit, screaming bloody murder to the first-base ump. Wilson takes off for third. The ball sits still on the right-field grass. "THE BALL!!!" we're screaming from the Yankees' bench. "GET THE BALL, KNOBBY!!!"

Now 57,000 fans are screaming the same thing. Knobby keeps at it, vapor-locked in his argument at first base. "GET THE BALL, GODDAMNIT!!!" Knobby's blowing gum bubbles as he argues. "CHU-U-U-UCK!!!" It's no use.

Enrique Wilson charges for home now but ends up taking a header so ridiculous it looks like something out of *America's Funniest Home Videos*. He trips. He stumbles. He splatters into home plate face first. Honestly, it would have been the funniest thing in the world if it weren't costing us this game. Knobby's still arguing, and by the time this whole ugly mess of a play is complete, we're down 2–1 with Travis Fryman smacking what amounts to the first bunt triple in the history of the sport.*

From there, with a rousing chorus of well-earned boos ringing in his ears, Knobby moves back to second, just in time to watch the Rangers crank out a pair of insurance runs. Down 4–1 now, we never get any closer. It's an ugly, embarrassing loss, and with this team now hitting the road, for three in a row at Jacobs Field, the series's momentum has moved in with Chief Wahoo.

Game 3. BLAUCH-HEAD!!! screams one New York headline. CHUCK BRAINLAUCH! screams another. And while the guy's got it coming, you can't help but feel bad. Even worse, with a day off to fill between Games 2 and 3, the televised replays of Knobby's brain-freeze have become just as relentless and wiseassed as the tabloids. Sportscasters are now adding wacky music under the footage, speeding up the tape for comic effect, adding *boings* and *cuckoos* and crashes to the soundtrack while simultaneously cutting back and forth between bubblegum closeups of Knobby and the swan-diving, face-busting Enrique Wilson. The clips are funny as hell, but there's no way I'm laughing (at least not in the clubhouse). Sure

---

* Fryman's bunt hit officially goes into the books as a single and a Tino Martinez error.

Knobby blew one. Sure we all wanted to smack him. But it's done now. We're past it. It's time to move on . . . almost.

Introduced to the Jacobs Field crowd just prior to Game 3, every one of us Yankees is greeted by a long, loud, merciless chorus of boos . . . except for Knobby. When Chuck Knoblauch gets announced, Knobby receives a long, loud, standing ovation. It's rude, and it's rotten, but it *is* kinda funny. A long line of Yankees tries hard not to smile. Some of us fail, miserably.

Bartolo Colon's on the mound for Cleveland, and Knobby quickly shuts up his Jacobs Field Fan Club by leading off the game with a solid single to left. He's booed immediately. After that, Derek Jeter bumps Knobby to second with a sac fly into right-center, and Paul O'Neill's groundout to short shuttles Knobby to third. At that point, Bernie Williams clips a lined single into left-center, scoring Knoblauch from third and giving us Yankees a 1–0 lead. Sadly, it's all downhill from here.

While Andy Pettitte's shaky all night long, Bartolo Colon's settles in to become practically untouchable. His fastball clocks in at 97 miles per hour. His change-up is *maybe* doing 70. He's hitting corners. He's throwing strikes. He's off and running toward a complete-game 6–1 victory, wherein we Yankees will manage to scrape out just two more hits over the final 8 innings. We're in *big* trouble.

Game 4. Dwight Gooden versus Orlando Hernández. Darryl Strawberry sends another pregame message. "Guys," he says, "do *not* lose this game to Doc, 'cuz if he beats us, I will *never* hear the end of it." With the order delivered, Paul O'Neill responds by smacking one of Doc's first-inning pitches *way* over the right-field wall. Back in New York, Darryl breathes a huge sigh of relief. Here in Cleveland, we Yankees ain't nearly that confident.

Here's the deal. We've got a rookie on the mound who struggled through the end of the regular season and hasn't pitched in a game for more than two weeks. Sure he's twenty-eight years old (or more), and sure he's been a star on the Cuban National Team, but can *any* rookie stand up to the pressure of a major-league, must-win, postseason start? "Listen to me," Hernández says through his translator, "you don't worry. My biggest game was getting on a raft and coming here. I can handle *this* one, easy."

He's not kidding.

El Duque has our eyes wide and our eyebrows rising right from the start of the game. Cool and precise and dominant on the mound, he thumps the Indians' lineup, top to bottom, all night long. *"Muy bien, amigo!!"* we shout at El Duque in horrible, phonetically learned Spanish. *"Muy bien!"* Taking the mound here in Cleveland, Orlando Hernández lifts this whole Yankee team on his back and carries us with him through one hell of an outing. It's a beautiful thing, and with our Yankee bats scratching out three runs against Doc, and one more for good measure off reliever Dave Burba, a well-earned 4–0 victory reknots this series at 2–2.

I've got the ball for Game 5, with Chad Ogea getting the start over the now unpredictable Jaret Wright. I can't wait. With Señor Hernández delivering a truckload of positive karma to the visitors' side of Jacobs Field, and laughter once again rolling through the Yankees' clubhouse, my Metallica's met with less horror than usual. Don Zimmer even makes a brief attempt at the world's worst air-guitar performance. Graeme Lloyd sings along, sounding a lot like a warthog in heat. Coney complains that his eardrums are bleeding. We're loose. We're relaxed. We're positive. We're ready to win ourselves a baseball game. I head to the bullpen on top of the world. Once there, however, it all turns to shit.

Good stuff in the warm-up; it's not the best ever, but solid. The fastballs are popping, the curve seems workable, but I couldn't care less. Right now, all I want to do is climb up the chain-link at the side of the bullpen and beat the snot out of a handful of screaming Cleveland idiots.

"You're an asshole, Wells! You suck! Fuck you!" they shout, hanging over the bullpen like a bunch of drunken, potbellied baboons wearing acid-washed jeans. Standard stuff, really. I barely even notice . . . until they shift gears. "Hey, Wells! Your mother's a whore!" they shout from above, laughing, and at that point I can't help but shoot them a glare. Bad move. They've struck a nerve, and they know it. Now the jackasses take it up a notch, laying out a long, steady, *completely* obnoxious string of mom-centered insults, *none* of which I'll reprint for you here. I'm dying to break a nose.

More dick-heads join the glee club. More insults get thrown, and by the time I've finished my warm-ups, I'm astonished to find that a bunch of *little* kids, just eight or nine years old, are now mimicking the older morons, reshouting every bit of filth the alpha mooks dish out. The "adults" all crack up at the sight. Welcome to Cleveland, ass-wipe capital of the USA.*

It *really* bothers me. I know it shouldn't, but it does. Insults aimed at *me* just roll off with no effect. It's part of the territory. But here, today, with the rifle sights shifting to my mom, I've become furious to the point of distraction. Min-

---

* I know the knee-jerk response: "Yankee Stadium fans are the rudest in baseball!" Wrong. Trust me on this one. I spent nine years pitching in the American League, and never once did *any* Yankee Stadium fan attack my family. It's only *ever* happened in Cleveland.

utes later, hands still balled into tight, homicidal fists, my head still spinning, I sit in the Yankees' dugout, stewing and staring, barely cracking a smile, even as my teammates are jumping all over a wild, tentative Chad Ogea and gifting me with a quick, 3–0, first-inning lead. In just a few moments, I'll give most of that back.

Taking the mound to my usual chorus of boos, I'm now raging inside. Sweating, scowling, *still* looking to fracture a skull, I'm knocked off my game. I'm distracted. My mechanics are off. My delivery sucks, my fastball is up, and I pay for it all through the first. The assholes have won.

Kenny Lofton leads off with a home run to right. Omar Vizquel and Travis Fryman both follow that shot with singles into center. Now I'm reeling, and Cleveland smells blood. Vizquel steals third. "Fuck!" Lost now, I uncork a wild pitch that sends Travis Fryman streaking into second. Manny "Mr. Home Run" Ramirez steps in. Time out.

C'mon, buddy, I say to myself. Shake it off! Forget about the idiots back in the bullpen and think! Your fastball is up, but the breaking stuff looks pretty sharp. Time to mix it up. Time to hit your spots and get back to basics. Good mechanics, move the ball around, this is how you win ball games. Suddenly, from out of nowhere, I've got a giant Rob Schneider in my head shouting, "Yewww can *Dooooooo* EEET!" I laugh out loud on the mound. Manny Ramirez stares at me like I've got two heads. Jorge thinks I've finally cracked. I couldn't care less. The ice is broken. The deep breaths finally come. It's time to stop thinking and toss.

The pitches come easier now, but that doesn't mean I'm out of the woods. Ramirez lofts a good curve into right, just shy of the warning track, more than deep enough to score Vizquel. Mark Whiten steps into the box, and on a first-pitch breaker, Travis Fryman steals third. He stays there as Whiten strikes out on my first *really* good fastball of the night. Jim Thome stomps in now, with smoke blowing out his nostrils and a bat the size of a telephone pole squeezed into his meat-hook hands.

Damn, are there *no* bad hitters on this team? I wonder on the mound. Curveballs. Away. Away. Away. This guy's not getting those gorilla arms extended. I lose him to a walk. Now Richie Sexson steps in, and again I'm throwing at the corners. This time I get lucky, with Sexson swinging and missing at a "strike three" curve that *should* have been "ball four." Bullet dodged, I'm out of the rotten inning with my head clear, my stuff working better, my one-run lead still in place, and a *very* good outlook on the rest of this game.

I feel even better when my teammates once again dog-pile Ogea for another run in the second. Up 4–2 now, Jaret Wright comes in early to return a Game 1 favor and relieve Ogea. *Much* more relaxed and effective than he'd been in the Bronx, Jaret will get tagged for just one run over his six innings of work.

Meanwhile, with a solid lead, solid stuff, and my unruly fastball back under control, I'm having *way* too much fun to stay pissed. In fact, as the game wears on, and Chili Davis smacks a solo home run that puts us up 5–2, I actually find myself feeling kinda goofy. Chasing after a foul ball that ultimately drifts over the Yankees' dugout into the crowd, I end up teetering at the edge of the steps. A dozen Yankees run up to make sure I don't fall.

"Hey, Skip," I shout over to Joe, "what's the big idea? I'm not allowed to dive for foul balls?" Joe Torre stares at me in horror, then laughs.

"Sure you can. Just make sure it's headfirst. That way you can't get hurt."

I make just one real mistake through the rest of my start, but, boy, is it ever huge. Having spent the last inning stomping all over Tokyo, Jim Thome's back at the plate now, breathing fire and screeching at the airplanes that are currently circling round his head. I don't even blink. He's mine, and with the fastball back in my arsenal, and nobody on base, I decide to challenge the man's green, scaly ass. Fastball, fired dead center. WHACK!!!

Thome hits a ball that knocks the MIR space station out of orbit. "Wowwwwwwwwwwww!" is all I can think of to say as it flies *way* over my head. "WOW!" Getting through the rest of that inning unharmed, I run back to the dugout, bragging. "Did ya see that, boys? Now *that's* the way to give up a major-league home run! *That* sucker was a *bomb*!"

"Some of your best work," Coney replies.

Eighth inning. Heading back to the mound, I've made the mistake of telling Joe and Mel that my gas tank is now getting low. With that in mind, they're taking no chances. They get Jeff Nelson up in the pen right away, and they tell me he'll come into the inning as soon as he's warm. No problem.

Problem. I hit that mound for the eighth inning riding a second wind of gigantic proportions. I feel great. I feel strong. I feel like Ernie Banks. "Let's pitch two!" I strike out Omar Vizquel to start the inning, but here comes Joe. "No! No, wait!" I shout as he approaches. He taps the arm. The gate opens. Nelson hits the outfield grass. Jorge trots out to the mound. Derek and Brosius join him.

"Great game, Boomer," Joe says, reaching for the ball. I squeeze it as tight as I can.

"No, you don't understand, I feel great now. Let me stay in!" Derek's laughing into his mitt. Jorge just laughs out loud.

"Don't be nuts. I already called for Nelson. You have to go."

"No, come on. Lemme pitch. I want to stay one more batter. There's still time. Maybe you can send Nelson back to the pen. Is that legal?"

Joe's lost it. He's laughing hard, still trying hard to twist the ball out of my clenched palm. "C'mon, just go off and get your big, warm, standing ovation."

"Yeah, right." Nelson arrives. I give up. Heading off the field as the huge Jacobs Field crowd boos me with all they've got, I stop on the grass, take off my cap, wave it to both sides of the stadium, and take a little bow. They're ready to lynch me. Jeff and Mariano close out the game in no time flat. We're up 3–2, with the series going back to the Bronx and Coney taking the mound for Game 6. I smell World Series.

Bounding into the postgame clubhouse, I find George Steinbrenner already holding court with a bunch of reporters. He's in mid-sound-byte as I arrive.

"Y'know, I don't know how many Christmas dinners I'm gonna share with the Boomer, but I like him a lot. I'm even starting to like The Metallics."

I smack my own forehead.

"It's Metallica, George."

"Yeah, that's what I said. Anyway . . ."

And he's off. I roll my eyes now and dive into my own gaggle of beat writers, making sure to tell them all about those heckling, pregame idiots, and to send the message "Hey morons, this win's for you." Maybe, if I'm lucky, their friends in the unemployment line will kick their asses for me tomorrow.

Game 6. The champagne's on ice. It's hidden away, but we all know it's there, and having now waited a full year to erase the nasty memories of our '97 collapse, we Yankees are *dying* to start popping corks. Coney's on the mound, we're home in Yankee Stadium, and it's a beautiful day to become AL Champs, but there's just one small problem. Somebody forgot to tell the Indians it's over.

Three innings into this sucker, we Yankees are walloping the bejesus out of Indians starter Charles Nagy. Everybody's hitting, everybody's running the bases, and as the final nail in Chief Wahoo's coffin, Scotty Brosius caps off the third with a monstrous 3-run blast over the fence in dead center to put us up 6–0. Break out the bubbles, boys. It's party time!

"Not so fast!" say the Indians.

Coney doesn't have his best stuff tonight, but he's been battling, and fooling, and out-thinking the Cleveland bats all night long. Indians on base? No problem. Coney works out of jams in every inning of this game . . . until the fifth. Still carrying a 6–zip lead, Coney gives up back-to-back-to-back singles to Enrique

Wilson, Kenny Lofton, and Omar Vizquel, who dinks a little infield dribbler that ends up loading the bases.

David Justice steps in, hearing the crowd shout, "HAL-LE, BERRRRY! HA HA! HA HA!" as loud as they can. He bears down, waiting for his pitch, and never gets it. Coney walks Justice, forcing home the Indians' first run. Bases still loaded, the Indians biggest home run threat steps in. Coney goes to work against Manny Ramirez.

Working the change, and a couple of pretty fastballs, Coney sends Ramirez down with a big, hacking, breeze-inducing K. Here comes Jim Thome (aka Sasquatch in cleats). Coney winds and fires. Thome snorts and clocks yet another monster shot, this time a grand slam, way past the wall in right field. By the time the inning's over, Coney's done for the day, and our 6–zip laugher has become a 6–5 nail-biter.

Every single Yankee now carries his own personal stomach knot. Every single Yankee knows that we need to stomp the momentum out of these Indians, fast. Let 'em tie this thing up and they may start getting crazy ideas about comebacks, and fairy-tale finishes, and knotting this series at 3 games apiece. We can't let that happen. At this point, Ramiro Mendoza rides in like the Dominican cavalry.

Though he's been invited out of the pen just once this whole postseason, Ramiro hits the mound at the top of his game. Showing *no* signs of rust, the man's flat-out unhittable through the sixth, seventh, and eighth. That's all we can ask, and more than we need. And when Mariano Rivera shows up for the ninth, it's time to start hanging plastic all over the clubhouse. Three Indians come up. Three Indians go down. The stadium explodes. The dugout empties, and we stomp out of this series with a sweet 9–6 victory.

Back in the clubhouse, halfway between scoring a direct champagne hit to Derek Jeter's left ear, and squirting Paul O'Neill square in the mush from a distance of twenty-five feet, I'm told that I've just been named the MVP of the ALCS. I never saw it coming, and honestly, as far as I'm concerned, *every* guy on this team qualifies as a Most Valuable Player. Of course, with that said, there's no way in hell I'm sharing my trophy.

From there, huddled around the phone in the trainer's room, we Yankees call Darryl Strawberry and take turns shouting into the phone at him, "This is for you, Straw!!!" Mike Stanton shouts as he holds the phone up to his bottle of champagne and drenches Chuck Knoblauch. Seconds later, Jeff Nelson and Ramiro Mendoza treat Darryl to the stereo sounds of their own surprise, double-barreled spritzing of yours truly. Laughing like hell, Straw's ready to pop a stitch. I serve as Darryl's surrogate victim with a huge, more-than-willing grin.

Final shining moment of the day? I shake, and I shake, and I shake, and I shake, and then, when the moment is right, I unload a full magnum of Perrier-Jouët smack into the back of Boss Steinbrenner's head. "Hooooo! Hoo! Hoo! Hoo! Hoo! Hoooooooooey!" he shouts as he runs, sounding an awful lot like a gray-haired Daffy Duck. It's a direct hit. George, who's always been labeled as "off-limits" in the Yankee clubhouse champagne wars, never once gets a glimpse at his fizz-shooting assassin, and quite frankly, now that I've printed this, I'm scared. I know how George thinks, and trust me on this one. Someday, sometime, somewhere, probably when I least expect it, the payback on this one's gonna be a real bitch.

October 14. The San Diego Padres beat the Braves 5–1 to become National League Champions, and that officially registers me as the happiest guy on the planet. Pitching for the *Yankees*, against the *Padres*, in my *hometown*, in the biggest sporting event of them all, this thing is gonna fulfill every single baseball fantasy of my youth . . . well, except for that one where I give Joyce DeWitt a sponge bath in the bullpen at Jack Murphy Stadium.

I was a weird kid. What can I tell you?

October 15. I've got two days to kill before the start of the Series, and bored out of my skull, I jump at the chance to drop in at the *Howard Stern Show*. There, after running through the standard material about Robin's mammoth breasts and Baba Booey's giant teeth, the studio conversation finally turns to the subject of baseball. As the reigning "King of All Marys," Howard knows less about sports than your average rhesus monkey. At the same time, however, he's a radio genius, and he quickly gets me in trouble. Relentlessly belittling the Padres, Howard digs hard for controversy, demanding that I make a Series prediction. "How many games?" he wants to know.

"Can't do that, Howard. I'll get into trouble."

"C'mon. C'mon. C'mon. C'mon. Don't be a pussy."

"I can't!'

"Pussy!"

We go back and forth like that for the better part of ten minutes until finally the man's incessant whining bores a hole in my head. I crack. "All right, Howard," I tell him. "If I *was* gonna make a prediction, which I'm *not*, I'd probably say five games? Will *that* get you to shut up and leave me alone?"

"Five games! You heard it here!"

I love Howard. I think he's honest, and smart, and funny as hell, but now, thanks to big-nose, I'm tits deep in trouble. The local tabloids turn my prediction into thick, black, 72-point headlines ("WE'LL WIN IT IN FIVE!" WELLS BRAGS!). San Diego pitching coach (and ex-teammate) Dave Stewart *reads* those headlines, throws a fit, and quickly posts photocopies all over the Padres clubhouse. My words become a war chant, a rallying cry for an entire Padres team that now hates my guts. George is pissed too. So is Joe. Curled up in the doghouse, I'll shut up until game time.

Game 1. It's my ball, my rules, my time of year, but as first pitch approaches, I've got a *swarm* of last-minute butterflies fluttering through my digestive tract. This has *never* happened to me before. I'm nervous. I'm shaking. I'm long overdue. Look at the facts: I'm pitching *Game 1*, of the *World Series*, for the *New York Yankees*, in *Yankee Stadium*, against my *hometown team*, and despite rumors to the contrary, I *am* a human being. With all that in mind, I've *earned* these heebie-jeebies, which quickly get worse in the bullpen.

Warming up, my stuff's flatter than last week's champagne. My breaking ball is mushy. My two-seamer won't sink, and while my location seems workable, it's not *nearly* as dead-on precise as it's been over the past few weeks. The heart pounds. The jitters set in. This may not be pretty.

Kevin Brown's on the mound for San Diego, and while he's had a monster season (18–7, 2.38 ERA), Yankee spies tell us he's now sick as a dog with a really nasty flu. Advantage, Yankees. The information brings evil, drooling grins to the entire Bombers lineup, and by the end of the second inning, with Brown's early stuff looking every bit as shaky as my own, the boys have me staked to a quick 2–zip lead. I blow it in no time.

Top of the third. Padres shortstop Chris Gomez beats me for a leadoff single into left. No big deal. From there, I get two quick outs from Quilvio Veras and Tony Gwynn, and that's when superslugger Greg Vaughn steps in. My chest puffs up. My nostrils flare. I'd piss on a tree if I had one. This is *my* territory.

One year after being rejected by the Yankees as "damaged goods," Vaughn's spent the '98 season whomping *50* home runs. Big and ugly, he shoots me a hard stare from the batter's box. I sneer back. It's go time. I rear back now, heaving a pretty curveball, low and away. SMACK! Ugly home run, high and *far* away, 420 feet into right. Vaughn circles the bases. I swear like a drunken sailor. We're tied up at two.

From there, while Kevin Brown goes superhuman, shaking off the effects of his flu and settling into a comfortable, dominant, almost untouchable groove, I just keep right on struggling. By the top of the fifth, I'm in hot water again.

Two outs. Quilvio Veras on first. Tony Gwynn steps up to the plate and wastes absolutely no time in spanking a massive, two-run homer off the facing of the upper deck in right.

Big Ugly Vaughn steps in now, and one pitch later, he kicks my ass again, *this* time clobbering a pretty good fastball right *over* the bullpen in left. My head drops. My heart sinks. A shouting, raging, high-volume stream of profanity rolls out of me and reaches all the way up to the mezzanine. Down 5–2, it looks like my fairy-tale season may have a *really* unhappy ending.

But never fear, people. This is 1998. We're the New York Yankees, the baseball gods love us, and as you've probably figured out by now, "happy endings" are what we do best. *This* time around, the magic happens in the bottom of the seventh, just moments after I've left the game for good, hit the dugout, and beaten the crap out of two watercoolers, one bat rack, and an entire case of Double Bubble. Being the goat is a bitch.

I sit on the bench, steam now rising out of both ears, while out on the field, Scott Brosius leads off the bottom of the seventh with a routine groundout to second. "Damnit!" This is my fault. My stuff's been bad. My butt's been kicked, and barring some late-innings magic, we're just gonna . . . hey, wait a minute, Jorge just singled into right. Kevin Brown hung a fastball that had "smack me" written all over it. Is flu-boy finally getting tired?

Ricky Ledee gets into the box now, and with my fingers crossed and my inside-out rally cap now resting comfortably atop my head, I watch Ledee walk on five pitches. Here comes Padres manager/former-David-Wells-rehab-catcher Bruce Bochy. He signals the pen, and Donne Wall trots on in relief. Now the *real* fun starts.

Chuck Knoblauch comes to the dish, and while a generous chunk of the Yankee Stadium faithful are still chanting "Blauch-head!" as loudly as possible, Knobby quickly turns those jeers into cheers by walloping a *humongous* three-run homer over the left-field fence. The stadium goes absolutely berserk. Donne Wall looks ready to crawl under the nearest rock. This game's tied 5–5!

Knobby takes a curtain call, and with chants of "Knob-BEE, Knob-BEE!" now echoing through the park, Derek Jeter steps in, takes one pitch, then singles with a sharp line drive into center. Here comes Bochy, again. He signals the pen, *again*. Donne Wall gets thrown overboard, as nasty lefty Mark Langston jogs to the mound. In the on-deck circle, Paul O'Neill is waiting with his standard, impatient glare screwed on tight.

With the stadium faithful screaming at earsplitting levels now, a nervous Langston begins his outing with a wild pitch that sends Jeter to second. From there, he gets lucky as O'Neill takes a *huge* cut at a bad pitch but ends up skying a routine pop fly into left. Two away, Paulie comes back to the dugout and finishes murdering my pair of well-beaten coolers. Bernie Williams heads for home plate.

Four pitches. "Take your base." Bernie receives an intentional walk. Chili Davis follows him to the plate, and he *also* takes a free pass, this time of the *non-*intentional variety. Bases loaded, Langston's rattled, the table is set for Tino Martinez, aka the coldest hitter in the Yankee lineup.

Just 5 for 32 this postseason, Tino steps into the box and digs in, ultimately battling Langston to a 2–2 count. At that point, Langston reaches deep and delivers a gorgeous fastball, right down the middle for strike three . . . only it's *not* "strike three." Instead, home plate umpire Rich Garcia inexplicably signals "*ball* three." Langston's jaw drops. *My* jaw drops. Zimmer shouts, "Holy Toledo!" The Yankees get lucky.

Knocked *completely* off his nut now, by the crowd, and the pressure, and the blown "strike three," a visibly spooked Langston moves back to the rubber, rears back, and fires a *big* mistake. It's a hanging, beachball-size fastball that Tino clobbers high into the upper deck in right for a grand slam. Derek scores. Bernie scores. Chili scores. Tino scores. All four get mobbed in the dugout, and with the stadium now just *completely* insane, Tino's tossed out for our second curtain-call-moment of the inning. Magic. Up 9–5, with my ass-kicking avenged, I end up going home with a *completely* undeserved W, once again securing my rank as the single luckiest human ever to walk the face of this planet.

Game 2. The Padres are down. Time to start kicking . . . hard.

Giving up three runs in the first, three more in the second, and one more for good measure in the third, Padres starter Andy Ashby (17–9, 3.34 ERA) hits Yankee Stadium with all the success, confidence, and good luck of Ed Whitson. He's caught the Kevin Brown flu.

Sweating profusely on the mound, Ashby can't swallow, or breathe through his nose, or throw an effective pitch. He's gone after 2⅔, and to be brutally honest, so is this World Series. Heads down, shoulders slumped, bats flat, these sickly Padres might as well raise the white flag and call it a season. They're shot. And while nobody in either dugout would ever *dare* tempt fate by making that simple little statement out loud, we all know it's true. San Diego's no longer hoping to *win* this World Series, they're just hoping to avoid being *totally* destroyed.

On the *Yankees* side of the field, one week and one day after his massacre of the Indians, Orlando Hernández is back on the mound, as nasty and merciless and flat-out beautiful as ever. Giving up just one scratched-out run over seven innings pitched, El Duque stomps all over the Padres, getting into jams here and there, but toughing them out without ever breaking a sweat. Told his start will be televised throughout all of Cuba, Hernández just beams on the mound. His family is watching. His two small daughters are watching. He needs to look good. One 9–3 victory later, he's more than accomplished that goal.

Two games into this series, we Yankees have exploded for 18 runs, 25 hits, and a pair of impressive victories. With that in mind, we fly Air Steinbrenner cross-country feeling happy, and invincible, and maybe just a little bit cocky. Two days later, it'll take just one tough Padre pitcher to slap us all back down to earth.

Game 3. First of all, let me just say this is *not* "Qualcomm Stadium." Instead, it always *has* been, and always *will* be "Jack Murphy Stadium." I don't care how many millions some faceless corporation throws at the place, I ain't playing their name game. This is my home. I've been coming to this park since I was eight years old, watching guys like Nate Colbert and Willie McCovey and Randy Jones from the cheap seats, while dreaming about someday growing up to wear a butt-ugly yellow and brown uniform just like theirs. Honest to God, I know this sounds phony, but as a kid, my fondest baseball dream was that someday, the Yankees and Padres would square off in the World Series, here in this ballpark, with me introduced as a real, live Yankees pitcher. I've got chills as I step on the field. Yet *another* dream is about to come true. That's when the booing starts.

I should have seen it coming, and looking back, it probably shouldn't have bothered me so much, but I swear, after the good season, and the perfect game, I fully expected to waltz back into San Diego as a sort of "Hometown Boy Makes Good" case. Y'know, I could have been a "local hero," a "success story," a "beloved son" . . . not bad for a former shopping cart wrangler who lived in a Chevy.

But this is baseball, and as part of the 114-game-winning, Padre-smashing Yankees, I'm no longer a cute, loveable "home-grown big-leaguer." I'm an enemy, a threat. I'm Satan in pinstripes. Introduced on the field with the rest of the Yankees, I'm greeted with huge waves of booing, and insults, and cries of "traitor" that just about crush me. "Aw, come on, guys!" I shout. "It's me, Boomer!" Never before have I been so anxious for the national anthem to start.

Coney leans in as the jeering continues in my direction. "Are these *all* former roommates?" he asks.

"Aw, shut up and go pitch!" I shout back at him.

Coney's got the Game 3 start for two reasons. First, sliding backward a day has given Grandpappy Cone an extra day to rest his arm, his toothpick legs, and his aching sacroiliac. Second, Joe Torre knows that Coney tends to lose the feel for his breaking ball in cold weather. That could be a problem in October in the Bronx, but here in San Diego, where it's 72 degrees 365 days a year, Coney can go with his full 904-pitch arsenal. He'll need it.

Getting the start for the Padres is former Yankee Sterling Hitchcock, and though he really *does* throw like a girl, this guy's got frightening stuff. So far this postseason he's outpitched Randy Johnson (throwing for Houston in the ALDS) *and* Greg Maddux, *and* Tom Glavine, racking up a 1.23 ERA, and 32 strikeouts over 22 postseason innings. And while a lot of these Padres look ready to pack up their stuff and head home for the winter, Hitchcock roars in, breathing fire. He plows through his first three innings of work without allowing so much as a base runner. Coney matches him pitch for pitch.

We're scoreless through four, then five, with Hitchcock rolling, and the Padres beginning to smell their first real shot at victory. You can see the change in their body language. You can see their eyes brighten. You can see the weight of intimidation lifting right off their shoulders. And when Hitch works himself out of a bases-loaded, one-out jam in the sixth, the Pods leave the field with a huge emotional lift. Now it's a ball game. Now it's a Series. Now they get to Coney.

Padres' sixth. Sterling Hitchcock comes to the plate with the Murph rolling out a big, appreciative, standing O. Hitchcock responds by cracking a single to right, for the Padres' first hit of the game. *This* guy's a gamer. Quilvio Veras follows Hitch to the dish, and he works out a walk that moves Hitchcock to second. Tony Gwynn follows up with a single to deep right, and as Paulie gives chase, Hitchcock brings home his own 1–0 lead.

At this point, Paul O'Neill fires a wild relay throw right over the cutoff man and into the Yankees dugout. When the smoke finally clears, Veras has scored, and Tony Gwynn's safe at third. Nobody out, two runs in, but Coney hangs tough, getting Greg Vaughn to ground out to short with a nasty laredo slider. From there, while Ken Caminiti brings home Gwynn with a long sac fly into center, a pretty curve from Coney handcuffs Wally Joyner, who ends the inning with a check-swing grounder to Tino. Done for the day, Coney's given up only 2 hits in his 6 innings of work, but he exits at the short end of a 3–0 score.

Top of the seventh, and the Padres take the field feeling strong. Scotty Brosius steps up to the plate. Sterling Hitchcock looks in and makes his first real mistake of the day. Having now spent the better part of the past half-inning sprinting around the base paths, Hitch is still huffing, and as any pitcher can tell you, that's a recipe for disaster.

Run out of gas, and your muscles *will* crap out on you. Your mechanics *will* get sloppy, and as you go through your motion, you *will* start releasing your pitches early. That translates into high, hanging fastballs, and long, *long* home runs. Scotty Brosius proves that theory by smacking Hitchcock's second pitch up and over the left-field wall. Shane Spencer follows that up with hard double into center. That brings Bochy out to the mound. Hitchcock's done, leaving the field to one more, well-deserved, standing O.

Joey Hamilton runs in, and while he focuses on a pinch-hitting Jorge Posada, Shane Spencer swipes third. Unshaken, Hamilton gets Posada to whiff, then jams Chili Davis, who bounces a weak ground ball that a muscle-bound Ken Caminiti can't stoop to pick up. Spencer scores easily, putting us Yankees within one. And while Hamilton gets out of the inning without any further damage, you can feel the tide turning our way. One inning later, San Diego goes down for the count.

Yankees' eighth. Randy Myers hits the hill for San Diego, and when he quickly walks Paul O'Neill, Bruce Bochy guzzles some Maalox, runs to the mound, and swaps out Myers for supercloser Trevor Hoffman. AC/DC's "Hell's Bells" rocks through the stadium at a *ridiculously* loud volume. I'm *totally* jealous. Up in his box, George Steinbrenner slaps his hands over his ears and complains that it sounds like WWF wrestler "The Undertaker" is coming into the game. It's a really cool entrance. At the mound now, Hoffman warms up with a dozen high-caliber bullets. He's ready.

Bernie Williams steps in, and he gets us all off our asses with a *deep* fly ball to right . . . that gets caught at the warning track. Tino hits the dish now, and with Hoffman showing a lot of uncharacteristic wildness, he's gifted with a walk. With Hoffman's last work coming in the NLCS, he's clearly rusty. O'Neill goes to second. Tino's on first. Scott Brosius is back at the plate. The drumroll starts again.

Hoffman's given up just two home runs through the entire 1998 season . . . but we're the Yankees. And with that in mind, the gods of baseball come down from the heavens. They smack Trevor Hoffman in the back of the head, and this *great* pitcher serves up a ball to Scotty Brosius that your grandma could have cracked for a fat, three-run homer. "That wasn't a baseball," Hoffman says later of the pitch. "I put a *football* up over the plate." Scotty's shot flies out of the park in straightaway center. The stadium goes dead. The Padres go a sort of sickly green. We take this sucker, 5–4.

Get out your brooms.

Game 4 (aka victory 125). Kevin Brown's back on the mound, looking to turn three days' rest and a fistful of antibiotics into the Pods' first Series victory. Warming up, he looks like an overripe cadaver. At the same time, Andy Pettitte is making his first start since the four-home-run beating the Indians laid on him back in Cleveland. It's been a long twelve days for Andy, made even longer by the news that his dad's been forced to undergo an emergency double bypass back home in Texas. Neither one of these guys looks ready to pitch.

Brown is gray. And with doctors allowing Tom Pettitte to return home early, just in time to catch Andy's Game 4 start on TV, tonight's starting pitcher has one *helluva* distraction. Though he's poised to be the winning pitcher in the '98 World Series, Andy's thoughts are clearly a thousand miles away.

This one *should* have been ugly, it *should* have been a mess, but somehow, against all odds, *both* these guys rose to the occasion, gutting it out to pitch the greatest games of their seasons, maybe of their careers. Andy's cut fastball just *kills* the Padres all night long, at one point mowing down nine in a row. At the same time, Kevin Brown retires his first *ten* Yankees, four of them with strike-outs. With dual classics being tossed, we're halfway home before either man blinks. Honestly, the real highlight of this game's first half comes when Knobby clocks a sharp foul ball into the field boxes behind the Padres dugout, and spectator Mark McGwire bare-hands it in the crowd. In unison 66,000 Padres fans go, "Woooooooooooooooo!"

Top of the sixth. With one out, Derek Jeter knuckles a little squibbler off the handle of his bat, then beats the play to first for an infield single. From there, Brown tosses one of the only mistakes he'll throw all night, a 1–1 curve to Paul O'Neill that stays out on the table just long enough for Paulie to crank it into right-center for a double, sending Jeter to third in the process. The score is still knotted at zero. Bernie Williams steps in, and when he's jammed by an awesome fastball, he ends up dinking a bouncer off home plate that ricochets forty feet into the air. Jeter streaks home and scores before it even comes down. By the time Brown gloves the chopper, his only play is to first. Look up the phrase "hard luck" in *Webster's* and you'll see a little drawing of that play.

Brown's hard luck continues in the eighth. Tiring now, and still looking like a super-size helping of death, Brown walks Derek Jeter to lead off the inning, then throws yet another beautiful fastball that yet another not-so-beautiful New York Yankee chops into trouble. This time it's Paul O'Neill, and when he bounces an infield hopper down the first-base line, Jim Leyritz makes a running grab of the ball, then races O'Neill to the bag, and loses. Remember how mad that hare was after losing his race to the tortoise? Same deal. Leyritz can't believe he got beat by old "Cement Legs" O'Neill and flat-out tosses a fit. Kevin Brown joins him, and together they both come thisclose to being tossed from the game by umpire Tim Tschida. Slapped down by the man in black, both guys retreat to their positions, where their day will quickly get worse.

Bernie Williams is at the plate now, and he advances both runners with a slow-rolling groundout to third. That brings Tino to the plate, and he takes the obvious IBB to load up the bases. One down, the Pods looking double play, Scott Brosius is back to play hero one more time. Only this time, his "big hit" will travel all of 80 feet.

Brown winds, delivers a nice-looking curve, and at that point, though I still have absolutely *no* idea how Scotty did it,* Brosius somehow manages to tip the bottom side of that pitch with exactly enough friction to send a slow, arcing, graceful, dying swan of a blooper two inches beyond the reach of the diving, extended glove of shortstop Chris Gomez. Jeter scores. O'Neill goes to third. Tino goes to second. Kevin Brown's brain explodes. There's not a decent hit in that rally, and when Ricky Ledee steps in and lofts a soft sac fly into left that scores Paulie, Brown's outing has now *got* to rank as the single most frustrating in World Series history.

Up 3–0, Mariano Rivera shows up to shut the door one last time. With two down in the Pods' half of the ninth, bets are being placed all over the Yankees dugout. For days now, Scott Brosius has been talking about how each night he keeps dreaming about making the last putout of this World Series. Will Brosius do it? Do you believe in his vision? If so, are you willing to bet me a twenty? Odds are running about 7–1 against Scotty's clairvoyance, as pinch hitter Mark Sweeney steps in and promptly smacks a nice clean grounder to Scotty. One grab, one toss, and the greatest season in Yankee history . . . is history.

The Padres scatter as the Yankees swarm, dog-piling on the field in a sea of

---

* Years later, with the benefit of twenty-twenty hindsight, all signs point to some sort of shady deal with Beelzebub.

elbows and legs and happy, victorious tears. Mariano goes down, beneath a huge stack-up of Knoblauch, and Girardi, and Derek, and a nosediving Chili Davis. I make a leap toward Coney and Graeme Lloyd. It's pandemonium. It's chaos. It's the single greatest moment of my career—125 victories, 50 losses. If Jeff Nelson's knee wasn't currently squashing my head, I'd be the happiest man alive.

Group-hugging all the way into the clubhouse, we can't help but laugh at the sight of Joe Torre and George Steinbrenner locked up in a huge, slow-dance of an embrace, both of them crying as they hug. I swear to God, this is the exchange that passes between them:

George: *I love ya, Joey! I LOVE ya! You're the best manager I ever had!*
Joe: *Awwwww, thanks, Boss. Now kiss me!*

And at that point, with both guys laughing, they keep right on hugging.

The champagne flies one more time, and this time the scene is soggier than ever before. Derek Jeter stands giggling (yes, giggling) as he unloads a full magnum on Steinbrenner, at which point George grabs a bottle himself and runs after a large group of his own infielders. "That's it!" the Boss shouts. "You're all in BIG trouble!" Only then does George realize he's holding an *empty* bottle.

Now he's like Wyle E. Coyote having run off the cliff. He knows he's dead, but there's a weird silent lag time before it happens. "Uh-oh" is all George can say before he's group-squirted from five different directions. How great is this? Minutes later, as Orlando Hernández starts passing out gorgeous Cuban cigars to everyone in the clubhouse, he quickly becomes the most popular guy on this team.

"Gracias! Mi amigo!!!" we each shout, hugging and kissing El Duque while hoping like hell he might give us an extra smoke.

For the next full hour we drink, we laugh, we freeze to death in wet shirts that now smell like the morning after a New Year's Eve party. Yanked up onto the network's TV podium, with my own thoughts running back to Darryl Strawberry in New York, I shout to the room, "We FINALLY did it! We did it GREAT! We did it TOGETHER! And right now, speaking for everybody in this room, I just wanna say . . . This one's for you, Straw Man!" The whole room swigs. Steinbrenner cries again. And at that point we all launch into one final chant of "Straw MAN, Straw MAN, Straw MAN!"

Much later, with "The Murph" empty and the crowds all gone home, we

Yankees take one last trip to the diamond together. Boom box in one hand, champagne in the other, El Duque's cigar still clenched tight in my teeth, I herd guys through the dugout 'til we're *all* at midfield. Soaking wet, dirty, in T-shirts and uniform pants, with towels wrapped round our necks, we walk in the grass one last time, together, the enormity of this season and our accomplishment finally settling in. We're quieter now, arms around one another, our thoughts all reflecting on what an absolutely incredible ride this has been.

The boom box plays Green Day's "Good Riddance" loud enough to choke every one of us up. *It's something unpredictable, but in the end it's right. I hope you had the time of your life.* Here at midfield, we're all trying hard not to cry. Trying hard to hang on to this moment, and this *feeling*, and one *another* for as long as we possibly can. Singing together now, like the most god-awful glee club you can possibly imagine, we're huddled up tight in a final embrace. *For what it's worth, it was worth all the while. It's something unpredictable, but in the end it's right. I hope you had the time of your life.*

Canyon of Heroes

It's not ticker tape. It's toilet paper, and whole reams of computer paper, and cut-up magazines, and McDonald's napkins, and ripped-up newspapers, and classified documents that got shoved through the office paper shredder. For about a half block, hundreds and hundreds of photocopies of some guy's ass join in the garbage hail as well. It's a much grimier avalanche than I'd expected. I'm not complaining.

There's not a Little Leaguer on the planet who hasn't dreamed of exactly this moment. World Champions, in the greatest city on earth, with 3.5 million of the greatest *fans* on earth, lined up twelve deep along Broadway. They're whooping and cheering and screaming their heads off. They're stacked up on one another's shoulders. They're hanging off light poles. They're waving brooms. They've got bad poetry on cardboard signs (BROSIUS IS FEROCIOUS! PARTY HEARTY, GIRARDI! PAUL O'NEILL, LET ME COOK YOU A MEAL! THERE'S NOBODY SWEETER THAN MY MAN DEREK JETER!). With Brandon and Nina riding shotgun, we're laughing and/or groaning at 'em all. That's when it hits me.

Babe Ruth's been here, and Gehrig, and Mantle, and Whitey, and Yogi, and DiMaggio, and Reggie . . . and now me. After two seasons in the Bronx, I finally feel like I've joined "the club." The ghosts are with me, and with the confetti raining, I'm now officially, indelibly, and irrevocably a Yankee. It's in the books.

I belong forever, and *that* sinks in hard. Damn! All this paper and not a Kleenex in the house.

We hit city hall now, where seventy zillion more fans have packed in to celebrate our season. The Rockettes dance. Michael Kay and John Sterling introduce the team. With a gigantic smile on his face, Mayor Giuliani shouts to the crowd, "I believe this will go down as the greatest team in baseball history!" Minutes later, when the roaring finally dies down just a bit, Joe Torre speaks.

Joe talks about how this team has played hard, smart, gutty baseball all year long. He talks about how united these Yankees have been, playing together, and growing closer all through the season. "I saw it right before Game Four of the playoffs against Cleveland," Joe says. "I was in my office when I heard David Wells's heavy metal music booming through the clubhouse. I knew it wasn't his day

Making the date
(© Reuters 1998/ Mike Segar)

to pitch, so I went over and turned it off. Well, nobody would stand for that. The whole rest of the team was shouting, 'Turn it back up! We love that stuff!' That's when I finally realized I had lost control of this game and this team to Boomer! I never thought that would happen!"

"Boomer! Boomer! Boomer!" they're chanting now. I'm shaking. Acceptance, belonging, adulation, a World Series ring, what more could a boy ask for? The crowd keeps chanting my name. They want me to speak, and overwhelmed with the emotion of the day, I try my best. "What do you say we make this an annual event?" I ask the crowd, bringing on yet another eruption of noise. "Okay, then, it's a date! We'll do this again, one year from today."

Unfortunately, I won't be invited.

FIFTEEN

Dumped and Dangerous

How can you not like
Roger Clemens? That's like saying you
don't like chocolate ice cream.

—*George Steinbrenner*

FEBRUARY 1999: LEGENDS FIELD, FOURTH
FLOOR, GEORGE STEINBRENNER'S OFFICE

"Aw, Boss, what the hell did you do to me? What did you do?" George looks up from his desk with wide, red, genuinely sad eyes. I'm standing in his doorway, having stiff-armed a secretary and two assistants to get this far, looking every bit like your classic, disgruntled postal worker. It's an ambush. George has no idea I'm coming. But I need to do this . . . now.

An hour earlier, rolling down Tampa's Dale Mabry Drive, with the AC on max and Godsmack blaring out of the dashboard, I speed past the strip clubs, past the burger joints, past the used-furniture warehouse, pulling into the Yankees' parking lot like a kid on Christmas morning. I jump out of my truck, and with every great memory of the '98 season rerunning over and over through my head, it's all I can do not to flat-out sprint to the clubhouse. I've been looking forward to this day for months. I can't wait to get back in uniform. I can't wait to get back on that field. I can't wait to start pitching, and winning, and working toward another ring. I'm whistling "Voodoo" all the way to my locker.

It's 8 A.M. and with the clubhouse still just about empty, I start unpacking some junk into my locker, making sure to grab out my shaving kit, so that I can finally hack off my beloved winter goatee. I've spared the life of the hairy little sucker for as long as I possibly can. Yankee rules insist he's gotta go, and as of this morning, me and the Bombers are officially back in business. That's when Brian Cashman taps my shoulder.

"Hey, Brian."

"Hey, Boomer. Listen, Joe wants to talk to you in his office."

"Ohhhhh, shit," I reply with a smile "It's day one. I'm here two minutes. I'm in the principal's office already?"

Cashman doesn't laugh. So now I'm wondering, Has Joe already seen the beard? Maybe I'd better go shave real fast. I say to Brian, "No problem. I'll be there in two minutes. I've just gotta hit the bathroom." I grab my shaving kit and head off.

Brian knows exactly what I'm up to, and he stops me. "No, Boomer, Joe wants to see you *now*."

"Hold *on*," I tell him. "I have to go visit the bathroom."

"C'mon, David. It really can't wait. Joe needs to see you *right away*."

"All right, all right." I drop the shaving stuff and head to Joe's office. Cashman follows me in and closes the door behind me. Already, I know this is not good. Joe's face sags. My stomach tightens.

Joe says, "Sit down, Boomer, we've got something to tell you," at which point Cashman finishes Joe's thought with "There's no easy way to say this, but uh . . . you've been traded."

Boot meets head. The room spins. "WHAT?!" is the first thing out of my mouth. Maybe I heard wrong. Maybe Allen Funt is hiding behind Joe's desk.

Cashman repeats himself. "We traded you."

I'm numb in an instant. "Oh *REALLY*?" I grumble. "Where'd I go?"

"Toronto."

"FUUUUUUUUUUUUUUUUUUCK!" Boot number two meets my head. Insult gets added to injury. Not Toronto! Anyplace but Toronto!

"I'm sorry. Really."

Joe tells me he's been in his office since 6 A.M., trying to figure out how the hell to give me the news. He then lays out the details for me.

"It's you, Graeme Lloyd, and Homer Bush, for Roger Clemens." All the air leaves my body. I'm stunned. I'm ready to punch a wall, or a GM, or a manager. I feel like I've been fired.

"My God," I tell them. "You're kidding!"

I don't understand this. Why make this trade? This team won 125 games in 1998. This team had a .714 winning percentage last season. If it ain't broke, you don't fix it. Granted, Roger Clemens is a great pitcher, but Derek Jeter and Scott Brosius have taken beanballs from this guy, and a huge percentage of this team hates Clemens's guts. But there's no point in arguing. I'm out. It's done. Game over. I shake my head and sigh. It's been a great run.

"Whatever . . . ," I say to those guys, dead. "I know this is a business. And I hope you match me up with Roger every time." At that point I stand, I hug Joe, and I tell him, "Thank you. These were the best two years of my life." He nods back, swallowing hard, clearly having a hard time with this.

Cashman's next. In midhug, I tell him, "Listen, that was smart of you, not letting me shave. 'Cuz if you gave me this news *after* I'd lost the goatee, I'd have pulled your arms and legs off."

Brian laughs nervously as I exit, not quite sure if I'm kidding . . . which, at the moment, pleases me.

Straight line to my locker. Let me out of here, fast. No reporters, no teammates, not now. . . . Oh shit, there's Graeme Lloyd, all bright eyed and smiling and ready to be a Yankee again. Graeme may be the one guy in the world who loves New York City even more than me. The news of this trade is gonna *kill* him. I intercept him at mid-clubhouse.

"Boo-MER!!!" He hugs me hard. "We're back, baby!"

"Yeah, listen, Graeme, there may be a little change in plans this year. Come with me." I walk Graeme into Joe's office, where the news gets spilt one more time. Graeme really takes it hard, crying and shouting and throwing shit. It's a bad scene, but together the two of us end up sneaking off into a corner, trying hard to calm each other down. "We just have to stay cool, and roll with the punches," I tell Graeme. "What else can we do?"

Graeme needs air, and he bolts the locker room, slamming every door he possibly can. I have other plans. I head upstairs, taking the elevator to the fourth floor and the Yankees' executive offices. George is at the end of the hall, in the corner. I brush past a handful of outer-office underlings; it's time for my unscheduled meeting.

"Aw, Boss. What the hell did you do to me? What did you do?"

George rises fast, and two seconds later, I'm wrapped in yet another hug, this one big, and genuine, and heartfelt. The ex-Boss and I will go on to spend maybe a half hour together in his office, reminiscing about the perfect game, and the Babe Ruth hat, and last year's postseason, and our near fistfight back in '97, and the Jameson's shots we've been known to share on occasion. George makes sure that I know this deal was designed and pursued and orchestrated by Cashman. He also tells me that when asked to vote yes or no on this one, for the first time in his career, George had to abstain. It was too hard. Too personal. George simply didn't want to be responsible for pulling the trigger on any deal that'd knock me out of pinstripes.

Less than a week ago, as we sat together at the ESPY Awards (sharing some of that previously mentioned Jameson's), my perfect game won an award for "Dramatic Individual Performance of the Year." In making my acceptance speech, I talked about how much I loved New York, and the Yankees, and how, after all the stops in Toronto, and Detroit, and Cincinatti, and Baltimore, I finally felt at home. As I sit in George's office, he tells me about how those words kept haunting him all through this deal, and how he literally picked up his phone several times last night, half-dialing Cashman's number to call off the whole thing.

Obviously, George stopped himself every time. He knows better. He knows you can't run a ball club with your emotions. He knows you can't play soft. I have no problem with that, but *none* of it makes this trade any more tolerable.

I take the elevator down, alone, still feeling dumped. Feeling like some kid whose parents have just decided to give him away to the chain-smoking, wool-hat-wearing, hockey-loving neighbors down the street. There's a herd of reporters milling outside now. The news has leaked. I run back to the clubhouse to grab my stuff and get out of Dodge. There's no way in hell I'm talking to any-body right now. Nine o'clock in the morning and all I want to do is go home to bed. That's when I literally run into Coney.

Head down, sunglasses in place, I never even noticed him come into the clubhouse. He grabs my arm. "Scumbag, what the hell's going on in here?"

"I'm traded."

"No way."

"Me and Graeme and Homer Bush for Roger Clemens."

"No fucking way."

Yet another bear hug follows, and this time both of us crack. Tears fall. We end up just standing together, in silence, for a long time, neither one of us knowing what to say. "Lemme just pack my shit and get out of here," I say to Coney.

"All right. I'll talk to you in a little while."

"Thanks, man. I think I may need that."

By now, a few more pitchers and catchers have arrived to work out (thank God the position guys haven't reported yet). Jorge, Andy Pettitte, Mariano, El Duque, and I bust through fast, numb, no-nonsense, forced-smiling "good-byes" and "good lucks" all around. I don't make eye contact. I don't let my voice waver. I'm dying inside. I just want to get out as quickly and painlessly as possible. Finally I kick open the exit, plowing outside, right through the middle of a swarm of reporters.

"How do you feel, David?" they ask over and over again.

"Who got the better of the deal?"

"You look as if you've been crying . . . is that true?"

"Did you know you weren't the Blue Jays' first choice?"

It's like a scene out of some really terrible TV Movie of the Week. The reporters swarm in. Camera flashes pop. My head spins. I can't keep up. I say nothing. I stammer. My eyes dart from camera to camera until finally I can't take any more. "Guys, please!" I shout. "It's not a good time. I'm a little emotional right now. Give me a couple of days. It's just too tough right now. Come over to the Blue Jays camp in a couple of days, and I promise, I'll answer all your questions."

I keep moving forward relentlessly, eyes down, ignoring more shouted questions all the way to the players' parking lot, where I dive into my car and screech away. Silent now, no Godsmack, no AC/DC, I'm lost in my own thoughts, with shock rapidly shifting to anger. "Fuck!" I scream behind the wheel. "How FUCKING dare you! I gave this team *everything* I had! This was everything I'd ever wanted! How dare you take my dream away from me!" I punch the roof of my car over and over and over again as I roll toward home.

The first thing I do is unplug the phone. The second is to collapse into my sofa. I'll lay there, eyes closed, silent, for a long, *long* time. I don't want to move. I don't want to talk. Angry, depressed, and devastated, I've basically shut down. Finally, there's a buzz from the front entrance of my gated community. I punch the intercom button and bark, "Yeah, what?"

"Hey, lemme in, Scumbag!"

I smile for the first time in hours. His workout complete, Coney shows up with bad food and beer, and over the next four hours he lends an ear, a voice of reason, and about 5,000 smart-ass jokes, which all combine to really help talk me down. Coney points out that since the Blue Jays don't open camp until Monday, at the *very* least, I've earned myself three extra days of winter vacation. "You should go down to Miami and hit Doral," Coney tells me, and for once in his life the man's hit on a fantastic idea. I replug the phone. I call the golf resort. I book myself a suite. I book myself a flight, and I'm all set to go. "Might as well enjoy my last weekend of freedom."

We talk about the trade, and Clemens, and how pissed off I am at getting tossed overboard. And at that point, Coney starts spilling whatever details he's been able to dig up. Clemens has been demanding a trade out of Toronto ever since last November. He also wants a *huge* contract extension from whatever team wins his services. With that in mind, the Yankees, Indians, and Texas Rangers quickly rose to the top of the contenders' list. From the Yankees, Gord Ash was originally demanding either Orlando Hernández or Andy Pettitte, along with any two of Ramiro Mendoza, Homer Bush, Ricky Ledee, or Alfonso Soriano. Cashman refused, mostly because all those guys put together earn like a third of Roger's salary. No deal. That was it; Cashman figured the trade was dead, and Clemens would simply end up someplace else.

Flash-forward to February, and with Roger *still* not moved, Gord Ash is desperate. He wants no part of a big, ugly spring training distraction, and with that in mind, he gets flexible. The pieces get juggled, and when Ash calls Brian Cashman proposing an offer of Wells, Lloyd, and Bush (aka an All-Star, a solid lefty reliever, and a genuine major-league-ready prospect), Cashman says "my knees buckled." The deal keeps the Yankees starting lineup undiminished, and once Ash tosses *my* name into the pot, Cashman's salary swap becomes a little more equal. Cashman calls an emergency meeting.

The Yankee suits gather in Cashman's office during the late afternoon hours on Wednesday. They meet for almost two hours before moving on, as a group, to an upscale Tampa steakhouse called Malio's. There congregating over platters of rigatoni and New York strip steaks, with glasses of red wine poured all around, the Yankee bigwigs vote on this deal, looking like rejects from the cast of *The Godfather*. By a 4–3 margin (with Steinbrenner refusing to vote), the deal goes through. Cashman confirms the trade at 11:42 Wednesday night with a phone call to Ash. That's the story, and as hard as it is to accept, business is business.

I *still* hate the deal. I *still* feel betrayed. I *still* feel rejected. I'm cursing the Yankees for trading me away. I'm cursing Gord Ash for wanting me . . . and now the phone rings. It's Gord Ash.

"Hi, David," he tells me, knowing full well that I've taken the news hard. "Listen, I just wanted to check in and tell you how happy we are to have you back with the team, and y'know, we're gonna leave you alone this time around. You do what you've gotta do to get ready for the season. We're not gonna have you weigh in anymore." That old Toronto smoke has once again begun coming out my nostrils.

"What the . . . *that* would be a very good idea," I say. "I've won thirty-five games over the past two years without 'em, and besides, I think you guys worried enough about it the first time around. Don't you?"

There's nervous laughter now. "Heh-heh, right . . . uhhhhhh . . . okay then." And now Ash clears his throat, and makes an excuse to get off the line. "All righty, Boomer, we'll see you in Dunedin on Monday."

"Yes, you will," I say, hanging up.

Yes, he will. *Wow*, that's a depressing thought. Coney's got a half slice of pizza shoved into his face when I come back. "Go okay?" he asks, still chewing.

"Yeah, wonderful," I reply deadpan. The front doorbell rings now. No buzz from the security guard at the front entrance? That should be impossible inside a heavily gated community called Safety Harbor. I open up. There stands a guy with helmet hair and a microphone. Somehow he's under the impression that after busting into a gated community and inviting himself onto my private property, I'll be happy to sit down for an exclusive "up close and personal" chat.

"Ahhh, Mr. Wells. Hi there. . . . " I stare, silently. "I'm here from Bay News Nine in Clearwater, and uhhhh, heh-heh, I was wondering if maybe I could interview you for a—"

"How the hell'd you get in here?"

"Well, see—"

"Get outta here! Take a hike!" My door makes a nice, loud KABOOM as I slam it.

Back inside now, I'm moaning to Coney about the Jays' new, butt-ugly, bright blue and red uniforms, when maybe twenty-five minutes after the first weird, unannounced doorbell ring, there's another.

"Not again!" I shout.

"Lemme get it," Coney orders. "You're liable to strangle the paperboy."

"Oh, no way. I want this one." Coney and I race for the door, and because Coney's slower than any human being on earth, I beat him there, with no problem. I yank open the door now, and there's not one but two reporters waiting for me this time. Two chicks. Their video cameraman is out by the curb, smiling at my house. A woman named Sam Marchiano is there from the MSG cable network, and next to her is Lisa Olson, from the New York *Daily News.* Both are polite. Both are talented journalists, but *both* of these women were *right* in front of me at the Legends Field complex this morning, when I specifically asked to be left alone. Now it's snap time.

I shout, "You *heard* what I said at the complex. Honor my wishes. I'll talk to you on Monday." And STILL they keep pressing.

"But it's such a big story. Can't we just chat for a few minutes?"

"No! And how the hell did you find out where I live?"

Lisa explains to me that every community resident has their address on file at the local court of clerks. It's a matter of public record, and they had every right to look me up.

"Oh well, if that's the case . . . ," I tell them, "get the fuck out of here, you dirty motherfuckers!" And that was just the first ten seconds. I ended up venting on these two women for the better part of ten minutes. The trade, the frustration, the anger, the betrayal, I took it *all* out on them. Talk about being in the wrong place at the wrong time. These two took it in the face with both barrels. "If being a reporter means behaving like you two, then being a reporter is a sleazy, slimy business," I shout at them from high atop my soapbox. "I ought to call your editors and get you chicks fired, or demoted back down to *secretaries.*"

That one did it. Whoo! They wanted to cut my balls off. I got the evil eye in stereo as they both stormed back to their car and pulled out of my driveway. "You have dirty jobs! You should find another line of work!" I'm shouting at them from my front porch now, like some kind of escaped mental patient. Inside the house, Coney's rolling his eyes and shaking his head at me. I don't care. This venting of aggression feels great.

A local police cruiser rolls by now. And though he's currently just making a standard run around the neighborhood, this guy's timing couldn't possibly be better. "Yessss!" I shout from my porch, waving the cruiser into my driveway as the reporters take off, down the street. The officer rolls down the window. We'll call him "Officer Jimmy,"* so he won't get into trouble. "Hey, Jimmy! Listen," I tell him. "If you do me one favor, I'll *sign anything* you want. Balls, shirts, cards . . . I don't care."

"What is it?"

"Y'see those two reporters up there? They were just trespassing. And they're reckless drivers too. I bet they're speeders. I want you to follow 'em outta here and give 'em a ticket."

"Deal," says the cop, smiling. He pulls their car over less than a mile down the road.

"Scumbag, that was rotten," Coney tells me.

"Yeah, I know," I say with a smile.

Coney baby-sits me right up until I've gotta run to the airport for my plane to Miami and the Doral golf resort. I thank him a hundred times for being there. I thank him for putting up with me for the past few hours. I thank him for putting up with me for the past *two years*. I thank him for being such a good friend. One more bear hug. One more deep breath. And I think it's right now, right here, that I finally accept I'm no longer a Yankee. It's like taking a frying pan to the face.

For the next three days, down in Miami, all I do is play golf, eat, and sleep.** I don't talk to the Yankees. I don't talk to the Blue Jays. I don't talk to reporters. I simply escape from *everything* and decompress. It gives me a chance to clear my head. It gives me a chance to catch my breath. It gives me a chance to slowly but surely begin thinking about life with the Blue Jays. Midday on the seventeenth green, I've once again got Sparky-Wan Kenobi in my head, talking to me about how I'm gonna have to stay focused, and get tough, and rise to the occasion, and behave like a professional. Back in Detroit, Sparky was forever preaching about making the best of whatever this game feeds you, because "no matter how bad it gets, it still beats working for a living." Here in Miami, those old words, from that old man, really helped turn me around. Like it or not, life goes on. Things change. Shit happens. Life is just a box of chocolates. Somebody stop me! I can't stop spewing lame, but applicable, catchphrases.

Dunedin. Tanned, rested, but still feeling like I've just gone from dating the prettiest cheerleader in school to sleeping with the goalie for the girls' field

* Not his real name, duh.
** With my bud Mark Fessler, who should have taken pity on me and at least let me win a round or two.

hockey team, I hit the Blue Jays locker room bound and determined to convince the world that I'm perfectly happy with this trade. I fail, miserably. Hitting the locker room for my standard physical, I discover that the Jays have invited reporters and photographers in with me. They're tossing lame questions at me even while the Jays' team nurse is busy jabbing all over my arm with a syringe. Apparently this guy's *completely* incapable of tapping a vein. Finally, with one crooked stick that nearly pops the eyeballs out of my head, I'm gushing.

"Hey, Dave. What's the cholesterol count of that blood?" one reporter asks, guffawing, proud of himself as the rest join in.

"Heh heh . . . right. Good one."

"Never mind the cholesterol . . . what's the blood-alcohol level." Now it's a hyena convention.

"Right. Blood-alcohol. Funny." Oh my God. Who let these assholes in here?

With my arm still bleeding, the flashes keep going off right up until I end the impromptu little photo shoot by giving this whole room the finger and asking Jays officials to get rid of the crowd. I mean, really, unless the American public has some overwhelming desire to view color glossies of my prostate exam, there's really nothing more to see.

Now comes the press conference. First up, I've gotta change. Team officials slap a really, and I mean *really* dumb-looking, bright red Jays' hat onto my head. From there, a smiling Gord Ash presents me with a shiny, royal blue team jacket that's got garish red, white, and blue ribbing at the collars and neck. It *screams* 1987. The New Kids on the Block would have given this thing to Goodwill. I hit the podium feeling awkward, and silly, and more than a little bit depressed that I'm not down the road in Tampa.

Face facts. I'm now the ace of a decent staff, on a decent team, with a semi-legitimate shot at becoming this year's American League Wild Card. Most guys would happily lose a nut for this opportunity, but for me, it's a big step down. There's no question. But while I *do* carry a torch, I've got to move on. With reporters gathering, it really *is* time to make the clean break. Time to kick off my first press conference as a born-again Blue Jay.

Stepping up to the podium, I can't help but notice all three of my front-porch reporters are now front and center, notebooks in hand, cheese-eating grins at the ready. Sorry, I'm not playing. I dig around the mike stand and unplug the microphones for MSG and Bay News 9. At that point, I'm ready to begin. "For starters," I say "I'd like to tell MSG and the New York *Daily News* and Bay News Nine to go fuck themselves." Gord Ash melts. His whole bald head starts sweating, and there's no way in hell he's not already having second thoughts about this deal.

From there, however, while reporters fire away, I do my best to behave, and smile, and say all the right things. "I'm clear-minded," I tell the press, "and ready to get started. I'm looking forward to the 1999 season, and I'm excited about helping this team win a pennant." I'm spilling all the standard clichés, but honestly, as lame, and half-assed, and dull as those statements are, they *do* contain some truth. With three days of grieving now behind me, with Sparky lingering in my head, and with no fucking way to turn back, it's time to rub some dirt on the wound and walk it off.

What else can I do? Whine? Retire? Ask for a do-over? I've got just one option: make the best of things, win some ball games, and stick a victory or two up the asses of the Yankees. Post–press conference, I head for the Jays clubhouse, where I meet my new manager, Tim Johnson, or as he's known in the locker room, "the Backstabber," "the Liar," "the Nut-Job," and "the Ex-Manager-to-Be."

Johnson came into the Blue Jays system portrayed as a tough-talking, nononsense Vietnam vet, a Marine who served in combat duty, a natural athlete so gifted he was offered a basketball scholarship to UCLA. Please make your own game-show-wrong-answer sound effects right here. NONE of those statements were true. Somehow, for the better part of thirty years, this guy had created a whole fantasy history for himself, and now, caught in his own lies, he was clinging to his job by a thread. Settling into the Blue Jays' locker room, I feel like R.P. McMurphy during the first act of *Cuckoo's Nest*. This is just too crazy.

Johnson calls an emergency meeting with his returning players. He apologizes profusely. He begs forgiveness. He talks with the players about the guilt he feels for his lies, and when all's said and done, Johnson exits that gathering telling anyone who'll listen that he was overwhelmed and all choked up by his players' support. He called the meeting "positive" and "great." Now, I'm not sure if the man came out of that meeting with the wrong impression, or if he was still just making up fairy tales, but I *can* tell you the Blue Jays of early 1999 wanted no part of this guy. He'd pass by his players and cuckoo-bird noises would ring out behind his back. Guys would twirl fingers up next to their temples whenever his name got mentioned. They didn't trust him. They didn't like him. They wanted him out . . . fast. Through the first weeks of the spring, Tim Johnson is as big a clubhouse distraction as I've ever seen.

So is the pain in my back. On Saturday, March 3, I throw off the mound for the first time this season. I throw well, at maybe 85 percent velocity, for all of eleven minutes, but by Sunday morning, I can't move. The lower right side of my back feels like somebody's hammered a nail into it. For the first time ever, my back *pain* graduates to *agony*. I gobble anti-inflammatories. I bend and stretch and get twisted up like a pretzel by the Jays' trainers, but there's no way in hell I'm gonna let this become an issue. Here with a new team, after the "big trade," I *am* gonna outpitch Roger Clemens. I *am* gonna make the Yankees admit they made a mistake. I *won't* backslide. I *won't* be defeated. I *will* succeed at all cost. It's gonna be a long season.

Exercise, heat, stretching, massage, all of these things get me through spring training in relatively good shape. I'm kneaded like bread dough three times a day. Chiropractors introduce my knees to my ears as often as possible. I'm in the whirlpool so much my skin's prunier than Marge Schott's. Still, with all this therapy, I'm actually feeling pretty damn good. With that in mind, I'm not complaining. I just wish I could get a handle on this team.

First of all, we've got babies all over the clubhouse. Shawn Green, Jose Cruz Jr., Shannon Stewart—all three of our starting outfielders are twenty-five years old. At short, Alex Gonzalez is twenty-six, as is our new second baseman, Homer Bush. DH Willie Greene and first baseman Carlos Delgado are twenty-seven. Young, and talented, but also sloppy, and used to losing after some lean, ugly years up here in the Skydome, this Blue Jays team is either gonna shape up as pretty good, or just about terrible . . . I'm not sure which.

On the mound, the always solid Pat Hentgen follows me in the rotation, but from there, we've got *big* question marks. Kelvim Escobar and Chris Carpenter are twenty-three and twenty-four, both with great potential but zero experience. Joey Hamilton is labeled a head case, just like I used to be. But he's a real gamer too, and last year in San Diego, pitching coach Dave Stewart loved his stuff so much that when Stew became assistant to Gord Ash here in Toronto, he made sure to bring Joey along for the ride. Again, this is a young and immature club, one that's not going to thrive under Tim Johnson's dented, rudderless, floundering leadership.

Every day the papers seem to catch Johnson in yet another lie. Every day his team drifts further away until finally, just about halfway through spring training, Gord Ash wisely elects to stop the bleeding. Johnson's sent packing, and in his place comes veteran manager Jim Fregosi, who turns out to be pretty damn great.

Loose, and likeable, he's also a tough guy. He immediately bans players from bringing golf clubs on the road (knowing full well that after eighteen holes, and ten hours in the sun, most players hit the baseball field for a night game at *maybe* 60 percent. "You can rent clubs," he tells us, laughing, "but I know *none* of you divas are gonna be caught dead on the course without your own custom-made Big Berthas, hacking around with a set of dented rentals." From there, in a move that elicits groans from all corners, Fregosi also bans the use of cell phones in the clubhouse. "I know that seems unfair, but trust me, if I walk into a locker room after a loss, and I find one of you guys giggling into a cell phone, I'm going to go off, and it's going to be ugly. So whatt'ya say we all just eliminate that problem right now."

But that's it. With those two simple rules in place, Fregosi couldn't care less about policing the rest of our postgame behavior. It's simple. You play your game, you try your best, Fregosi's your biggest fan. Get lazy, get comfortable, and your ass is gone. Wanna play cards in the locker room? That's cool, but you've gotta deal Fregosi in. Wanna hang in the hotel bar after the game? That's cool too, but you've gotta buy Fregosi a drink. This is a guy right out of the Sparky Anderson mold. *This* is a guy who's going to do a great job in motivating, and teaching, and energizing this young team. *This* is a guy I can play for. This season *could* be kind of fun after all.

We Jays are by no means a *great* team, but with the kids playing hard, and feeling genuinely enthusiastic about their run around the American League, there's a contagious joy fermenting in brewmeister Fregosi's loose, happy club-house. Guys are laughing. Guys are singing, badly. Other pitchers start blaring their own game-day music almost as loudly as mine. In short, this talented young team is having fun, and right through April, that translates into solid play, great effort, and more than our share of early season victories. Fregosi knows what he's doing.

He keeps this team up and excited by any means necessary. Honest to God, at one point in the season, as we head off to start a long West Coast trip, Fregosi has us leave Toronto a day early, weaseling the entire team a top secret, one-night stay in Reno, Nevada. "This team needs to get acclimated to the time change," he tells us, tongue planted firmly in cheek. "And if you guys *happen* to wander into the casinos while you're at it, well, that's okay by me." Again, *this* is a guy I can play for.

April. We baby Jays roll out of the gate at 12–4, while going on an 8–0 tear through Tampa Bay, Baltimore, and Anaheim. The kids are hitting everything in sight. Carlos Delgado begins a home run tear that'll put him at 44 dingers by

Hanging with Fregosi *(© Reuters 2000/Joe Giza)*

season's end. (He'll go into the clubhouse and smoke a big, fat, Cuban cigar after every one of them.) Shawn Green's run amok too, batting well over .300 while kicking off his own season-long home run derby. Shannon Stewart, Homer Bush, and Alex Gonzalez all prove they can hit well over .300, even if none of those guys are old enough to sprout a decent beard. Even more surprisingly, our lone old men are smacking the ball pretty well too. Catcher Darrin Fletcher is up near .325 all month long, and at the front of the Social Security line, my old teammate Tony Fernandez has creaked and cracked his way to a batting average of just over .375.

As you can imagine, the thrill of victory takes this colorful young clubhouse right up over the top. Boom boxes are rocking, high fives, chest-thumps, fore-arm smashes are being delivered left and right, and this very good team is really starting to feel like it can win. Heading into Yankee Stadium for the first time this season, we're the front-runners in the AL East, a full game and a half in front of the Bombers. We've won eight in a row, with our pitching staff on fire, and every slot in the batting order producing. The Yankees are about to take a beating . . . or so we think.

With my own record now standing at a sharp 3–0, I've pitched well in every April start, though my back has been sliding downhill. So far, I've avoided the cortisone syringe, toughing it out on the mound, while getting Jacuzzi'd and abused by our trainers between each start. Coming into New York, however, the back won't give me any trouble at all. Right now, I'm running on so much adrenaline, I could pitch seven innings with my whole damn spine on fire. Dressing in the visitors' clubhouse before the game, I've got my Metallica cranked up to absolutely paint-peeling levels. Tony Fernandez comes over trying to lower the volume. "Hey! My day! My day!" I shout at him over the super bass.

"You day? You day? My ears! My ears!" he shouts back before scurrying off to the relative peace and quiet of the weight room. Tonight I'm louder than ever, but I just don't care. Right now, I want this W more than anything else on the planet. I want to stick it to the Yankees with all my heart. I want to deliver a nasty personal message to the team that disowned me . . . but that doesn't happen. Instead, while I get beat in the Bronx, Yankee *fans* send a personal message of their own, and it just about wrecks me.

Bottom of the first. Seconds before I leave the dugout to take the mound, Fregosi taps me on the shoulder and points up to the big screen out past the fence. The Yankees are replaying the last out of my perfect game. When it ends, everybody in the place stands, and the stadium speakers begin blasting Van Halen's "Running with the Devil." I head to the mound in shock, wide-eyed, in the middle of a ninety-second standing ovation. "Boomer! Boomer! Boomer!" the crowd shouts, and with one quick glance round the upper decks, I can't help but notice a sea of number 33 T-shirts and jerseys. I'm touched beyond words, thrilled to death, and completely unsure of how I should react.

I'm the enemy now, aren't I? I'm the opposing pitcher. I'm a Blue Jay. I've got to focus. I can't play this halfway. Though I'm now thrilled to death, and once again amazed by the loyalty and heart of these Yankee fans, I decide against the crowd-pleaser-cap-wave. It just seems wrong. Instead, as the stadium cheers, I keep my eyes down, kicking at the dirt behind the rubber, like I'm digging to China. Finally, with the stadium faithful back down on their asses, I get down to the business of warming up. That's when the creatures get me.

"Roll call" takes place before every Yankees home game, when the regular inhabitants of the stadium's bleacher seats (aka "the Bleacher Creatures") begin to relentlessly chant the name of each Yankee player until they get a wave and/or a smile in return. Tonight, even though I'm preparing to kick their team's ass, my name is right at the top of their list. I ignore them as long as possible, but it's pointless, and I know it. Bleacher Creatures don't know fatigue, and they don't take no for an answer. If I don't wave at them, they WILL shout my name for the next three hours. I'll wake up tomorrow morning with them on the ledge outside my hotel window, *still* yelling. I've gotta give in. They get their wave, and now we get down to business.

In the first inning, with my friends and ex-teammates now stepping up one after another to *my* plate, I'm actually surprised at how much abuse I'm taking . . . all of it verbal. As I warm up, Chuck Knoblauch shouts from the on-deck circle, telling me that in my new red and blue uniform I look like something Superman threw up. Later, with Derek Jeter on first, Tino Martinez fouls off pitch after pitch after pitch. Eleven pitches into the at bat, I shout at home plate, "Jesus Christ, Tino! Enough already!" From first base Jeter adds, "Yeah, come on, the bartenders at Veruka can't wait all night!" I can see Coney inside the dugout laughing, shouting, "Just throw him some of your usual easy-to-hit shit!" And with that I launch a picture-perfect Laredo slider at home plate. Tino fouls it off. Inside the Yankees dugout, Coney's flipping me the bird.

The definition of bittersweet: Joe hands me my championship ring, spring 1999. *(© Steve Moore)*

I make it into the fifth with a 1–0 lead, and the Yankees held scoreless, but at that point, Chili Davis screws up my payback. Singling and scoring in the fifth, Chili comes back to the plate in the seventh, murdering me with two runs batted in, and another run scored. I love that guy like a brother, but that night I really wanted to kill him. I leave in the seventh, at the bad-smelling end of a 4–1 score. The cheering starts again. When I leave the field, there's another standing O in progress, and this time, despite the loss, I do manage a wave, and a tip of the cap, and a "thank-you." It's the least I can do.

From there, the Yankees go on to just plain spank us Jays, winning this first contest 6–4 before sweeping the series and booting our big busload of twenty-somethings right out of town. That Yankee sweep *kills* this team, leaving it intimidated, shell-shocked, beat-up, and flat. Mugged in the Bronx, the kids go down hard, playing depressed, tentative ball for a long, long time. Leaving New

With Brandon and Lars at the Skydome, 2000

York, we'll lose seven of eight as we stumble headlong into a truly lousy May.

May. We never really get back on track. Slumping badly, this team will ultimately go 11–17 for the month, and by Memorial Day weekend, we Jays will be *well* out of first place and floundering. I do nothing to stop the slide, spending the month pitching like a giant, corn-filled turd. My back is sore, my pitches are all over the map, my velocity seems down, and my ERA quickly soars to a morbidly obese 6.30. I'll lose ugly in Texas, Detroit, and Boston, and by month's end, with the Yankees rolling into Toronto, I'll be dipping toward the bottom of my worst slump ever, just in time to take an 8–3 beating at the hands of Hideki Irabu. It doesn't get a whole lot worse than that.

June. Our season's over, or at least that's how it seems in the local papers.

This is a "gutless" team, they write. We're soft. We're lazy. We don't care about winning. Fregosi needs to clamp down. Wholesale trades are in order. Time now to start rebuilding and rebounding into a more productive 2000. Dumber words have never been written. It's ridiculous. We're barely a third of the way through the season, with a young, exciting, talented team on the field, and these momos have already thrown in the towel.

No beat writers in any town that I've ever played in are as ignorant, muck-raking, or relentlessly negative as the guys in Toronto. In a region where baseball is just slightly less popular than hockey, football, basketball, curling, tobogganing, ice fishing, and snowshoe racing, the local sports-hosers have absolutely *no* idea what they're talking about. Writing about cigarettes, beer, and ugly wool hats, they'd win Pulitzers, but baseball seems entirely beyond their reach.

That's a bad thing, because while this team is busy fighting through its slumps and injuries, and hard luck, a lot of the younger guys actually seem to be buying this beat-writer bullshit. You can't help but notice how the early-season piss and vinegar has all but disappeared from this club. World-beaters in April, they've let a few bad weeks and a *lot* of bad press create a clubhouse filled with second thoughts and self-doubters by early June.

June 3. With my back still hurting, I finally break down and get my first cortisone shot of the season, which works wonders. One day later, I'll toss eight solid innings against Montreal, earning my first strong, pain-free W in weeks. Up in the stands, scouts from the Cleveland Indians and New York Mets are watching me pitch. Like the newspaper morons, Gord Ash, it seems, may have already given up on 1999 too. Yours truly is currently being dangled as trade bait.

Gord Ash tells the Indians it'll take Bartolo Colon, Richie Sexson, and Enrique Wilson to pry me loose. All of those guys have tremendous potential. All are cheap. All three are twenty-four years old. Can you smelllllllll the rebuilding plan that Gord Ash is cooking? The Indians politely decline. From the Mets, AAA ace Octavio Dotel, outfielder Roger Cedeno, and infielder Luis Lopez are the names on the table, but that deal never happens either. Instead, by midmonth, the baby Jays have shaken off their funk, and this team is actually bouncing back, winning eight out of nine from Philadelphia, Anaheim, Kansas City, and Cleveland.

Good breaks start falling our way now, fast. When Robert Person struggles mightily as this team's closer, a twenty-three-year-old kid named Billy Koch comes up from AAA, moves into the Jays pen, and immediately starts throwing

100 mile-per-hour fastballs and racking up saves. When shortstop Alex Gonzalez goes down with a shoulder injury, journeyman infielder Tony Batista rolls in from Arizona and promptly hits 10 home runs in a month. When Jim Fregosi gets himself black-eyed in a Philadelphia bar fight, the rock-'em sock-'em manager commands more respect than ever, and his middle-aged shiner lights an inspirational bonfire under this team.

By the All-Star break, the Jays will once again stand at four games over .500, just three games away from a Wild Card berth. With that in mind, wholesale rebuilding gets delayed. The negative press slows down. Wells comes off the table, and the '99 Jays go home for the All-Star break on a roll.

At 9–6 for the first half, with my ERA still hovering above the 5.00 mark, I'm hardly an All-Star this year, but things *are* looking up for me too. With a cortisone shot on July 10, I'm able to pitch a complete-game, two-hit shutout heading into the break, and another complete-game victory coming back on July 17. With my game now officially back on track, I'm pain free and pumped about this team's Wild Card chances. At the same time, in a petty, but perfectly human, turn of events, I'm equally excited over the fact that I've now racked up two more victories than Roger Clemens has down in the Bronx.

On the seventeenth, with Clemens on the mound, losing to Atlanta, Coney calls me from the Yankees dugout and leaves me a message on my voice mail. "Hey, Scumbag," he says, "Roger's on the mound . . . losing. Listen to this." And at that point, Coney holds the phone up in the air, allowing me to hear all of Yankee Stadium chanting, "Boomer! Boomer! Boomer!" Back north of the border, a big, evil grin crosses my face, at which point I start frantically redialing Coney's cell.

July 18. Without question, this is the toughest day of my season. Tossing batting practice to Brandon on the field at Skydome, I'm called over to the dugout by one of the clubhouse guys. "Hey, Boomer!" he shouts. "David Cone's got a perfect game going through seven, down at Yankee Stadium! You wanna watch the last coupl'a innings?" Brandon and I are off the AstroTurf and staring at the clubhouse TV in two seconds flat.

It's Yogi Berra Day at the stadium, and for that reason there's a whole heaping helping of Yankee greats peppered all over the house. Don Larsen's there. So are Whitey Ford, Don Mattingly, Bobby Richardson, Phil Rizzuto, and with all that Yankee magic now circling through the Bronx, I sit down to watch with a *very* good feeling about Coney's chances. I just wish I could help.

Coney broke with tradition last year, sitting with me, talking, teasing, calming me down through the last three innings of my own perfect game. Today as one of the only people on the planet who know exactly what's running through David Cone's mind right now, there's just no way in hell I can return the favor. With the TV cameramen catching Coney alone in the dugout, I'm dying to dive in with a joke. I'm dying to tease the guy, to taunt him, anything to help keep his mind off the monumental accomplishment in front of him.

But I can't.

With a lump in my throat, I watch Coney get his last out, a little, tipped pop-up to Scott Brosius at third. I couldn't be happier for the man. I couldn't feel worse about being so far away. I start dialing my cell phone immediately. Finally, maybe ten minutes after Coney's been carried off the field, I get my man. "Scumbag!" I shout. "That was a thing of beauty! I'm glad you did it! Welcome to the club!" At which point I pop the top off a tall boy and let Coney hear it gurgle down in his honor. "Honestly, dude, I think I've got big-

Yanking the chain of the Tigers' sportscaster/personal snack-fetcher Kirk Gibson
(© Reuters/Peter Jones)

ger goose bumps than you! Now if only you'd thrown that knuckler . . ."

Coney laughs, but as we chat, I can hear him being swallowed up in that same sort of glorious, happy chaos that swarmed all over me after my own perfect game. I've got no right to distract him. "All right, dude. I've gotta go!" I lie. "Go get drunk and have one or two for me!"

"Done deal." And with that the call's done. I won't get to chaperone Coney through Manhattan tonight. I'll miss the bars, and the food, and the laughter, and the excitement, and the whole celebration for my friend. We'll beat the Braves 3–2 tonight in a tight, well-played game, but I'll be distracted throughout. What I wouldn't give right now for a rain-out, a private jet, and a quick cab ride into Midtown.

But I can't complain. From the Fourth of July weekend right through the middle of August, we Jays are the single hottest team in baseball. Closing out July at 19–7, it's the winningest month in the history of the Toronto franchise. The locker room rocks. Our confidence is sky-high. We can't do anything wrong. Things gets so crazy that at one point, when Jim Fregosi's eight-year-old son tells him that the Willie Greene character in his PlayStation baseball game has been hitting like crazy, Fregosi takes a flyer and sticks the bench-warming Greene into our own lineup. Two home runs and a 4-for-5 day later, that strategy seems brilliant. As a result, all through the rest of that '99 season, Robbie Fregosi's PlayStation will become a valued contributor to our Blue Jays' offensive strategy. By the way, Fregosi *will* kill me for sharing that news.

By mid-August, the guys on *SportsCenter* are calling us Jays a lock for the AL Wild Card, and as you've probably learned by now, all through the history of baseball, perfect moments like these are almost always followed by disaster. We keep that proud tradition alive. We lose seven in a row, at home, to Seattle and Oakland.

Meanwhile, out in center field Jose Cruz Jr. hits a slump deep enough, and prolonged enough, and ugly enough, to smack him right out of the lineup. In his place, from the Colorado Rockies, comes Brian McRae, a guy who I swear to God, even *I* could beat in the one hundred-yard dash. With two gimpy knees, and one gimpy bat, McRae lasts just a couple of weeks before a desperate, disgusted Fregosi goes to plan C, yanking twenty-three-year-old Vernon Wells right out of Syracuse and tossing him into the fire.

Things are even worse on the mound. With mechanics problems up the ying-yang, Kelvim Escobar is now losing every start, and by mid-August Fregosi banishes him to the Siberian front known as the bullpen. At just about the same time, Joey Hamilton is forced to call it a season when his chronically achy shoulder finally explodes, and Chris Carpenter follows suit when one Amazonian bone spur and a bunch of his pygmy cousins all move into the big guy's elbow. That leaves Pat Hentgen, and me.

Correction, that leaves Hentgen. Facing the Red Sox, at home, in my last start of July, I seize up almost immediately, wincing through four bad innings while I get shelled for 7 runs on 11 hits. It's shot time, and with another start at Yankee Stadium right around the corner, I make sure that needle's good and deep this time around.

Feeling post-injection-fantastic, I take the mound against Andy Pettitte and toss yet another complete game . . . which I lose. Chili Davis kills me again, this time leading off the fourth with a solo homer to left. And four innings later, with Joe Girardi on second base, Derek Jeter smacks one to the exact same spot. In the end, I give up 3 runs and 7 hits over 8 innings pitched. Not a bad outing (especially against this Yankees lineup), but tonight Andy Pettitte's on fire. He too throws a full 8 innings, but with our Blue Jays bats gone to oatmeal, my team manages to scratch out just one, unimpressive, small-ball run. I *still* haven't beat those pinstriped bastards.

Five days later, on the mound in Arlington, my back's at it again. It's rigid and painful with every release, and I now feel a sort of grabbing, pinching sensation in my lower back every time I follow through, almost like a hook grabbing onto a nerve. The pain is worse than ever before, and that's got me scared . . . almost as much as the fact that my last cortisone shot was effective through all of *one* start. I'm gonna sit, missing a scheduled start for the first time in a long, *long* time.

Ten days down. Ten days of chiropractors, three times a day. Ten days of ice. Ten days of stretching with the team trainers. Ten days of hydrotherapy. Ten days of anti-inflammatories. Ten days of complete, uninterrupted rest. Come August 18, I hit the mound feeling better than I have since April, but *still* I'm not perfect. Still I'm not "right." With an achy loss in Seattle followed up by a *very* stiff, five-inning stint down in Oakland, my future is clear. Chiropractors can't fix me. Neither can ice, or whirlpools, or ibuprofen, or Miss Cleo. Fact: though the effects don't last *nearly* as long as they used to, my beloved cortisone shots still provide the *only* guaranteed cure for what ails me.

September 1. Shot up again, and one day later, that sweet stick-and-burn translates into another beautiful, dominant, complete-game victory. This one's a four-hitter, over the Twins, during which I feel all of seventeen years old. Loose, and strong, and completely pain free, I'm ready to play two. I just hope this feeling hangs on for a while.

It doesn't. Seattle kills me again on the seventh, with 7 runs scored in 7 innings pitched. Leaving the mound, I'm pinching badly now, with the old stick-up-the-butt posture back in effect, and pain bad enough to keep my breaths puppy-dog shallow. By the time I'm inside, I'm already jonesing for my next shot. With the Yankees coming to the Skydome, I've got just one more chance to beat them this season. I *will* be at full strength.

September 13. Thuh-uhhhh-uhhhhh Yankees lose!! Thuh-uhhhhh-uhhhhh Yankees lose! One massive shot right between vertebrae, and I've got 'em in the palm of my hand. Another complete game. Another four-hitter, and I come away with a soul-stirring, ego-pumping, chest-puffing, 2–1 victory over Orlando Hernández. Man, I've gotta tell you I practically cartwheeled right off that mound. *Sure* it took me four tries to beat 'em, and *sure* the Yankees are now fast approaching yet another postseason run, and *sure* Roger Clemens has now squeezed his ass into my rightful, postseason slot in the Yankees rotation; but for today, right here, right now, at least for a little while . . . I win. Actually, I win twice.

Maybe this last shot went in deeper or more precisely than the five that preceded it. Maybe the cumulative effect of all those injections has finally made a more permanent change. I have no idea. All I know is that for the first time in a while, I'm enjoying some long-lasting cortisone-injected relief. Three strong starts close out my season. And with one last shot for the road on October 2, my final start of the season is . . . you guessed it, a complete-game victory, in Cleveland, where just before game time, the local baboons are screaming their big red asses off again. That makes stomping their team extra sweet. So does the fact that with this victory, we've cost the playoff-bound Indians their home-field advantage for the postseason. Suck on *that*, Indians fans.

In the end, we baby Jays end our season at 84–78, good enough for third place in the AL East, but nothing more. Fighting off injuries, and fatigue, and inexperience, and a late-summer glut of batting slumps, this team still battled a whole lot longer, and a whole lot better, than anybody could have expected. The kids learned a lot, and with just another piece or two added to this puzzle, the Jays of 2000 really could shock all of baseball.

Personal stats. Even with a spine made of eggshells, I rack up 231⅔ innings pitched, highest in the American League, with a record of 17–10. Down in the Bronx, Roger Clemens ends his regular season at 14–10, which, were I a lesser person, I'd make note of, and remember, and stick into a book four years later.

Within hours, I'm the hell out of Cleveland and back in my woods, wandering through the brush with Kirk Gibson, king of the wild frontier, and Alan Trammell. Soaking in the peace and the serenity and the beauty of the land, I'm suddenly convulsed with a cold-turkey, bone-rattling, postseason withdrawal. During '95, '96, '97, '98, playing baseball in October had become an annual tradition with me, and this year, left out in the cold, I'm falling apart. I'm jonesing bad, digging through the local Michigan papers, looking for any Little League playoff game that might need a good lefty. Y'know, line up those ten-year-olds and I'll mow 'em down, baby. I want Game 1.

I can't even *watch* the playoffs this year; it's just too hard. Instead, I sit in a tree stand, alone, silent, clearing my head, recharging my batteries, drinking horrible coffee, watching and waiting for deer that never come. They're no dopes. Like the rest of the world, they're probably back in their living rooms, watching the Yankees win it all, without me.

By the time the ticker tape's once again snowing down over Broadway, Nina and I have already escaped to Hawaii, where I'll lay in the sun, motionless, for the better part of the winter. On several occasions, Greenpeace volunteers will actually show up to try and push me back out to sea, but they fail every time. I can feel my face turning to leather. I can feel the melanomas rising, but I don't care. This is just too great. Trust me on this one. If you're not gonna pitch in the World Series, paradise, with the woman you love, makes a damn fine alternative. Oddly though, even here in Maui, Gord Ash can *still* make me crazy.

November. Wholesale changes are in store for the Jays in 2000, and with infuriating, mind-numbing Canadian logic, every single one of them sacrifices on-field talent in favor of "fiscal responsibility." In early November, both Shawn Green (42 HR, 123 RBI, .304 batting average) and Carlos Delgado (44 HR) are offered *decent* but entirely unspectacular five-year deals. Both guys decline, and within minutes, Gord Ash is aggressively dangling *both* franchise players as trade bait. At the same time, in an effort to free up even *more* payroll, Pat Hentgen, Joey Hamilton, and I are *all* on the block, while Graeme Lloyd, a free agent after the '99 season, goes entirely unpursued. Tony Fernandez, and his .328 batting average, is left off Gord's 2000 wish list as well.

And now it gets worse. I wake up one morning in Hawaii, turn on *Sports-Center,* and hear that Shawn Green has been traded to the Los Angeles Dodgers for Raul Mondesi, a player I know nothing about, though the papers call him "moody," "unhappy," and a "malcontent." Mondesi spent 1999 hitting .253, with 33 homers and 99 RBIs, solid numbers, but a definite step down from Green's stats. I shake my head hard, hoping that maybe the sand in there had somehow made me hear this deal wrong. Worse, just a few days later, Ash works his penny-pinching magic again, this time shipping Pat Hentgen off to St. Louis for, get this, a mediocre lefty-reliever, a backup catcher, and an unloved, minor-league pitching prospect.

Well, that did it. I now officially blow my top and put in a phone call to Gregg Clifton, demanding that he call Gord Ash and get me the hell "oot" of Canada. The papers pick it up, the Canucks go crazy, and in retrospect, I probably shouldn't have made waves. Apparently, by the time I opened my big mouth, I was already the subject of preliminary trade talks between the Jays, the Mets, and the Indians. With that in mind, Ash, Clifton, and I are all forced to quickly eat my inflammatory comments and begin backpedaling, pretending all's well in the Great White North. Obviously, if interested teams know I'm desperate to escape, they won't offer *nearly* as much in return for my services . . . ultimately making it just that much harder to spring me.

I hide through the rest of the winter, blood pressure rising, duct tape slapped securely across my big mouth.

January 2000. With Shawn Green now gone, Carlos Delgado has his GM by the kumquats, and from that position, he's able to extract himself a three-year, $36 million deal. At about the same time, Mr. Ash succeeds in wringing another $3 million out of team ownership, allowing him to hold off on a fire sale of any more experienced players. The 2000 Jays will now run as is, with a payroll of just about $53 million. It's good news, in that the Jays' money-saving team gutting seems finished at last, and bad news, in that it's now official. I ain't going any-where.

In the end, the Jays of 2000 head into spring training with a lineup that seems *decent* but clearly not as strong as last year's model. We've made bad trades. We've lost key players. Management's refused to step up in building a winner, and it seems their lack of commitment has left us Jays even farther down the food chain than we were this time last year. We simply can't compete with the likes of the Yankees or the Red Sox. With that in mind, it's hard to work up a whole lot of enthusiasm for the 2000 campaign, and I head into spring training as one *really* unhappy camper.

February. "You *really* wanna know what I think?" I tell the reporters asking my opinion about the Green and Hentgen trades. "I think we got a big pile of shit in both trades! Half the guys I never heard of, and to be honest with you, I don't know this Raul guy from Adam!" Pitchers and catchers reported last week. Guess which one just wants to go home. But stay tuned; things change quickly down here in the land of free orange juice, Mickey Mouse, and skanky, ten-dollar lap dances.

If there's one unbreakable law of baseball, it's that *every* team looks good in March. Good, bad, piss poor, it doesn't matter. Inevitably there are young guys who look ready to step it up. Veterans looking sharper than expected. Question marks looking like exclamation points. Heading into the season, I'm once again seeing the glass as half full, convinced that if this team really works its ass off, a Wild Card berth is well within our grasp. I was wrong. Even with my optimism on overdrive, I flat-out underestimated this team. Let's jump way ahead.

July. We Blue Jays are 8 games over .500. We're surprising the world, and with the Yankees and Red Sox playing some *really* bad baseball, we've all spent the better part of the past month juggling first place like a hot potato. The kids are excited, and while the young arms in the Jays starting staff have been struggling, our bats have gone crazy. Delgado, Batista, Mondesi, and Jose Cruz have each smacked 20 homers or more by the All-Star break. Stewart, Delgado, Darrin Fletcher, and DH Brad Fullmer are all batting *well* above .300. We're averaging close to *seven* runs scored per game, and that kind of offense covers up a *lot* of mound mistakes. This season, being "good enough to win" basically requires showing up, breathing, and keeping your arms attached to your body, at least through the fifth.

In Yankee Stadium, with my back absolutely on fire, those smoking Jays' bats saved my achy ass big-time. Struggling through 5 painful innings, I'd hit the showers early, but with my teammates' superbats launching an impossible, 6-run scoring spree off El Duque, I'm ultimately gifted with a big, fat, butt-ugly W.

And speaking of "ugly." That win in the Bronx comes just days after Bernie Williams and I hit the *Late Show with David Letterman,* assaulting eardrums all over the country as that show's musical guests. No, that's not a typo. With Bernie on guitar and me on what some might generously describe as "vocals," the two of us roar through a version of "Take Me Out to the Ballgame" that makes Harry Carey seem like *Mariah* Carey. I'll take abuse for weeks, with Lars Ulrich phoning at one point, just to tell me I sing like a harpooned walrus on crack.

Or at least, cortisone. Coming off a prolonged stretch of back grief through the latter half of spring training, I stretched, twisted, and therapied myself into a stupor, but I was still unable to move, let alone pitch, without pain. I found myself lying in bed through the better part of each day. I was walking like a marionette and making old-man grunts with every move. After just one start, I got my first shot of the season, which bought me a painless, complete-game shutout over Texas.

But just like last year, the effects of my injections were becoming shorter and shorter lived. Facing Seattle, just six days after that first shot, I suffered through a 1-inning, 5-run disaster. From there, shot number two gifted me with a complete-game victory over the Angels. With that in mind, I'll spend the rest of this season becoming far less shy about getting shot up. Here at midseason, with David Wells Ws rolling in on a regular basis, the Toronto trainers are more than willing to serve as my enablers.

I'll pitch 9 complete games in this 2000 season, and every one of them comes right after a shot. And while I *used* to battle through at *least* one uncomfortable outing before hitting the juice, through May and June, I've been back on the table at the first twinge. It's insane, I know. And sooner or later, I *am* gonna pay the price, but for now, while I can, I'm gonna kick ass by whatever means necessary. It's working. At thirty-seven years old, with maybe one or two seasons left in my career, I find myself at 15–2 by the All-Star break with an ERA of 3.44. Thanks to one handy-dandy adrenal steroid hormone, I'm beating the clock, and the opposition, and I'm having a ball. I see no reason to stop.

All-Star break. Joe Torre calls. He wants me to start for his American League team in this year's "midsummer classic," and it's all I can do not to laugh, or shout "I TOLD you so!" into the phone. At 15–2, I'm an obvious, unavoidable choice. At 15–2, Joe comes to me like an ex-boyfriend, asking for a second chance. At 15–2, vindication is mine. At 15–2, with Clemens now struggling, the Yankee brass must all be second-guessing their votes back at Malio's. Brian Cashman must be sighing. Marge Schott must be swearing. Pat Gillick must be choking. Sure it's petty of me to be thinking in these terms, but it's also perfectly human. (*Don't even try telling me that you wouldn't do exactly the same thing.*) And while I'll behave myself well at the All-Star press conference, inside my own head, I've got Gloria Gaynor singing "I Will Survive" at top volume. I'm loving every minute of this.

I do slip once, telling a reporter that "yeah, I'm now *completely* over the trade that sent me to Toronto . . . although it did just hit me that right now, I am close enough to strangle Joe Torre." It gets a big laugh, but I can't help but notice the old "Mr. Wilson face" quickly returning to Mr. Torre. Grabbing his mug in my hands, I gift him with a big, loud, Bugs Bunny/Elmer Fudd–style kiss. At 15–2 I figure I've earned the noodge. Joe reacts like he's just eaten a bug.

Quality time at a Metallica concert with Nina, my kid Lars,
and the "other" Lars (Ulrich)

Just like last time, the All-Star game itself is a lot of fun, and I ultimately spend two innings heaving and praying with pitches to Sammy Sosa, Vlad Guerrero, Andres Galarraga, and a bunch of other guys who can easily crush any mistake I might toss. Two scoreless innings later, I'm done. Running to the airport, I shoot home for one blessed day of goofball parenting with Brandon, and my new guy, Lars, who's just begun that frantic running and squealing and crashing stage that always has moms worried their kid will lose an eye. Dads, on the other hand, love this phase, mostly because we know there's nothing on earth funnier than a full-speed toddler wipeout.

I'm home. They're home. We hit the pool together, and for the first time in my life, I *really* feel like an old man. There's a big water slide to fly down, but with my back feeling flimsy, I don't dare risk it. Chicken fights are off limits too. And while normally nobody on earth can even approach my belly-whoppering technique, the diving board's off limits too. Today I'm on the sidelines, edging into the shallow end, toes first, like your grandmother, while Brandon and Lars swim around, bored, trying their best to avoid looking openly disappointed. Later in the day, when Brandon catches me off guard with an absolutely beautiful top-rope, flying suplex off the back of the couch, I see stars. Pain shoots through me, and the era of cortisone immortality quickly comes to an end.

Dumped and Dangerous

It's not that I stop getting the shots. I'm just smacked in the face with their long-term, real-world effects. If I can't even roughhouse with my monsters anymore, something inside my spine is *clearly* falling apart. And while the injections *may* allow me to do my job, and function on the mound, I simply can't keep this abuse up. There is a *huge* downside to my current success. One look at the boys drives that point home, hard. Immediately I decide to give the stretching and the chiropractors and the anti-inflammatories another chance. Immediately, I decide to back off on the shots. Immediately, I start thinking seriously about retirement.

Back from the break, with Brandon's dive-bombing behind me, and just two All-Star innings under my belt this week, I hit the mound against Philadelphia, shot-less, and sore, muddling through 7 innings with flat, motionless stuff that the Phillies happily cash in for a 7–3 victory. Five days later, despite a ton of horizontal time and a huge amount of physical therapy, I'm worse, hanging on through just 4⅓ innings, while giving up five quick runs to Tampa Bay, aka the worst-hitting team in baseball. Now I'm scared. Now I get the shot. A five-hit, complete-game victory over Cleveland follows.

Meanwhile, though we Jays are still smack in the middle of a pennant race, we're averaging less than 20,000 fans per game. Those that do come seem to sit on their hands through all nine innings, as if they're just here killing time until hockey season begins. We Jays are young (except for me), we're exciting, we're playing good ball, we're hitting home runs like mad, and nobody seems to care. Gord Ash has a theory that in the hockey-obsessed Canadian marketplace, any team that falls short of making the playoffs is seen as a complete failure. I think he's right. Baseball fans in Canada simply don't understand what they're watching. I've seen these people boo players for moving up a runner with a well-hit sac fly. An oot's an oot to them. I've seen these same fans boo pitchers for walking a guy with one out and a runner on second. It's ridiculous. Stick, puck, ice, missing teeth; this is the stuff these Canucks understand. Baseball seems entirely too mysterious for 'em. Honest to God, there are nights where I just want to climb up into the seats at the Skydome and start slapping.

August. The annual Blue Jays' midsummer slide is threatening again. Having gone just 11–16 through July, Raul Mondesi closes out that already lousy month by going down for the season with bone chips in his right elbow. At the same time, while Shannon Stewart and Carlos Delgado continue clobbering everything thrown their way, the rest of our lineup is falling off fast. We're fighting hard. Nobody's giving up, but by the end of the month, with the Red Sox and Yankees both playing much better baseball, our long-shot dreams of taking this

Having "borrowed" my camera, my baby Jays teammates
now offer me this sincere and heartwarming gesture of friendship

division are gone. We now stand a full three games behind the Indians and A's in the Wild Card chase. Attendance drops off at the Skydome.

As for me, with my back getting worse, I spend the month of August juggling a few great outings, and a few horrible outings, with just a pair of cortisone injections. All told, I'll go 3–1 for the month, which puts my record at a stiff, fragile, exhausted 19–5 for the season. Hunching whenever I walk now, and often spending whole days staring up at the ceiling from my hotel mattress, I'm a walking disaster area. That's when the tendinitis sets in.

On the road in Anaheim, I'm staked to a quick 6–0 lead when the shoulder goes boom. It tightens fast, and that brings Fregosi to the mound. Achy back, stiff shoulder, I leave the field ready to call Dr. Kevorkian from the phone in the dugout. One start later, I'll wish I'd gone through with it.

September. Disaster. Absolute humiliation. Facing Oakland, with the shoulder on fire, and my back once again killing me, I'm also hampered by the fact I just plain suck. My stuff's rotten today, and very quickly I get massacred for 7 runs and 9 hits in just 1 inning. Hello, Mr. Fregosi. Hello, punched water cooler. Hello, kicked bat rack. Hello, horrified batboy. Good-bye, horrified batboy.

Hello, cortisone injection. Look, even this late in the season, even at a measly 71–66, we Jays are *still* just three behind Cleveland for the Wild Card. I've got to keep cranking. I'm also just one good start away from my first-ever 20-win season, and that's a *huge* motivator. Don't let the standard politically correct sports clichés fool you. We players are *always* aware of the milestones in front of us, and we really do bust ass to reach 'em. "It's really just about the team" we'll lie to the guys from ESPN. "I never even *thought* about the record." Don't believe us.

Twice in a row I'll go to the mound feeling good, looking to keep this team in the Wild Card hunt, *and* notch myself victory number 20. Twice in a row I'll pitch pretty well. Twice in a row I'll be disappointed. Facing Detroit at home, I take a 5–4 lead into the ninth, only to have the great Billy Koch blow a rare save in the ninth. When it happens, I actually feel worse for him than I do for me. All week long Billy's been chasing after me saying, "You go eight! I go one! I'll get you number twenty. I'll get it done." After the game, I tell him, "I haven't decided whether to give you a time-out, or send you to bed without supper."

"Very funny, Methuselah!" he shouts back, at which point I ground the little punk for the next two weeks.

Five days later, back in Yankee Stadium, Andy Pettitte and I duel head to head and pitch for pitch. We both hold the other team scoreless through seven. We both get touched for a run in the eighth. We both leave the game with the score tied at one. Three innings later, with a Carlos Delgado single and a Jose Cruz homer off reliever Randy Choate, my baby Jays really *earn* this victory. It's a huge one, because after falling back to four games off the Wild Card pace, this victory, coupled with an Indians' loss, puts us back within three. The Delgado stogie burns like a furnace. Shannon Stewart's dancing in his locker. Darrin Fletcher's hugging every human body that can't outrun him. Fregosi's slapping backs with both hands. You can *feel* the adrenaline rising. You can *feel* the kids discovering how good they really are. We're ready to go on a tear.

But then we hit Chicago for a nightmare of a weekend series against the Sox. On Saturday, Chris Carpenter gets hit in the face by a hard line drive off the bat of Jose Valentin. He goes down hard, screaming in pain, needing a dozen stitches to the inside of his cheek. We have no idea when or *if* he'll be back. Twelve hours later, having spent the better part of his season battling back from surgery, Joey Hamilton takes the mound for a Sunday day game and lasts all of three innings before his shoulder falls apart . . . again. This time, Hamilton's done for the season. Here in the homestretch of a race where *every* game has become a must-win, we've just seen 40 percent of our starting rotation go down in flames. Most teams would fold 'em up right here.

But wait, it gets worse. Heading home with one day off, before diving into a three game set against the Yankees, my body attacks me from *yet* another annoying direction. Back aching, shoulder sore, I wake up on that one blessed day off with somebody drilling a hole in my right big toe. The gout is back. I roar.

I bolt from my bed, but remember, with this goddamned bad back I can't even come *close* straightening up. At the same time, having now slept on my sore shoulder, my entire left arm is dead. Put those together, and you end up with a large, naked guy, hopping around on one foot, moaning in pain, with one useless arm flapping around at his side, and his entire body hunched over like some sort of hairy, lower-case *n*. I'm Dr. Frankenstein's Igor. I'm Quasimodo on crack. I'm supposed to start tonight.

Not gonna happen. Within an hour, I've got my first pair of naproxen coursing through my veins, and with this team's future on the line, I attempt to speed up my recovery, by doing something really dumb. I take a cortisone shot . . . this time, to the toe. This is the same digit that sent *lightning bolts* of pain through my body at just the touch of a bedsheet, and now I've somehow decided it would be a good idea to drive a large needle through it. I don't know if you've ever *seen* a six-foot-two, 270-pound man scream like a six-year-old girl, but it's a sight to behold, let me tell you. Even worse, while the shot makes my entire foot numb, the toe somehow remains in full pain mode. All I can do now is gobble more medication and hope for the best. Steve Trachsel takes my start.

A late-season acquisition from Tampa Bay, Trachsel's a streaky, struggling pitcher with a really bad habit of tipping his pitches (the same habit will *kill* him with the Mets in 2001). Tonight, however, with his team in desperate need of an inspiring, well-pitched victory, the man tosses a gem, scattering just 4 hits over 7 innings. At the same time, with Andy Pettitte on the hill for the Yankees, these Blue Jay kids explode for 16 runs in a soul-stirring, spirit-lifting bloodbath.

One day later, with 10–11 journeyman Esteban Loiaza getting the start, the baby Jays pull off yet another miracle, walloping the one-two punch of Coney and Doc Gooden in a 7–2 laugher. Now it's my turn.

Seventy-two hours after my toe first exploded, the combination of naproxen and cortisone has taken the lightning bolts of foot pain, and turned them into . . . well, imagine sticking your big toe in a light socket. With this team still within reach of a Wild Card berth, I can live with that kind of pain. I take the mound against Orlando Hernández, and while he's good, limiting us Jays to three runs on eight hits, tonight I'm even better.

With one last spinal injection taking me home, I toss another complete-game victory, this time holding the Bombers to one run on five scattered hits. Finally notching my 20th W of the season, I'm even more thrilled to hear that we've now

Enduring the Jays' "fans" (© *Mitchell Layton/Newsport*)

passed by Cleveland in the Wild Card hunt, and we now stand just two games back of the current front-runner, Oakland. With ten games left to play, the clubhouse is insane. We've destroyed the reigning World Champs with one hand tied behind our backs, and you can't help but wonder if destiny's calling.

But that's when the bottom fell out.

Maybe we got too high. Maybe we wore ourselves out. Maybe somewhere deep in our own psyches this young, unproven team just didn't feel *worthy* of playing in the postseason. Or maybe we just started sucking. Whatever the reason, having now beaten the living tar out of the best team in baseball, we Jays fell into that classic sports trap of following up gorgeous, unexpected victory with heinous, underachieving defeat. Our bats turn to snow. Our pitchers turn to shit. We close out the season losing 8 out of 10.

Tampa Bay beats the Jays for three of four, while the hometown fans boo this team, top to bottom. It's nuts. It's clueless, but it's been like this all season. Honest to God, the Toronto fans suck. If a batter makes an out, he gets booed. If a pitcher walks a batter, he gets booed. If the team loses a game, we all get booed . . . loudly. Even though this underpaid, understaffed, underloved little team is right in the thick of the hunt, right into the last week of 2000, these mouth-breathers in the stands have *no* idea what we've accomplished. The wool-hat-wankers just boo . . . relentlessly. I've *never* been so happy to end a season on the road.

October 1. Wanna end your season ugly? How 'bout traveling to Cleveland and having the mutant fans there throw food and batteries at you while you're warming up in the bullpen? How 'bout listening to those same morons shout their now traditional insults about Mom at you all through your game? How 'bout doing all that with an aching back and terrible stuff on the mound? How can all that be topped? Try getting hammered for 7 runs and 7 hits in just 2 innings, then having the Toronto media throw an insanely ignorant hissy fit that contends you're lazy, that you just didn't feel like pitching, and that you blew off your responsibilities and started your off-season early.

Forty-eight hours later, I'm back in my tree, alone, with Wildman Gibson off scavenging berries and roots from under a rock somewhere. The idiotic booing from the fans in Toronto still stews in my head. The ridiculous criticisms of the local press still haunt me, and right then and there I start planning my exit. Wrapped up in my own thoughts, I nearly shoot Kirk Gibson when he arrives bearing beer.

That would have been awful . . . all that perfectly good beer wasted.

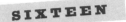
Socked and Sacked

Well . . . it was quick.

—White Sox manager Jerry Manuel,
summing up the "David Wells era"

DECEMBER 2000: WAIMEA BAY, HAWAII

Back again. The sun is high. My big, bald head is now pink. Me and Gibby have finally left the woods, and we're now bobbing up and down on long boards, side by side, maybe sixty yards off a stunning, white sand shoreline.

The sky is *too* blue. The surf is *way* up, and the waves are just plain *too* perfect. No, really, I mean *too* perfect. Eight-footers on Monday, *ten*-footers on Tuesday. You *can't* hit the sand when they're running like that. Sunburned and gimpy, we old fossils are now spending every waking moment of our days paddling into position, waiting for our wave, then kicking like hell, huffing and puffing like old steam engines in the hopes of catching a curl. Between sets, "Nature Boy" Gibson pontificates at length on subjects like "The Fascinating Life-Cycle of Kelp" and "Our Friend, the Plankton." I sit on my board, hoping a sympathetic shark will swim up and eat him.

Fast and furious, the breakers roll in, and by day three, my board-rust is *completely* gone. I'm back at Ocean-Beach-ability and flying like a screaming, waterlogged maniac through the foam. I'm Big Kahuna, baby! Gibby, on the other hand, is way too type A to ever *really* roll with the surf. He gets up okay, but he's tense on his board, tight, *fighting* the physics instead of allowing himself to relax, and glide, and become one with his wave. Still, despite his glaring board flaws, Gibby *does* have a world-class wipeout, high and deep, kinda like Goofy, head over heels with the exact same "Whoo-Hooo-Hooo" yelp.

Still, despite the surf, and the sun, and Kirk's *really* funny wipeouts, I'm *far* from serene here in paradise. Two months removed from the season, my Jays have clearly learned nothing from the mistakes of 2000. Once again, there's been a mandate from ownership forcing Ash to dump salary, *this* time to the tune of a whopping $8 million. Just like last year, step *one* in that process involves dangling the team's biggest names and trolling for nibbles. By November, rumors are already swirling that Raul Mondesi's on the block, and that yours truly may be heading for the Mets, or the Cardinals, or the Red Sox. Alex Gonzalez and Jose Cruz Jr. get branded as trade bait as well. Here we go again.

By early December, here in Hawaii, I'm hearing whispers that the Jays are now actively shopping me to the Mets, looking for decent starter Glendon Rusch and maybe a pair of good minor leaguers in return. It's maddening. After a surprising step forward in 2000 (despite the dollar-driven losses of Shawn Green and Pat Hentgen), my pitch-poor Jays seem headed toward yet another penny-pinching deballing in '01. Granted, attendance was down at the Skydome last year, but does *this* seem like a franchise committed to winning? I don't think so. With a lousy back, and my thirty-eighth birthday on the horizon, I know full well this may be my last run through the bigs. That said, I'm praying the Mets trade goes through, for two obvious reasons.

First, I just can't stomach going out on the bottom, with a big, fat Canadian yawn of a season. Honest to God, the prospect of playing for a weakened, rebuilding Jays team, in front of Toronto's silent, surly, cluelessly negative fans is just about killing me. Second, with the Mets in the hunt, I've got a shot at ending my career back in New York, with a pretty good shot at making the postseason one last time.

But wait, it may not be so easy. With the Mets' interest in me now public, the grapevine starts singing that the Cleveland Indians (of all people) plan on getting into the Boomer hunt as well. "No way!" I say laughing at the early reports. "As much as those fans hate me? I'd rather play for hell. The Indians have *gotta* know that." Apparently they don't.

"David Wells and Raul Mondesi go to Cleveland, in exchange for Roberto Alomar and Dave Burba." That's the proposed deal I keep hearing about. That's the deal that scares me. It actually seems plausible. And while the salary swap here is not quite as Toronto-lopsided as in the Mets' deal, bringing Roberto home would go over *big* with the Canucks, allowing Gord Ash and company to save a little cash, and a lot of face, all at the same time. Damn! That deal makes sense. I can't let this happen. Time to start working the New York press.

The way I figure it, I've got to make three points public. First, I've got to goose the Jays along in their efforts to dump me. Second, I've got to make it clear that I *do not*, under *any* circumstances, want to play in Cleveland. And third, I've got to jump up and down and cheerlead about coming home to New York City. Together, I'm thinking those three crystal-clear messages *should* combine to ship me to Shea . . . as long as I can clear up my own Bobby Valentine mess.

To be brutally honest, I *really* can't stand the guy. In the past I've called this Mets manager a "loser" in the press, and I've also talked openly about what a nightmare it'd be, playing for a dick like him. Constantly diving into the spotlight, Valentine's got a rep as being arrogant and obnoxious and conniving and a backstabber. A lot of players hate him. A lot of his fellow managers hate him. Valentine's *easily* the least-liked manager in the game. Trust me, the list of former Mets who hate this guy is longer than your arm, and I have a feeling a list of 2002 Mets who felt the same way about him would have knocked out your eyeballs as well.

I'm on the mound one time against the Mets, in a nationally televised game, and Valentine gets himself ejected, only to sneak back into the Mets' dugout an inning later, wearing a cheesy-assed pair of fake eyeglasses, and a stick-on mustache. He's not fooling anybody. He's not back to "lead his team" or pass some life-or-death message to his bench coach. He's shucking and jiving for the cameras, milking the moment for whatever screen time he can weasel. Big, white, phony smile beaming, he's playing for the cameras, thrilled with the attention, and the spotlight, and the chance to pass himself off as some sort of loveable character who'll do anything to help his players win. It's not working. Watching this jackass prance around in the dugout, I'm thinking, What a loser! Just get the hell out of the dugout, go back to your office, have a beer, and watch the game on TV!

Anyway, even with all that said, given a choice between Cleveland, Toronto, and New York, I'd *still* choose to play for the Mets. It's a no-brainer, and with that in mind, it's time for me and my agent to start spin-doctoring. Quickly Gregg Clifton dials his cell, chats with the *New York Post*, and earns us a back page by telling one reporter that I'd really *love* to come home to New York and play for the Mets. He also says that I'd have no problem at all playing for Bobby Valentine. Strategic Hit Number 1 is a bull's-eye. The press starts rolling. The

public gets excited, and Steve Phillips can't help but read between the lines. The Mets get serious.

One day later, my phone's ringing off the hook. Everybody wants a quote. Everybody wants an interview, and that's when we pull the trigger on Strategic Hit Number 2. With the Mets now primed to dive head-first into signing me, it's time to cool the jets of the Indians and Jays. This time around, I talk to the *Post* myself. Again we start off with a loud, clear, love-letter cover to New York City, but this time, I follow that sweet talk with a couple of carefully constructed controversies. Speaking out in print, I hit the *Post* with a quote about how there's no way in hell I want to get shipped to Cleveland. And from there, when I'm asked for a yes-or-no response to the question "Would you like to remain a Blue Jay?" I say "To

Beauty marries the beast . . .
I'll let you decide who's who

be honest, no." I then rub salt in the wound by simply telling the truth—making it clear that in my humble opinion, the fans in Toronto flat-out suck, and the front office does too, showing *absolutely* no commitment to winning. From there, with a couple more fictional quotes about how I'd be happy to play for Bobby Valentine, and a message to the Toronto front office saying "Do it now, make my wish come true and let me be a Met," I've done all I can. The skids are greased. The Indians and Blue Jays are big-time dissed. The ball is in play, and with any luck at all I *should* be a Met within days. With that settled, it's time to go home and get married.

Honeymoon: greeting the sheep in New Zealand

We're finally gonna do it. After *years* of her putting up with me, and caring about me, and not killing me when I probably deserved it, I've finally wised up and asked Nina to marry me. Amazingly, she's said yes, and with my heart soaring, our great, big, bells-and-whistles, fancy-schmancy ceremony is all set for this weekend, to be followed immediately by a honeymoon in Australia and New Zealand. That's where I get blindsided . . . and like it.

I'm on a little dot on the globe called the Hayman Island, just off the coast of Australia, when it happens. Once again, I've been traded. Once again I'm in paradise when the whole deal goes down, and once again I'm the last one to know about it. This time I get the news in a phone call to (of all people) Tom Arnold. Tom's been a friend now for several years, and he'd just served as an usher at my wedding to Nina. I call him just to say hello, and he answers by shouting, "Boomer! Hey, man, congrats on the trade!"

"It happened?"

"Hell yeah!"

"Mets?"

"Hell no!"

"Aw fuck, not Cleveland."

"No man, Chicago!"

"Sox or Cubs?"

"Sox!"

"Oh my God! I didn't even know they were interested! They're a really good club! I *love* going into Chicago. I *love* that town! Deep-dish pizza! Chicago dogs! Mustard, relish, onions, and sauerkraut! Holy shit, this is fantastic, way better than the Mets deal! Wow!"

"Sorry you're so disappointed, buddy," says Arnold, laughing.

"Hey, didn't the Blues Brothers live in Chicago?" I ask.

Arnold laughs hard now, shouting, "Oh my God, will you *please* shut *up*?!"

Here's how the deal happened. Way back in November, worried that the Indians might be in the running for my services, Sox GM Kenny Williams dove headfirst into the free-for-all, mostly as a blocking measure against his arch

With Bobby Higginson, John Salley, and Tom Arnold at my charity softball game, January 2002 *(Courtesy of Chris Kreski)*

rival, Cleveland. "I'd heard the Indians were interested in you," he told me. "And I saw no reason to let anybody in the AL Central improve like that, especially not Cleveland." With that in mind, Kenny makes a couple of quick, pitching-rich offers to the armless Canadians in Toronto, but Gord Ash isn't interested. At this point, if you believe Kenny Williams's side of this story, Ash begins pushing for an admittedly sore-shouldered, 15–10 Sox starter Mike Sirotka to be included in any deal. Williams obliges, countering with a four-player proposition including Sirotka, reliever Kevin Beirne (1–3, 6.70 ERA), outfielder Brian Simmons, who sat out the entire 2000 season with a torn Achilles, and Mike Williams, a mid-level, minor-league pitching prospect.

From there, however, Williams hears nothing, and right up until the last minute, it looks as though Steve Phillips and the New York Mets are going to win me, with a package that apparently consisted of Glendon Rusch, as well as a hot, right-handed prospect named Grant Roberts, and one more minor-league arm. The Mets have everything on the table. Rusch and Roberts can both contribute to the armless Jays of 2001, but somehow Toronto pulls the trigger with Chicago. Why? Simple. In my opinion, those guys were trying to stick it to me.*

I had gone on the record saying that I wanted to go to New York (*Make my wish come true . . .*) and the Mets had stepped up in good faith, but now, with another decent offer on the table, the Jays seem to believe they can send me out of town with one last "fuck you." I asked for New York, they're feeding me to Chicago. Done deal. Gord Ash may be smirking, but right how, he can't even *imagine* how badly this one spiteful moment will come back to bite him in the ass.

Sirotka's shoulder falls off. First injured pitching in last year's ALDS against Seattle, Sirotka nonetheless felt well enough to play right through a multigame, November All-Star trip to Japan. Coming home, he freely admits he knew his shoulder wasn't right. Visiting the Sox team doctors in early January, he's given a cortisone shot for his pain but receives no X rays or MRI. He's told to come back in ten days if the pain hasn't subsided.

Ten days later . . . Sirotka's officially a Blue Jay. He passes his routine team physical, but when the Jays look more closely at Sirotka's shoulder, a second MRI reveals tears in the pitcher's rotator cuff. A visit to Alabama and Dr. James "The Genius" Andrews confirms the stomach-churning diagnosis. Sirotka's out

---

* Apparently "sticking it to Wells" was a popular sentiment. When this trade was announced on the big screen at a Maple Leafs' hockey game, the entire crowd gave the new deal a long, loud standing ovation. I can't say that I blame them.

for the year. The Jays are *royally* screwed. Me, I'm laughing my ass off. Maybe regular weigh-ins will help the man heal.

And now comes the whining. "No fair!" the Jays shout. "We want a do-over!" Ash begs Commissioner Bud Selig to void the entire trade. But after a two-week investigation, Selig rules that the Sox dealt Sirotka in good faith and the deal will stand as originally constructed. Again I laugh my ass off, especially when Glendon Rusch launches into his own very impressive spring training with the Mets. Ash is crushed, and it couldn't happen to a nicer guy.

Spring 2001—Tucson. Here's how every single day of this spring goes down. I wake up stiff, bent up like a giant claw and *completely* unable to stand. At that point, I have to literally fall out of bed and hit the floor. To get on my feet, I have to pull myself up using the night table. Forty-five minutes and one long, hot shower later, I'm generally loose enough to get myself dressed, get into my car, and drive to my chiropractor's office. There, begging for treatment, I'm poked, pressed, twisted, and squeezed through an hour of torture that leaves me shell-shocked, raw, and just about ready to hit the field.

Back in the car now, I drive across town to the ballpark. There, with the sun burning down, and a pair of Sox trainers looking on, I'll do a lot of serious stretching before going through the motions of calisthenics and playing with a little bit of half-assed throwing. By 11:30 A.M., I'm done for the day. Time to go back to the doctor.

More bending. More twisting. And by lunchtime, the man's got me sweating, and rubber-limbed, and ready for back flips. Six hours into my day, I'm finally feeling great. Time to play golf with Coach Bo.

Serving as a White Sox spring training instructor this year, Bo (Mr. Jackson, if you're nasty) still knows baseball. Taking batting practice with the boys on the field, the big man's *still* cranking 400-footers in all directions. He's smart, and funny. He's every bit as ancient as me, and I like him a lot. By week two, we've got a standing, daily golf date, where he whups my ass for big cash on each hole. The eighteen holes aren't great for my back (or my wallet), but it's fun, and Bo's cool, and what the hell else am I supposed to do all day here in Tucson?

Right from the course, I head for my chiropractor's office one more time for a little postgame tenderizing. Three times through the ringer, I end each day being kneaded and pressed into a sort of human Jell-O mold. Every day's the same, and as we sweat our way through the last part of March, every day leaves me feeling a little better, a little stronger, a little more ready to pitch. By the day *before* opening day, I'm actually feeling fantastic . . . but that's when a horrible stomach flu turns me into a human equivalent of the Old Faithful Geyser.

I blame Gibby. Just before the season begins, we hit the Final Four together in Minneapolis, rooting for Michigan while gobbling down garbage before, dur-

NCAA Finals, March 31, 2001. Moments later, Gibby will poison me.
(© *Reuters/Sue Ogrocki*)

ing, and after the game. Somewhere in there, amid the hot dogs, and the beer, and the chicken wings, and the pizzas, and the steaks, and the fourteen other courses, a monster bug took hold. Four of the five guys in our group will spend the next twenty-four hours suffering through a raging, explosive, thoroughly embarrassing case of the stomach flu. Only one of us has to start a major-league ball game during the attack.

It's *really* ugly. Upstairs and down, my body's exploding all morning long. I'll take Pepto-Bismol, and ten minutes later, KABOOM! I'm puking in a lovely shade of pink. Water, warm ginger ale, crackers, Kaopectate, nothing helps, and everything that goes in quickly launches right back out. I'm cramped. I'm dehydrated. I'm ready to die but not willing to give up my opening day start. I head for the ballpark in Cleveland, hoping for a miracle.

By 11 A.M., I'm like a dishrag, draped over a bench. Like clockwork, every twenty-two minutes, my body explodes. Standing on a pitcher's mound in front of 42,000 fans could prove horrifying for all 42,001 of us. By 11:30, I've thrown in the towel. I find Jerry Manuel and tell him. "I'm really sorry, Jerry, but I don't think I'm gonna be able to . . . excuse me a minute . . . Blaaaaaaaaaargh!!!!!!!!!!"

Enter one very brave trainer with a suppository gun. Instantly qualifying for sainthood, this brave soul risks his own life to go where no man has gone before and take a last-ditch, desperate stab at saving my start. One blast later, I'm shocked, wide-eyed, and maybe even back in business. My digestive tract is once again my friend. I can actually ingest Gatorade and keep it somewhere within the confines of my body. I feel better. I feel stronger. I feel like Popeye after a can of spinach. And by the time I hit the bullpen, I'm pumped and ready for yet another Cleveland ass-kicking, this time assisted by one major imbecile in the crowd.

"Hey, asshole," he yells into the pen. "Where's your mother?" at which point he runs like hell. Once again, I'm greeted by the Cleveland welcome wagon. Once again, it stings. Once again, my blood boils. The morons won't *ever* say this stuff to my face, that'd take a nut sack. Instead, they hit and run, and my only recourse is to beat up on their team—which happens again, today.

Two runs, four hits, six innings, one victory, one asshole smacked down. Not bad for an opening day's work, especially coming off an overtime shift of driving the porcelain bus. The back feels strong, the legs feel good, and despite the fact that I resume my twenty-two-minute puke schedule just moments after leaving the game, all things considered, it's a really good day.

This is a *good* team. This is a team that won 95 games last season, and should better that record this year. This is the kind of team the Jays *should* have been, young and fearless and building on last year's momentum with the addition of key players wherever they can help. We've got Paul Konerko moving in at first, with Frank Thomas grudgingly headed for a DH slot. Ray Durham is at second, Royce Clayton is at short, and anonymous .302 hitter Herbert Perry is at third. Carlos Lee hit .301 last season in right. Jose Valentin mans center, and the great Magglio Ordonez takes over in right. Behind the plate, Cleveland refugee Sandy Alomar Jr. makes *everybody* on the pitching staff better.

Behind me in the rotation are Cal Eldred, James Baldwin, and Jim Parque, who are all coming off strong 2000 performances. Even our number five, a kid named Mark Buehrle, seems like a really strong candidate to move up the food chain. Honest to God, any one of these guys could move into Toronto right now and be that team's ace. Out in the bullpen, wiseass deluxe Keith Foulke is well on

April in Chicago
(AP Photo/Duane Burleson)

his way to becoming one of the very best closers in baseball, and with Kelly Wunsch, Sean Lowe, and Antonio Osuna setting him up, we starters can hand the ball off without freaking. Still, with all that said, this team cannonballs into 2001 only to find there's no water in the pool. We're 8–15 by May 1.

Everybody's pressing. Nobody's hitting. On the mound, we're making bad pitches, and at home plate, we're swinging at worse. The kids look nervous. The vets look sleepy, and out on the mound, I pretty much stink. Coming off the opening day party, I hit the mound twice more, feeling good, feeling sharp, but somehow my game's inside out. Where normally i'd come straight at batters, I'm falling behind. I'm less aggressive. I'm making mental mistakes, and the result finds me lit up for two straight piss-poor losses. Even worse, after losing a 9–4 mess to the Twins, my back seizes up for the first time this season.

This one's bad. This one crimps me into a sort of modified fetal position twelve hours a day. This one keeps me from ever standing upright. This one draws sad, sympathetic, entirely infuriating faces from my teammates. This one's gonna need a shot. I take it April 18, one day before I'll toss my first complete-game victory of the year. This one's a 3–1 beauty against the Detroit Tigers, where I throw 81 of 100 pitches for strikes, and I'm into guys' kitchens and ahead in the count all night long. Five days later, still feeling great, I go 9 more against Oakland, this time scattering 5 dink hits and giving up just 1 run. However, when I leave the game after 9, the score's still tied up at 1–1. Two innings later, Paul Konerko will win it for us with a game-winning monster blast that's got every guy on this 7–12 team convinced we're ready to turn our season around. We lose seven of our next eight.

And that's just the tip of the iceberg. Two starts into his season, number two starter, Cal Eldred, goes down with an elbow injury . . . forever. Honest to

God, with a five-inch screw holding his previously repaired elbow in place, this flare-up effectively stomps out the man's entire career. From there, complaining of a sore left shoulder, number *three* starter Jim Parque hits the DL, and he's quickly joined there by DH Frank Thomas, who's complaining of a sore *right* shoulder. One blink of an eye later, reliever Antonia Osuna is gone for good, nursing yet *another* shoulder gone rotten. Here in Chicago, when it rains, it typhoons. And though we're barely a month into this season, this team's already in big, *big* trouble.

May. I'm on the radio, getting into big, big trouble myself. I've begun hosting a little weekly show on a Chicago sports radio station, and Frank Thomas is my hot topic of the day. Still riding the pine with some mysterious arm pain, Frank's made a statement saying, "I don't want to embarrass myself by playing at less than a hundred percent." Fans are angry. Fans are confused. Fans are accusing Frank of dogging it. I toss my two cents into the controversy and almost immediately my argument has me chomping loafer. It starts when I make the mistake of using me, Coney, *and* Frank Thomas as examples in making a bigger point.

It's this simple. Guys like the three of us, guys who are impact players for our teams, we *need* to go out there and play hurt. Perfect example. All through last season, I played hurt in just about every start. Sometimes I'd get my ass kicked, but more often than not, I was able to keep things together well enough to come out on top. In my mind, unless you're *really* falling apart, you've gotta bear down, forget about your own pain, and be in it to win it.

Our *opponents* won't know that we're hurt, and with a so-called big-gun stepping in at the mound, *or* at the plate, one simple little act of deception can change the entire complexion of a game. If Coney's playing hurt, guys on the other team will *still* be thinking, Oh shit, David Cone is out on the mound today. We've gotta bring our best game or he'll kick our ass. That can make 'em press, or swing early, or fall off balance. By the same token, if Frank Thomas is up at bat, playing hurt, showing his usual intensity, and digging in like he always does, I don't care *who's* on the mound, that pitcher's sweating. He's thinking, Oh shit—throw this guy junk and he's gonna walk. Throw him anything too fat and he's gonna yank it five hundred feet.

Even at 75 percent, a guy like Frank can *easily* intimidate a pitcher, make him tentative, make him lose a little confidence. As a result, that guy may change his game plan. He may start aiming the ball, and *all* of those things can result in some really bad, really hittable pitches. Sure nobody likes to look bad at the plate, but even at three-quarter speed, a guy like Frank

Thomas can help his team win. Sometimes 75 percent is more than enough. I go on to say that if Frank really *is* afraid to embarrass himself on the field, then he's embarrassing himself with that statement. That's when all hell breaks loose . . . or at least that's what the media would like to see happen.

Later that day, I get to the ballpark just in time to find a bunch of reporters already in Frank's ear, telling him everything I said on the radio and spinning it in whatever way makes it juiciest. "David says you're dogging it," they tell him. "He says you've got no guts. He thinks you don't belong on the DL." Mind you, I never said any of those things, but that's the spin they're throwing. By the time I show up, Frank's already gifted their muckraking with a beauty of a sound byte. "Wells ain't no fucking doctor," he grumbles. "If I *could* be out there, I'd be out there." Fearing the man might soon live up to his nickname as the Big Hurt, I pull him aside right away, and when I explain the point I was *trying* to make, Frank's totally cool with me. "Don't even worry about it," he tells me. "I trust you. I'm not pissed." Big handshakes are offered and accepted. Case closed.

But with papers to sell, this thing hangs in the air, and days later, when Frank's lingering injury finally gets diagnosed as a torn tricep, I catch hell in the papers for kicking the guy when he's down. Even worse, Big Hurt's out for the season, and we Sox are sinking, fast. By mid-May we're at 14–29, and our season, for all intents and purposes, really does seem over. At the same time, the same papers that were busy trying to get me and Frank Thomas into a Hell-in-the-Cell free for all are now busy spouting off that GM Kenny Williams is already looking to unload me for prospects, white-flagging 2001 in hopes of rebounding big in 2002.

Braves, Cardinals, Phillies, Mariners, Brewers, Red Sox, Mets, Indians, and Yankees; *all* these teams are mentioned as possible suitors (the *Brewers*?). Every day, it seems, reporters have some new rumor for me to try on for size, and with my back getting worse and my attitude following suit, I hang on for the better part of two weeks before I finally crack. "Apparently, I'm just a pitcher for hire now," I shout in the general direction of anyone carrying a notebook or tape recorder. "I'm a piece of meat, tossed on the grill." Going a step further, I make it clear that while I've heard nothing from Chicago management about any deals in the works, the rumors and the lack of communication have me "ready to snap." Kenny Williams pays me a visit the following day and does something no GM has ever done with me before . . . he just plain tells me the truth.

"Look," he tells me, "I know you're hurting, and *you* know this season's falling apart on us. So, yeah, we're listening to offers. I wish I had better news, but that's the truth."

You could have knocked me over with a feather. I had every expectation that the Sox were shopping me around, I just never expected my GM to be so cool with me about it. "Listen," I told him, "I love Chicago. I like the guys on this team. But I understand, and to be totally honest with you, I *am* hurting, pretty bad. And if you really want to move me, I'd say do it soon, while you can still get something back."

We shake hands, and by my next start, there are scouts from a solid half-dozen teams in the stands.

June. How's this for pathetic? I go back into Toronto. I sleep on a crappy, hotel mattress. I wake up crumpled like a cheap fender. I rock back and forth 'til I flop out of bed, at which point, still unable to stand, I have to sort of crab-walk into the shower. Later, after I've slowly but surely begun once again returning to some sort of human posture, I hit the streets of Toronto for a pregame stroll. Six blocks from my hotel, I'm recognized by some fans. "Hey, you're David Wells!" one tells me.

"Uh, yeah, I am."

"Yeah? Well, fuck you, motherfucker. I'm glad you left town."

"Ohhhh-kay then." I turn and head down the street. Now the others start shouting at me too. These guys are kind enough quickly to inform me that I apparently suck, that I smell, and that, at least according to them, I am now, and always have been, a practicing homosexual. Never have I been so glad to get back to a bad hotel. I stay there 'til game time.

Back on the *Brady Bunch* AstroTurf of the Skydome, I'm booed incessantly for the better part of two hours. And while in and of itself that's no big deal, it *does* start to grate on you when you have absolutely no curveball, your back hurts, and you're currently neck deep in giving up 8 runs and 13 hits in just 5⅓ innings pitched. I'm pathetic, but even *that's* not the low point of this day.

First inning. Two runs have already scored, and with one out, I've got Raul Mondesi on second, and Brad Fullmer at the plate. Fullmer grounds one to the right-hand side of Paul Konerko at first. Konerko grabs the one-hopper, I cover first, and we've got the routine out. At this point two things happen. I feel something pull in my groin while in an entirely separate bodily disaster, my brain freezes cold.

"That's three," I say, smiling as I toss the ball casually back to first-base ump Jerry Crawford, who quickly dekes himself out of the way. "That's two! That's TWO!" Konerko shouts as Mondesi scores from third. At this point, 19,000 normally silent Jays fans rise as one to laugh and mockingly cheer for their fallen, humiliated, boneheaded alum.

Not exactly a scout-wowing performance. It also marks the White Sox' eighth loss in a row.

Nine days pass, and I miss one start while the mild strain in my left groin heals. Shockingly, almost all of the scouts who'd watched me implode up in the Skydome are back in attendance today, and this time (freshly cortisoned) I don't disappoint. Holding the Tigers scoreless through five, I get tagged for a pair of homers in the sixth that brings Manuel to the mound with a one-way ticket to the showers. Leaving the field with a 5–3 lead, Manuel tells me he doesn't want me to risk restraining the groin, but I mean, really, look at this situation. Scouts in the stand, shaky trade bait on the mound, there's no way in hell he's gonna let me blow this one.

Within forty-eight hours, the Yankees and Red Sox have *both* turned up the heat in trying to reel me in. Orlando Hernández and Andy Pettitte are *both* hurting in New York, and with Coney having a hard time in Beantown, both franchises are now chomping at the bit for some solid, dependable innings-pitched. One outing later, I'll prove to both teams I'm probably not their guy.

Two runs, three hits, zero innings pitched. That's the line score of my June 8th start against the Cubs. Testing my back from the start, Eric Young leads off the game with a little bunt in front of home plate. I run. I grab it. I pivot. Pain explodes right through me. I toss to first and throw the ball away. The Comiskey faithful groan. Young goes to second. The faithful keep groaning. Here comes Miguel Cairo, who bunts *another* little squibbler to my right. I run again. I pounce. I pivot. The same pain explodes all over again. I toss. I grimace. I've thrown away another one. Now my back's tightening up. I can't follow through. My motion's a mess. I walk Sammy Sosa. Ron Coomer singles. Rondell White does the same. My trade value plummets. Here comes Jerry Manuel again, at which point I just nod and get the hell off the poor guy's field.

The cortisone shot goes in deeper than usual this time, a bull's-eye, with that same little twinge, then the sting, then the burn, just like always. Relief rolls in immediately, and this time around, I manage to wring one shutout and two passable outings from just one syringe. Amazingly, during this two-week period, the Yankees come calling yet again, this time offering up a respectable boatload of minor leaguers in exchange for one thirty-eight-year-old, broomstick-backed, left-handed geezer. *Somebody* over there still likes me.

June 27. With my back grabbing, I know it's time once again to feed the monster his cortisone. Gotta keep pitching. Gotta hang on as long as possible. Another nice stick, long and smooth, right between disks. The twinge comes hard, then the sting, then the burn, and all that's followed by . . . nothing. It's a dud. Ten minutes *after* the shot, I feel every bit as bad as I did ten minutes *before*. This is scary.

June 28. We do it again. Same shot. Same sting. Same burn. Same lack of results. Only now there's a whole new doomed, depressed sadness coursing through me. I need to work through this. I need to get loose. Anything less and my career is simply over. I stretch with the team trainers all day, and by game time, while I'm not great, I *am* loose enough to pitch. Out on the mound in Minnesota, I last all of two innings before I seize up completely.

Warming up before the third inning, I follow through on one simple four-seamer and simply can't straighten up. Finally, with a whole lot of effort, and a

Falling apart at Wrigley *(AP Photo/Ted S. Warren)*

whole lot of pain, I do manage to stand erect, wave to the dugout, and take myself out of the game. I won't be back at all this season.

July. I'm done. With two weeks of shots and stretching, and rest, and chiropractors, and every therapy known to man all failing me miserably, I can no longer stand up straight. I can no longer sit in a normal chair. I can't put my own socks on. I can't walk comfortably. And there's no way in hell I could ever, *ever* survive ten minutes with my kids. That's what puts me over the top. That's what makes me finally pull the trigger on surgery. Put into that context, the decision is simple.

I've talked with the White Sox team physician, James Boscardin, for hours this week. He's explained my situation in layman's terms, and he's told me that my chances of a complete recovery are quite good. He's also let me know that with proper postop care, exercise, a ton of physical therapy, and the dropping of some significant weight, another year or two of major-league pitching is well within my reach. I go under the knife on July 18, with the bare outline of a long-range plan already in effect.

August 8. With the surgery a success, I've barely begun the painful process of recovery and rehabilitation, but today I've got business to attend to. With the Yankees playing Tampa Bay, I make sure I "just happen to be in the neighborhood" of Tropicana Field, dropping in on my old teammates "just to say hello." Trying my damnedest to look healthy, and agile, and well on my way to a full and uncomplicated recovery, I get hugs from Jeter and Bernie Williams. I get the old eyeball roll and an "Aw geez, will you look what the cat dragged in" from Don Zimmer, and I have a very carefully worded conversation with Joe Torre in his office.

Unable to discuss my baseball future at all without getting himself in hot water for tampering, the two of us are quickly speed-reading between the lines, each trying to make sure the other guy's getting the correct subliminal message.

"Boomer! You look terrific!" Joe shouts at me.

"Thanks, Skip. I feel really good, and the doctors tell me I should be better than ever by spring."

Joe smiles. Message received.

"Did you lose a little weight?" Joe asks.

"Yeah, I'm working hard at it."

"Holy cow, I guess an old dog can learn some new tricks."

Another smile. Another message received. Here comes Paul O'Neill.

"Jesus, Boomer," he says loudly, consciously within earshot of Joe. "You look fantastic. I wouldn't be surprised at all to see you back here, in camp with the Yankees next spring."

"Yeah, you never know." I laugh, wanting to kiss the old guy for setting me up with that spectacular, 360-double-reverse slam dunk.

The seed is planted. But now I've gotta go. Heading for the door, I shout out a quick, collective good-bye. "See ya, guys," I shout. "I've gotta roll. I don't want to be late for my workout with my personal trainer."

Forty Yankees just stare at me like I've got two heads. The "new me" may be a little hard to swallow.

SEVENTEEN

Home!

Pitching,
number thirty-three,
David Wells.
—*Bob Sheppard*

APRIL 18, 2002:
PITCHER'S MOUND, YANKEE STADIUM

I can hear them from all the way inside the Yankee clubhouse. "Boo-MER! Boo-MER! Boo-MER!" they roar. My heart is pounding. I've been awake, nervous, and ready to burst since 3:51 this morning. I'm bouncing off the walls, and now in

(© *Reuters/Mike Segar*)

just about two minutes I'm gonna be back on that magical field making my first home start as a member of the 2002 New York Yankees. My hands literally shake, but with pinstripes in place, I exit the Bombers' dugout as the big crowd explodes. I hop the line, just like always, crossing the grass toward the single greatest spot on this planet—the pitcher's mound in the house that Ruth built.

My heart soars. It's hard to catch my breath. Standing there on the mound, I look up into the stands and try to soak in the moment. It's too big. Too loud. Too Kodachrome perfect. Nine months ago, as I gingerly tiptoed off that field in Minnesota, I really thought my career might be over. With that in mind, to stand here today, feeling *great*, with my Yankee dream revived, I'm overwhelmed with joy and pride and gratitude, but more than anything else, I'm bombarded by memories.

I think about December and January, and the endless sessions of long-toss I enjoyed with my neighbor, buddy, and former major leaguer Darnell Coles.* Right out on my street, like a couple of giggling, shit-shooting, stickball-playing ten-year-olds, we'd air it out for an hour a day, slowly but surely working my arm back toward full velocity. I think about February, and how flat-out great it felt to speed down Dale Mabry Boulevard, toward Legends Field for my first spring workout as a born-again Yankee. I think about the fantastic look of disbelief on Joe Torre's face when I showed up to camp a full thirty pounds lighter than I'd been back in August. I think about March, and how natural it felt to be back, pitching to Jorge Posada, who still (thankfully) calls the smartest game in baseball. Right from the start, I've been strong and focused, throwing pain-free smoke, while having the absolute time of my life. Having come so close to hanging 'em up for good, I know I'm on borrowed time. I know how precious these Yankee days are. I'm not gonna waste them.

I think about that day in the Legends Field weight room, where I'm sweating profusely, AC/DC blasting, working through an intense, unsupervised, upper body workout. Halfway through four sets of curls, I look up to find Joe Torre staring at me in the doorway, mouth open, eyes wide, astonished at the sight. Newspaper in hand, he's here to ride the stationary bike for a while. Quickly I head for my boom box.

"Sorry, Skip." I tell him, turning down the volume. "You want me to put something else in the CD player?"

---

* He's an awesome guy. The dude played seven positions for eight teams over a fourteen-year major-league career. He also gives out great Halloween candy.

Joe's mouth opens wider. He does a broad double-take. Finally, he speaks. "Well," he says, "you got any Sinatra? Maybe some Tony Bennett?"

"No."

"Al Martino? Perry Como?"

"No."

"Liza? Sammy? Dean?" He's smiling with every suggestion. Joe knows what's in my CD case. Joe knows I'd rather listen to nails on a blackboard than adult contemporary.

"Can't help you."

"Got any Yanni?" He's laughing out loud. I make a gagging noise in response. "All right then," he tells me, "just leave your loud stuff on. Maybe it'll get me working as hard as you. Maybe I'll even like it."

I crank the volume. "You Shook Me, All Night Long" blares.

"Excuse me," Joe asks, "but did that man just say 'She was a sex machine, who kept her motor clean'?"

Even in a Yankees uniform, spring training is *still* a pain in the ass
(AP Photo/Kathy Willens)

"Yeah. She was the best damn woman that he *ever* seen."

"Oh . . . well . . . okay then." Joe goes back to his paper.

Two minutes later, with Joe reading on the bike, and me still burning through curls, I notice that *both* of us are now gently bobbing our heads to the same heavy metal beat. Me and Joe Torre, brother-headbangers to the end. I stifle a laugh. I say nothing, but I can't help appreciating Joe's effort.

Jeter, Posada, Bernie, Andy Pettitte, Mariano, El Duque, Mussina, I'm thrilled when my boys finally hit camp, but at the same time, I have to get myself adjusted to a whole lot of new faces too. From my vantage point on the mound it just plain seems *wrong* for

DAVID WELLS

Robin Ventura to be standing on the third-base bag that we all know belongs to Scotty Brosius. It's even stranger to see Knobby's old spot manned by Alfonso Soriano, and Tino's filled up with monster-boy Jason Giambi. It makes me feel sad. It makes me feel old.

Out in left field, Darryl's long gone, beaten once again by the demons he can't seem to shake, and as much as I like Rondell White, I can't even *begin* to fathom right field populated by *anybody* but Paulie. I imagine him at home now, retired, smashing up the coffee table when he can't finish the *TV Guide* crossword puzzle.

And of course, there's the Rocket. Once and for all let me go on the record as saying I don't have a prob-

Me and Mariano
(AP Photo/Kathy Willens)

lem with Roger Clemens. Was I *happy* when he came to town and I ended up north of the border? Of course not, but that doesn't mean I ever made *him* the focus of my anger. The man's a fantastic pitcher, easily the best *right*-hander of our generation. And while in the past I haven't always agreed with his behavior on the field (trust me, if I were Mike Piazza, that broken bat would still be shoved up Roger's ass), we *are* teammates. We *are* Yankees, and from this day forward, I will have *no* trouble at all supporting the man wholeheartedly.

The *other* "new guy" I should probably mention is Giambi. This is gonna be bad. We're getting along *way* too well. We're having *way* too much fun. We're a giant *New York Post* headline waiting to happen. He's loud. He loves Linkin Park and Godsmack. He occasionally has some problems with overbearing authority figures. He likes motorcycles. He likes cheeseburgers. He throws a great punch. He's been known to occasionally enjoy an adult beverage . . . it's amazing how we opposites attract.

Still, even with all these old pals and new faces dotting the Yankee land-scape, my *closest* friend is nowhere in sight. Even amid this great spring reunion,

I miss Coney to death. Nobody calls me "Scumbag" anymore (at least not to my face). Nobody crushes my grapes. Nobody makes me laugh the way he can. Honestly, the *only* way this 2002 reunion tour could get any better, is if that weird-looking, skinny-legged, gimpy old guy was right here next to me, where he belongs . . . and where I can keep my eye on him.

Back in the Bronx, I roll through my final warm-ups as the chants of "Boo-MER!" continue. My stuff feels strong today, biting, and sharp, popping into Jorge's glove with a nice, loud *thwap!* All through spring training, and three previous starts on the road, my new improved spinal column seems entirely incapable of having a bad night (knock wood).* Six tosses to go. I can't wait to get started.

Squinting up into the stands, I spot Nina and the boys. None of them notices me; they're all too busy digging through Brandon's giant box of Cracker Jacks. It doesn't matter; they make me smile just by being here, and caring about me, and making my future seem every bit as exciting as today. Honestly, at thirty-eight years old (thirty-nine, or maybe even forty, by the time you'll read this) I know my days are numbered. I've got one season left, maybe two, but at the same time, I *could* break down tomorrow . . . and that'd be fine too. I've wrung far more than my fair share of laughs from this game, and with that one gorgeous woman, and those two insane monkey-boys waiting for me at home, I know that once I leave this field for good, I'm never, ever gonna look back with regret.

I've even got a job lined up once I'm out of baseball. I'm gonna be a roadie for either Creed, or Cheap Trick, or Metallica. It's all set up. I'll lug stuff, help set up, be a gopher, whatever it takes to hang with the band. Honest to God, just once before I keel over I want to know what's it's *really* like to be a rock star, and with that in mind, I *will* be coming soon to a stadium or arena near you. Even better, Lars Ulrich has now begun a no-holds-barred campaign aimed at getting me to learn how to play bass. He wants me to jam with Metallica. How awesome is that gonna be? "Stone Cold Crazy" . . . the David Wells mega-jam. Better get your tickets early . . . and your earplugs.

I'm ready now, warm-ups tossed, and with the crowd cheering louder than ever, the Yankees and I get set to make my homecoming really ugly for the Orioles. Upstairs in the owner's box, George Steinbrenner watches intently,

---

* By the start of the home opener, I'm already 2–0, having beaten the O's and Blue Jays with a no-decision against the Bosox. I've also allowed just 7 runs in 21 innings of work. Does this kid rock or what? Sorry.

hoping for the best. Win or lose, I won't let him down. Good friends don't do that to each other. Upstairs even higher, *way* past the nosebleeds, Attitude Annie's got her scorecard in hand. Her lawn chair's unfolded, and any minute now she's more than likely gonna start shouting at the umpire.

Last, here on this beautiful night, in this gorgeous, soul-stirring monument to baseball, the Bomber ghosts are with me too. You can't help but feel them. Out in Monument Park this morning, I paid my usual respects to the Bambino, and tonight, just like always, I know he's got my back. But they're *all* here this evening. Gehrig, Mantle, Joltin' Joe, Thurman Munson, Billy Martin, Roger Maris, Casey Stengel, the list goes on forever, and just to stand here, on *their* field, in *their* stadium, never fails to give me chills. Those guys will always be the *real* magic behind the New York Yankees, and I can't *begin* to adequately tell you how thrilled I am just standing here on this little clay hill, knowing that I'm once again a small part of this team's incredible tradition. To steal a quote from the Iron Horse, "Today, I consider myself the luckiest man in the world."

With Metallica's Lars Ulrich . . .

. . . and Creed's Scott Stapp

With six months of baseball ahead of me, I'm hoping that sentiment has a very long shelf-life.

April 30, Yankees at 16–10

One month into the season, this kid is most definitely *back*. Pain free, strong, skinny, and looking *particularly* hunky in my pinstripes this year, I haven't felt this good on the mound since half past 1978. I'm 3 and 0 on the hill with a whole lot of run support* and a whole lot of confidence. I want the ball every night. Pitching at home against the A's and Barry Zito this evening, I bounce into the clubhouse with the pearly whites gleaming.

Hit the Yankees locker room, walk six feet in any direction, and chances are you'll not only bump into a great player, but a great *guy* as well. Nowhere on this team will you find laziness or complacency. Nowhere will you find the standard-issue scumbag who cares more about padding his stats than winning ballgames. Nowhere will you find the muttering underachiever, pissing and moaning and second-guessing the manager as a way of justifying his own lousy performance.** Those guys may be infesting the majors like *cucarachas* these days, but trust me on this one, they just don't play ball in the Bronx. This team's jackass population is absolutely nonexistent, and that fact alone speaks *volumes* about Joe Torre, Brian Cashman, and Boss George. With World Series rings up the ying yang, these guys obviously know their baseball, but even more importantly, they know their people. Wanna job playing baseball in the Boogie Down? Get in line, but I should warn you right now, you'd better be special. Assholes, crybabies, losers, and long-haired freaky people need not apply.

Still, even though this '02 team is hands-down more focused and talented than any I've ever seen . . . by *no* means are we perfect. Case in point: Derek Jeter, who's right now standing in his locker singing at the top of his lungs. Headphones in place, he bobs to a thumping hip-hop beat, sounding an awful lot like Jay Z . . . *if* Jay Z was tone-deaf with his nuts in a blender. Derek may be an amazing shortstop, but he's also an amazingly *bad* singer. The dude's got *no* voice, whatsoever. He's Al B. Sure on crack. Batboys cover their ears. Coach Zimmer runs for cover. The bathroom mirrors are cracking, but *still* Derek keeps singing, and *smiling*, actually seeming to enjoy the fact that he's torturing us all. My fellow Americans, I'm sorry to stomp on your "golden-boy" illusions, but it's high time somebody exposed the evil dark side of our picture-perfect shortstop.

"Hey, where you guys going?" the evil soprano shouts.

"Shut *up!*" comes the reply.

"Aw, come on. Don't be like that. Y'all *know* you *love* my voice."

Earth to Derek. "Wrong!"

Eardrums bleeding, I duck into the trainers' room, where Gene Monahan and Steve Donohue have a rub and a hot pack and a big glob of heat gel all wait-

---

* Thirty-nine runs in my first five starts. *You* might win fifteen games pitching in front of these guys— even though you *do* throw like a girl.
** I think those guys all ended up in Queens this season.

ing for me. I touch nothing. That's the rule, and I know from experience that I'd be insane to even think about breaking it. It is written in blood that shall any Yankee mess with the equipment, supplies, first-aid kits, sprays, pads, tapes, bandages, shavers, ointments, gels, or athletic cups neatly stacked and organized by our two anal-retentive trainers/miracle workers, said player shall die, slowly and painfully, most likely hanged by the neck with a soiled Ace bandage. Gino and Steve don't mess around. They're Felix Unger, squared. I'll bet you a million bucks that at home their couches are covered in plastic slipcovers. Even money says their wives and kids are too.

Flopping onto the nearest open table, I'm massaged, and cooked, and at the twenty minute mark, I'm topped off with a mega-hot balm that slowly but surely turns my lower back into a George Foreman grill. "Hot enough for you?" Monahan laughs, not caring that his rotten joke was originally told by witty stegasauruses. "Hey, do I smell bacon?" Donohue adds. I roll my eyes and continue sweating. Somewhere, Henny Youngman is rolling around in his grave.

Lousy stand-up aside, Donohue and Monahan might just as well be named Dumbledore and Merlin. Their wizardry is awe-inspiring, and if *ever* there was a team in need of such witchcraft, it's us '02 Yanks. Right from the start of spring training, we've been dropping like flies. Jason Giambi's tree trunks have gone gimpy. Derek Jeter's neck has fallen off. Andy Pettitte's shoulder has crapped out. Roger Clemens has seen one hand become a pancake.* Ramiro Mendoza is stiff from *cabeza* to *culo*. Sterling Hitchcock has been sent back to the manufacturer for repair. And ever since one really bad neck twist, El Duque's whole head just seems kinda crooked. At the same time, Robin Ventura's been battling a bad back, *and* a bad *face*, having taken a knee to the jaw, in mid-double-play. The fact that most of these guys are on the field at *all*, let alone thriving, stands as pretty solid proof of our trainers' powerful black-magic voodoo juju.

Dressing now, in the locker that used to belong to Tino Martinez, I'm told by reporters that a victory tonight would push my Yankees' winning percentage to a whopping .730.

"No way!" I respond, eyebrows shooting straight up.

"Absolutely true," I'm told. "If you win, you'll have the highest-winning percentage of any pitcher in Yankees history."**

"No &;%$& way!"

---

* Flattened by a nasty-ass comebacker on opening day.
** With at least fifty or more starts.

I'm stunned. A half-gallon of adrenaline immediately shoots into my heart. My eyes go wide. My chest blows up to the size of a Winnebago. I gasp like Uma Thurman, taking John Travolta's hypodermic needle in *Pulp Fiction*. "Highest-winning percentage of any Yankee pitcher . . . ever?" How exciting is *that*? How pumped am I?

I'm *way* too charged up to sit still. And when one quick scan of the clubhouse reveals that Joe Torre's already out on the field watching batting practice, an evil smile slides over my face. Ever since February, I've been promising Joe that my game-day heavy metal will be funneled through a pair of headphones this year. Right now though, I'm feeling *way* too juiced to behave like a civilized human being. Sevendust is roaring through the clubhouse speakers in less than thirty seconds. I'm air-guitaring in forty-five. Joe's back in the clubhouse at the three-minute mark. Eyes meet. Joe shakes his head with a grin, sighs, then throws up his hands, bolts to his office, and shuts the door in his wake. He knows my brain. He knows I need this. It's good to be home.

POSTGAME NOTES: I told ya so. Decent stuff tonight, but I really wouldn't even need it. Our bats are burning these days, and even by the time I took the mound in the first, this mega-team had staked yours truly to a big, fat 6–zip lead. Got burned for just two runs over five innings, then hit the showers early, when a thunderstorm blew us all into the clubhouse for a 1:47 rain delay. From there, while I happily lounged about the warm, dry players' lounge, Ramiro Mendoza took my place on the mud-hill formerly known as the pitcher's mound, slamming the door on Oakland while gifting me with a sweet, 8–2 W, and a 4–0 start for the '02 season. The perfect end to a perfect day.

It just doesn't get any better than this. One month into this '02 campaign, I remain *completely* pain free, flexible, strong, and well on my way to pitching 200-plus innings (knock wood). I should probably send roses to Doc Boscardin.

May 17, Yankees at 26–15

Last night I felt better on the mound than I have all season long. Last night I pitched my first complete game in over a year. Last night my breaking ball was biting with fangs, and my location was as locked-in perfect as it's ever been. Last night I tossed 84 of 112 pitches for strikes, with the Devil Rays scratching out just 3 hits on their way to taking a butt-ugly 13–0 stomping. Last night I upped my record to 6 and 1. Last night seems like a million years ago. As of seven o'clock this morning, I can't move.

Flying high after last night's game, I iced, showered, dressed, talked crap with the press, and cracked open a tall boy or two, all without ever *once* thinking about the old spinal column. Exiting the Yankees' clubhouse, with *no* pain, and *no* stiffness, my thoughts were fast commuting toward the China Club, Veruka, Dorian's, and every other great Manhattan nightspot that seemed overdue for a late-night, postgame Boomer invasion. Minutes later though, *long* before my imaginary party's had a chance to get started, the urge to celebrate gets yanked right out of my body. In the blink of an eye, it's there; a motherfucking twinge of back pain. Same spot as last year. Same pain as last year. Something's catching, deep and low . . . same as last year. My heart sinks. My gut tightens. Quickly, I try to talk myself into believing it's nothing terrible, nothing that can't be chalked up to 112 pitches over the course of two hours and forty-eight minutes. The club plans get trashed. Tonight, I'm gonna party with takeout Chinese, Advil, and a heating pad at home. In three days, I'm gonna be thirty-nine. Tonight, I feel every bit of seventy.

Morning rolls in faster than it should; my eyes open wide as a pair of invisible vice grips clamp down on my lowest vertebrae. I'm in mid-spasm, and right at the moment I dare to imagine that things can't possibly get any worse, the almighty whammy kicks in, and my back locks up, completely. At this point, the phrase "Ohhhhhhh, shit" moans out of my lungs for the better part of a half hour.

Struggling just to flop out of bed, I'm wracked with the exact same symptoms that crushed me last year in Chicago. I'm sure a disc must be herniated. I'm sure my career is now officially over. Cinderella Wells has now gone to the ball, only to get hit by a bus just outside the castle. Alone in my apartment now, every movement requires a huge amount of effort, grunting and agony. It's déjà vu all over again, and it really, *really* sucks. "Okay, buddy," I say to myself when I've finally managed to get as far as the bathroom. "You made it this far. You had a good run, but now you blew it out. You're cooked. Don't get stupid. Don't mess around with more cortisone. Just go home to your kids before you make yourself worse." *That's* a tough statement. Apparently the sum total of surgery, and a year's worth of rehab, sweat, pain, cardio-training, dieting, self-denial, and incredibly hard work is now equal to shit.

Or maybe . . . not? Staring into the bathroom mirror, I realize that even though my back's on fire, and I can't seem to turn one millimeter in any direction without making my eyes bug out like a frog, I'm not crooked. A year ago, after shutting it down with the White Sox, I had the posture of Dr. Frankenstein's Igor. Today, I'm not bent. And while that's not exactly cause for noisemakers and birthday cake, it *does* give me hope. Fingers crossed, I do a handful of simple body experiments. I can lift my arms. I can get into and out of a chair. I can walk in a *perfectly* straight line without crying like a baby. None of that would have been possible last time around.

Semi-mobile now, I tiptoe to the stadium, where a batallion of doctors, trainers, and massage therapists waits for me, ready to pounce, ready to work me over like an overly caffeinated Indy 500 pit crew. Deep down, I'm still expecting the worst, but I also know that if there's even *one* more miracle left in this spine, these guys *will* pull it out.

Monahan and Donohue swoop in first, ordering an MRI, while pulling out all the stops in their gung-ho crusade to loosen me up. And though their heat, their rubs, and their endless regimen of gentle new stretching exercises initially make just a *tiny* bit of progress, that's a *very* good sign. If I'm getting better—even *slightly* better—with their treatment, chances are my injury is muscular, as opposed to *structural*. If I'm treatable, it's beatable, in all likelihood *without* surgeons, scalpels, or early retirement. It's a great moment, but not nearly as great as the one that's gonna end tonight's game.

May 17. On a *very* cold night, with rain pouring down, and the Twins pulling out to a 12–9 lead in top of the *fourteenth* inning, these Yankees *still* refuse to roll over and play dead. Shane Spencer leads off the bottom of the fourteenth with a single, and after Alfonso Soriano flies out to left field, Derek Jeter comes to the plate, working deep into the count before cracking a single that puts runners at the corners. Bernie Williams checks in the dish now, representing the tying run, but because Bernie's already gone boom twice in this game—including a game-tying solo shot in the bottom of the ninth—Twins reliever Mike Trombley ain't tossing *anything* worth hitting. Five pitches later, Bernie's on first with a scared, semi-intentional walk. And now, while every player in a Twins uniform starts praying for a groundball double play, Jason Giambi stomps up to the plate with the chance to *finally* play the role of Yankee hero. It seems like a long shot.

Jason's been struggling in his early adjustment to the Big Apple, pressing too hard, swinging too hard, working out too hard, never once allowing himself to just relax, enjoy the ride, and play the game that made him so awesome in Oakland.* Tonight however, all that's gonna change. With sheets of rain rolling in

---

* It's gotten so noticeable that Mark McGwire has recently called Jason on the phone with a message along the lines of "Dude, chill, can't ya?"

over Yankee Stadium, Giambi drills the first pitch he sees deep into the right-field stands, for a grand slam, walk-off victory.* I jump up in the clubhouse, whooping. A nasty bolt of lightning shoots through my spine. I just plain don't care. Five hours and forty-six soggy minutes after this game began, Jason sends us all home walking on air, and immediately goes on a white-hot tear. Already this feels like a team of destiny. Once again, I'm thinking October in May.

Back in the clubhouse, three days pass slowly, but with continued improvement, and MRI results now confirming my not-dead-yet status.** I'm listed as day-to-day, twinge-to-twinge, spasm-to-spasm. This is where Mel Stottlemyre gets busy.

Tuesday morning, May 22. I show up at Yankee Stadium as a stiff, sleepy, pessimistic pain in the ass and yet somehow Coach Stottlemyre still manages to lure me toward the Yankee Stadium bullpen for a brief short-toss session. Neither of us is expecting much, but we *both* know it's time for me to get back on the horse. Throwing tentative, half-assed versions of every pitch in my arsenal, I've got pressure† and some tightness in my back but no real pain. Nothing blows out. Nothing flares up. I'm smiling. Mel's smiling. I'm quickly penciled in for Saturday.

"If you can pitch, you'll pitch," advises an equally pleased Joe Torre. "If you can't, just tell me. Don't push it. Don't take chances, and don't worry about it." With Andy Pettitte and Orlando Hernández *both* riding the DL right now, it takes a hell of a manager to be that careful.

Wednesday: Fenway Park. This morning I beat Mel to the bullpen by a solid ten minutes. We're throwing from the windup today, and from the stretch, with a lot more velocity than we cranked out yesterday. "You're ready to throw, huh?" Mel asks, smiling at my unusual display of punctuality.

"You know it."

"Well then let's do this, Brutus."

Thirty pitches follow, and by the time we're half-done I'm already anxious for Saturday. The pressure in my back's not so bad today, and the only real *pain* I run into comes with my high leg kick from the stretch. It's not a prob-

---

* Jason has set a trap, purposely laying off the first pitch in every at bat tonight—hoping to lure the Twins pitchers into a false sense of safety. He's hoping they'll feel brave enough to toss him a nice, fat, first-pitch fastball. Trombley finally gives it to him in the fourteenth. The only other player in the history of the Yankees to come to the plate with his team down by three and end the game with a walk-off grand salami is Babe Ruth. Jason's jaw falls off when we tell him.

** I've officially got a "bulging disc," which sounds bad, but really isn't all that disastrous. Truth be told, I've probably had some form of a "bulging disc" for the better part of the last 7 or 8 years.

† Press your thumb into your lower back. Press hard. Now press a little harder. That's what it felt like—uncomfortable, but not really painful.

lem, at least not for Mel. Watching me throw, the majors' best pitching coach tinkers with my mechanics, and two minutes later, my stretch kick's a breeze. If I lay on my back foot a little longer than normal, then kick with a bit less altitude than your average Rockette, the back stays happy, the ball moves well, and in a perfect world, this new, revised motion may even allow my delivery to be quicker than normal. I'm at a solid 90 percent, and thanks to a whole lot of hard work from a whole lot of unsung Yankee heroes, I'm just about ready to go.

Saturday. The big day. The big game comes, and I stink . . . but there's great news. The crap-start has nothing to do with my back. Honest to God, the creaky old vertebrae felt great warming up, but here in Boston, my head's just not working. A little sluggish, a little off, I've missed one start, and it's now been nine days since my last live pitch. As any pitcher will tell you, that layoff ain't good. I'm aiming the ball today, struggling with control, movement, and an umpire who seems to believe that pitches right down the middle of the plate should be called "Ball four!" It's a frustrating combination. First batter of the game is Rickey Henderson, who *knows* I haven't pitched in a while, and *knows* I'm coming off an injury, and *knows* I'm nervous, and with all that in mind, he's not swinging at *anything* until he sees for himself that I can throw a strike. Some things never change. I get down 2–0, and of course, Rickey's smiling at me. But from there, with a couple of tipped breakers and one nice fastball, we end up locked up at 3–2. At that point, I rear back, toss, and deliver a message. Solid fastball, right through the middle of the plate; this sucker blows past Rickey before he ever gets the bat off his shoulder. Overacting through his standard, hammy "Whoa, that was inside!" fake-out schtick, Rickey's grasping at straws. He's cooked, and he knows it.

"Ball four!" shouts umpire Jim Reynolds.

"What?!" I shout

"What?!!" Jorge shouts.

"Take your base." Even Rickey looks surprised by this call.

I crack now. Fighting a bum back, nine days off, and location that seems kinda ferkakta today, my biggest problem is now an umpire. It hardly seems fair.

"Where was that fucking pitch?!!" I shout into the plate.

"Inside, low."

"What? Where the hell's your strike zone, man? Section twenty-two in the loge?"

Reynolds heads toward the mound now, shouting all the way. I return the favor, steaming toward home plate and this obviously nearsighted umpire with obscenities flying.

Joe's mouth hangs open in the dugout. He's seen this before. He and I have argued about this in years past. If I get tossed now, after pitching a grand total of zero and zero-thirds innings, our bullpen's in deep trouble. Joe bolts onto the field ready to strangle me, but Jorge, Derek, Nick,* Alfonso, and Robin have all beaten him to the mound. They're already gang-shooshing their pitcher, which leaves Mr. Torre free to visit Mr. Reynolds, collaring the umpire into a gentlemanly conversation about the fairness, objectivity, and parameters of the American League strike zone. Together, over the course of the next several minutes, the six-man, two-pronged peacekeeping mission saves me a trip to the world's earliest shower.

Crisis averted, but my stuff still stinks. Wobbly and off-target on the hill, every count seems to end up at 3–2, every batter seems to be repeatedly fouling off my best stuff, but I hang in there. Fighting the urge to get mad and sloppy, and keeping my pitches well chosen if not always well tossed, I manage to survive a 93-pitch outing with just two runs scored. The fact that every single one of those 93 pitches got tossed within the span of just 3⅔ innings should give you some idea of just how lousy my stuff really was. Still, with my back in one piece, my team leading by a score of 3–2, and Ramiro Mendoza now tossing fireballs in my relief, it's hard to feel all that bad about this particular train wreck. Our thirty-second W follows.

Two games back of the overachieving Bosox in the AL East.

June 15, Yankees at 43–24

Bed. The first thing I'm aware of is the foot in my face. Next comes an elbow, a leg, then fingers, a knee, and finally another foot, this one significantly bigger than the first. Coverless and pillow free, I'm literally hanging off one side of the bed, with my head resting on a night table. School's out. Brandon and Lars are with me now in New York, and though I haven't had a decent night's sleep in a week, I couldn't possibly be happier. Nothing in the world feels better than waking up in the middle of a great big dog pile of knuckleheads. With Nina already up and dressed and out of the bedroom, me and the boys can now squeeze in one rip-roaring pillow fight without ever getting into trouble. I win this one

---

* Jason Giambi was the DH that day, which is a good thing. He told me after the game that if he'd been at first during my blow up with Reynolds, he'd have tackled me and sat on my head 'til I either shut up or suffocated. Thanks, buddy.

hands down, with a sort of breaking curve that nails Brandon square in the back of the head. Hours of Cap'n Crunch, Power Rangers, and video hockey will follow, but at that point, I've gotta head out. I'm due at Shea Stadium for a rumble.

You know the story. Piazza owns Clemens. Clemens beans Piazza in the head during the 2000 regular season, then heaves a hunk of broken bat at the guy during Game 2 of that year's Subway Series. Now, a full twenty months after the fact, Roger's gonna have to pick up a Louisville Slugger and face the chin-music at Shea. Knuckle-draggers all over Queens are calling for his head. With nothing else to cheer for in their vast lost mess of an '02 season, Mets fans are treating this thing like a public execution. There's just no way Roger's going home without a bruise.

Shawn Estes is on the hill for the Mets today, and by the time Roger steps into the batter's box, Shea Stadium is ready to explode. The attendance numbers show that 54,347 are packed in here today, and every one of them is lusting for blood. The noise is deafening. Roger stares at Estes. Estes stares back. Every Yankee is up on the top step of the visitors' dugout ready to go. Estes delivers and throws a purpose pitch right behind Roger's . . . ass? What the hell was that? Only at Shea could a starting pitcher take aim at a six-four, 220-pound target and miss by eight inches. Talk about missing your spot. The crowd roars. Estes gets a warning. And that's when I realize that maybe, just maybe, Estes was smarter than *everybody*. Maybe the guy's location wasn't nearly as bad as it looked. In missing the ass of Clemens, Estes had made the perfect pitch. The guy won the respect of his teammates. But at the same time, he didn't hurt anybody. He'd embarrassed the Rocket, but at the same time, he didn't get suspended, fined, or beat up. Estes just made his point, sent his message, and moved on. Roger, on the other hand, may have avoided getting knocked on his butt, but he was clearly knocked off his game.

Freezing up in the field with a mental error in the third, Roger forgets to cover home and allows a Shawn Estes bunt to score Rey Ordonez from second. Later, with Estes at the plate again, Roger serves up a fastball that Estes cracks over the wall in left for a two-run dinger. An inning later, with Piazza at the plate, and the Shea Stadium crowd howling like a pack of orangutans, Roger sees his low, split-fingered fastball take a ride all the way to the back of the left-field bullpen. He's out of the game before that inning is over. The Mets go on to beat us 8–0. Tomorrow's my turn.

Feeling strong now, after slowly but surely blowing off the back problems of May, my record now stands at 7 and 3. My ERA is at 3.74. I'm tossing quality innings, I'm making good pitches, and with all that in mind, I come into Shea

Stadium ready to stomp on the Mets without mercy. And that's exactly what happened . . . right into the eighth inning.

Bottom of the eighth, with a 2–0 lead, I've scattered just six hits while striking out seven. Still feeling tough, I look into home plate now to find my old friend Roberto Alomar smiling back. One pitch later, he's ripped a solid line drive into left, for a double. Here comes Piazza, whom I manage to beat with a nice cutter, down and in. Piazza hacks, clubbing the pitch into the dirt and bouncing a tapper toward first. Jason Giambi boots it, making his very first error of the season. That brings up Mo Vaughn, a man whose lifetime batting average against me stands at a whopping .455 (30 for 66). He's also ripped me for nine career home runs, including three in one game.

I love this stuff.

First and third, game on the line, no outs, *big* challenge in front of me. Crowd standing, fans cheering, beers being totally ignored in the stands, this is what baseball's all about. Front and center now, this is my game to win or lose. My chance to shine.

Mo digs in, wobbling a bat over his head that's just about the size of your average dining room table. I push a quick fastball past him, 0–1, at which point Mo stomps himself back into the clay. I look in. I wind up. I toss. Looking for the grounder that will buy me a double play, my pitch is a nice cut fastball inside. With any luck at all, Mo should just bounce that sucker toward the left side of the infield.

Wrong.

Somehow, while my cutter spins well, it never quite breaks, and that brings a murderous gleam to Mo's big ugly eyeballs. He stays with my pitch, rears back and croquets a moonshot over the wall in right. Not again! I can live with the loss. I can live with the goat horns, but, Mo, dude, listen to me. When your career's finally over, you don't owe me dinner, you owe me a car.

All-Star Break, Yankees at 55–32, First in AL East

Seventy-two hours of freedom are now staring me in the face, and while in years past that kind of downtime might signal the start of one *hell* of a party, these days I'm a lot more interested in kickball. I'm also charged up for swimming, tubing, water-balloon fights, freeze tag, farting contests, and every other dumbass activity that my kids and I can possibly cram into three whole days of chaotic, responsibility-free fun. Jetting off to my ranch, this year's "Camp Boomer" rocks the Michigan woodlands with a three-day festival of good food, bad jokes, good times, bad kids, and above all else, a whole lot of family downtime. Still, late at night, here in the woods, where the only sounds you can hear are the crickets, the toads, and Lars snoring like some sort of wild boar with an adenoid problem, I can't help thinking about what a great first half it's been. Let's start at the top.

134 HOME RUNS: That's not a typo, it's a long-ball-swatting miracle. *Seven* different Yankees now have ten home runs or more. Everybody's crushing the ball. Everybody's a monster. Everybody's helping us pitchers win games. Look at this lineup and I dare you to find a weakness. Jason Giambi's now blown off the butterflies (and idiot boo-birds) of his slow New York start to become a nightmare for any pitcher dumb enough to challenge him. Derek's ridiculous, as always. Bernie's amazing, as always. Alfonso's unconscious. Jorge's just the best offensive catcher in the American League. And ol' Grandpappy Ventura's already got more RBIs this year than he did all last season with the Mets. Granted, Nick Johnson and Rondell White and Shane Spencer may be struggling right now, but does *anybody* actually believe those guys won't bounce back hard as we fly through the back half of this season?

The answer to that question may actually be yes, because just days ago, in an effort to make this lineup even more ironclad, the Boss and company found a way to bring Raul Mondesi to the Bronx. Raul, of the big-bat and rocket-arm school, has never made a secret of his desire to be a Yankee, and up in Toronto he was *forever* quizzing me about life as a Bomber. This deal may end up being damn good for us Yanks.

PITCHING: We may be old enough to have played AA ball with Moses, but so far, Roger, Moose, El Duque, and I are all holding up pretty well.* Scattered senior moments aside, we're all still capable of kicking ass on a fairly regular basis. At the same time, Andy Pettitte's back off the DL, and hoping to make a monster run right through the second half. Mariano Rivera's still limiting opposing batters to a pathetic .177 batting average. Ramiro Mendoza's racked up six wins from the pen. Karsay and Stanton seem just plain unhittable, and as if all that weren't *way* more than enough, just days ago, smoke-throwing, baby-arm Jeff Weaver joined the team as a humongously intimidating insurance policy.

We're now officially invincible.

PREDICTION: October now feels like a lock. I may get my fairy-tale ending yet.

---

* As of the break, I'm 9–5 with a 3.66 ERA.

Four games in Anaheim, and for the first time all year I've crashed off the wagon of low-fat, healthy eating. I swear it wasn't my fault. In and Out Burger was calling my name and as always, I was powerless against her sweet, seductive, high-fat charms. Two 100 percent pure beef patties, hand-torn lettuce, tomato, spread, two slices of American cheese, with or without onions, stacked high on a freshly baked bun . . . this is the Double Double. This is what I grew up on. This is my crack. Salad and skinless chicken be damned. There's just no way in hell I can be within twenty-five miles of one of Southern California's In and Out cholesterol dens without indulging in a great big red-meat overdose.

I knew I was an addict when I sat, dripping a combination of ketchup and semi-congealed grease onto one of Gene Monahan's spotless training room tables. He throws a hissy fit immediately, threatens to murder me, then goofs on me relentlessly for being such a glutton. Halfway through my back rub, I just don't care at all. Eyes rolled back in ecstasy, mouth hanging open like Homer Simpson, I'm high on beef, baby!

Truth be told, though the burger is doing wonders for my psyche, I really *do* need this backrub today. Ever since the All-Star break, each of my starts has been followed by a bit more stiffness, a bit more pain, and a slightly longer recovery period. It's nothing major, nothing I can't play through, but five months into this season, my body is clearly slowing down, feeling a bit more of the effects of my age, my job description, and twenty full years of horsehide-slinging abuse. Tonight, however, for the first time since May, the pain in my buttock is gonna become a royal pain in the ass.

Here's how it works. I'm 12 and 5 coming into this game, and I've got family and friends crammed into seats right up and down the Big Ed's third-base field boxes. Every one of those old pals is now expecting their hometown buddy to toss 'em a gem. They won't get it. Just moments into the game, I find my back knotted up even lower and deeper than usual. It's come on hard and fast, and the end result leaves me almost completely unable to follow through on my pitches. That translates into breaking balls that stay flat, and cutters that just wobble in toward home staying belt-high and hittable. Two innings later, having been quickly embarrassed by an onslaught of five runs, six hits, and a pair of walks, Joe kindly performs euthanasia on my outing.

Now flash-forward with me. Two days later, the Yankees and I are all back in New York, for the start of a short home stand against Kansas City and Oakland. With me is Scott Yeckenevich, the very same guy who baby-sat me through last summer's rehab, then drilled me like a crazed boot camp sergeant through my workouts last fall and winter. With my back gone kablooey (that's a technical medical term), and a reunion with cortisone still out of the question, my hope is that some extra work with Scott might help keep me pain free and flexible for as long as humanly possible.

Working with Scott at my apartment, every morning come hell or high water, we try out some new exercises aimed at keeping me loose, flexible, and butt-pain free. From there, I'm off to the stadium, where Yankees strength coach Jeff Mangold puts me through the paces of his own power regimen. From there, I'll hit the stationary bike, then Gino's table for my standard heat pack, rub, and magic thumbs. Finally, when all *that's* done, though my body's pretty much got the consistency of well-kneaded bread dough, I inevitably feel better and stronger and much more positive about the rest of my season.

At that point, just when I'm dying for a giant corner piece of Sicilian pizza, there's Scott again, cutting me off at the pass, cooking healthy meals, full of broiled fish, chicken, and a whole lot of strange, green, vitamin-packed plant life. With a sigh and a burning desire to make it through this season healthy and with at least 200 innings pitched, I dive back into his rabbit-food regimen head-first, allowing myself just a tiny bit of food fudging each Sunday.

The program flicks a switch. I feel tangibly better, almost every day now. But even with all that work and all that health food, my starts are still falling flat. My curve is spinning, but not dropping off the table. My other pitches have developed a nasty habit of sitting too fat and too high in the strike zone, screaming "Hit me! Hit me!" on their way to the dish. On August 8, the A's tag me for ten hits and seven runs over six. On the sixteenth, the Mariners slap me around for three runs and seven hits and six walks over 5⅓. Two days later, Mel's back on my butt.

For over a month now, with my back stiff and my brain half-expecting a blowout, I've stopped throwing in the bullpen between starts. Today, however, Coach Stottlemyre end runs the pen in favor of a nice long session of sideline scrutiny.

Going through the motions, literally, with my delivery, Mel uses his super-human powers of perception to notice that while I'm standing in the set position, my legs are not quite as far apart as they should be. It's a tiny posture issue, but changing my stance ultimately allows me to crank up a lot more power from the set position, while keeping my weight back, making my motion toward home a lot quicker, and my entire delivery a lot more efficient.

Just like last time, Mel's genius pays off big-time. My slightly revised delivery helps me close out the month of August with a pair of monster starts against the Angels and Red Sox at home (15⅔ innings pitched, 2 earned runs, 9 strikeouts, and 0 walks). With a back that now feels stronger, and more flexible than it has all season long, my stuff sharp, my mechanics fixed, and the Yankees coasting into September at 87–47, I can't help scanning the trees for the first signs of Autumn gold.

September 6, Yankees at 87-53

The roll continues, this time with a complete-game five-hitter against the Tigers that translates into a fast, easy, 8-1 victory. At 16-7, with a month left to play, my goal of 200 innings now seems like a lock. Twenty wins now seems like an outside possibility as well. (Don't ever believe a pitcher who says he doesn't care about that goal.) I'm loose, I'm pain free, I've lost four pounds this week, and with all that in mind I leave Yankee Stadium just before midnight feeling a whole lot better than any semibroken thirty-nine-year-old pitcher should feel.

Dinner follows with Scott Yeckenevich, and from there, after a club stop or two, the two of us decide to close out the night in a diner I love. Called Gracie's Corner, the place is just steps from my apartment, with good food, twenty-four-hour service, and like most New York diners, a whole lot of sit-down-eat-shut-up personality. It's just about 5:30 A.M. now—very late night, or early morning, if you're a farmer. Scott and I enter the diner and take a booth, me with my back to the door, Scott on the opposite side. Straight in front of me now, filling another booth, are three guys, all of them loud, all of them making noise like they're pretty well toasted. Two face away from me, and on the opposite side, there's a little guy, staring, squinting, and whispering to the others.

"Hey," he's saying, "I think that guy is David Wells." Two seconds later, I've got all *three* of these guys staring and squinting.

"What guy?"

"That guy, right there in the booth."

"What are you, outta your mind?"

"Naw, I'm fuckin' serious."

"Get out. That ain't him." It's like listening to Paulie Walnuts chat with Bobby Bacala and Johnny Sack. Two booths away, I'm trying my best not to laugh, hoping these knuckleheads will ultimately decide I'm just some random bald guy, and leave me alone.

"Hey over there," shouts the little guy. "You ain't David Wells, are you?"

"Uh, yeah. Yeah, nice to meet you."

Now these geniuses put their heads together, muttering and giggling under their brewery-fresh breath. Almost immediately, they begin lobbing insults toward my table.

It's all standard stuff. I suck, and I'm old, and I ain't no pitcher, and my record this year would be lousy if the Yankees weren't scoring so many runs for me . . . nothing clever, nothing original, nothing I can't endure. Ordering an egg-white omelet, I hear "Why don't you order a cheeseburger, you big fat fuck?!" And then they hit the topic of my mother. Now *clearly* trying to poke at my last nerve, they're reaching their goal, fast. Honestly, I really do believe there ought to be a law that says if some drunken joker starts talking shit about your mom, it's absolutely legal to beat his ass. Scott sees me doing a not-so-slow-burn now, and he immediately starts trying to get our waiter's attention. "Check please?" he's asking loudly, hoping we can still get the hell out of Dodge without a showdown. Meanwhile, I get up to visit the bathroom, making sure to stop at the numbskull booth along the way. I lean in, toward the two larger nudniks on one side of the booth.

"Listen, guys, enough is enough," I tell them. "You wanna talk about me, that's fine. But leave my mom out of it. She's dead and she can't defend herself, so just do me a favor and shut the hell up."

BAM! The littlest asshole, the one I'm not even looking at, just hauls off and sucker punches me. His tiny little fist clocks me square in the mouth. I never see it coming. I go down hard, hitting my head on their table as I fall. My forehead's busted open. My two front teeth are cracked, and even as I'm wobbling back to my feet, this asshole's waving a butter knife, smiling and shouting, "C'mon! You want a piece of me?! You want a piece of MEEEE?!"

Fire shoots from my eyes. Lightning shoots out my ears. Right now I'd like nothing more than to turn this guy into a grease stain, but I don't. Sober, grown up, and honestly fearing that one solid shot to the head might kill this overly aggressive little mini-me, I back off.* Scott dives in and puts some distance between us all, and even before we've made it outside to the sidewalk, I'm dialing 911 on my cell.

Not very David Wellsian, I know. History says I should have flattened the punk, probably breaking a hand or a finger, and getting into big trouble with

* The little guy's lawyer will ultimately try to make a case that I was intoxicated on the night of "the incident." Trust me on this one, the very fact that his client still has a head will stand as irrefutable proof to the contrary.

Joe Torre and Brian Cashman and George Steinbrenner in the process. This morning though, with the sun now rising, I know I did the right thing even if it does seem kind of wimpy. Is one punch worth the aggravation and time and expense of the trial that'll follow when this guy inevitably sues me? Do I really need that? Does my wife? Do my kids?

Yikes, all of a sudden I'm sounding mature, levelheaded, and well reasoned. I may start wearing sweaters any day now.

At any rate, there I stand, bleeding and fuming on the corner of Eighty-sixth and First, but still very much under control. The police reports get filed. The little guy, who's name turns out to be Rocco Graziosa, gets hauled off to the pokey, and I head home to start thinking about dentist appointments, legal proceedings, and the inescapable "reprimand" that's sure to come from the Yankee brass. A few hours later, I head to the ballpark knowing full well that sooner or later, my teammates are gonna give me a whole lot of shit for this too. One day later, it hits the fan.

The New York *Daily News* runs a photo of Graziosa, all five-feet-six of him, standing and smiling at the camera beneath a headline that reads I BEAT UP DAVID WELLS, BARKEEP BRAGS TO BOSS. That's all they need. Hitting the training room that morning, I find that *somebody*—and you know who you are, Derek Jeter*—has carefully clipped Graziosa out of the picture, added some fake arms and legs, and stapled the little slugger up onto a locker-room corkboard. Next to Graziosa is an equally doctored photo of me. Teeth missing, eyes crossed and black, nose bleeding, I lay on my back while the little paper Graziosa stands over me, arms raised, like Ali over Liston. The word *Owwww* is markered into a thought balloon over my head.

It's gonna be a long week. Everybody wants to see the teeth. Everybody laughs when I show them. Everybody in the Yankees clubhouse who's ever been goofed on by me (and that's pretty much everybody) now has an open invitation to bust my balls. They wanna know if Graziosa climbed a stepladder before he punched me. They wanna make sure I know that Graziosa still lives at home in his parents' basement. They wanna know if he head-butted me in the nuts. They wanna know when Sky Lo Lo** came out of retirement. I just wanna know when they're all gonna finally climb out of my ass.

---

* Turnabout may be fair play in this one case, because on more than one occasion, some teammate has enjoyed making paper-cutout Mariah Carey gags at the expense of our beloved shortstop. I won't tell you the culprit's name, but he's a left-handed starter who's recently written a book.
** Late, great World Champion Midget Wrestler. He reigned from 1949 to 1975.

Days pass, the ragging subsides, the teeth get fixed, the police report gets filed, and finally, the GM calls me in for a sit-down. Cashman's glad to see that the report backs up my version of the story, and he's thrilled with the idea that I controlled my temper and didn't deck the guy. He's none too thrilled with the idea that I was out running around Manhattan until six in the morning, but since there's no home curfew in effect for us Yanks, his decision is that no disciplinary action will be necessary. Case closed. Crisis passed. Time to clinch a division.

September 12, Yankees at 92–54

I'm pitching today against the Orioles, and with our magic number at eight, there's an easy, relaxed confidence rolling through the dugout these days. Sure, everybody's looking forward to the postseason, but at the same time, we're all really enjoying these final weeks together. In the past couple of days, Shane Spencer and I have learned that it can be a lot of fun to spend entire games whipping pumpkin seeds at Lee Mazzilli's ass as he stands trying to do his job in the first-base coach's box. We fling. He tries to ignore it. We fling again and again and again. He waves "cut it out" gestures back toward the dugout without turning around. We double the ammo, flinging the little suckers now with nearly machine-gun frequency. Maz gives us a head spin. We immediately look off into another direction and try to appear innocent. We fail badly. Maz returns to the pine threatening to take batting practice on our faces.

Across the field though, Willie Randolph is actually dishing out more grief than he gets. Sign any autograph for any woman, and Willie will *relentlessly* accuse you of trying and failing to land yourself a date. "I know what you're doing," he'll holler from across the field, "but trust me, you're *way* too ugly for a girl like that. Maybe you'd get luckier if you have Derek sign a ball for her." At the same time, since Willie thinks *every* base runner sprinting and panting and chugging toward third should be capable of scoring, he never holds anybody. With that in mind we're forever flashing hold signals at him from the Yankee bench.

"You're gonna kill somebody, Willie. You're gonna give some poor son of a bitch a coronary going from first to home." He just laughs. If one measly death will win us a ball game, it's more than acceptable to Coach Randolph.

Meanwhile, even though it's already September, here amid the laid-back comfort of a big lead in the AL East, I find myself learning something new about my teammates almost every day. For example, a quick round of baseball trivia tells me that Nick Johnson, today's rookie contestant, knows practically nothing about baseball. He's never heard of Johnny Vander Meer. He's never heard the story of Babe Ruth's called shot. He's fuzzy on Sandy Koufax. This Billy Zane–looking dunce is gonna be a pet project in 2003. The only roadblock may be that by next season, with his rookie status behind him, Nick won't actually be forced to attend my history lessons.

At the same time, I've learned that I really like Jeff Weaver. He's smart and funny, and I find out this kid actually grew up within two hours of me. Strange though, all Jeff's great Southern Californian stories seem to take place a full decade after mine, and for some reason they contain a lot less hair gel, headbands, leg warmers, and *Miami Vice* sportcoats with the sleeves pushed up.

And finally, here in the waning days of the '02 season, I've learned that Shane Spencer is indeed Dorf. You know who I mean. I'm talking about that stupid-ass little "Dorf on Golf"/Tim Conway guy. Shane's just like that—all torso with legs that look as if somebody sliced 'em off at the knee and just screwed a new pair of feet onto the thigh bones. However, despite his stubby little condition, Spencer is nonetheless remarkably flexible. Like Dorf, Shane can literally sit on the bench of the dugout and lift either stumpy leg straight up over his head. I laugh every single time he does it, which is bad, because now that he knows my weakness, Spencer can perform that stunt during whatever inappropriate moment he chooses. Down by three? There goes the leg. Out comes the laugh. Here come the stares from our coaching staff. Only human, I'm powerless against his evil, squatty-bodied little scheme.

Now it's game time, but this one's over early. Gifted with five runs in the first, I'm also blessed with strong stuff tonight, and a back that feels flat-out great. That translates into bad news for the O's, who go down quietly, 7–3, in a game that doesn't even last two hours and forty-five minutes. I'm 17 and 7 for the season now and am really having the time of my life.

September 21, Yankees at 97–58

We clinch the division today with Andy Pettitte tossing a short, sweet, 3–2 gem against Detroit. Even better, as of today's eighth inning, Mariano Rivera is back off the DL (for the third time this year), looking healthy, sharp, and *more* than ready to kick ass in the postseason. Now officially at full speed, we Yankees need to turn up the heat for October . . . but first we need to bust into the clubhouse and go nuts.

Steve Karsay is the first man to kill me, dousing me over the head with beer that I never saw coming. Derek's next, then Jorge, and even with my eyes sting-

The happy ambush: You know you're getting old when a guy as slow as Steve Karsay can blindside you (*AP Photo/John F. Martin*)

ing from alcohol, it's great fun to watch guys like Jason Giambi, Nick Johnson, Robin Ventura, Raul Mondesi, and Jeff Weaver enjoying this brave new world of Yankee success. Having been here twice before, I know exactly how incredible these moments are, but for these guys, it's a mind-boggling experience. I can't wait to see their faces after we win this year's World Series.

Jason just stares, openmouthed, grinning from ear to ear while he slowly twirls at the center of the room. It's a bad move—one that leaves him open for one hell of a blast from my champagne bottle. Whoosh, right in the mouth. I've still got the touch.

An hour passes and slowly but surely the high-fives and face-blasts of champagne give way to a whole lot of Yankees in search of a late-night celebration. Guys make dinner plans, guys make party plans, and right in the middle of it all . . . there's me without a single bash on my dance card. I'm pitching tomorrow, and with a freakish 12 P.M. start, I know that I'm now officially too old to burn the candle at both ends. With that in mind, and with my kids and my wife all along for the ride, my big night consists of mall shopping, venison kabobs at a local restaurant, and bed.

No one on earth can imagine me being this responsible.

Rested or not, that 12 P.M. start flies in fast, and despite the fact that I get my eighteenth W with a solid, 4–3 outing, I never quite feel comfortable on the mound. Day games have never been my strong suit. Things are better for me on September 28, when I get to beat up on the Orioles one more time, giving up just two hits and no runs over six. I'm ready. Stick a fork in this regular season, people, it's time to move onto the really good stuff.

We Yankees end this season at 103 and 59, with a *huge* September run of 19–8. My own final stats clock out at 19–7 with an era of 3.75 and 206 innings pitched. Not too shabby for a guy who sent the better part of 2001 as flexible and athletic as your average Jell-O mold. It's a proud moment, not just for me, but for Doc Boscardin, Scott Yeckenevich, Gene Monahan, Steve Donohue, James Mangold, Mel Stottlemyre, George Steinbrenner, Darnell Coles, Gregg Clifton, Nina, and everybody else who helped yank this tired, broken-down old carcass back into fighting, pitching, winning shape. To everybody who kept me going, I can't possibly say anything more appropriate than thank you. Thank you from the bottom of my heart.

October

"Yankees Will Sweep." "Bombers in Four." "Angels Outclassed in ALDS." You pick the newspaper, sports-talk station, website, or smarmy TV sports guy, and *everybody,* it seems, is looking right past the ALDS and into the League Championships, where a Yankees vs. A's rematch is all but guaranteed.* About the only place I know where the Angels are being taken seriously is right here in the Yankee clubhouse. We Bombers have taken four of seven from the Angels this season, but except for my two-inning debacle at the Big Ed, the contests were tight and well played, and often nail-bitingly close. We know better than to get complacent.

Our clubhouse is businesslike now, focused and hungry. And while there are no pep rallies, no gung-ho battle cries, no Paul O'Neill, or Tino or Scotty or Knobby pumping their fists and shouting up at the ceiling this year, an unspoken confidence is everywhere. This is a veteran team that's won 103 regular season games. This is a team whose bats and pitchers both seem to be peaking at exactly the right time. We know our roles. We know what's expected of us. We *know* how to win. There's no reason to doubt we'll be every bit as successful in October.

Game 1: Roger Clemens vs. Jarrod Washburn

Nearly fifty-seven thousand Yankee fans have the house the Ruth built roaring, and before this sucker's all over they're gonna get a whole lot louder. Tied up at four, heading into the eighth, we Yankees have spent the night playing long ball, with all of our runs scoring on moonshots from Derek, Jason, and Rondell White. At the same time, Anaheim's playing little ball, sticking close to a game plan that seems almost entirely lifted from the Joe Torre/Yankee playbook, circa 1996. Bunting, stealing, fouling off a ton of pitches, and working deep into

---

* The Twins, it seems, stood no chance of survival either.

every count, the Angels seem entirely focused on manufacturing one run at a time, whenever and wherever possible. With the exception of a sixth-inning dinger from Troy Glaus, the Angels have earned their runs tonight by scratching and clawing, one base at a time. Somewhere tonight Jim Leyritz, Gerald Williams, Wade Boggs, Mariano Duncan, and Joe Girardi are feeling entirely ripped off.

Top of the eighth inning, with Ramiro Mendoza working his third inning of relief* and Troy Glaus once again flexing his twenty-four-inch pythons at the plate. Ramiro fires. Glaus connects, and *bam,* the dude's second home run of the night ends up flying all the way out to the screen that covers Monument Park. That's the end of Ramiro's night, and when Steve Karsay comes on to blow through the next three batters, we head to the bottom of the eighth down 5–4. It's magic time.

Ben Weber comes on to pitch for the Angels, and he takes out Rondell White and pinch-hitter John Vander Wal pretty quickly. From there, however, he walks Alfonso Soriano, who promptly steals second base, then walks Derek Jeter as well. That's all Angels manager Mike Scioscia can stand. With Jason Giambi coming to the plate, he yanks Weber, bringing in lefty Scott Schoenweiss, who immediately gets scorched for a nasty single, right off the glove of first baseman Scott Spiezio.

Here comes Scioscia one more time. With Bernie Williams in the on-deck circle, the whole wide world is expecting the call to go out to supercloser Troy Percival. Instead, Scioscia calls an audible, bringing in Brendan Donnelly. Williams steps in. Donnelly delivers, and one fraction of a second later, Bernie's clocked a three-run blast that becomes the game-winning hit when Mariano Rivera slams the door in the ninth.

High drama, excitement, and one of the best damn ball games you'll ever see played. . . . It's October as usual here in the Bronx.

Game 2: Andy Pettitte vs. Kevin Appier

Though we're poised for yet another come-from-behind gem, the magic runs out tonight. Andy's game is off right from the start, and by the top of the third, we're already down 3–zip. But we're the Yankees and this being October, you can rest assured that by the time this sucker's over, we'll have found *some* way to crank out yet another miracle.

---

* Roger ultimately lasted 5⅔, giving up 4 runs on 8 hits, with 3 walks and 5 Ks.

We start chipping away in our half of the third, when Derek unleashes yet another solo blast, then add two more in the fourth. Down 4–3 in the sixth, our standard, everyday impossible dream keeps rolling when Alfonso Soriano clocks a two run homer. Up 5–4, the universe is once again at peace. The Yankees are on top. But not for long.

With back-to-back blasts at the top of the frame, Garrett Anderson and Troy Glaus put the Angels back on top, chasing Orlando Hernández, who's been solid in relief of Andy Pettitte. Steve Karsay comes on in relief, but before this inning's done, the Angels will have added an insurance run, heading into the bottom half of the eighth with a 7–5 lead.

Time's running out, but remember, we *are* the Yankees, and . . . damn, we're shut down in the eighth.

Ninth inning. Jeff Weaver relieves Karsay, but when Garrett Anderson, Troy Glaus, and Scott Spiezio go single, single, double on his ass, we head into the bottom of the ninth facing an 8–5 deficit. This is *not* supposed to happen.

Troy Percival's on the mound. Jason Giambi's at the plate. Fingers are crossed all over the tristate area. A cry of "Let's go, Yankees!!!" rings through the house. Jason comes through, singling to left. Here we go. Percival K's Bernie, but never fear, Robin Ventura and Jorge Posada both follow that whiff with singles, and the end result sees Giambi closing the gap to 8–6. One out now, two on, cue the dramatic come-from-behind miracle now.

Nick Johnson K's. Wow, this comeback victory is gonna be especially dramatic tonight. Two down, bottom of the ninth. Raul Mondesi at the plate and . . . he pops out to second. Game over. Series tied up at 1–1 and heading into Anaheim with the Angels gathering momentum.

Rocky starting pitching? Miracles that fall flat? Who wrote this postseason, anyway?

Game 3: The Wrath of the Rally Monkey— Moose vs. Ramon Ortiz

This one's nuts. Up by a score of 6–1 after three, we Yankees have quickly chased Ramon Ortiz off the field, and we're starting to believe this series might contain at least one easy victory. Ain't gonna happen.

With two in the third and another in the fourth, the Angels cut our lead to 6–4, while John Lackey, who's come in in relief of Ortiz, settles into a groove and just plows through our lineup in the third, fourth, fifth, and sixth. Jeff

Weaver's not that lucky, and by the end of six, our 6–1 laugher has become a 6–5 Maalox moment . . . and it's about to get worse.

With Mike Stanton taking the hill from Weaver, the goddamn Angels keep hitting. Solid doubles, bloop hits, dink singles, perfect bunts, this team is hitting both good pitches *and* bad, depositing just about everything their bats touch into some area of the field that we Yankees can't reach. Every break is going their way. Every guy on their team is hitting. Paul O'Neill would have had an aneurysm by now. And still it continues. By the end of the seventh, we're all tied at six. The first real seeds of doubt are now germinating. Momentum's a bitch when it's on the other side of the field.

Eighth inning. Stanton on the mound. Second baseman Adam Kennedy leads off by blooping a sweet cutter into right field. Raul Mondesi charges toward it at roughly 166 miles per hour. He lunges. He grabs. He comes up short. The ball bounces off his glove and Kennedy ends up with the world's crappiest double. I smack my own forehead. This is insane. The gods have turned against us. Two pitches later, David Eckstein sac flies Kennedy to third. Frustration is setting in fast. Maybe we're pressing. Maybe it's fate. Maybe our pitchers are just getting hammered. Whatever the reason, at this point it really does seem that God must be rooting for his Angels.

Darin Erstad at the plate now, and with Eckstein waggling his ass off the bag, he laces a 1–2 pitch down the right field line for a double. Eckstein scores. Angels lead 7–6. Stanton hands off to Steve Karsay, who lasts all of two pitches before giving up a two-run blast to Tim Salmon. Angels lead 9–6. Troy Percival's on the mound in the ninth, and this time around, with a little less swagger and a little less confidence, we head quietly toward a two-games-to-one deficit.

Tomorrow, it'll be my job to turn this whole thing around.

Game 4: Me vs. Jarrod Washburn

Happy thoughts. Happy thoughts. Sure, we may be down two games to one. And, sure, momentum may be riding squarely on the side of the stupid-ass monkey. And, sure, the commisioner's office and Fox TV have made a last-minute switch and turned this sucker into a day game in Anaheim, where my career numbers aren't exactly brilliant. It doesn't matter. I don't care. None of that's gonna make one bit of difference in the game I'll pitch today. I figure if I just keep telling myself all this stuff I may sooner or later start to believe it.

Taking the mound at the bottom of the first, my pregame worries get blown off pretty quick. Feeling strong, pumped, and ready to kick red-and-white ass,

I get Eckstein and Erstad and Salmon, 1-2-3, all on pitches that spin and move and land exactly as I've asked. One inning down, I take my first deep breath of the day. My first smile follows quickly after that. Jorge and Robin turn their second-inning single and double into an early one-run lead. We'll stay like that into the third.

Fighting now against an Angels lineup that seems hell-bent on making contact with anything and everything even vaguely hittable, DH Shawn Wooten clips a pretty good curve and ends up dinking himself a shallow single to center. Lucky. Then catcher Bengie Molina sac bunts Wooten to second with a perfect little nubber that just kind of dies in the grass near home plate. One down, man on second, and here comes second baseman Benji Gil, who raps a clean single into left, moving Wooten to third. David Eckstein comes to the plate and my obvious goal is the DP grounder . . . which is exactly what I get. Eckstein clocks a roller to Soriano at second, but here in bizarro-world, the normally routine double-play ball ends up bouncing under the normally sure-handed Alfonso's glove and then through his legs, which of course brings Wooten home, and moves Gil to third. Tie game. First and third. I still need the double play, and this time I get it, when Darrin Erstad grounds into a 4-6-3 gem. Bullet dodged. Time to regain this lead.

Jarrod Washburn's tough but tired, and with that in mind, our Yankee bats are now working him into the count as deeply as possible, as often as possible. By the end of the fourth, with the game still tied up at one, Washburn will have thrown his seventy-fifth pitch. I'll be closing in on fifty and starting to feel pretty confident.

Top of the fifth—Juan Rivera rides an error to first and Alfonso doubles him over to third. A picture-perfect sac fly from Derek Jeter brings Rivera home and stakes me to a born-again lead. It'll last all of three pitches. Join me now as we revisit the bottom of the fifth, also know as "the Single-Most Mother-Effing, Ball-Busting, Frustrating, Mind-Boggling Inning of My Career!"

It starts off bad when Shawn Wooten's back at the dish, cracking a fat 2–0 fastball over the wall in left center. Then I get a fly-ball out from Bengie Molina, before Benji Gil and David Eckstein beat me for back-to-back singles. The lid stays on. I refuse to lose my cool. And with runners at the corners, I've got Darin Erstad standing on top of home plate. An inside fastball jams the dish-hog. Erstad swings, and right off his hands, he lifts a dying quail up over my head just beyond second base. Too shallow to score Gil, this sucker should belong to Bernie, or maybe Al-

fonso, orrrrrrr no, wait, it's gonna be Bernie, no it's Alfons-oh—SHIT!*
Somehow this nothing little bloop in-betweener manages to find grass. Gil scores to put the Angels up 3–2. I try to stay calm, but with Tim Salmon and Garrett Anderson following with back-to-back RBI singles, I don't think I'm succeeding. Now down 5–2, I get Troy Glaus to fly out before Scott Spiezio completes my nightmare with yet another RBI smack. It's 6–2 Angels and Joe's out. Mendoza's running in. I head to the clubhouse, where I can finally start shouting.

"Are you fucking kidding me?!!" I'm shouting in the club-house. I'm throwing my glove now. I'm tossing my cap. I'm just railing at the whole world but first and foremost myself. Losing does not come lightly, especially with an entire season on the line. Two hits allowed over the first four innings, and then I'm lit up for eight in the fifth. "How is that even fucking possible?!"

I call Kirk Gibson. "Gibby!" I shout into the phone "We blew it. I'll see you next week at the ranch!" For once in his life Mr. Gibson is speechless.

Ahhh . . . pinstripes
(*Courtesy of Chris Kreski*)

I spend the rest of the game in the clubhouse, pissed and depressed and ultimately feeling even worse when Orlando Hernández, Steve Karsay, and Mike Stanton combine to blank the Angels through the sixth, seventh,

---

* The New York papers went a little nuts declaring that the blooper should have been caught, but I'm not so sure. Somehow, with the hand of God nudging all four of these games toward the Angels, I have a feeling that if either Bernie or Alfonso had actually touched that thing, a bolt of lightning might have taken them out.

and eighth. Erase the fifth inning, and we'd have won that game 5–1 with the series heading back to New York, Roger Clemens on the mound, and the rally monkey ready to be hunted down and stuffed. It's not a happy afternoon.

But life goes on. We all survive. And at the risk of trotting out the first lame cliché of this book, we can all go home with our heads held high.

Post-Postseason

So we didn't get the ticker tape. We didn't win it all. Hell, we didn't even make it to the ALCS, but that doesn't mean this sucker can't have a happy ending.

I mean it. Sure, it'd be great to add one more World Series ring (or two) to my fingers. Sure I'd love the chance to go out on top, throwing the smoke and winning the games that ultimately bring baseball's world championship back to the Bronx. But trust me on this one, even if that stuff never happens, I'm still gonna go down in history as the single luckiest human being on the face of the planet. I mean, really, people, you're reading a book written by a guy who used to saw through the legs of dead cows for a living.

Win or lose, every second I spend in a Yankee uniform is amazing, and every second I spend with my wife and my kids is even better. I'm healthy. I'm content. And pitchers and catchers report any day now.

Can you think of a happier ending than that?

I didn't think so. I'll see you in the Bronx.

Your pen pal,

Dave

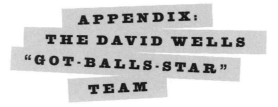

I'M AN OLD GUY, AT LEAST BY BASEBALL STANDARDS, AND AFTER TWO full decades of bouncing around the bigs, I know for a fact that stat sheets don't mean dick. Want to come in fourth place? Build yourself a team by the numbers. Want a ring? Build yourself a team of hard-nosed, hard-hearted, hard-fighting (and possibly hard-living) monsters. The major leagues are littered with solid, talented, entirely complacent athletes, but it's a whole lot harder to find the real assholes. These are the guys who can win you some ball games. They're bullies, they're blowhards, they're the kind of dirt-eating, spit-spewing, sweat-stained freaks who'd stomp a mud hole in their mom to score a run. Gather enough of these antisocial mutants in your clubhouse, and I promise you'll be playing ball in October.

With that in mind, I spent a few hours digging through some of my old team rosters in assembling my own personal, all-time, can't-miss, *dream* lineup. This mofo's a flat-out dynasty. Take a look:

First Base

CECIL FIELDER—Big Daddy may not have racked up the most impressive career stats of all time, but with a big game on the line, there was *nobody* tougher. With men on base, there was *nobody* more intimidating. With your sandwich within stealing distance, there was *nobody* meaner. Well-motivated and playing every day, the big moose could be an unstoppable force. He was also fantastic in the Tigers' clubhouse, with most guys simply too scared to ever slack off and risk one of Cecil's plus-size, postgame ass-whuppings.

TWO HONORABLE MENTIONS

MO VAUGHN—He's never been a teammate, but nobody on this planet kicks my ass as badly as Mo does. I knock him down. He gets up, smiles at me, and hits a 400-foot home run. I hit him in the elbow. He gets up, smiles at me, and hits another. Time and again, the man just *spanks* my best stuff. In my opinion, that officially qualifies Mo as the single greatest player in the history of the game.

JASON GIAMBI—I've known Jason for only a year, but I *guarantee* you, the dude's a repeat MVP-to-be (maybe even in 2003). Huge stick, solid glove, he's also the speediest of my first-base nominees . . . which in this case, is kinda like saying that Curly was the handsomest of the Stooges.

Second Base

ROBERTO ALOMAR—The one no-brainer in the bunch. No second baseman hits like Robby. No second baseman in the history of the game has ever come close to fielding the position like Robby. Nobody I've ever played with comes through in the clutch nearly as often as Robby does. And as John Hirschbeck can attest, the man's a really bad loser. Forget 2002, the guy's awesome—it's just too bad he's stuck playing for that AAA team in Queens.

Shortstop

CAL RIPKEN JR.—A perfect swing, a perfect glove, a perfect physique, a perfect gentleman (at least in public)—the man's "Gallant" to my "Goofus." Cal was eighty-nine years old in 1996, and *still* he led us Orioles, by example, day in and day out. He never yelled. He never kicked a watercooler. He just went out on the field and quietly played to the very best of his ability . . . almost *always* making a lot of our younger guys look like shit in comparison. *Bonus Points:* I also liked his haircut.

HONORABLE MENTION

DEREK JETER—Bear with me on this one, because while I know the classic argument says that A-Rod and Nomar are both better all-around short-stops, I couldn't care less. Put Derek in a big game and he *will* win. Need a game-winning, walk-off home-run? Ask Jeter. Need somebody to dive into the stands, flip over a couple of times, have beer poured on his head, and still catch a foul ball? Ask Jeter. Need somebody to play "Heart and Soul" with Eddie Layton on the Yankee Stadium organ? You know who to call.

Third Base

TRAVIS FRYMAN—I know what you're thinking. You're thinking: Travis Fryman? And let me address that now by saying, "Yeah, dumb-ass, *Travis Fryman*! Got a problem with that?" Back in Detroit, the man chewed turf. The man busted up double plays with his own patented "knee to the second baseman's nuts" technique. The man stole signs. The man was a snarling beast in any given bench-clearing brawl. The man slid headfirst, even into his hotel room. In short, the man was *the man*. In spring training 1995, with me looking on as a witness, *the man* made himself a vow to play every single inning of all 162 games of the upcoming season. Seven months later, bruised, bashed, beaten, and busted, he became the only man in all of major-league baseball to accomplish that feat.

Catcher

JORGE POSADA—Darrin Fletcher, Pat Borders, Benito Santiago, Sandy Alomar Jr., Mickey Tettleton, Joe Girardi; over the past two decades, I've been caught by some pretty good backstops, but none of them have ever come *close* to calling a game as well as Jorge. I swear to God, the man's psychic. He *knows* what I'm thinking. He *knows* when I'm struggling. He *knows* when I'm gearing up to throw something dumb. We're on the exact same wavelength, and out on the field, there are times where I actually feel like we're sharing one brain *(feel free to insert your own obvious joke at my expense right here . . . you big jerk)*. I trust Jorge completely. I rarely, if *ever*, shake him off, and with this dude calling my shots, I've so far been able to dodge Father Time and remain dominant, even as a semi-broken-down thirty-nine-year-old.

Left Field

KIRK GIBSON—First, let me go on the record and state that the fact that this man is often standing next to me, in the wilderness, holding a large-caliber gun, has *nothing* to do with his selection to my team. He's actually an obvious choice. You want the toughest man in the history of major-league baseball on your team? You call Gibby. You've seen the footage. You saw how the man hobbled out onto the field at Dodger Stadium, stared down Dennis Eckersley, and hit the single most memorable home run in World Series history. That's Gibby. The man's a gamer, and a leader, and if you look up the definition of *winner* in *Webster's* you'll find a picture of Kirk. Oddly, his picture can *also* be found alongside the words *verbose, gassy,* and *homely.*

Center Field

DEVON WHITE—Put this guy in center, and your other outfielders should probably bring lawn chairs to work. The dude's faster than a speeding line drive. More powerful than a loco Mo Vaughn. Able to leap tall outfield fences in a single bound. Look, out in center field. It's a bird. It's a plane. It's Devo! And that dude just turned your 400-foot homer into a useless, fly-ball out. Lovestruck pitchers tend to kiss this man on a semiregular basis.

Right Field

DAVE WINFIELD—Huge bat. Huge arm. Huge heart. Huge teeth, but don't let that blinding smile fool you. The man was ruthless, destroying pitchers like Skydome seagulls, and picking off runners with shotgun blasts from right. He's smart, he's strong, and I've never met anybody who could read pitchers the way Winfield did. Hold your glove two centimeters off-kilter when you're throwing your curve? Winny would pick it up. Blink differently before you throw a slider? Winny would take you downtown. Well-liked, well-respected, and always cool, Winny's still the guy I want to be when I grow up. *Bonus Points:* He *always* picks up the check at dinner, and/or the tab at . . . uh . . . Starbucks, yeah, that's it.

Designated Hitter

PAUL O'NEILL—Choosing Paulie as my DH, instead of my everyday right fielder, is gonna drive that man nuts, and it may very well end ugly. I can see it now, me in a headlock, turning purple, while Paulie just squeezes tighter and asks me over and over again, "*Now* would you pick me over Winfield? *Now* would you pick me over Winfield?" Paul O'Neill ranks as the single most ambitious, most driven, most insanely gung-ho guy I've *ever* played with, and that's *exactly* why he's in my lineup. Honestly, if this dream team were to ever actually take the field, Paulie would probably take a lead pipe to Winfield's knee, then jog right over him on his way to the outfield.

Pitching Staff

I've left myself *out* of my own rotation, in what I believe is a very generous gesture, aimed at keeping the rest of my staff from looking shabby.

STARTERS

DAVID CONE—The gamer of all gamers. Coney's the toughest son of a bitch I've ever played with. Shoulder on fire? Coney's still throwing. Vein graft barely stitched into place? Coney's still throwing. Cannonball lodged in his left ear? Coney's still throwing. He's an inspiration. He never quits. He throws 147 different pitches, and I miss him to death. *Bonus Points:* Next to Coney, the rest of us would look really handsome in our team picture.

MIKE MUSSINA—The Moose and I have played together on two squads now, and I have to admit, we don't always see eye to eye. We're not pals. We don't hang, but there's no way in hell I can leave this guy off my staff. I've *never* seen a pitcher with stuff as naturally fluid, and effortless, and consistent as Mike's. Year after year after year, the guy just heads to the mound every fifth day and mows down whatever batters haven't written themselves out of the lineup to avoid facing him. He's durable. He's tough, and he wins . . . a *lot*.

JOHN SMILEY—If the Yankees are the filet mignon of baseball, *this* guy spent his entire career playing for bologna. At the top of some really bad staffs in

Pittsburgh, Minnesota, and Cincy, Smiley was a tobacco-chewing, ball-busting, blue-collar ace who never got anywhere *near* the recognition he deserved. A bone-deep tough guy, Smiley was also the funniest, bluntest, and most outspoken dude in the bigs. As legend has it, with the hated Marge Schott and her equally hated Saint Bernard, Schottzie, *both* approaching him on the field one time, Smiley yelled, "Get that disgusting animal off the turf!" When Marge protested, Smiley replied, "I was *talking* to Schottzie."

ANDY PETTITTE—The one "nice guy" on my team. A stand-up, honest, clean-living Sunday school teacher, Andy's Attila the Hun on the mound. He pitches up. He pitches in. He brushes guys back off the plate, and somehow, standing there with his clean-cut, "Up with People" good looks, he gets away with murder. Never a warning, never an ejection, he's like the "perfect" brother your parents loved best. Loaded with natural ability (I *hate* that), he's also gutty, consistent, and a great role model for the rest of the animals on my staff. *Bonus Points:* He's good friends with God.

JIMMY KEY—He's soft-spoken. He's buttoned down. He's one pocket protector away from full-blown nerd status, but don't let any of that fool you. The guy takes no shit on the mound or off. Let's put it this way: on the one occasion I made the mistake of seriously goofing on this guy, he shoved my face into a team bus window. You've gotta *love* that.

The Bullpen

SETUP GUYS

DUANE WARD/MIKE STANTON—Neither guy chokes . . . *ever*. Neither guy has an off night . . . *ever*. Neither guy can stomach blowing a lead . . . *ever*. Neither guy can tolerate being anything less than "big dog in the kennel." They'd kill each other within two weeks. *Bonus Points:* Back in the Skydome, Duane Ward was a master at getting us flashed by hot girls in tank tops. This skill cannot be underrated when building a squad.

CLOSERS

TOM HENKE/MARIANO RIVERA—Why *two* closers? Simple. These two are the two best relievers in the *history* of baseball. Period. Case closed. Done. Argue with me about that statement, and I'll be happy to throw a fastball behind your head.

Coaches

PITCHING COACH

LARRY HARDY—So how does an AA coach make this dream team? Simple. He's the best. When I was a thrower, he made me a pitcher. When my mechanics looked more like a seizure than a major-league pitch-delivery, he spent literally dozens of hours correcting my faults. When I was still just cluelessly attacking batters with fastballs and a prayer, Larry taught me about pitch selection, and patterns, and the concept of a big-picture game plan. Finally, on that one occasion when my left arm had turned into taco meat, and I was seriously ready to quit baseball, Larry Hardy's the guy who talked me out of it. I really *do* owe him my career.

HONORABLE MENTION

MEL STOTTLEMYRE—There is a breed of major-league pitching coach whose entire job description consists of sitting on the dugout bench, yawning, eating a lot of sunflower seeds, and every once in a while shouting some pointless, asinine cliché at their pitcher like "C'mon, baby! *Throw* that ball!" That ain't Mel. Mel stares intently as you warm up. Mel picks up even the tiniest hitch in your mechanics. Mel knows you're running out of gas long before you have any idea. Mel makes you a *much* better pitcher. It's really that simple.

Manager

SPARKY ANDERSON—I met Jack Nicklaus one time and quickly came to the conclusion that the guy was a total asshole. The same thing happened with Gene Simmons, and even that little cock-sack Fred Durst from Limp Bizkit. My point here is that a lot of times, when you actually *meet* a person you really admire, they end up disappointing your ass. Not Sparky. For years I was stepped on and/or ignored in the Blue Jays' clubhouse, but Sparky found a way to jump-start my whole career. He cared about me. He talked with me. He laid out exactly what he expected from me. He walked me, batter by batter, through each and every upcoming lineup. We enjoyed each other's company, and honest to God, out there on the mound at Tiger Stadium, I was forever digging deep, challenging myself to win games, not just for my team, or myself, but for Sparky. He trusted me. He believed in me, and I never wanted to let him down. There's a reason some guys become legends

HONORABLE MENTION

JIM FREGOSI—He drank. He smoked. He gambled. He got into fistfights. He won ball games. How cool is that? A great strategist, a great motivator, a hardboiled tough guy, and a laid-back clubhouse presence, Fregosi took some *very* green, marginally talented Blue Jays teams, taught them how to win, and turned them into surprisingly solid overachievers. Of course, playing in Toronto, his efforts, talents, and achievements went entirely unappreciated by the idiots in the stands and the front office. He deserved a lot better.

And there you have it, a team that could very easily win you ten pennants in a row, or end up in jail before the end of your first road trip. Either way, it'd be a helluva ride.

ACKNOWLEDGMENTS

SPECIAL THANKS HAVE TO BE TOSSED AT THE FOLLOWING PEOPLE, who supported, encouraged, and put up with us throughout the writing of this book:

Mauro DiPreta, our editor, whose patience, talent, humor, and red pen never slept.

Gregg Clifton, whose memory for details, numbers, and *really* embarrassing stories has made this manuscript shine.

Peter Sawyer, Carmen LaVia, and of course the incredible force of nature known as Fifi Oscard, whose competence, compassion, and honesty might one day give literary agents a *good* name.

Joelle Yudin, whose smile has now proven *entirely* unshakeable.

Julien Rouleau, who went above and beyond the call of duty in securing our photographs.

Guy Nicolucci, who provided good ideas, bad punch lines, and smart-assed criticism when *all* were sorely needed.

Jack Helmuth, who happily provided the creative insights of your average, everyday, raging, gung-ho, borderline-nut-job Yankee fan.

The staff of the Monroe, Connecticut, Public Library, who never yelled at us, even though we crashed their Internet portals, turned a whole lot of their microfilm into spaghetti, and spent nearly eight months hogging their one really good table (up near the window). And especially Dawn Kreski, the brilliant, beautiful slave driver, without whom *none* of this stuff would *ever* get done.

Sincere thanks are also extended to Octagon's Patrick McGee, Tom George, and Mel Sirois, as well as Kirk Gibson, Rob Ducey, Doc Gooden, Darnell Coles, David Cone, and Jason Scheff.

Your time, patience, and generosity were all greatly appreciated.